# THE LINUX® BOOK

**David Elboth**

PRENTICE HALL PTR
UPPER SADDLE RIVER, NJ 07458
WWW.PHPTR.COM

Library of Congress Cataloging-in-Publication Data

Elboth, David.
[Boken om Linux. English]
The Linux book / David Elboth.
p. cm.
ISBN 0-13-032765-4
1. Linux II. Title.

QA76.76.O63 E42 2001
005.4'32--dc21

2001016420

Editorial/Production Supervision: *Laura Burgess*
Acquisitions Editor: *Mark Taub*
Marketing Manager: *Kate Hargett*
Manufacturing Manager: *Alexis R. Heydt*
Art Director: *Gail Cocker-Bogusz*
Interior Series Design: *Meg VanArsdale*
Cover Design Director: *Jerry Votta*
Translator: *Svein Erik Tosterud*

Prentice-Hall, Inc.
Upper Saddle River, NJ 07458



Prentice Hall thanks the Marketing Unit for Norwegian International Non-fiction (MUNIN), Oslo, for the financial support for the translation, which made the publication this book possible.



The publisher offers discounts on this book when ordered in bulk quantities.
For more information, contact

Corporate Sales Department,
Prentice Hall PTR
One Lake Street
Upper Saddle River, NJ 07458
Phone: 800-382-3419; FAX: 201-236-7141
E-mail: corpsales@prenhall.com

Printed in the United States of America

10 9 8 7 6 5 4 3 2 1

ISBN 0-13-032765-4

Prentice-Hall International (UK) Limited, *London*
Prentice-Hall of Australia Pty. Limited, *Sydney*
Prentice-Hall Canada Inc., *Toronto*
Prentice-Hall Hispanoamericana, S.A., *Mexico*
Prentice-Hall of India Private Limited, *New Delhi*
Prentice-Hall of Japan, Inc., *Tokyo*
Pearson Education Asia, Pte. Ltd.
Editora Prentice-Hall do Brasil, Ltda., *Rio de Janeiro*

*For my father, Rolf Bruno Elboth,*
*and mother, Enid Madeline Donald Mills*

# Contents

# Foreword

This book will serve both as an introduction for newcomers to Linux and as a reference for professionals. The book starts with the basics and goes through the most important Linux commands. If you are an IT manager wondering if Linux would make a good client or server operating system for your company, you will find it very valuable to read Chapter 25, "Cost/Benefit Analysis."

I started with Unix 15 years ago and have written three books on UNIX3: *UNIX: From User to System Administrator, UNIX: An Introduction,* and *UNIX Commands by Example: A Desktop Reference for Solaris, UnixWare, and SCO UNIX*. In the past four years, I have also written two books on Linux: *Linux Installation and Configuration,* and *Introduction to Red Hat Linux 7.0.*

I was first introduced to UNIX in 1985, when the operating system was called Microsoft XENIX (a UNIX clone). At that time the machine hardware was based on a PC with a 4.77 MHz Intel CPU, 640 KB RAM, and a 10-MB hard disk. Later I worked with both BSD and System V-based solutions like SCO XENIX, SCO UNIX, ISC UNIX, Novell UnixWare, Solaris 1.x, Solaris 2.x, IBM AIX, SCO UnixWare, NCR Unix V.4, and of course, Linux.

Early in 1997 I started working on an Intranet/WEB-development project for a Norwegian company called Telenor Marlink. In this project, the development platform was based on Sunsoft Solaris 2.5. A colleague named Knut Ranheim was also working on this project and wanted us to use Linux and PC hardware as the workstation platform. Since then I have been hooked on the Open Source model and Linux.

Today, I work as a project leader for different Linux software projects. In my part-time, I am Contributing Editor for the Norwegian Linux magazine, *Open Source Linux Magazine.* I also write books and am a well-known lecturer. If you would like to know what I use Linux for, check my homepage: http://home.c2.net/delboth

It's impossible to thank all of the people that have helped me with this book but I will give it a try.

I would like to thank Christian Schaller for all his input on X-Window and GNOME.

A special thanks to Nicolay Langfeldt, who greatly helped in making sure this book is technically sound. His insightful comments, suggestions, and tips did much more than just correct my technical oversights. Also thanks to Nicolay for using part of his NFS HOWTO. I would also like to thank David Wood for using part of the SMB HOWTO and give credit to every contributor to the SMB HOWTO.

I would like to thank Ottar Grimstad, Bjørn Roland, Vegard Veum, Kjartan Maraas, and Harald Brombach for reviewing different chapters.

An overwhelming thanks goes to Svein Erik Tosterud (Editor-in-Chief for the Norwegian Linux magazine, *Open Source Linux Magazine*) for doing most of the translation from my Norwegian book to the English version.

Thanks also to the Marketing Unit for Norwegian International Non-fiction (MUNIN) who subsidized the translation of this book into English.

I would also like to thank the Prentice Hall PTR team, who made this book a reality. They are the people who turned my text files into the book tyou are now holding in your hands.

Undertaking a project such as this places an equal if not greater burden on the people closest to you. My wife, Vigdis Enge, provided her patience and understanding. But above all, she provided her love.

Finally, a thanks to the more than 10.000 readers of my previous books. Without your continued support, I couldn't write these books. Thanks for all the email.

*David Elboth*

CHAPTER
1

# The Linux Book

## 1.1 Using Linux

This book has been written for anyone who wants to learn how to use the Linux operating system (OS). The book will also be useful to advisors, IT managers, IT directors, and other professionals who influence decisions in organizations that are evaluating Linux. To understand this book fully, you should have experience with PCs or workstations and have some knowledge of at least one OS like DOS, OS/2, Windows 98, Windows NT, Windows 2000, SCO UnixWare, Solaris, HP-UX, etc. Linux is a large system that cannot be covered fully in one single textbook. I have chosen to focus on central functions that you will use daily. Although Linux is a large and fully functional OS, it is simple to use. However, before you learn the basics, Linux may seem complicated. Fortunately, you don't need to learn a lot to get started. When you've finished Chapter 8, you will understand a lot!

## 1.2 Try and fail

To fully understand and be able to use Linux, you must go through all the exercises yourself and get hands-on experience. I will explain what you have to do and use examples. Practical training is essential to learn and remember. Go through all the exercises!

When you have reached a basic understanding of Linux, most of the chapters in this book can be read separately. After learning the basic skills in the first few chapters, you can go on reading any chapter. If, for instance, you want to learn how to use the text editor vi, you can go straight to the chapter on the vi editor without reading the preceding chapters. The exercises at the end of each chapter give you a chance to practice your new skills.

## 1.3 Explanations in this book

Most chapters start with a short summary of their contents. This makes it easier to find what you are looking for.

This book explains how to execute the various commands. For instance, if you want to know date and time, I will explain the method like this:

1. Type **date.**
2. Press **RETURN**.

Linux now shows the current date on your display, for instance:

```
[david@nittedal david]$ date
Sat Nov 24 20:23:28 CET 2001
```

The text you must type and the keys you must press are always set in boldface type. Messages from Linux are set in italics as shown above.

Most commands in Linux are executed by pressing the RETURN key. As you move through the chapters, I will stop writing "press RETURN" when I explain commands, presuming that you know that this is how you execute commands. If I use the graphical user interface (GUI) of Linux, you have the option of using the mouse to execute commands.

Other commands may relate to the command I am currently explaining. I refer to these like this: See also `chmod` and `find`.

## 1.4 Linux and GNU

Linux is based on the Unix OS. The budding start of a free version of Unix was initiated by a group of computer specialists at the Massachusetts Institute of Technology (MIT) in 1984. They founded the Free Software Foundation and developed the GNU GPL (General Public License), which allowed anyone to distribute, change, and even sell the product without paying any license fee. The GNU project developed most of the accessories and applications for a free Unix system, but the most essential part, the core, was missing.

A Finnish student, Linus Torvalds, developed the core of the Linux OS. The project started in 1991, when Linux version 0.02 was released. Version 1.0 of the Linux core was not ready until 1994 (see Figure 1-1). The OS should probably have been named GNU/Linux, but Linux is now well-established. Over the years, a number of volunteers on the Internet have contributed in the further development of Linux. Today, Linux supports most popular microprocessor architectures like Intel I386, Sun SPARC, Digital Alpha, PowerPC, MC680XX, and StrongARM.

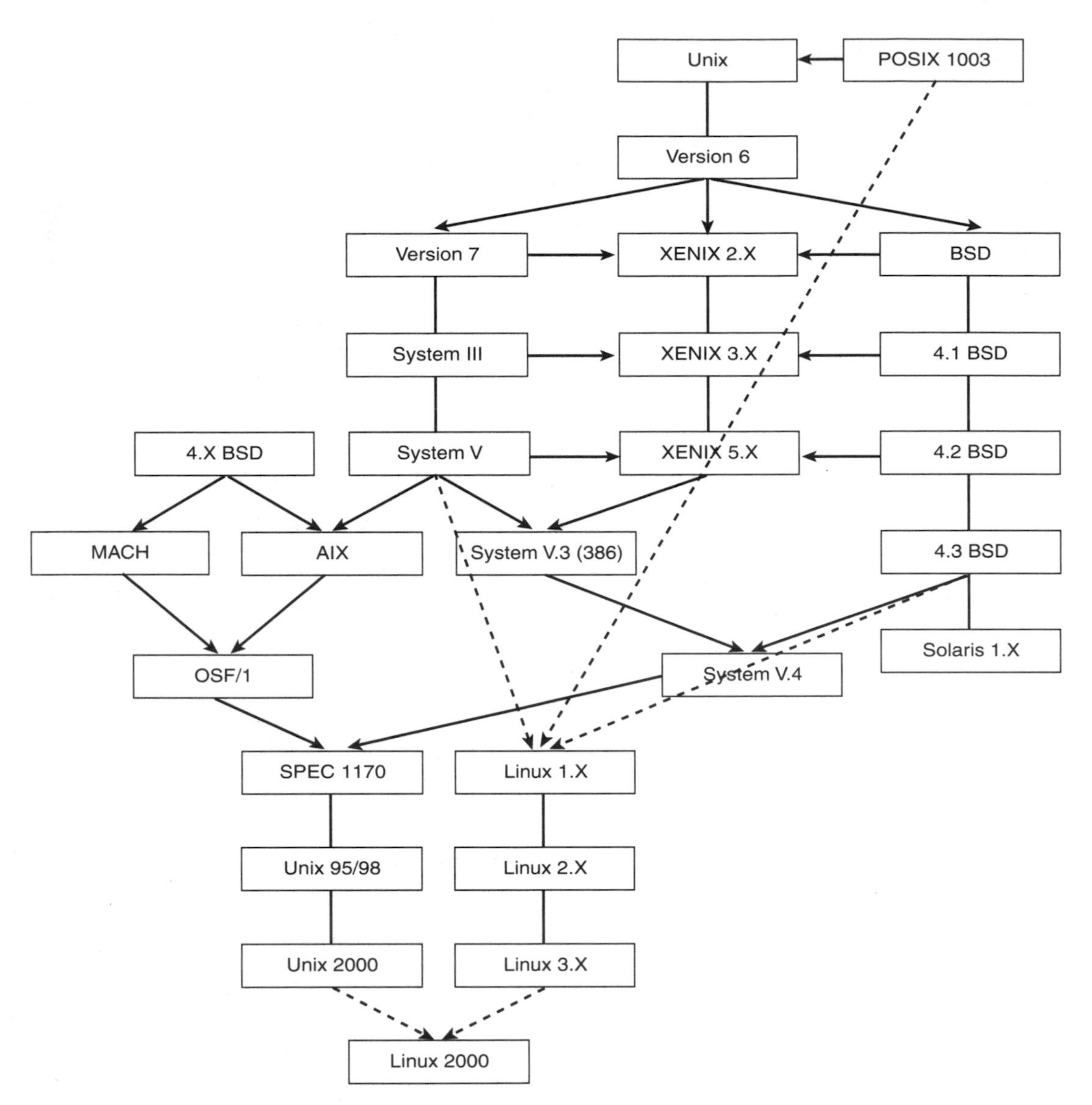


**Figure 1-1**
*Linux has inherited features from several Unix systems. The sketch gives you some history and indicates how I believe Linux will develop in the next few years.*

Linux is a multitasking, multi-user OS with a lot of "Unix-like qualities."

Today you will find a variety of Linux packages. The major differences are normally limited to installation procedures and the choice of control software (device drivers) and accessories (see Figure 1-2).

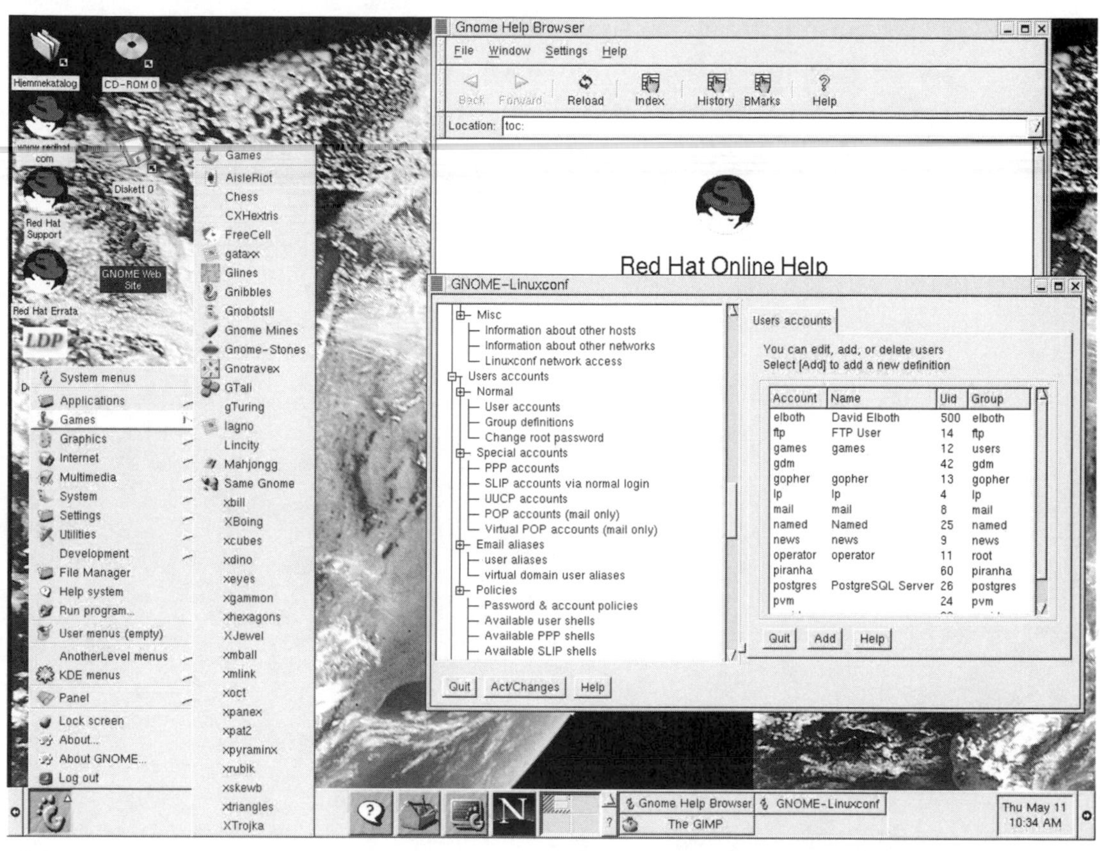


**Figure 1-2**
*A display showing a modern Linux GUI environment. This is the GNOME GUI. There are several other, similar interfaces.*

The most popular Linux distributions today are:

- Caldera (www.caldera.com).
- Craftwork (www.craftwork.com).
- Debian (www.debian.org).
- DosLinux (www.tux.org/pub/people/kent-robotti/index.html).
- LinuxWare (www.trans-am.com).
- Linux Pro (www.wgs.com).
- Mandrake (www.linux-mandrake.com).
- Red Hat (www.redhat.com).
- Slackware (www.cdrom.com).
- SuSE (www.suse.com).
- Corel Linux (www.corel.com)

Whatever distribution you decide to install, you will end up with essentially the same Linux kernel and environment. When explaining commands and exercises, I had to choose one version, so Red Hat Linux is the basis for this book. The creator of the original Linux OS, Linus Torvalds, is a user of Red Hat Linux. Red Hat Linux today has a more than 50% market share.

CHAPTER 2

# The Operating System

## 2.1 The Linux operating system

Without programs, your computer is quite useless, being just a collection of electronic and mechanical components that you cannot use for anything. Programs can be split into three levels: basic control programs built into the computer (BIOS), the OS, and the user applications that you run. The BIOS (Basic Input/Output System) starts when you switch your computer on. This program runs some checks to make sure that the computer functions okay. When the tests are completed, the OS is activated. The OS is not necessarily just one program; it may be a collection of programs. It is the OS that makes it possible to run the computer. It functions as an administrator for the computer and other hardware like printers and storage devices, for your applications and for you and other users. We'll have a look at the various tasks that the OS takes care of in this chapter.

### 2.1.1 Linux Controls

When you press a key on your keyboard, the OS translates the electrical signal from the keyboard to the computer so that the right symbol is displayed. When you print a file, the OS starts the printer and transmits the text from your computer to the printer. When you want to use an accessory belonging to the OS or an application, the OS makes the necessary code available for you to do your work.

### 2.1.2 Linux Interprets

Most commands in applications like word processors, spreadsheets, and databases cannot be understood directly by your computer. The OS acts as an interpreter.

The OS also works as an assistant to the applications. Applications are always designed to work with a certain OS, not with a certain type of processor or computer. This makes it easier to develop versatile software that can solve many different, complex tasks, as the application exploits the OS.

### 2.1.3 Linux Performs Tasks

The OS also executes a number of practical tasks. Floppy disks can be prepared for use (formatted), you can find indexes for hard disk drives and floppy disks, and you can copy and delete files. As I will show you later, an advanced OS like Linux has an array of possibilities.

### 2.1.4 Linux Finds Faults

A central task for the OS is to check that your computer and applications work properly. The OS finds faults and reports them to you. The OS can fix some minor faults, more complicated problems are reported, and it is up to you to handle the trouble-shooting.

## 2.2 A multi-user operating system

Linux is a multi-user operating system, meaning that several users may use the same computer at the same time. The principle of time-sharing accommodates for this, by literally distributing time between users.

If, for instance, two or more users send files to the same printer at the same time, the OS organizes a queue and admits the users one by one. If one single user runs different programs that utilize the same resources in the computer, the OS distributes time between the programs.

The OS also monitors the data flow and prevents data from different users from mixing. It also ensures that different users don't disturb one another. If two users operate the same program, for instance a word processor, the OS organizes each user's access to the program. Although they run the same program, they work with separate data files. The computer is so fast that you normally won't notice that there is someone else using it at the same time.

## 2.3 Concepts and technology

I will now take a closer look at some of Linux's features and explain some of the words and phrases that are used in connection with Linux.

### *2.3.1 Programs and Processes*

Tasks done by a computer are often referred to as processes. A process may be to read data from a file, print a document, do a calculation, or run a large program. One user may run several processes at the same time.

### *2.3.2 Background Processes*

Some processes are called background processes. This means that they run in the background as seen from the terminal (the system unit or X terminal) that you are working at. For instance, if you wish to run a program that will last several minutes, you will be bored sitting at the terminal waiting for the program to finish. You can run the program in the background instead, and run other tasks on the terminal while the program finishes.

### *2.3.3 Shared Resources and Priorities*

The resources you have at hand are, for instance, the computer's processor (CPU), internal memory, hardware like printers, plotters, and external storage units, software, etc. Linux will distribute the access time to these resources between users and between each user's programs.

Linux gives each pending process a priority. This priority list decides in which order the processes will be executed. In most cases, the order will be decided based on the order in which the processes requested access to the resource. However, priorities can be decided in other ways.

As a user, you can influence the priorities. Linux may also have set up mechanisms that decide priorities, or the system may be configured to give certain priorities.

### *2.3.4 Swapping and Paging*

Linux is designed to store only the active part of a program in the computer's main memory. Those parts that are not in use remain on the hard disk. The Linux kernel transfers processes to memory only when needed. When they aren't needed, the processes are returned to the disk.

Other large programs can be moved between disk and memory in the same way.

One of the methods that some operating systems use for this switching is called swapping. Swapping means that a complete program is loaded into the main memory. Paging is another method for transferring processes between disk and memory. Paging moves only parts of a program. The size of these parts is normally 1KB, 2KB, or 4KB (1KB is approximately 1000 characters). Linux uses paging as its switching method.

### *2.3.5 Instruction Part and Data Part*

If, for instance, four users run the same part of Corel WordPerfect 9, we say that they are utilizing the same instruction part of the program. If the size of this part is 100KB, you don't multiply by four and find that they in sum use 400KB. The real figure is a lot lower, say something like 250KB. The reason is that the instruction part is common, and only the data part is special for each user.

## 2.4 Linux and architecture support

Linux is a portable OS that today is supported on the following platforms: Intel, SPARC, Alpha, PowerPC, MCXXX, StrongARM, and IBM Mainframe CPU architecture. This means that a large number of computer architectures are able to run the Linux OS. This is beneficial because most user applications (programs) are designed for use on a certain OS rather than on certain computers.

The practical benefit is that "programs" (source codes) that you have stored in your computer running Linux can be used on any other computer that also runs Linux.

## 2.5 The Linux kernel

Linux is a comprehensive program that is composed of a number of small and large programs. The most important part of Linux is called the kernel. The core is loaded into the internal memory of your computer when you boot it up, and remains there until you turn it off. It is the kernel that is responsible for most of the resource distribution between users and applications.

Most other parts of the Linux OS are not in use all the time. The kernel transfers other parts of Linux from your hard disk to the internal memory whenever necessary. You communicate with the Linux kernel via a program called the shell. This is illustrated in Figure 2-1.

## 2.6 The Linux shell

The part of Linux that is most obvious to the user is the program known as the shell. It is an interpreter placed between the user and the Linux kernel. You type your commands, and the shell translates them into a form that the Linux kernel and other programs can respond to.

There are several different shells that can be used in conjunction with Linux. Some of them are: the Bourne again shell (bash), C shell with filename completion and command-line editing (tcsh), and Z shell (zsh). The most popular shell is the Bourne again shell (bash). Chapter 16, "Shell Programming," is based on the bash.

## 2.7 Utilities

Linux contains a number of programs in addition to the kernel and shell. These are normally referred to as utilities. They may be used individually, but you can also combine them and make more complex Linux programs that use several utilities.

You can use these utilities standalone, or you can use many tools together and create small Linux shell programs. There are also many other tools that can be used as part of the Linux OS.

A certain group of useful applications are programs like word processors, spreadsheets, and databases. There are lots of programs in this category that can be run under Linux. "To be run under Linux" means that these programs are able to communicate with Linux, i.e., that you can use these programs if Linux has been installed on your computer. You can start the programs from Linux and the programs will use Linux to execute certain functions like printing documents.

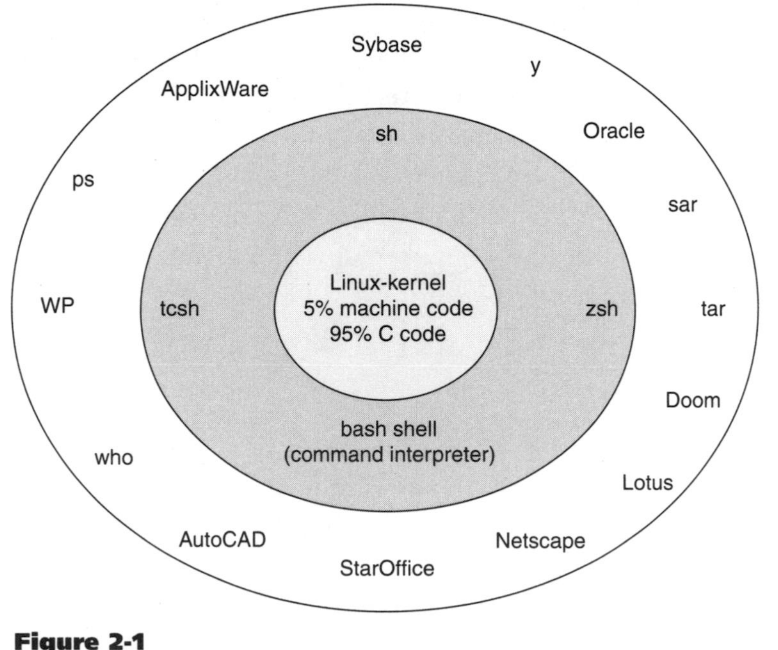


**Figure 2-1**
*The composition of Linux.*

## 2.8 How to use Linux commands

You send commands to Linux via the shell. For example, to print the index of a directory, follow this procedure:

1. Type the index command **ls**.
2. Order Linux to execute the command by pressing **RETURN**.

The index will show on your display. It may look like this:

```
batch
c-files
dhry.c
dok
mbox
text
usr
```

Most of these commands come in different variations. The variation that will be executed is decided by one or more supplementary commands. Supplementary commands are referred to as options or arguments. When I want to show you that a command may have options and/or arguments, I use this notation:

```
Command: ls [option] [argument]
```

`Command` is the name of the program or function that you want to execute, and is always printed first. Normally there must be a space between the command, option, and argument.

Where I've typed "`option`," you can add one or more additional commands, which may have the form of one or more characters. `option` means that you can add details on how you want the command to be executed.

**[ ]**

When an option is inside brackets, the main command does not need more information, and it is up to you whether you want to give additional commands.

**...**

If an option or argument is repeated, I show this with ... (an ellipsis).

**-options**

In most cases, the first option starts with – (hyphen).

`argument` means that you can give additional information about how the command should execute. When an argument is placed inside brackets [ ], it is optional.

To separate what the user types and what the program displays on your monitor, I've used the following conventions in my examples:

- What the user types is printed in bold typeface.
- A message from the program on your display is printed in italics.

For example:

```
[root@nittedal /root]# ls -la
total 16
drwxr-xr-x 4 root   root   1024 Nov 24 20:52 .
```

```
drwxr-xr-x 19 root  root  1024 Nov  8 19:15
-rw-r—r—    1 root  root  736 Nov 24 21:02 .FVWM2-errors
-rw-r—r—    1 root  root  1126 Aug 23  2000 .Xdefaults
-rw-r—r—    1 root  root  2069 Dec 30 12:01 .bash_history
-rw-r—r—    1 root  root  24 Jul 14  1999 .bash_logout
-rw-r—r—    1 root  root  238 Aug 23  2000 .bash_profile
-rw-r—r—    1 root  root  176 Aug 23  2000 .bashrc
-rw-r—r—    1 root  root  180 Mar  4  2001 .cshrc
drwxr-xr-x 2 root  root  1024 Nov  8 20:45 .prognet
drwxr-xr-x 2 root  root  1024 Nov  8 20:56 .seyon
-rw-r—r—    1 root  root  166 Mar  4  2001 .tcshrc
-rw-r—r—    1 root  root  324 Nov 24 20:52 Xrootenv.0
[root@nittedal /root]#
```

This is an example to show how a command with an option and an argument may display:

```
ls -t htm*
```

`ls` is a command that is used to display a list of files in a directory. The option `-t` means that the list will be sorted chronologically by year, month, and time. The newest files are listed first, the oldest ones at the end. The argument `htm*` means that all files starting with "`htm`" will be listed on your display.

A command may also be typed without options or arguments. The command will be executed in its standard form. This means that the command has a standard form and a standard argument that will be used unless other options or arguments are included. I'll use the `ls` command as an example:

```
ls
```

When no options or arguments are added, this command will list the files in the current working directory.

## 2.9 Pipes, filters, and redirections

In Linux, you may create new commands by combining commands. Here is an example that shows a combined command:

```
ls | wc -l
```

The `ls` command displays a list. The next command, `wc -l`, counts the number of lines in this list.

These combined commands in Linux are referred to as pipes. I think of it as a system where the result of the first command is transferred in a kind of pipe to the next command, where a new function is executed.

The symbol | denotes a pipe. When this symbol is placed between two commands, the second command will be executed on the basis of the results of the first command.

Pipes can be used to combine a large number of programs in a pipeline. Each program will execute certain operations. These programs are also called filters, as each program filters the data before transferring it to the next program.

Each command has certain standard functions. The commands get data via a certain input channel and output them via another channel. The `ls` (list) command gets its information from the keyboard and outputs it via the display. The keyboard is the standard input channel for the `ls` command and the display is the standard output channel.

It is possible to change the standard input and output channels. If you want to output data somewhere else, you may use the following command:

```
ls > /dev/lp0
```

which outputs the list to your printer rather than to your display. The following command:

```
ls > datafil
```

writes the list to a data file rather than to your display. Changing the standard input or output channel is called redirecting data.

## 2.10 Editing text

Linux contains several programs for editing text. The most common ones are ed and red (line-oriented editors), vi, pico, and emacs (screen-oriented editors), and xedit (an X-based editor). The editors are used to type, delete, add, or move text. You can also copy text from other files. The very popular vi editor has very advanced text-processing facilities.

## 2.11 The system administrator, or root

The system administrator can start and terminate Linux, add or delete users, and maintain and manage the Linux system. A number of commands are used to monitor the status of various parts of the system. If the system is running out of storage capacity, the system administrator can ask the users to go through their files and delete files that are no longer needed. When you have installed the Linux OS on your computer, you can be the system administrator and/or a normal user.

To execute system administration functions, you will use some commands that are not accessible to normal users. A person with access to these commands is called a system administrator, or root. System administrators have a certain user ID and group ID that give access to the system administrator commands.

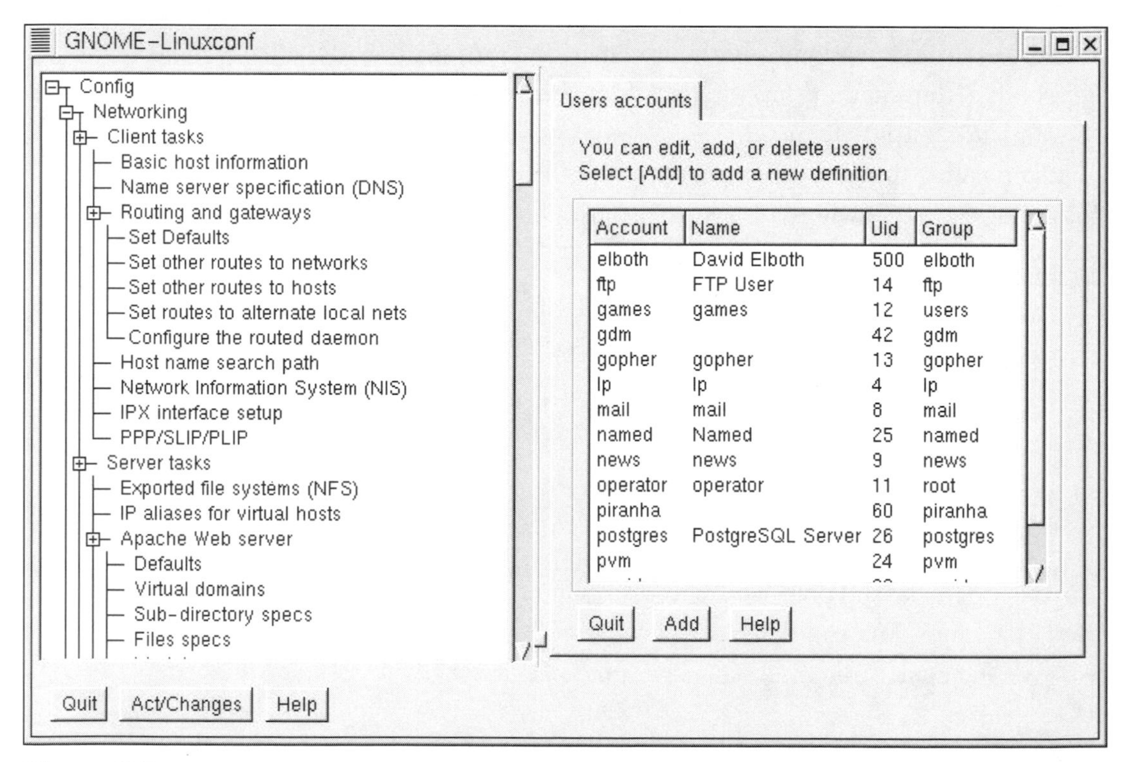


**Figure 2-2**
*The administrator shell Linuxconf.*

Some of the material in this book is intended for system administrators (roots) only (see Figure 2-2). This material is a bit more complicated. If you are a normal user and have an already configured computer, you may just skip these sections.

CHAPTER
3

# Installation

## 3.1 Introduction

In this chapter, I will explain how to install Linux. Linux is free and no organization or unit is responsible for publishing new versions and distributions of the software. Anyone can make and produce Linux distribution. I have focused on how to install Red Hat Linux. You can download the latest ISO image of Red Hat Linux from www.redhat.com. From the ISO image you can create bootable CDs. I will not discuss all available installation variations—that would make a separate book. The instructions are focused on a "standard" installation.

## 3.2 Preparing to install Linux

It is important to plan the process before you start installing Linux. This is especially significant if you are already running other operating systems on your PC.

Using a PC that contains standard components simplifies the process, as you will find Linux device drivers for the most popular PC components. If you want to use Red Hat Linux, you should check Red Hat's online resources to make sure your hardware is compatible and supported. You will find the hardware compatibility list at http://www.redhat.com/hardware.

Prior to installation, you should get an overview of how the main board and cards are set up with memory addresses, I/O addresses, DMA channels, and hardware interrupts. If Windows is already installed, you will find the necessary technical specifications in Start> Settings> Control Panel> System.

Here is a simple checklist:

- Machine architecture – Type (ix86, SPARC, Alpha, PowerPC, MC68XXX, MIPS, StrongARM).
- Hard disk drives – Type (IDE/SCSI), size (2GB/1000GB), parameters.
- BIOS type.
- Size of memory.
- CD-ROM – Type (IDE, SCSI), parameters.
- Display card – Type, parameters (amount of RAM).
- Monitor – Make, model, technical data.
- SCSI card – Type, parameters.
- Network interface card – Type, parameters.
- Audio card – Type, parameters.
- Tape drive and card – Type, parameters.
- Mouse – Type, parameters.
- I/O ports – Type (RS-232, parallel port, USB).

It is essential that you take note of everything that you do and enter during both the entire Linux installation process and during the configuration setup. If things go wrong, you will know where in the process it happened. Make sure that you have all documentation on your hardware on hand as well as the documentation for the Linux distribution you are about to install. These suggestions are useful no matter what OS you are installing.

## 3.3 Installation overview

In this chapter, I'll describe how to install Red Hat Linux. However, the general procedure is identical no matter which Linux distribution you have chosen.

You will do the following:

- Repartition your hard disk drive(s) to make room for Linux.
- Boot the Linux installation media (floppy, CD).
- Define Linux partitions.
- Define filesystems and swap.
- Install Linux software in the new filesystems.

Red Hat Linux has two installation programs, one character-based and one with a GUI. Both installation programs will lead you through the process and automate one or more of the steps mentioned above.

The installation process is described in detail on the Red Hat home site (www.redhat.com). You can also download the documentation and make your own documentation CD.

## 3.4 Linux and the keyboard

During the Red Hat installation process, keys and function keys have specific functions (see Table 3-1). You can move between different fields with the arrow keys or with the mouse.

If you choose the character-based installation, you can move field by field forward by pressing Tab and backward by pressing Alt and Tab at the same time. When you want to select a field, just press the Spacebar or the RETURN key.

**Table 3-1**
**Function Keys During Installation**

| Screen | Keys | Screen Description |
|---|---|---|
| 1 | Alt + F1 | Installation dialog. |
| 2 | Alt + F2 | Command line (bash shell). |
| 3 | Alt + F3 | Installation log. |
| 4 | Alt + F4 | System log (messages from the Linux kernel and other active programs). |
| 5 | Alt + F5 | Other messages. |
| 7 | Alt + F7 | X Window System. |

When using the character-based installation, you indicate a selection or remove an existing selection by pressing the Spacebar. If you press the function key F12, the field value is stored and you can go on to the next field.

When you boot Linux with the installation disk, you already have a multi-tasking and multi-user OS that allows multiple virtual screens.

At any time during the installation process, you can change between these screens. During the installation process, Screen 1 is important as it displays the installation dialog. Screen 3 is also important because it displays the installation log. If you choose to install via the GUI, you should stick to Screen 7 (X Window). When using the GUI installation, you just use the mouse to indicate when you want to move forward (Next) or backward (Back) during the installation process.

## 3.5 Different installation methods

Red Hat Linux has four major installation methods:

- Local installation disk.
- Installation disk for network installation.
- Installation disk for PCMCIA unit.
- Installation CD-ROM.

The last option is used when the machine is capable of loading the Linux OS directly from a CD-ROM with a boot track. You must have a relatively new PC (BIOS) that supports the CD-ROM standard El Torito.

If your machine is not capable of loading the OS from CD-ROM, you must make an installation disk. If you have a traditional PC with a standard CD-ROM drive, you must make a local installation disk. This is the most frequently used disk option. When the disk has loaded the Linux kernel, including the CD-ROM device drivers, the rest of the OS is read from the Red Hat Linux CD-ROM.

With the "Installation disk for network installation" or "Installation disk for PCMCIA unit" options, you can use these copying methods: hard drive, NFS, FTP, or HTTP. If you copied the Red Hat Linux files to a local hard drive, you may use the hard drive method. If a Linux or Unix machine[1] is set up on your

[1]It is possible to run an NT server as an NFS server, too.

network, you may install via NFS. The external NFS filesystem may be a part of a hard disk drive, the entire hard disk drive, or a shared Linux CD-ROM. If you have set up an FTP server and it contains the Linux files, you may install directly from the FTP server. The FTP server may also be on the Internet. The last option is an HTTP server. You can install Linux on a PC from an HTTP server.

Select "Installation disk for PCMCIA unit" if your machine requires PCMCIA support during installation (portable computer) or if your machine does not have boot support for a CD-ROM. It is possible to set up PCMCIA support later if you have installed the PCMCIA package.

You make the installation disks from a DOS-based machine or from the command line in Windows by following this procedure:

1. Put an empty, formatted disk in your PC's floppy drive.
2. Use the `rawrite` command from the Red Hat Linux boot CD-ROM.

For example:

```
C:\> d:
D:\> cd \dosutils
D:\dosutils> rawrite
Enter disk image source file name: ..\images\boot.img
Enter target diskette drive: a:
Please insert a formatted diskette into drive A: and
press —ENTER— : ENTER
D:\dosutils>
```

When applicable, replace "d:" with the drive letter of your CD-ROM drive. For example:

```
C:\> rawrite -f e:\images\boot.img -d a:
```

In the last example, you need a search path to the `rawrite` command. E is the drive letter of the CD-ROM drive. A is the floppy drive. With the option `-f`, I specify the disk image file. The option `-d` specifies the diskette drive to use.

| BOOT File | Description |
|---|---|
| `BOOT.IMG` | Local installation disk. |
| `BOOTNET.IMG` | Installation disk for network installation. |
| `PCMCIA.IMG` | Installation disk for PCMCIA unit. |

Each installation disk offers various installation methods for the Red Hat Linux OS. You will find a more comprehensive description of how to make installation disks on the Red Hat Web site, www.redhat.com.

When using a Linux installation disk, the device driver for the CD-ROM drive will be loaded from the installation disk. You may also select this option when installing from a local hard disk drive.

The rest of this installation description is based on the assumption that you either selected the option "Local installation disk" (copies the OS from the CD-ROM) or that you start directly from the CD-ROM (bootable CD-ROM).

## 3.6 Installation disk or CD

You start installing Red Hat by placing the Red Hat Linux installation disk in your PC or workstation and switching your machine on. If your machine is capable of booting directly from a CD-ROM (most modern PCs are), you of course use the CD-ROM rather than a floppy.

When starting the Linux installation from a floppy or a CD-ROM, a startup menu will pop up on your screen. The screen will contain some options. You can choose from among the following function keys:

- F1 displays the original window.
- F2 offers help and explains available options.
- F3 offers help on "Expert mode." In this mode, you must select device drivers.
- F4 offers help on how to set Linux kernel parameters when booting.
- F5 offers help on emergency boot via the CD-ROM.

Press the RETURN key. The process of unzipping and running the Linux kernel starts. (The Linux installation program of course runs under Linux.) A new menu window tells you to insert the Red Hat CD-ROM in the CD-ROM drive, unless you have started directly from the CD-ROM.

Here are some boot prompt examples:

```
boot:
```

Linux will give you various messages in connection with several boot options. When you press RETURN, the default Linux system will load. This normally is sufficient to install Linux.

```
boot: text
```

You are running a character-based installation.

```
boot: dd
```

You have a separate driver disk (fd, hd, CD-ROM).

```
boot: rescue
```

You are entering Emergency mode. In this mode, you can rescue an earlier Linux installation. Use this mode when the Linux system does not load in the normal way.

```
boot: expert
```

You are running in Expert mode if Linux does not find all the hardware components in standard mode.

```
boot: linux mem=256M
```

The Linux kernel uses the entire RAM in a 256MB system. (RAM is the machine's internal memory.)

## 3.7 CD auto-boot from DOS

If your machine is not capable of booting directly from a CD-ROM (most modern PCs and SPARC workstations/servers boot from CD) and you have a device driver in MS-DOS that accesses the CD-ROM, follow this procedure:

1. Boot MS-DOS.
2. Place the Red Hat Linux boot CD in the CD-ROM drive.
3. Go to the CD-ROM mapping, e.g., *C:\>*D:
4. *D:\>*cd \dosutils
5. *D:\dosutils>*autoboot.bat

You will now enter the Installation menu. This method will not work from MS-DOS in Windows, Windows 98, Windows NT, or Windows 2000. You must boot in pure MS-DOS. Remember that you also need space for the Linux partitions on your hard disk drive. If the MS-DOS partition occupies the entire hard disk drive, the disk must be repartitioned.

## 3.8 Selecting the language and character set

After pressing ENTER, you are welcomed to Red Hat Linux. The Language Selection window opens and offers several installation language options (see Figure 3-1).

The next window (see Figure 3-2) is for keyboard configuration, which consists of three parts: model, layout, and variation. The most frequently used keyboards are Generic 101-key PC and Generic 102-key (Intl) PC.

After installing Linux, you may change your keyboard by running the `kbdconfig` command.

Example:

```
[root@nittedal /root]# /usr/sbin/kbdconfig
```

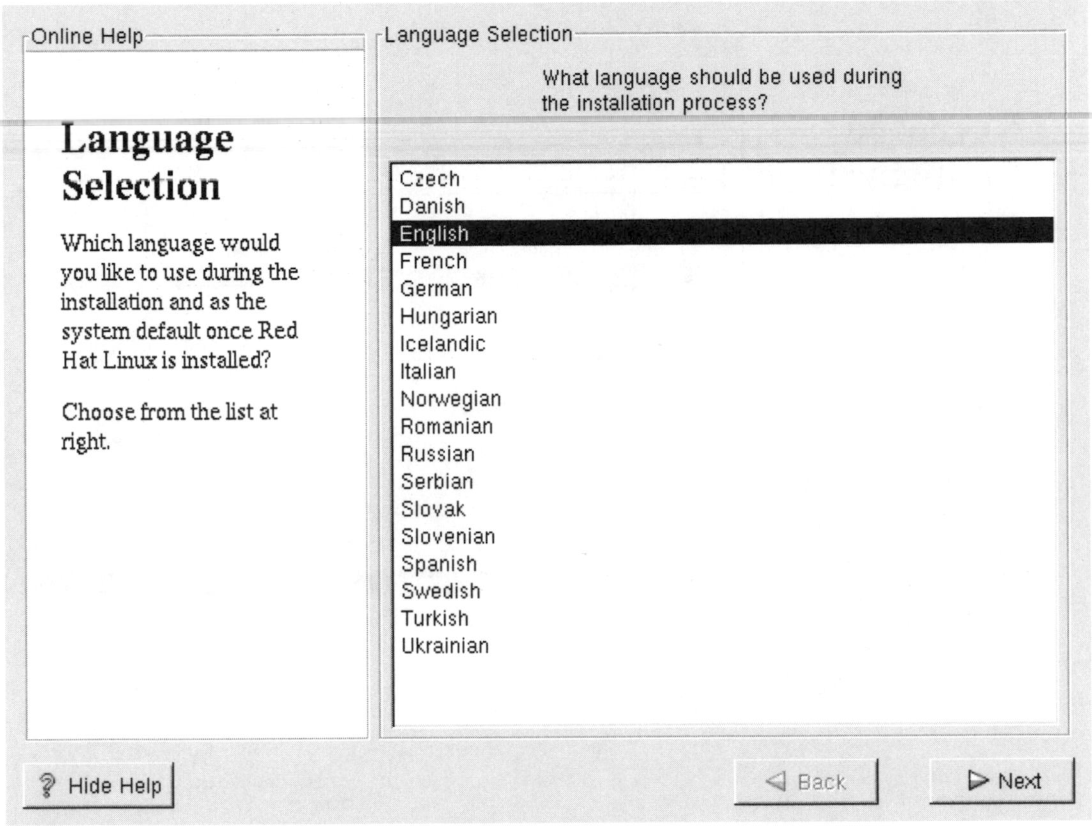

**Figure 3-1**
*Here you can choose which language you would like to use during the installation.*

If you later prefer to change to a language other than English, I recommend that you run the **`locale_config`** command and select the required language. Some programs will use your local language better.

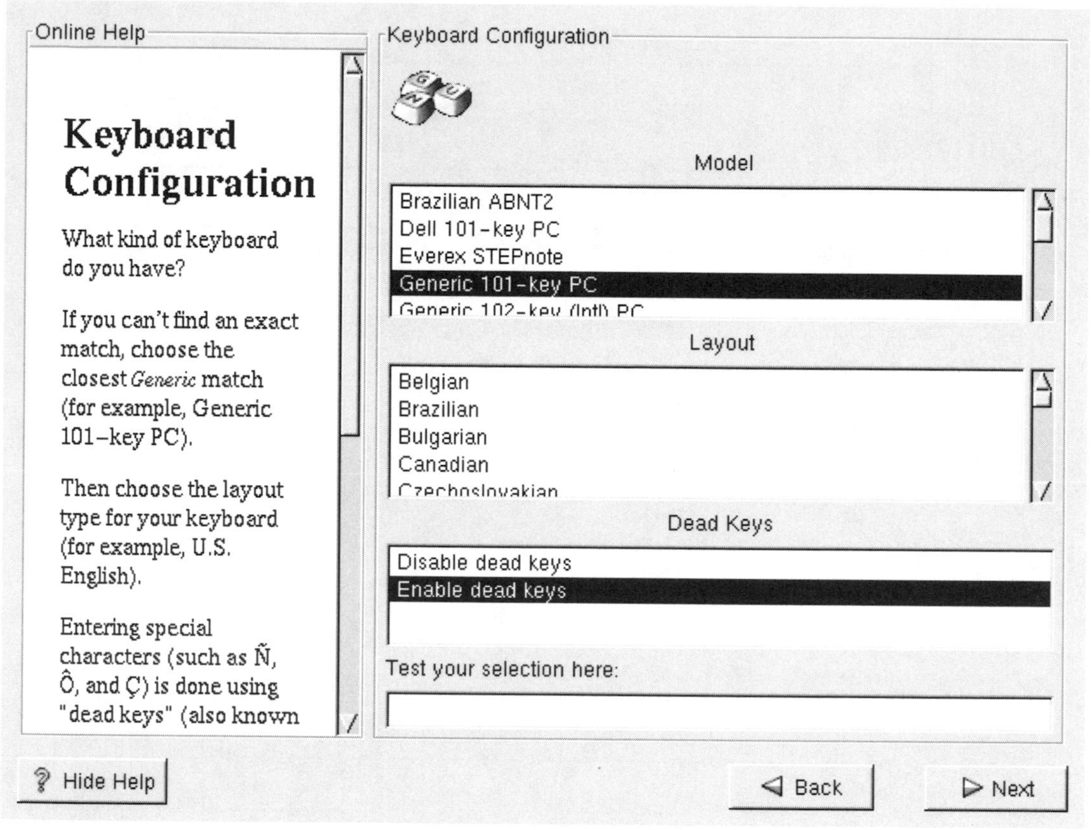

**Figure 3-2**
*Here you choose which kind of keyboard you have.*

## 3.9 Configuring the mouse

Most mice will be recognized automatically. If this is not the case with your mouse, you will be asked about what kind of mouse you have. Pick the right one from the list (see Figure 3-3). If you cannot find your mouse on the list, you must pick a compatible mouse. Red Hat Linux 7.x also supports a mouse and keyboard connected via the USB port.

If you have a two-button mouse, you will be asked if you want the mouse to emulate a three-button mouse. As X Window is based on a three-button mouse, it makes sense to select three-button mouse emulation.

After installing Linux, you may change your mouse by running the **`mouse-config`** command.

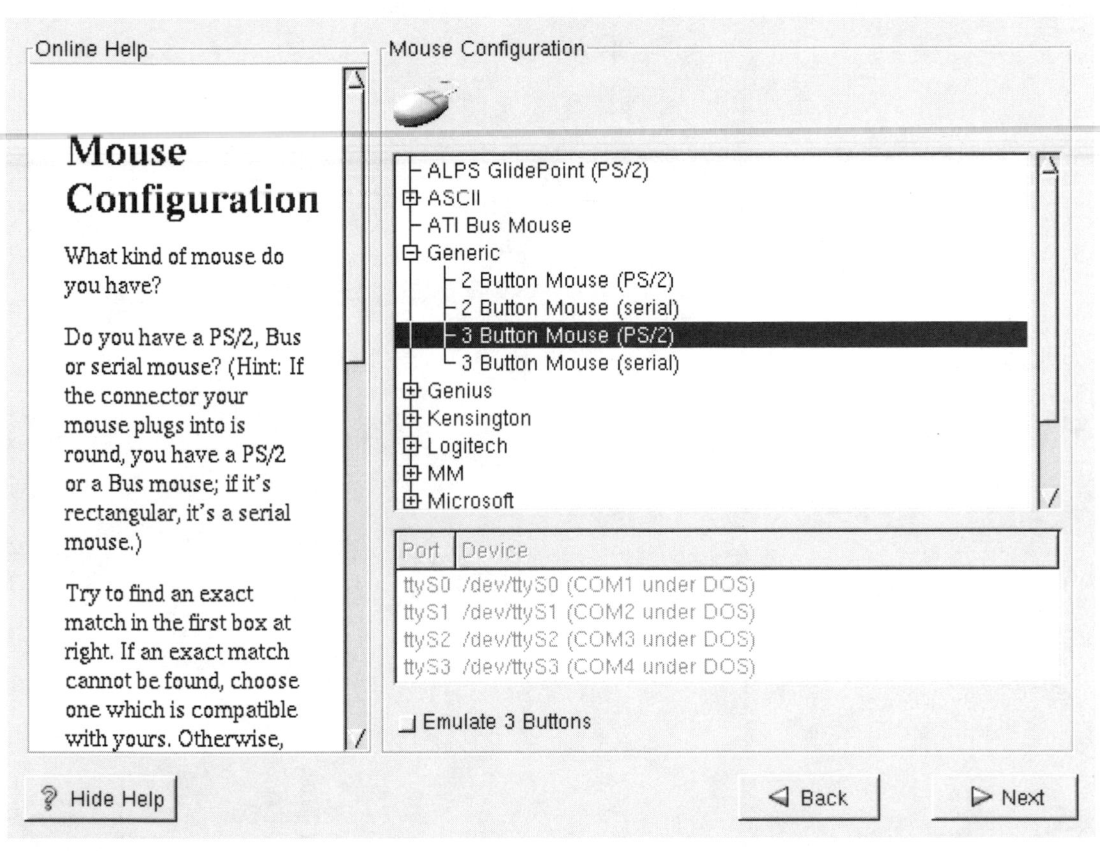


**Figure 3-3**
*Here you specify which kind of mouse you have.*

Example:

```
[root@nittedal /root]# /usr/sbin/mouseconfig
```

You will find more information about setting up a mouse in Chapter 19. If you have problems with Microsoft Intellimouse Logitech Pilot+ or Logitech Mouseman+ (the middle button), you can get help at http://www.inria.fr/koala/colas/mouse-wheel-scroll.

## 3.10 Installation classes

After Red Hat's Welcome screen, you enter a menu window for selecting the installation class (see Figure 3-4). This menu window gives you the options of

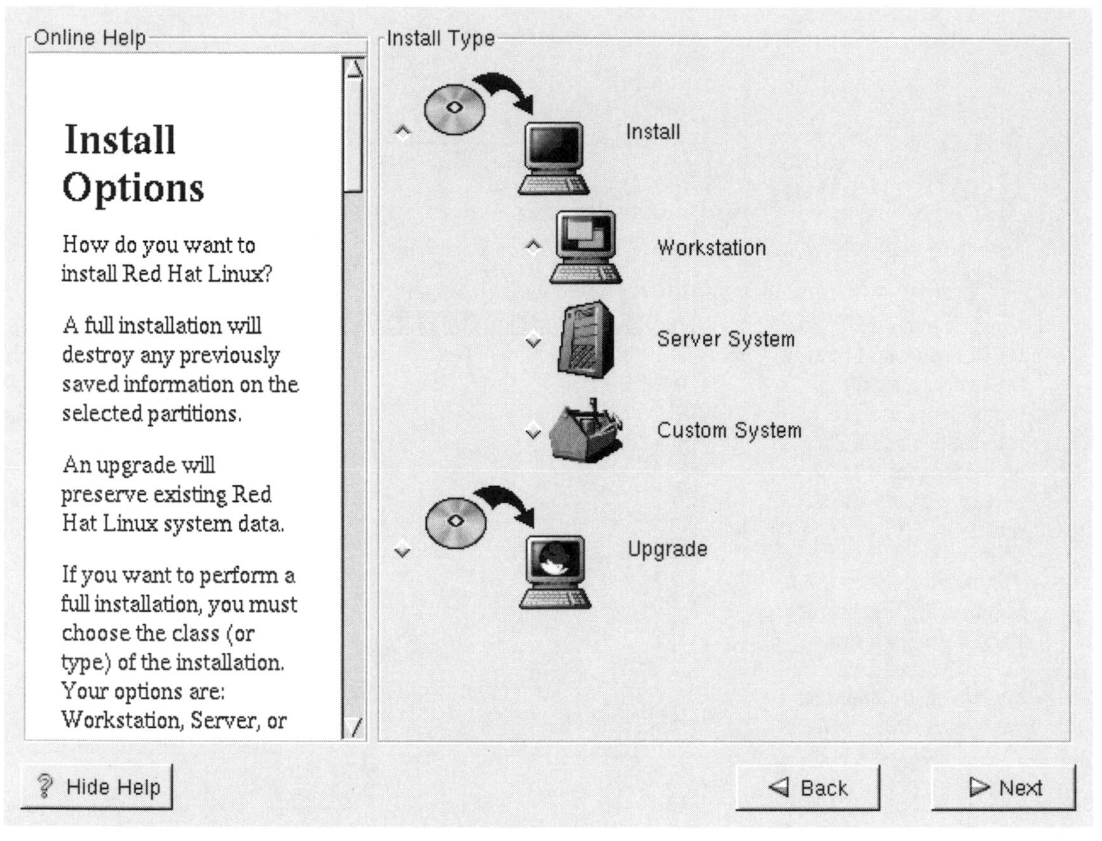


**Figure 3-4**
*Here you choose how you want to install Red Hat Linux.*

making a new installation or upgrading an existing Red Hat system.

A new installation method is called "no partition." If you select "no partition," you can install Red Hat Linux on a DOS or Windows partition. There will be more on partitions later.

If you select to upgrade, you keep the existing filesystems and data, whereas a new installation removes existing filesystems and data. In addition, you can choose from among the following installation classes:

- **Workstation (GNOME/KDE).**
- **Server System.**
- **Custom System.**

These are parallel to what is offered by SCO UnixWare and Sunsoft Solaris on their installation CDs with Unix operating systems. When you select

"Workstation" or "Server System," respectively, the number of filesystems, swap areas, applications, and OS services will be set up as a function of a workstation (client) or server solution. For example, the NFS, FTP, and SQL processes will be set up when you select the "Server System" option, while only the client software will be set up when you select the "Workstation" option.

If you select "Workstation," Linux will remove all existing Linux partitions. If you select "Server System," Linux will remove all existing Linux partitions and other operating systems, like Windows 98 or Windows 2000.

If you wish to set up a workstation but don't know whether to choose GNOME or KDE, you should read Chapter 10 before making the decision.

The hard disk drive is normally divided into partitions. One or more partitions may be dedicated to an OS. One hard disk drive may have multiple partitions for different operating systems like MS-DOS, OS/2, Windows (Linux may be installed on a DOS/Windows partition), and Linux. If there are already other operating systems on the system, you may have to change these partitions to make room for Linux[2]. Then you make one or more Linux partitions in the freed area. The minimum requirement is one filesystem, for Linux (/=root) and one swap partition. This process is called repartitioning.

If you don't need to control the repartitioning in detail, you may just select the "Workstation" or "Server, System" option, and the rest of the installation will be considerably simpler. In the rest of this chapter, I will take a closer look at a custom installation.

## 3.11 Defining filesystems

After defining the type of installation that you want, you will go directly to the menu for partitions and filesystems (see Figure 3-5). Here you will specify at which mount points (filesystems) you will install Linux. Red Hat offers two different tools that can be used to modify partition tables: Disk Druid (Manually partition with Disk Druid) and `fdisk` (Manually partition with `fdisk`). The `fdisk` program is completely comparable to the DOS-based `fdisk` program and is simple to use. I recommend using Disk Druid, which is more advanced and gives you better control. If you are running a graphic installation, you will

[2]Only a separate Linux partition will give 100% Linux functionality.

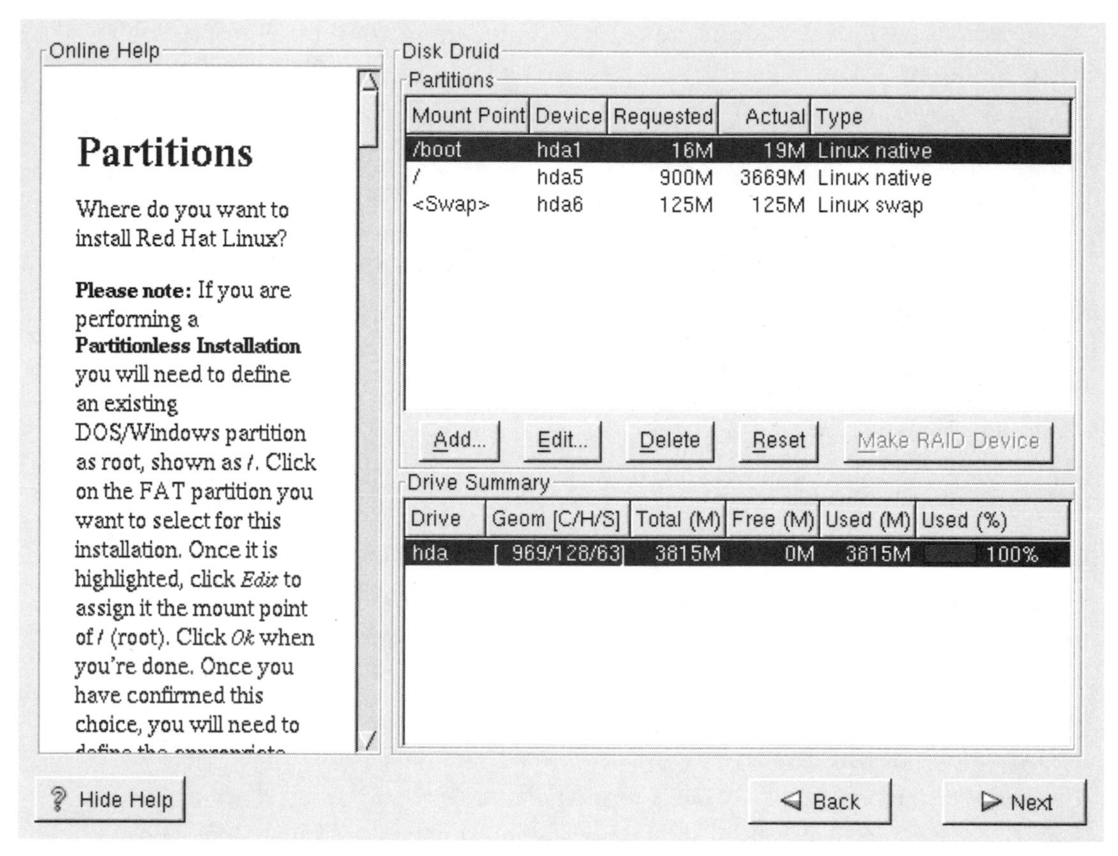


**Figure 3-5**
*Here you specify where you want to install Red Hat Linux.*

go straight into an X Window-based version of Disk Druid.

Each line in "Disk Druid Partitions" represents a hard disk drive partition equal to a DOS partition. If you have one DOS partition that uses the entire disk, this partition will be identified as C:. If you have more than one partition under DOS or Windows, these will be identified as D:, E:, etc.

The first sector of the disk will always have an MBR (Master Boot Record), together with a partition table. As the name indicates, the function of the MBR is booting the system.

The partition table contains information about the size and location of partitions. Under Linux, the files are stored in a filesystem, which is a part of the hard disk drive. Each filesystem is defined in a separate partition on the hard disk drive. You can view these partitions with the Disk Druid program. Each line has five different columns:

- **Mount Point.**
- **Device.**
- **Requested.**
- **Actual.**
- **Type.**

The Mount Point field lets you decide where to mount the partition in the filesystem. Linux has a different filesystem model from what you probably know from DOS and Windows. In Linux, all partitions are mounted into a complete filesystem and all filesystems (partitions) are located somewhere under root (/). Under Device, you will find the name of the partition. Partitions are named according to disk type, disk controller, and the port at which the disk is located. The first disk on the first IDE port is called `/dev/hda1`. SCSI disks get names like `/dev/sdX`, where `X` indicates the SCSI controller to which it is connected and which SCSI ID number it has. Requested shows the minimum partition size that was set when defining the partition. Actual tells you how much space that has been allocated to the partition so far. The last field, Type, defines the partition type.

In the Drive Summary section, you will find technical data for the hard disk drive. In the Drive field, you will find the name of the device driver for the disk. The Geom [C/H/S] field shows the disk's total number of cylinders, disk heads, and sectors. Total tells you the disk's total capacity. Used shows the portion of the disk allocated to the partition at the moment. Free tells you how much free space there is on the disk. The red graph below Used gives you visual information about hard disk usage.

The following menu options are available in the Disk Druid program: Add, Edit, Delete, and Reset. Use Add when defining a new partition (see Figure 3-6). With Edit, you can edit an indicated, existing partition. Delete removes an indicated partition. Reset brings back the original partitions.

When installing Linux, you need at least two partitions (/ and Linux swap). If you have a large hard disk drive (6GB or more), it makes sense to have separate partitions (filesystems) for `/ (root)`, `/boot`, `/usr`, `/home`, `/prog`, etc. You should also assess the need for separate partitions for `/tmp` and `/var`. `/tmp` is unique because every user has read and write access to it. This could be a problem because users can fill up the disk. `/var` contains logs and e-mail queues. If you intend to use the machine as an e-mail server, I recommend that you keep `/var` in a separate partition or on a separate hard disk drive. The size of partitions is set at n MB, where n is a whole number. When defining a partition, you may define a fixed size or make it growable, i.e., extendable. You may set multiple partitions as growable as long as there is free space on your hard disk drive. Under Type, you can select Linux swap or various filesystems. The Linux native or DOS filesystem (max. 32MB or larger than 32MB) is the most usual setting. The DOS filesystem will be mounted when the Linux system boots, just like the Linux native filesystem.

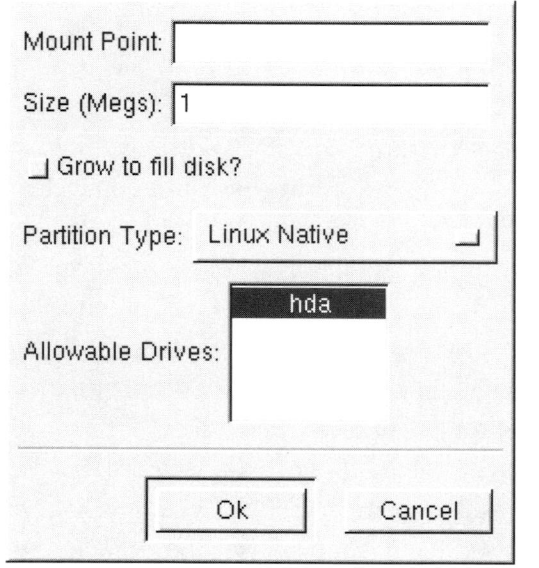


**Figure 3-6**
*Here you specify your file system mount point, size, and type of file system and allowable drives.*

In the Allowable Drives field, there is a list of the hard disks that are installed on the system and that have been checked and accepted by the installation program. Here you can select the hard disk drives that you want to be accessible to Linux. When you are satisfied with the partitions, select Ok. If you don't want to define the current partition, select Cancel.

I recommend that you start by defining Linux's swap area (the technology is paging). On older Unix machines, the rule of thumb was defining swap as *2.5 x RAM*. This is not valid for Linux as the virtual memory (VM) of Linux is *VM=swap+RAM*, whether swap is larger than or smaller than RAM. If you have 64MB RAM, define the swap area to 128MB. 128MB is a handy size as it is the maximum swap partition size under Linux 2.2 and there is plenty of room for it on all modern hard disk drives. The partitions are connected to each defined filesystem (/, /boot, /usr, /usr/src, /var/spool/lpd, /stuff, and /usr/local).

The Linux kernel will automatically be placed under / (root) if you don't have a /boot partition. You will find partition size limitations on many PC BIOSes. Creating a small /boot partition to hold the Linux kernel is therefore a good idea. But, don't make this partition larger than 16MB.

The swap area is always defined by multiples of 128MB. You can have as many 128MB swap partitions as you like.

If you are upgrading Linux, the Linux installation must find already defined Linux partitions. Root (/) is the most important one. If there is no root partition, you cannot upgrade; you must make a completely new installation. All existing data will then be erased.

## 3.12 Format and partitions

When all partitions and the swap area have been defined, you can select Next. The next menu picture lists your partitions (see Figure 3-7).

Now you can choose whether or not to format the partitions and check if there are defective areas in the partitions. I recommend that you run both options, as this is the only way to be absolutely sure that all data has been removed and that bad blocks have been listed to prevent data from being written to them.

## 3.13 Installing LILO

If you have selected either the "Workstation" or "Server System" installation class, you will not be asked any questions connected to LILO (see Figure 3-8). The installation will run automatically.

LILO (Linux Loader) is a program that is installed to the MBR of the hard disk drive. LILO can boot a number of operating systems, including Windows, DOS, and Linux. When booting, LILO lets you choose which OS to run.

There are two alternative locations for LILO under Linux:

- **MBR (e.g., /dev/hda).**
- **First sector of boot partition (e.g., /dev/hda5).**

Online Help
Choose Partitions to Format
Choose the partitions that you would like to format for Red Hat Linux.
Do you want to check for bad blocks?
Checking for bad blocks can help prevent data loss by finding the bad blocks on a drive and making a list of them to prevent data from being written to them in the future.
Choose partitions to Format
/dev/hda5 /
/dev/hda1 /boot
Check for bad blocks while formatting
Hide Help
Back
Next

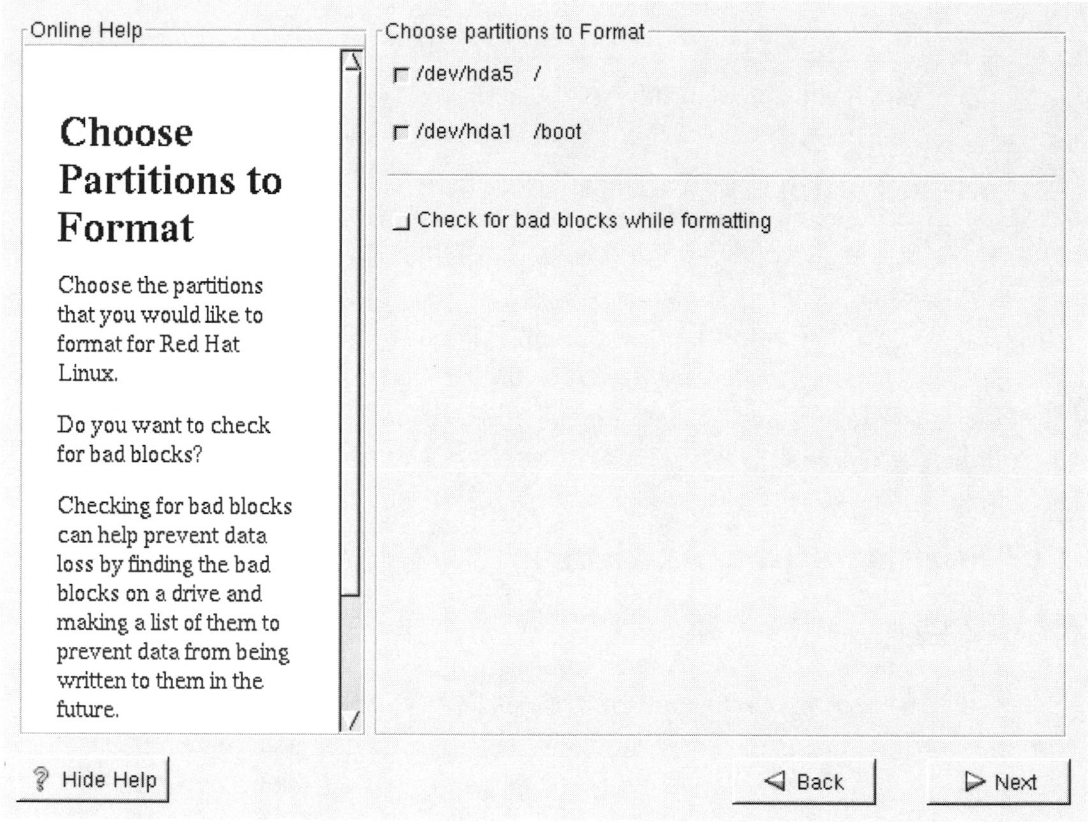

**Figure 3-7**
*Here you specify partitions to format.*

You can also choose not to install LILO.

I recommend that you install the MBR boot program unless you are running another operating system's boot program like System Commander or OS/2 from IBM. The exceptions are Windows NT and Windows 2000. If you are using either of these operating systems and would like to install LILO, you should install it on the first sector of the boot partition rather than on the MBR. You will find more information on dual-boot Linux and Windows NT at http://www.linuxdoc.org/HOWTO/mini/Linux+NT-Loader.html.

If you choose the MBR, you can be sure that Linux will boot as the MBR loads, immediately after the BIOS has been loaded. LILO will display the LILO command line that gives you the option of loading other operating systems. If you have another boot program that can be configured to start LILO, you should install LILO on the first sector of the boot partition. The last option,

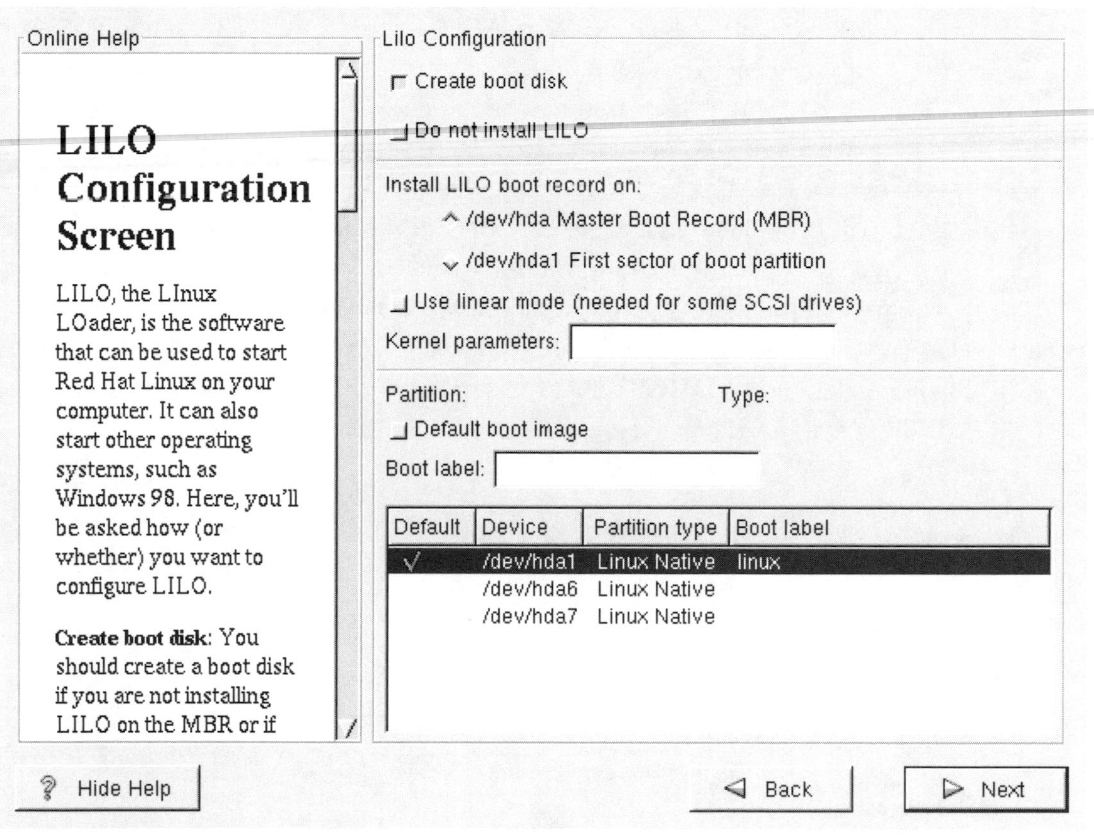


**Figure 3-8**
*Here you specify the configuration of the Linux Loader (LILO).*

not installing LILO, is only applicable if you intend to load Linux from a boot disk (floppy disk) every time.

In this menu, you can also apply options to the Linux kernel when the system is booting. In a standard installation, this is not necessary.

If you don't want LILO to load your Linux system, there are several alternatives. You can, for example, create a boot disk. It is also possible to load Linux from a DOS partition using LOADLIN or SYSLinux. You will find more information on LOADLIN and SYSLinux at ftp://metalab.unc.edu/pub/Linux/system/boot/dualboot.

## 3.14 Network configuration

After you have installed LILO, you are asked about configuring your network interface cards (see Figure 3-9), unless you have already done this (for example, when installing using FTP, NFS, or HTTP, or using PCMCIA support). If you don't set up any network communication, your Linux machine will be unable to communicate with other machines via the network interfaces accessing a LAN (Local Area Network) or WAN (Wide Area Network).

When you have selected your network configuration, the installation program will try to analyze and identify your network card. If you have a familiar card, the installation program will find it and the correct hardware parameters. The next step is setting up the IP address.

You can choose between a DHCP and fixed IP address. If you choose DHCP, you need to have a DHCP server on your network that gives you an IP address. If there is no DHCP server, you must choose fixed IP address.

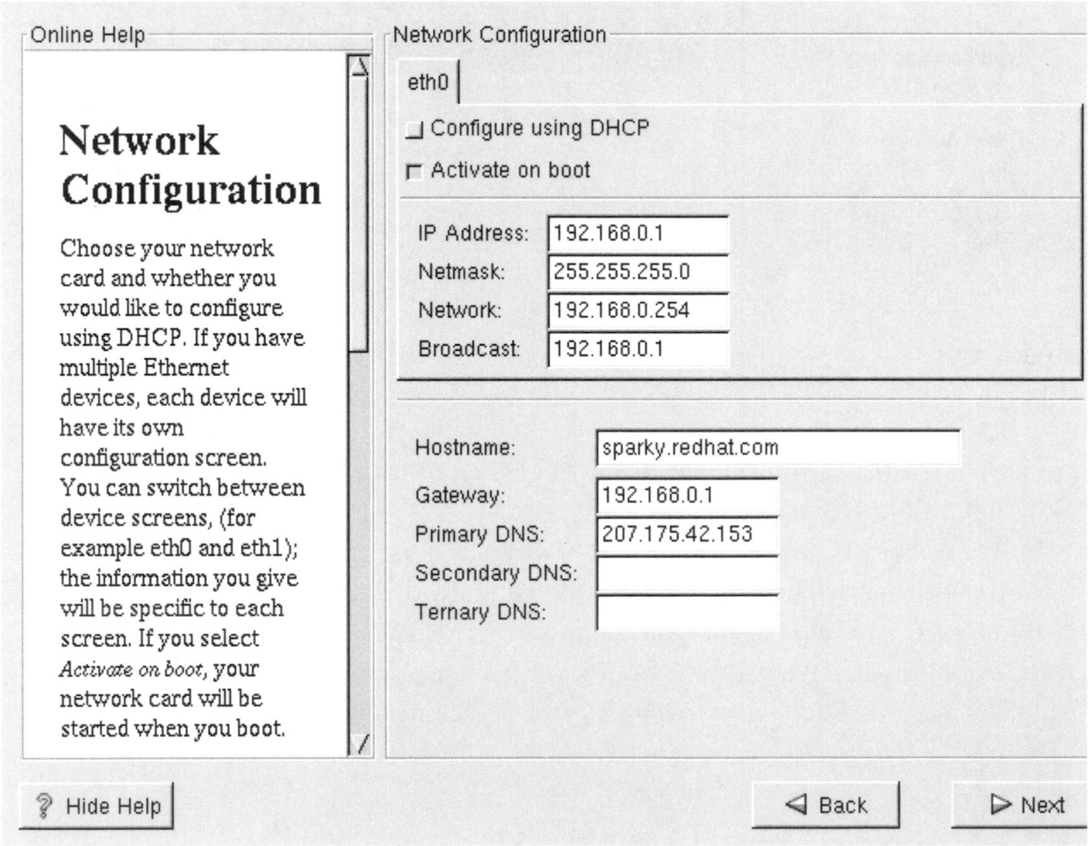

**Figure 3-9**
*Here you specify your network configuration.*

## 3.15 Setting up TCP/IP

The first part of the TCP/IP setup consists of the following TCP/IP parameters: IP address, netmask (specifies the number of nodes per subnet), network address, and broadcast address (an address for communicating with all servers on this network or the subnet.) In the lower part of the screen, you set the hostname with its complete domain name, default gateway (specifies which IP address to use when accessing machines in other networks), primary DNS (specifies the machine (name server) that converts your domain name to the correct IP address), secondary DNS (reserve name server), and tertiary DNS (a second reserve name server).

| Field | Example Value |
|---|---|
| IP Address | 207.117.119.15 |
| Netmask | 255.255.255.0 |
| Network | 207.117.119.0 |
| Broadcast | 207.117.119.255 |
| Hostname | delboth.c2i.net |
| Gateway | 207.117.119.1 |
| Primary DNS | 193.216.1.10 |
| Secondary DNS | 193.216.69.10 |
| Tertiary DNS | 193.216.69.12 |

## 3.16 Configuring the time zone

Now the installation program asks whether you want to set the CMOS clock (see Figure 3-10) in the machine related to UTC (Universal Coordinated Time) or as a function of a physical location. I recommend that you choose to set the clock as a function of a physical location, e.g., North America/Chicago. You will find this option in the list.

You can change the time setting after the Linux installation at any time by running the setup program (see Chapter 19) or directly from `/usr/sbin/timeconfig`.

Example:

```
[root@nittedal /root]# /usr/sbin/timeconfig
```

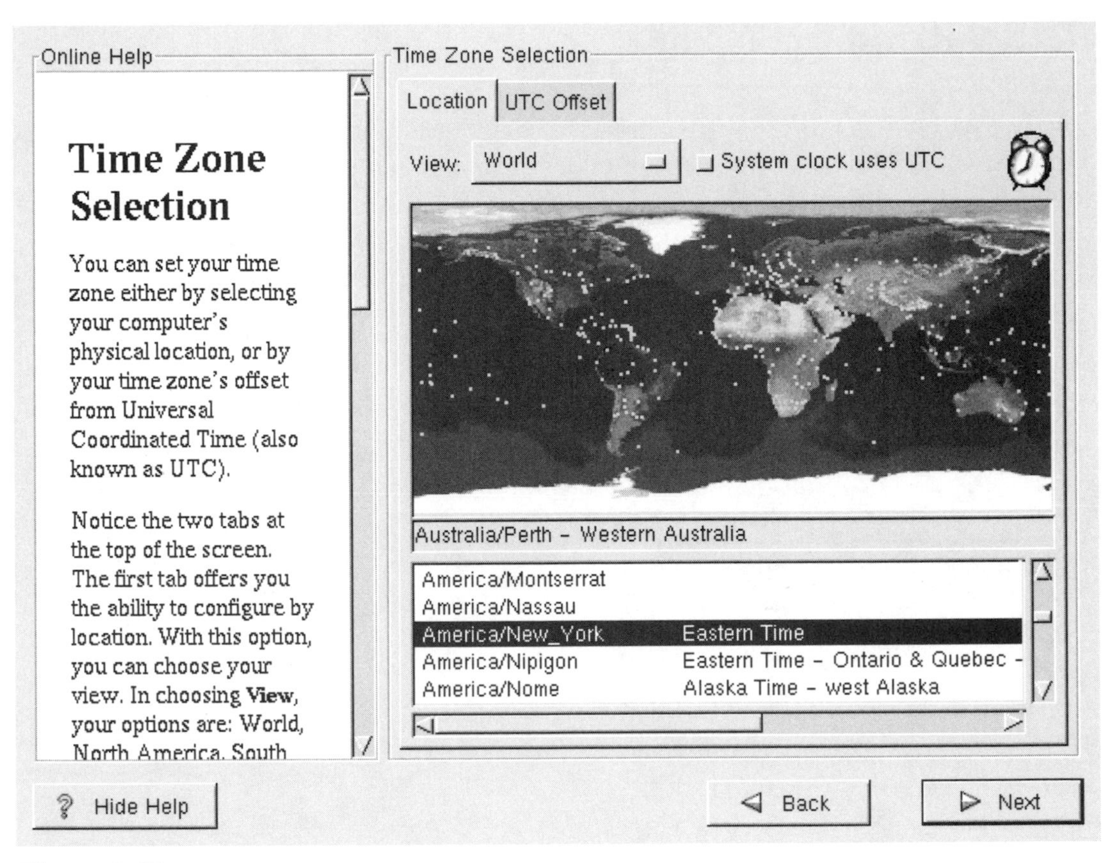


**Figure 3-10**
*Here you specify your time zone.*

## 3.17 Defining the root password

Next (see Figure 3-11), the installation program asks for the root password (system administrator's password). You will need this password whenever you log in to configure the Linux system, define users, install program packages, etc. The root password must be at least six characters and you need to enter it twice. Pick a password that is easy to remember, but hard for others to figure out.

The password can be letters as well as numbers. You cannot use control symbols in the password. The system differs between lower-case and upper-case characters. A good password is a mix of letters and numbers. Note that forgetting the root password will make it hard to get into your system, at least if you don't have physical access to the system. If you have physical access to the machine, you can reboot and enter `linux single` on the LILO command line.

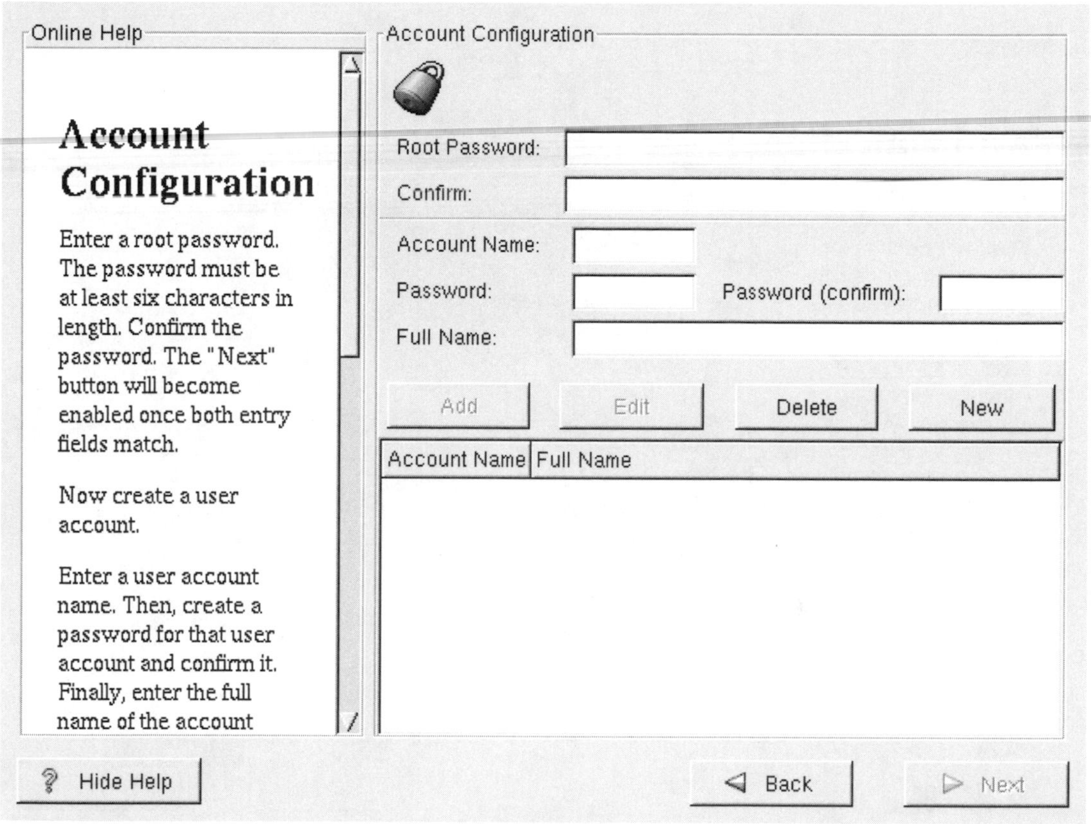

**Figure 3-11**
*Enter the password for your root account. Also, add your normal user account with a password.*

This will give you a shell with root privileges and you can set a new password for root. When logging in as root, you have access to all services. Be cautious! Do not log in as root unless you are planning to do work that requires root access.

When you have defined the password, you can define other Linux users. First, define yourself as a user.

## 3.18 Defining authentication

The next menu (see Figure 3-12) lets you choose the authentication level for passwords in the Linux system. The options are MD5, shadow password, NIS, LDAP, and Kerberos. Select the first option, MD5, if you need passwords with up to 256 characters. Selecting a shadow password gives a slightly higher secu-

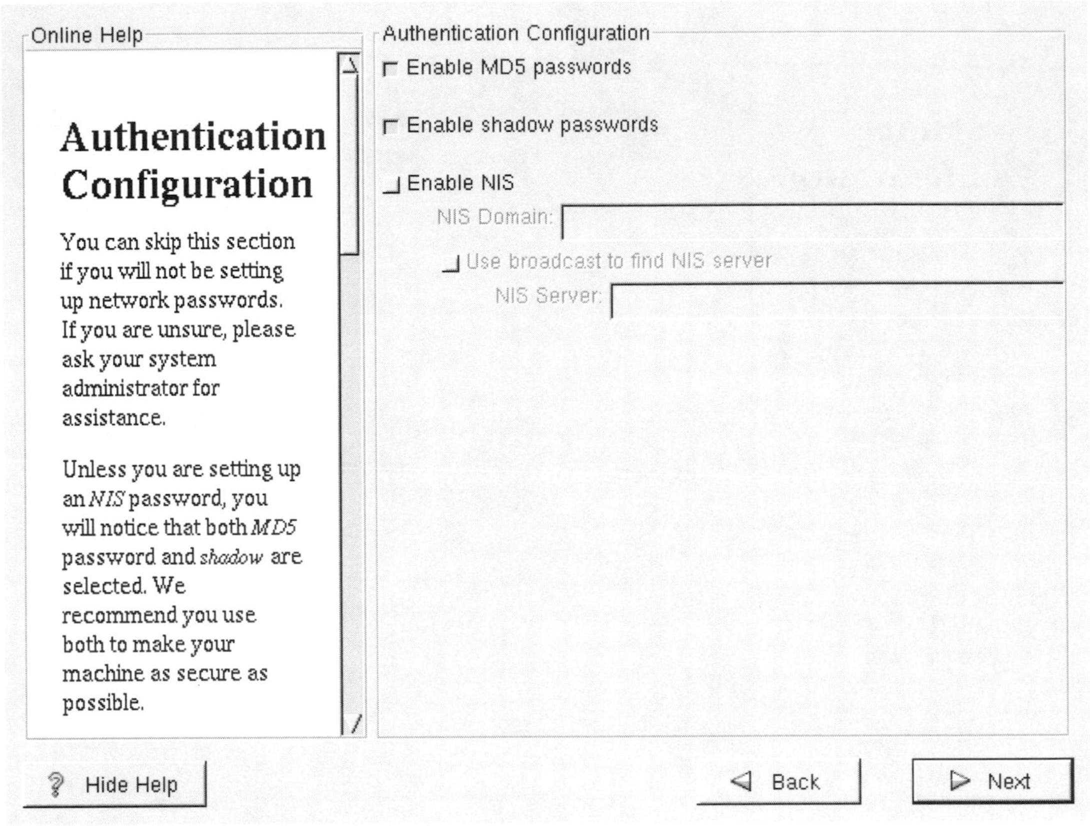

Online Help

Authentication Configuration

You can skip this section if you will not be setting up network passwords. If you are unsure, please ask your system administrator for assistance.

Unless you are setting up an *NIS* password, you will notice that both *MD5* password and *shadow* are selected. We recommend you use both to make your machine as secure as possible.

Authentication Configuration

Enable MD5 passwords

Enable shadow passwords

Enable NIS

NIS Domain:

Use broadcast to find NIS server

NIS Server:

Hide Help

Back

Next

**Figure 3-12**
*Here you choose your authentication configuration.*

rity level as the encrypted password is placed in the `/etc/shadow` file instead of in `/etc/password`.

The NIS alternative consists of two subgroups: NIS domain and NIS server. If your machine is not connected to an NIS (yp)-based network, you can skip this alternative.

If you already have server components that talk LDAP, you can reduce user administration to a minimum by registering all users and services to a central LDAP server. Ask your system administrator whether you are using LDAP and if there is an LDAP server in the system.

The last option is Kerberos (not shown on Figure 3-12), which you can choose if all network services and their authorization are administrated with a Kerberos-based system.

## 3.19 Selecting Linux components

When your partitions have been configured and formatted, you are ready to select the Linux components and packages that you need (see Figure 3-13). Linux components are categorized according to their functionality:

- **Printer Support.**
- **X Window System.**
- **GNOME.**
- **KDE.**
- **Mail/WWW/News Tools.**
- **DOS/Windows Connectivity.**
- **Graphics Manipulation.**
- **Games.**

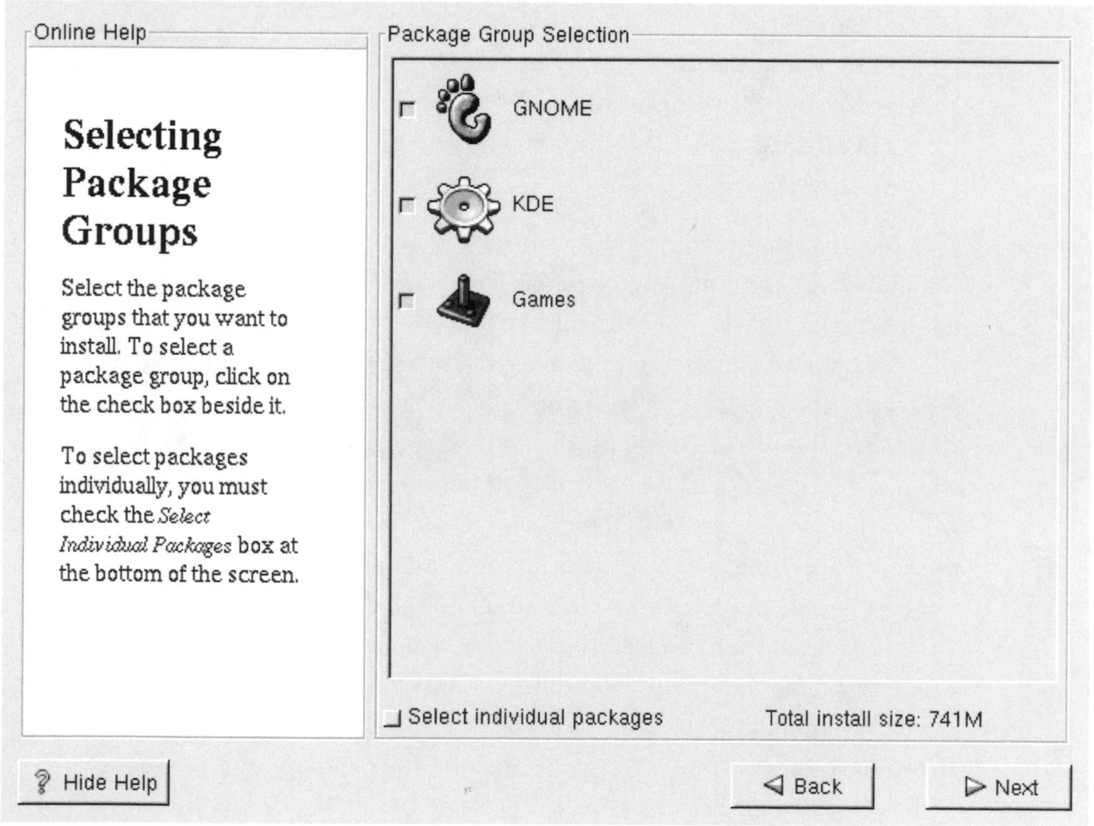

**Figure 3-13**
*Here you select your package groups.*

- **Multimedia Support.**
- **Laptop Support.**
- **Networked Workstation.**
- **Dialup Workstation.**
- **News Server.**
- **NFS Server.**
- **SMB (Samba) Server.**
- **IPX/Netware ™ Connectivity.**
- **Anonymous FTP Server.**
- **Web Server.**
- **DNS Name Server.**
- **Postgres (SQL) Server.**
- **Network Management Workstation.**
- **Authoring/Publishing.**
- **Emacs.**
- **Development.**
- **Kernel Development.**
- **Utilities.**
- **Everything.**

Select the components that you need. If you have a large hard disk drive, you can choose Everything. Just click the Everything button. For this purpose, you need some 2000MB. Even if you have the space required, I recommend that you consider your real needs. Unless you need them, it is not a good idea to install the server packages (you normally won't need them on a workstation). If you install the server packages, the system bootfiles (`/etc/rc.d` subdirectory) will also be updated. The next time you boot the machine, the server processes will start automatically. This means that resources are spent for no purpose, and there are also some possible security problems connected to this.

Most people think that they will not need the development packages, as they are not programmers. But these packages contain compilers that you will need when installing programs from source code (which is normal in the Linux world) or compiling a new or adapted kernel (which you will do at some point). If you have the required disk space, include the development packages.

To select or not select individual packages, click the Select individual packages button and make your selections. When you select a package group, you can select single components from the package group.

You will see that some packages cannot be deselected, as there are dependencies to other packages and to parts of the OS (see Figure 3-14).

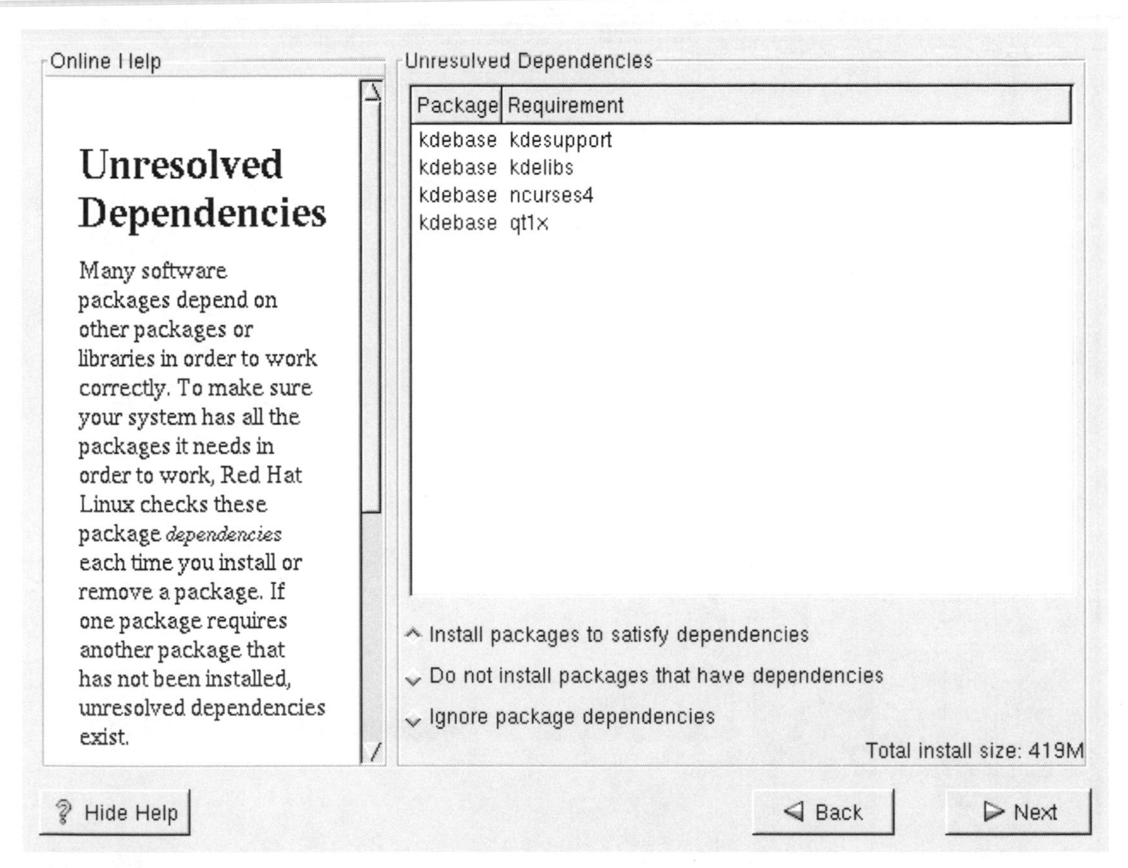


**Figure 3-14**
*Many packages depend on other packages. This figure shows an example of unresolved dependencies.*

## 3.20 Configuring the X window system

If you have already selected to include X Window components, you will now be able to adapt X Window to your purposes. In most cases, Xconfigurator will find your video card as well as your monitor (see Figure 3-15). Here you can test the configuration that Xconfigurator has performed. Just click Test this configuration. If you have special needs, you can adapt X by clicking the Customize X Configuration button.

You can choose the screen resolution and number of colors (bits per pixel). Your resolution selection as well as the number of colors you choose will depend on the amount of memory on the video card, what kind of monitor you have, and finally, what your preferences are (640x480, 800x600, 1024x768, 1200x1024, 1600x1200, etc.). For a 15" monitor, 800x600 or 1024x768 is suitable. A 17" monitor will do fine with 1024x768 pixels. 19" and 21" monitors perform well with 1200x1024. Some high-quality 19" and 21" monitors allow for 1600x1200 pixels.

Now save your X Window settings. The X Window settings are saved in the `/etc/X11/XF86Config` file. You will find more about installing X Window in Chapter 10.

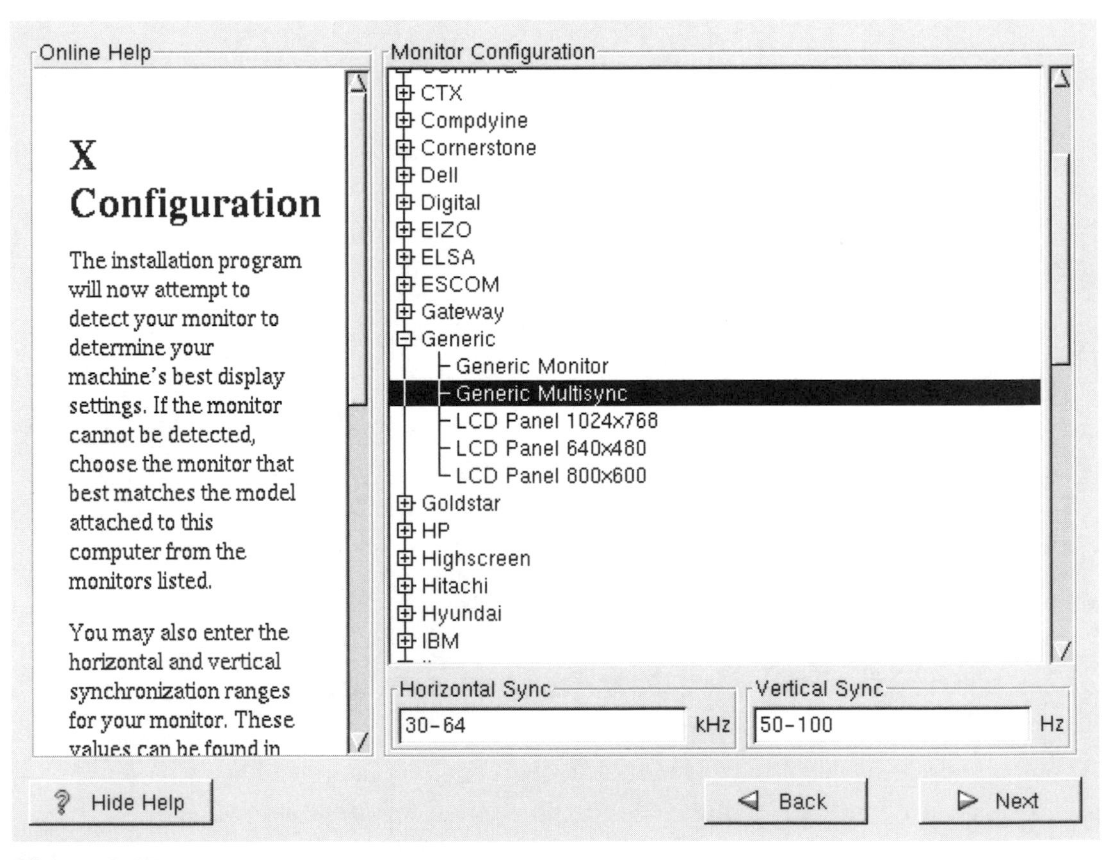


**Figure 3-15**
*Here you can choose which sort of monitor you are using.*

If you select "Use Graphical Login," your login and work environment will be graphical instead of character-based. If you have forgotten to set up a graphical login, you can start the graphical environment later by entering `startx` from the terminal prompt (e.g., *[david@nittedal david]$* **startx**).

## 3.21 Installing packages

Click Next to start installing Red Hat Linux (see Figure 3-16). You will find a complete log of the installation in the `/tmp/install.log` file after rebooting the system. This log is a handy record of what has actually been installed.

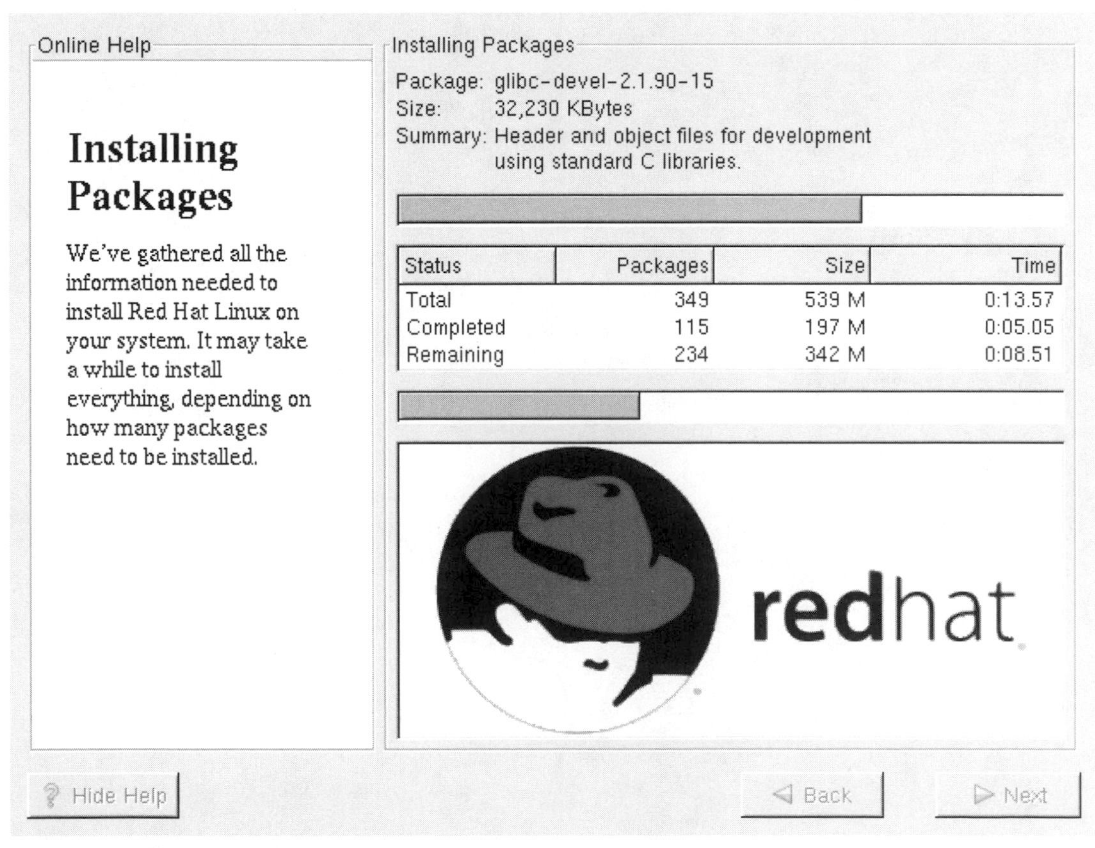


**Figure 3-16**
*Here you see that the installer begins installing your packages.*

Now the installation program will start to install each package. The installation status will keep you continually updated about the contents of each package, how much is left before the installation of the package is completed, and how much is left before the entire installation is completed. The complete Red Hat Linux 7.x is contained on two CD-ROMs, so keep CD #2 ready!

## 3.22 Linux boot floppy disk

The next menu option (see Figure 3-17) gives you the opportunity to make a Linux boot floppy disk. You should make one, as this makes it possible to boot your Linux system without using LILO. This gives you the possibility of booting even if LILO is damaged, for example, because a different OS has over-

Online Help
Boot Disk Creation
Insert a blank, formatted diskette into your floppy drive, and click **Next** to continue.
Bootdisk Creation
Please remove the install floppy (if used) and insert a blank floppy in the first floppy drive. All data on this disk will be erased during creation of the boot disk.
Skip boot disk creation
Hide Help
Back
Next

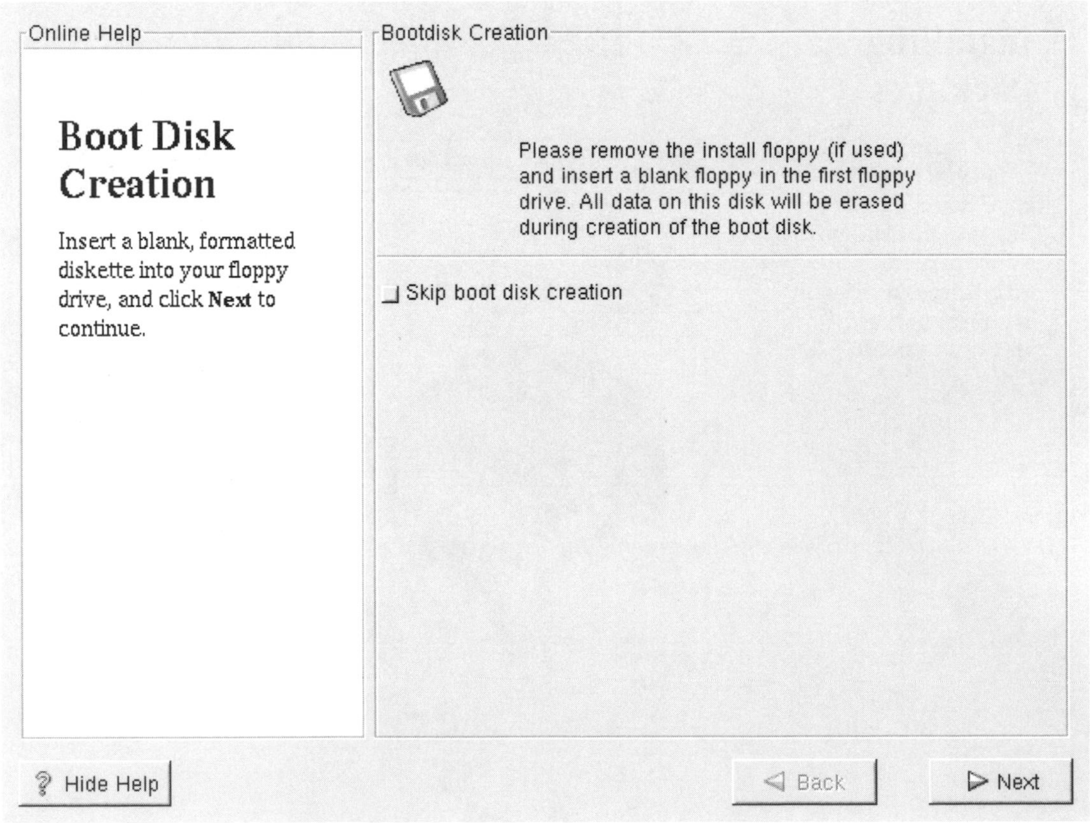

**Figure 3-17**
*Here you insert a blank floppy. The installation program will make you a Linux boot disk.*

written LILO. This happens, for example, if you reinstall Windows after installing LILO.

I always choose to create a Linux boot disk. If you change the Linux kernel at a later time, you should generate a new Linux boot. Running the `mkbootdisk` (see Figure 3-18) command does this.

Example:

```
[root@nittedal /root]# mkbootdisk --device /dev/fd0 2.4.5-15
```

```
Terminal
File  Edit  Settings  Help
Hold down left mouse button and drag to move this Window.
Double click left mouse button to [un]shade this window.
-rwxr-xr-x   1 root     root       164797 Apr 17 00:49 libresolv-2.1.1.so
lrwxrwxrwx   1 root     root           18 May  3 19:05 libresolv.so.2 -> libresolv-2.1.1.so
-rwxr-xr-x   1 root     root        72090 Apr 17 00:49 librt-2.1.1.so
lrwxrwxrwx   1 root     root           14 May  3 19:05 librt.so.1 -> librt-2.1.1.so
lrwxrwxrwx   1 root     root           12 May  3 19:20 libss.so.2 -> libss.so.2.0
-rwxr-xr-x   1 root     root        21774 Mar 21 21:13 libss.so.2.0
lrwxrwxrwx   1 root     root           19 May  3 19:08 libtermcap.so.2 -> libtermcap.so.2.0.8
-rwxr-xr-x   1 root     root        14907 Mar 21 16:37 libtermcap.so.2.0.8
-rwxr-xr-x   1 root     root        46431 Apr 17 00:49 libutil-2.1.1.so
lrwxrwxrwx   1 root     root           16 May  3 19:05 libutil.so.1 -> libutil-2.1.1.so
lrwxrwxrwx   1 root     root           14 May  3 19:20 libuuid.so.1 -> libuuid.so.1.2
-rwxr-xr-x   1 root     root        10659 Mar 21 21:13 libuuid.so.1.2
drwxr-xr-x   5 root     root         1024 May  3 21:09 modules
drwxr-xr-x   2 root     root         1024 May  3 19:22 security
[root@davelin /lib]# cd modules
[root@davelin modules]# ls -la
total 7
drwxr-xr-x   5 root     root         1024 May  3 21:09 .
drwxr-xr-x   4 root     root         3072 May  3 21:33 ..
drwxr-xr-x  11 root     root         1024 May  3 23:10 2.2.5-15
drwxr-xr-x  11 root     root         1024 May  3 21:08 2.2.5-15BOOT
drwxr-xr-x  10 root     root         1024 May  3 21:10 2.2.5-15smp
[root@davelin modules]# mkbootdisk --device /dev/fd0 2.2.5-15
Insert a disk in /dev/fd0. Any information on the disk will be lost.
Press <Enter> to continue or ^C to abort:
```

**Figure 3-18**
*I generate a new Linux boot disk by running the Linux command* `mkbootdisk`.

## 3.23 Finishing the installation

At this point, the installation program will tell you that the system is ready to reboot the Linux OS (see Figure 3-19). Remove all CDs and floppies and shut down the system. This may take a few minutes.

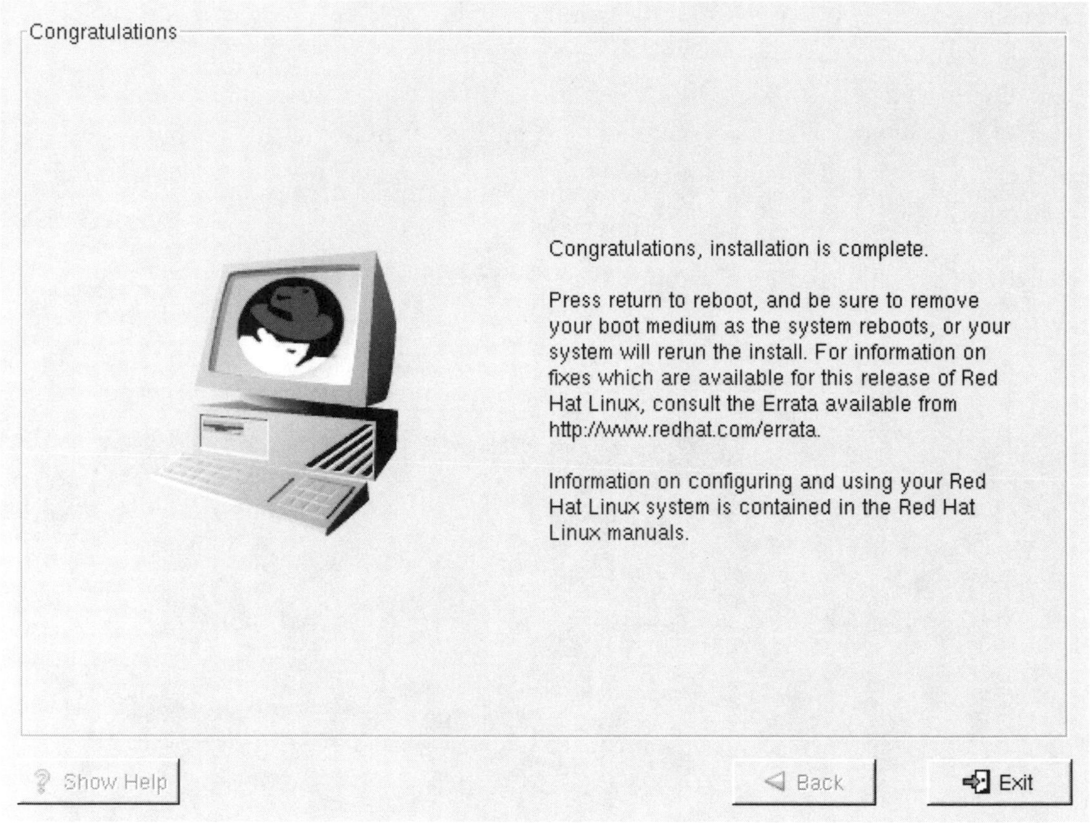

Congratulations
Congratulations, installation is complete.
Press return to reboot, and be sure to remove your boot medium as the system reboots, or your system will rerun the install. For information on fixes which are available for this release of Red Hat Linux, consult the Errata available from http://www.redhat.com/errata.
Information on configuring and using your Red Hat Linux system is contained in the Red Hat Linux manuals.
Show Help
Back
Exit

**Figure 3-19**
*Congratulations, you have just installed Red Hat Linux.*

If your PC switches off automatically, just restart it. When your PC has run through the normal boot sequence, you will see the LILO command line, which is `boot:`

To start without special parameters, press RETURN.

```
Linux

LILO boot:
```

The graphical login picture should appear after a few minutes if you installed the X Window System with either the GNOME or KDE interface.

Look at the messages as the system loads. Note error messages, if any. If you experience installation problems, I recommend that you look at the Red Hat Web site, www.redhat.com, and various newsgroups.

| Newsgroup | Description |
|---|---|
| comp.os.linux.admin | Linux administration and installation. |
| comp.os.linux.answers | Various answers to Linux-related problems, including installation. |
| comp.os.linux.hardware | Linux installation/device drivers and support. |
| comp.os.linux.help | General Linux help. |
| comp.os.linux.setup | Hints on how to set up Linux. |
| linux.redhat.* | Dedicated newsgroups for Red Hat Linux. |

I also refer to Red Hat's Frequently Asked Questions (FAQs) for answers to questions and problems that may occur before, during, or after installation. Check the FAQs online at www.redhat.com/support/docs/faqs/rhl_general_faq/FAQ.html.

If the installation fails, you may need a revised diskette image. In some cases, Red Hat makes special images available via the Red Hat Linux errata listing. From http://www.redhat.com/support/errata, you can read the latest support news online and download revised diskette images. You will also find documentation updates at http://www.redhat.com/ support/errata/doc_errata/.

## 3.24 After the installation

After the installation of Linux, you are all set for installing other software or hardware. Each distribution has its own mechanisms for this. In some distributions, you must mount filesystems in certain directories and copy the software manually. Many distributions have dedicated programs that lead you through the installation. Red Hat uses rpm, which is described in detail in Chapter 19.

When you want to take the system down, use the `shutdown` command.

Example:

```
[root@nittedal /root]# shutdown now
```

You will find a more detailed description of how to shut down the system in Chapter 19. If you need to define users, you can run the `useradd` program. This is also described in Chapter 19.

## 3.25 Removing Linux

To remove your Linux partition, there are several alternative methods. The most dramatic option is to low-format the hard disk drive. Most hard disk drive vendors offer low-format software. Low-format software is also available on the Web. When using the low-format option, everything that has been installed on the machine will be removed. All partitions will disappear, including whichever OS you are using. Low-format software is normally supplied on special boot disks. These are normally based on MS DOS. When you have booted you can just follow the menu options.

If you only want to remove Linux you don't need to low format. In Linux, you can remove LILO from the MBR by running the LILO program (`/sbin/lilo`).

Example:

```
[root@nittedal /root]# /sbin/lilo -u
```

By using the –u option, you get back to the original MBR configuration. You can also use Microsoft's `fdisk`. If you want to remove Linux from a machine that runs both Linux and Windows, you should make sure that you have a Windows boot disk. You can start the machine with this disk and use the `fdisk` command with the `mbr` option.

Example:

```
C>fdisk /mbr
```

This sets the MBR to point to the primary DOS partition and Windows will boot normally. Removing a Linux partition with Microsoft's `fdisk` is sometimes problematic. If so, you can start the machine with a Linux boot disk and use Linux's `fdisk` to remove the partition. After rebooting the machine, you can use Microsoft's `fdisk` to make a Windows partition.

CHAPTER
4

# A Linux Work Session

## 4.1 After the installation

To use Linux, you must be a registered user with a username and password on a computer running Linux. If you installed Linux yourself on a PC, probably only one user was registered, the system administrator (root). In Chapter 19, you'll find a description of how to define new Linux users.

I strongly recommend that you start by defining a normal user. You should only log on as root when configuring the system. My advice is that you log on as a normal user for all other purposes. This gives you better security.

## 4.2 Username and password

Every user registered on a Linux computer has a logon name and probably a secret password. Each user has a personal area on the disk called the home directory. The default home directory in Linux is `/home/logon name`. All users are members of one or more groups.

The logon name (also called the `user-id`) is usually a name with some connection to the user's real name. I normally use my first name, surname, a project name, my initials, company name, etc. The username/logon name must contain a minimum of five characters and a maximum of eight characters (some systems allow longer names). The logon name cannot contain capital letters, and cannot begin with a number or special character.

Your password can contain up to 256 characters. Capital letters and small letters are allowed, but no special characters.

## 4.3 Logging in

This is the login procedure in Linux:

1. Switch the computer on.
2. The initial screen appears. It may look like Figure 4-1.

The initial screen may also be character-based.

### 4.3.1 Comments on the Password

For security reasons, the password will not be shown on your display. To prevent unwanted access to your system, it is advisable to change your password (using `passwd`) frequently. If you type a wrong password, you'll get a message like this:

```
Red Hat Linux release 7.0 (Guinness)
Kernel 2.2.16-22 on an i686


delboth login: david'^H^H^H
Password:
Login incorrect


login:
```

**Figure 4-1**
*The login screen under the GNOME environment.*

Try and log in again. Remember that you must press **RETURN** after typing each command.

### 4.3.2 The Terminal Prompt

If you log in to a GUI, you can pick commands via icons, menus, and mouse clicks. I will guide you through a character-based interface. From the GUI, you can call a character-based interface in three different ways:

- Open a terminal window in the GUI.
- Terminate the GUI by using the Control-Alt-Backspace command or by a menu command.
- Switch to a screen-based console by the Control-Alt-F1 command (to F6).

The character-based interface brings you to the Linux shell. The shell is the part of the program that handles the communication between you, the user, and the Linux OS.

The terminal prompt (shell prompt) shows that Linux is ready to receive your commands. The appearance of the prompt depends on the shell you use.

The prompt *[david@nittedal david]$* shows that I am running the Linux bash shell, the most widely used shell under Linux. The Bourne shell can also be indicated by $. If you are the system administrator (root), the prompt will be #. Under Linux, it is normal that both root and users have bash as their standard shell, but you are free to choose other shells like tcsh.

### 4.3.3 Commands from the Linux Shell

When the terminal prompt is activated, you can give commands. This is how you do it:

1. Type the command. For example, if you want a calendar for 2001, type **`cal 2001`**.
2. Press **RETURN**. Your 2001 calendar will appear on your screen.

In the rest of the book, I will not explain in detail how to give commands. The calendar command will appear like this:

```
[david@nittedal david]$ cal 2001
```

This means that you first type **`cal 2001`**, then press **RETURN**.

### 4.3.4 Edit Keys in the Shell

Edit keys may vary from system to system. The following keys are in general use:

| **Edit Key** | **Function** |
|---|---|
| Backspace | Deletes character. |
| <Ctrl-U> | Deletes one line. |
| <Ctrl-C> | Interrupts a command/program. |
| Del | Interrupts a command/program. |
| <Ctrl-S> | Temporarily stops the execution of a command/program. |
| RETURN | The shell seeks the user's PATH for a command/program and executes any task that is found. |

## 4.4 Linux help functions

To assist you, Linux has several help systems.

If you type `man` (or `xman` in X Window; see Figure 4-2) and a Linux command, you will get a full description of all options and arguments that can be used with the command. You can use `man/xman` as a reference at any time. The syntax is: *man [command]*.

Some examples:

```
[david@nittedal david]$ man ls
```

Gives information about the ls command.

```
[david@nittedal david]$ man bash
```

Gives information about the bash shell.

If you want a hardcopy, type:

```
[david@nittedal david]$ man -t bash | lpr
```

which will send the man page for the bash shell to the console as a PS (PostScript) file. If you are worried by the amount of paper this requires, you can use the command `psnup` (which is part of the GNU `pstools` package). The `psnup` command takes a normal PS file, processes it, and outputs a PS file with multiple pages of the source file on each output page. For example, `psnup -6 source.ps destination.ps` will reformat `source.ps` so that six pages fit on a sheet of paper and store the result in `destination.ps`.

```
[david@nittedal david]$ man -t bash | psnup -2 | lpr
```

Here, we print the bash man page with two pages per sheet. If you want help about the bash shell, simply type:

```
[david@nittedal david]$ help
```

This give you access to the resident Linux bash shell help function. You will find help about all parameters that can be set under the bash shell. The syntax is: *help [command]*.

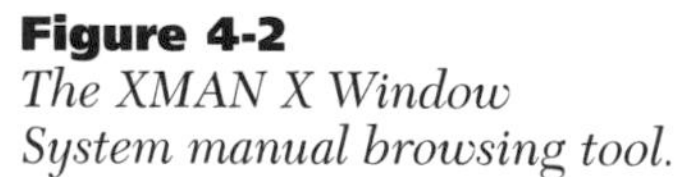

help
Options
Sections
Xman Help
XMAN is an X Window System manual browsing tool.
GETTING STARTED
By default, xman starts by creating a small window tha
"buttons" (places on which to click a pointer button).
buttons, Help and Quit, are self-explanatory. The thi
creates a new manual page browser window; you may use
open a new manual page any time xman is running.
A new manual page starts up displaying this help infor
manual page contains three sections. In the upper lef
menu buttons. When the mouse is clicked on either of
menu is popped up. The contents of these menus is des
Directly to the right of the menu buttons is an inform
This display usually contains the name of the director
being displayed. It is also used to display warning m
current version of xman. The last and largest section
information display. This section of the application
list of manual pages to choose from or the text of a m
To use xman pull down the Sections menu to select a ma
When the section is displayed, click the left pointer
of the manual page that you would like to see. Xman w
directory listing with the manual page you selected.
That should be enough to get you started. Once you un
basics of how to use xman, take a look at the rest of
the advanced features that are available to make using
efficient.


**Figure 4-2**
*The XMAN X Window System manual browsing tool.*

```
[david@nittedal david]$ help history
```

Gives information on the `history` command in the bash shell. If you just type `help`, you will get an overview.

If you want more in-depth information than what `man` (`xman`) and `help` offer, you should try the GNU hypertext document system, `info`. The syntax is:

*`info [infotext/command]`*.

Typing just `info` will bring you to the top of the information tree.

```
[david@nittedal david]$ info
```

You can use the arrow, Tab, and RETURN keys to move up and down through the information tree. If you need to know more about the Linux `tar` command, for instance, you can type:

```
[david@nittedal david]$ info tar
```

The Linux commands `less`, `more`, and `cat` give you access to the documentation database. When you want to know more about compressed files, this is the command:

```
[david@nittedal david]$ cd /usr/doc/zip-2.1
```

This brings me to the zip documentation directory.

```
[david@nittedal david]$ less *
```

The command above sends all the documentation files on zip to your display, where you can read them. If you want the information in HTML format, go to the /usr/doc/HTML directory. Frequently asked questions and answers are available in the /usr/doc/FAQ directory.

In the /usr/doc/HOWTO directory, you will find a description of how to set up a variety of Linux services and functions. The files are compressed with the gzip program. To read the HOWTO files directly, type the command zless. If you want to know how to set up an audio card, follow these commands:

```
[david@nittedal david]$ cd /usr/doc/HOWTO


[david@nittedal david]$ zless Sound-HOWTO.gz
```

The last command unzips the files and lets you read them on the screen. If the file is not compressed, type this command:

```
[david@nittedal david]$ less Sound-HOWTO
```

In the /usr/doc/HOWTO/mini directory, you will find an ASCII version of the HOWTO documentation. It is less comprehensive than the original HOWTO documentation. The /usr/doc/HOWTO/other-formats/html directory contains a complete HTML version of all HOWTO descriptions, a comprehensive guide to installing Linux, and an explanation on how to get going when you have finished the installation.

## 4.5 A work session in Linux

A work session used to consist of giving commands to the Linux shell. Today it is used to apply a GUI (X11; see Figure 4-3) between the user and the shell. If you are logged into a character-based interface, you only need to type startx:

```
[david@nittedal david]$ startx
```

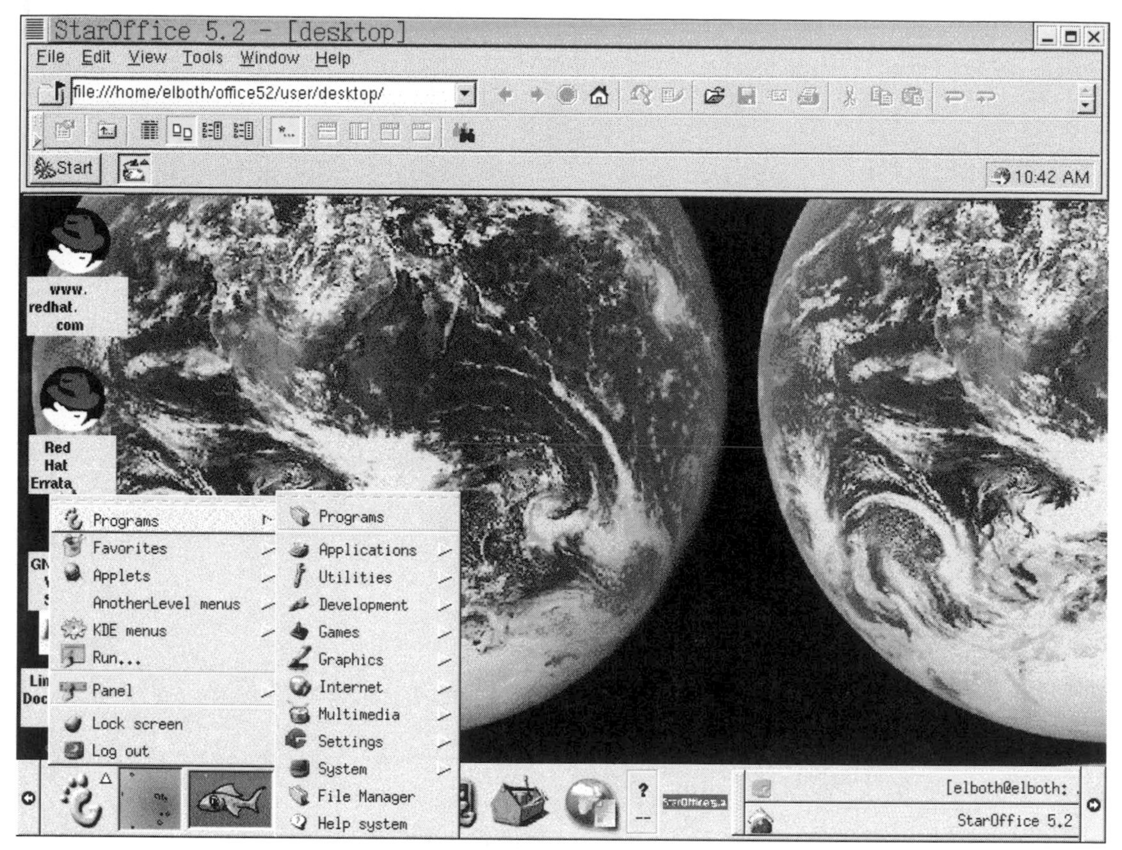


**Figure 4-3**
*The GNOME desktop environment.*

Quite often, you will log on to a Linux machine to use an application rather than give Linux commands. If you want to start the database server `sqlora`, for example, all you need to do is type `sqlora` and press RETURN. But many applications can only be run directly from X Window.

If you want to run an external program, the first thing you do as root is install the program. As a user, you must know the path to where the program is installed. After using the program, you can continue to work with Linux, or you can log out.

## 4.6 Logging out from Linux

If you are logged in as a user in bash, zsh, or tcsh, you log out by simply pressing <Ctrl-d>:

```
[david@nittedal david]$ <Ctrl-d>
```

This means that you hold down the Control key and press d (lower-case d). When in tcsh, you can use the command `logout`:

```
[david@nittedal david]$ logout
```

Remember to press RETURN after typing the command. You can also log out by typing `exit`:

```
[david@nittedal david]$ exit
```

You will now be logged out of the system, and the logon image will appear on your screen. If you are logging out of X Window (GNOME), choose the Log out option from the quick menu (see Figure 4-4).

Remember your `user-id` and password!

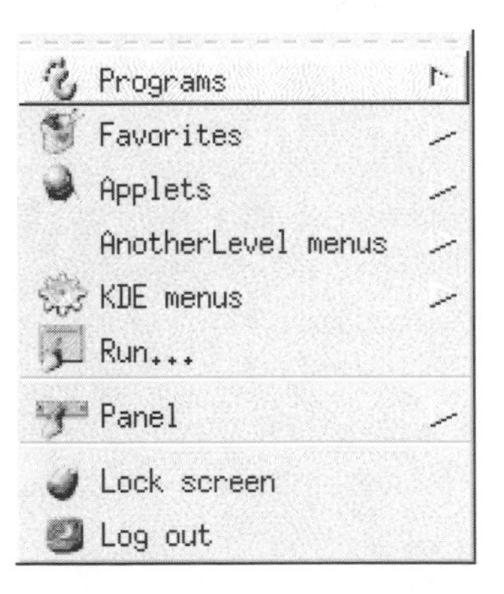


**Figure 4-4**
*The main menu button on the panel. Last option is Log out.*

## 4.7 Taking the Linux system down

A Linux machine cannot just be turned off; it needs to be shut down. You must log on as root or have access to the shutdown routines if you wish to close down the system. In Chapter 19, you will find more detailed information on the different methods of shutting down the system. If you want to shut down the system from X Window (GNOME), first choose Log out, then choose halt. You can also type this command from command mode:

```
[root@nittedal /root]# shutdown
```

When the text "System halted" or "System down" appears on your screen, you can switch the machine off. This is the last message that appears on the screen, and it may take anything from 15 seconds to 10 minutes before you get this message. If you get an error message when typing `init 0`, this could mean that you are not logged in as root.

## Exercises for Chapter 4

1. After logging in, start X Window. What is the difference between X Window and a traditional terminal session?
2. Log in with the username and password that you have been given. Which shell are you using?
3. Which edit key pauses the system when you are executing a command or program?
4. How can you get help regarding the various Linux commands? Practice to master the various methods!
5. How do you terminate a terminal work session?
6. On which day of the week were you born? (Tip: Try `cal`.)

CHAPTER

5

# Information from the Linux System

## 5.1 Commands that gather information

The Linux commands that you will learn in this chapter are easy to use. Even if you make mistakes, there is hardly any risk of damage. These commands simply gather information. By using these commands, you practice using Linux and learn a bit more about the system.

## 5.2 Calendar - cal

The `cal` command gives access to an overview calendar for a day, month, or year.

**cal Command – Shows Overview Calendar**

| | |
|---|---|
| Command | `cal [month] [year]` |
| Function | Gives you a calendar overview of a day, month, or year. |
| Argument | Month and/or year. |
| Options | None. |

Examples:

```
[david@nittedal david]$ cal
```

Gives you the calendar for the last, this, and next month.

```
[david@nittedal david]$ cal 5 2000
      May 2000
Su Mo Tu We Th Fr Sa
    1  2  3  4  5  6
 7  8  9 10 11 12 13
14 15 16 17 18 19 20
21 22 23 24 25 26 27
28 29 30 31


[david@nittedal david]$
```

Gives you the calendar for May 2000.

## 5.3 Echo to the screen - echo

The `echo` command sends codes to your screen. The `echo` command expects an argument in the form of text or codes.

**echo Command – Displays Text/Code on your Screen**

| | |
|---|---|
| Command | `echo [argument]` |
| Function | Sends a string of text or codes to your display. |
| Argument | Text or control code and/or wildcards. |
| Options | See the Linux man pages. |

The `echo` command without arguments only sends an empty string to your display.

Here are some codes that can be added:

| | |
|---|---|
| -n | Do not output the trailing newline. |
| -e | Enable the interpretation of the following Backslash-escaped characters in each string: |

| | |
|---|---|
| '\a' | — Alert (bell). |
| '\b' | — Backspace. |
| '\c' | — Suppress trailing newline. |
| '\f' | — Form feed. |
| '\n' | — Newline. |
| '\r' | — Carriage return. |
| '\t' | — Horizontal tab. |
| '\\' | — Backslash. |
| '\NNN' | — ASCII code NNN (octal). |

Examples:

```
[david@nittedal david]$ echo Linux is fun
```

Sends the text string " Linux is fun" to your screen.

By entering the appropriate code, you can send characters from the ASCII or ISO table. If NNN is not a valid octal number, it is printed literally. For example:

```
[david@nittedal david]$ echo -e '\07'
```

Sends the code <Ctrl-g> (bell) to your screen.

```
[david@nittedal david]$ echo -e  '\063'
```

Sends the number "3" to your screen.

```
[david@nittedal david]$ echo -e 'A'
```

Sends the letter "A" to your screen.

```
[david@nittedal david]$ echo -n "Hi, how are you!!"
```

Sends the text string "Hi, how are you!!" to your screen, without the trailing newline.

```
[david@nittedal david]$ echo *
```

Functions like the `ls` command (see below). It lists all files in the current directory. If you include special characters in the text, you must use quotation marks.

```
[david@nittedal david]$ echo "*! are special characters"
```

See also: `bash` and `ls`

## 5.4 List files - ls

`ls` lists an overview of files and directories. It is equivalent to the MS-DOS `DIR` command. You will also find the `DIR` command in Linux (see Chapter 15). However, using `ls` rather than `DIR` gives you more options in Linux. Not all flavors of Unix support `DIR`, so being familiar with `ls` will be helpful when you use some members of the Unix family.

**ls Command – Lists Files**

| | |
|---|---|
| Command | `ls [-aCilrRt] [argument]` |
| Function | Lists files and directories. Without options, you get a list sorted by name. Various options also list owner, group, size, last updated, etc. |
| Argument | File and/or directory with or without wildcards. |
| Options | See the Linux man pages. |

**ls Command – Lists Files (*Continued*)**

| | |
|---|---|
| `-a` | Shows all files, including system files that begin with a dot. Examples: `.profile`, `.login`, `.cshrc`, `.mailrc`, etc. |
| `-C` | Displays the files and directories in a multi-column format. |
| `-i` | Displays the appropriate inode numbers. |
| `-l` | Displays complete format, including:<br>- Permissions.<br>- Number of links to physical files.<br>- Owner.<br>- Size.<br>- Date. |
| `-r` | Sorts in reverse order. |
| `-R` | Displays all assigned directories. |
| `-t` | Displays files in chronological order. |

The arguments may be files and/or directories. The `ls` command without arguments displays all standard files and subdirectories in the current directory on your screen.

System files begin with a dot. These are not listed. If you add the argument `-a`, the system files will be displayed. The reason why you need an extra parameter to display files beginning with a dot is that the dot is what Linux uses to hide files. Programs that create configuration files, etc. normally define these files with a dot first. This means that the files are kept hidden because you normally don't want to change them. Examples:

```
[david@nittedal david]$ ls -la
```

Lists all files and directories, including system files (see Figure 5-1). The list is displayed in a complete format.

```
[david@nittedal david]$ ls -lt
```

This only lists standard files and directories. If I use the option `-t`, the list is displayed chronologically.

See also: `dir`, `vdir`, `chmod`, `find`

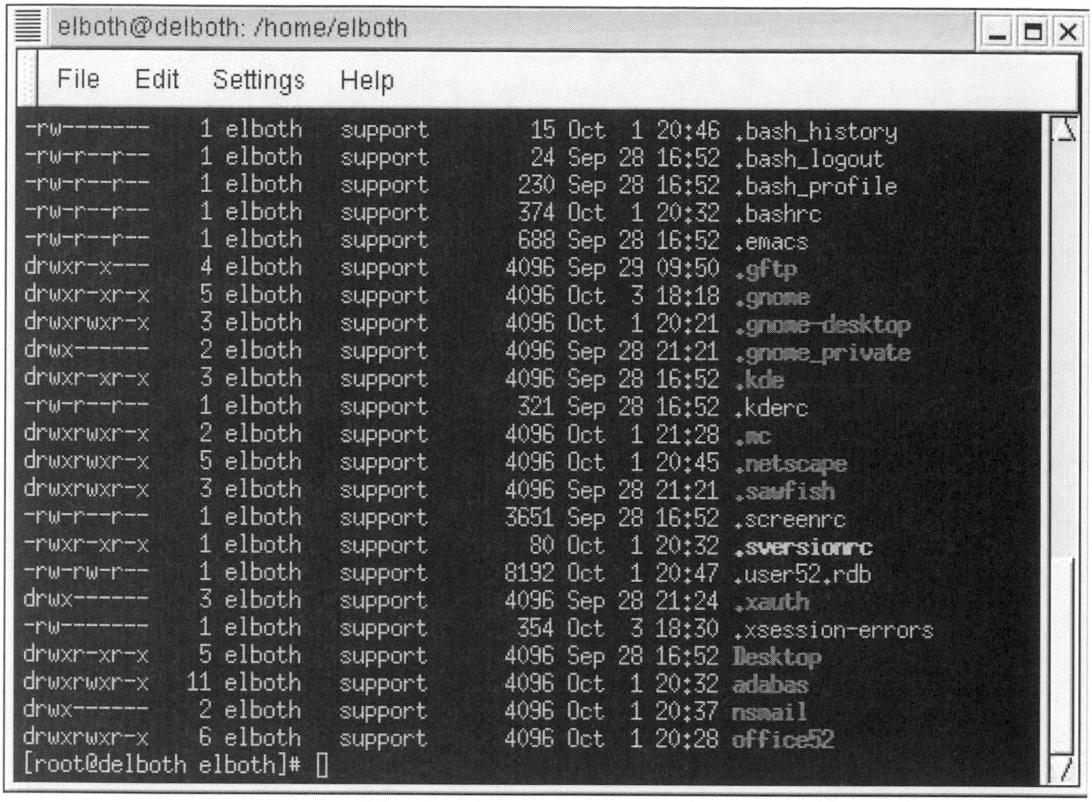

```
elboth@delboth: /home/elboth
File  Edit  Settings  Help
-rw-------    1 elboth   support        15 Oct  1 20:46 .bash_history
-rw-r--r--    1 elboth   support        24 Sep 28 16:52 .bash_logout
-rw-r--r--    1 elboth   support       230 Sep 28 16:52 .bash_profile
-rw-r--r--    1 elboth   support       374 Oct  1 20:32 .bashrc
-rw-r--r--    1 elboth   support       688 Sep 28 16:52 .emacs
drwxr-x---    4 elboth   support      4096 Sep 29 09:50 .gftp
drwxr-xr-x    5 elboth   support      4096 Oct  3 18:18 .gnome
drwxrwxr-x    3 elboth   support      4096 Oct  1 20:21 .gnome-desktop
drwx------    2 elboth   support      4096 Sep 28 21:21 .gnome_private
drwxr-xr-x    3 elboth   support      4096 Sep 28 16:52 .kde
-rw-r--r--    1 elboth   support       321 Sep 28 16:52 .kderc
drwxrwxr-x    2 elboth   support      4096 Oct  1 21:28 .mc
drwxrwxr-x    5 elboth   support      4096 Oct  1 20:45 .netscape
drwxrwxr-x    3 elboth   support      4096 Sep 28 21:21 .sawfish
-rw-r--r--    1 elboth   support      3651 Sep 28 16:52 .screenrc
-rwxr-xr-x    1 elboth   support        80 Oct  1 20:32 .sversionrc
-rw-rw-r--    1 elboth   support      8192 Oct  1 20:47 .user52.rdb
drwx------    3 elboth   support      4096 Sep 28 21:24 .xauth
-rw-------    1 elboth   support       354 Oct  3 18:30 .xsession-errors
drwxr-xr-x    5 elboth   support      4096 Sep 28 16:52 Desktop
drwxrwxr-x   11 elboth   support      4096 Oct  1 20:32 adabas
drwx------    2 elboth   support      4096 Oct  1 20:37 nsmail
drwxrwxr-x    6 elboth   support      4096 Oct  1 20:28 office52
[root@delboth elboth]# 
```

**Figure 5-1**
*Using the Linux* `ls-` *command from a terminal session.*

## 5.5 Date and time - date

With the `date` command, you can view and change the date and time.

**date Command – Displays/Adds Date and Time**

| | |
|---|---|
| Command | `date [MMddhhmm[year]] [+format]` |
| Function | Displays date and time. You can format the result as you prefer. If you are root, you can also change the date and time. |
| Argument | Date and/or time. |
| Options | See the Linux man pages. |

The format is defined by a set of field codes. These are the abbreviations for date and time:

| | | |
|---|---|---|
| MM | — | Month. |
| dd | — | Date. |
| hh | — | Hours. |
| mm | — | Minutes. |
| yy | — | Year. |

You can use several field codes for the format. Each field code sets conditions for the way the data is displayed. A % character separates each field code.

Format field codes:

| | | |
|---|---|---|
| n | — | Forces a line feed. |
| t | — | Forces a Tab character. |
| m | — | The month is displayed in the form 01 to 12. |
| d | — | The date is displayed in the form 01 to 31. |
| y | — | Only the two last digits of the year are displayed. |
| H | — | The hours are displayed in the form 00 to 23. |
| M | — | The minutes are displayed in the form 00 to 59. |
| S | — | The seconds are displayed in the form 00 to 59. |

If the format starts with +, the printout is user-controlled.

Examples:

```
[david@nittedal david]$ date
Fri Nov 30  17 11:39:37 CET 2001
(CET is Central European Time.)
```

Displays the present date and time.

Ordinary users can only display the current date and time. Root, however, can set a new date and time for the system:

```
[root@nittedal /root]# date 07291545
```

Here, root sets the date to July 29 and the time to 15:45.

If the system clock is incorrectly set, this will influence all commands related to time. Root must make sure that the clock is correctly set. If you want to set time and date, you can also use the X Window program `Linuxconf`.

Finally, here is an example that shows how to use the `date` command with format field codes:

```
[david@nittedal david]$ date'+Today's date:%m/%d/%y%n
Time: %H:%M:%S'
```

which produces:

```
Today's date: 07/13/2002
Time: 22:01:49
```

See also: Chapter 11, "Processes," and Chapter 16, "Shell Programming."

## 5.6 Who is logged in? - who

If you want to know who is logged in to the system, you can use the who command.

**who Command – Who Is Logged In?**

| | |
|---|---|
| Command | who [-u] [-T] [-q] |
| Function | Gives information about users and terminals that are using the system. The command lists usernames, terminals, login time, and the elapsed time since the last activity. |
| Argument | None. |
| Options | See the Linux man pages. |
| -u | Lists users that are logged in only. |
| -T | Displays the status of all terminals. |
| -q | Displays reduced print format. |

The who command without any option displays the names of users who are logged in and performing activities. The time when they logged in is also displayed. Using the option -u lists the processes associated with the user (see also Chapter 11).

Examples:

```
[david@nittedal david]$ who
david          ttyp0        Nov 17 11:34
root           tty2         Nov 17 11:44
erik           tty6         Oct  9 00:46
```

These are the names of the users who are logged in. Notice that you get the activity and the time of login.

```
[david@nittedal david]$ who -u
root       tty1      Nov 27 10:48 00:04
```

```
david       tty6      Nov 27 12:21    .
david       ttyp0     Nov 27 11:00    .    (207.117.119.220)
```

Users who have been active in the last minute are indicated by a dot. Terminals that have not been in use for the last 24 hours are marked `old`. The number on the far right is the IP address (`207.117.119.220`) of the user who is logged in.

```
[david@nittedal david]$ who -T
root     -     tty1        Nov 27 10:48
david    +     tty6        Nov 27 12:21
david    +     ttyp0       Nov 27 11:00 (207.117.119.220)
```

The `-T` option displays the status of the terminal. The + character indicates that anyone can write to the terminal. (See the `mesg` command.)

See also: `date`, `login`, `whoami`, `ps`, `mesg`

## 5.7 Who am I? - whoami

If you have more than one `user-id`, it is easy to get mixed up. The `whoami` command is very useful in these situations!

**whoami Command – Who Am I?**

| | |
|---|---|
| Command | `whoami` |
| Function | Who am I logged in as? |
| Argument | None. |
| Options | None. |

Example:

```
[david@nittedal david]$ whoami
nittedal.c2i.net!david ttyp0 Nov 27 11:00 (207.117.119.220)
```

The result of this command shows that I am logged in with the username `david`. My domain name is `nittedal.c2i.net`. I am logged in via the terminal line `ttyp0` (first virtual console over TCP/IP). My IP address is `207.117.119.220`. The device name of my terminal session is `ttyp0`. I logged in at `11:00` on `Nov 27`.

The `whoami` command is an option of the `who` command. The Linux command `ID` is a simplified variation of `whoami`. Try `id`, too!

See also: `date`, `id`, `login`, `mesg`, `who`, `ps`

## 5.8 User information - finger

The `finger` command (see Figure 5-2) displays system information about users who are logged in to the system.

**finger Command – Who Is Logged In?**

| | |
|---|---|
| Command | `finger [username@hostname]` |
| Function | Displays system information on users. |
| Argument | Username and hostname. |
| Options | See the Linux man pages. |

```
[david@nittedal david]$ finger
Login       Name            Tty   Idle   Login Time    Office
Office Phone
david       David Elboth    6     1:17   Nov 27 12:21
Nittedal 67075694
david       David Elboth    p0           Nov 27 11:00
(207.117.119.220)
root        root            *1            Nov 27 10:48
Nittedal    67078944
```

The display will depend on the security level of the system. Here is an example from Red Hat Linux. The display tells me that there are three users logged in to the system. I can see the full names of the users, which terminal program they are using, how long they have been logged in, login time, and their office address and telephone number.

Here is an example where I have used the hostname:

```
[david@nittedal david]$ finger david@nittedal.c2i.net
[nittedal.c2i.net]
Login: david                                Name: David
Elboth
Directory: /home/david                     Shell:
/bin/bash
```

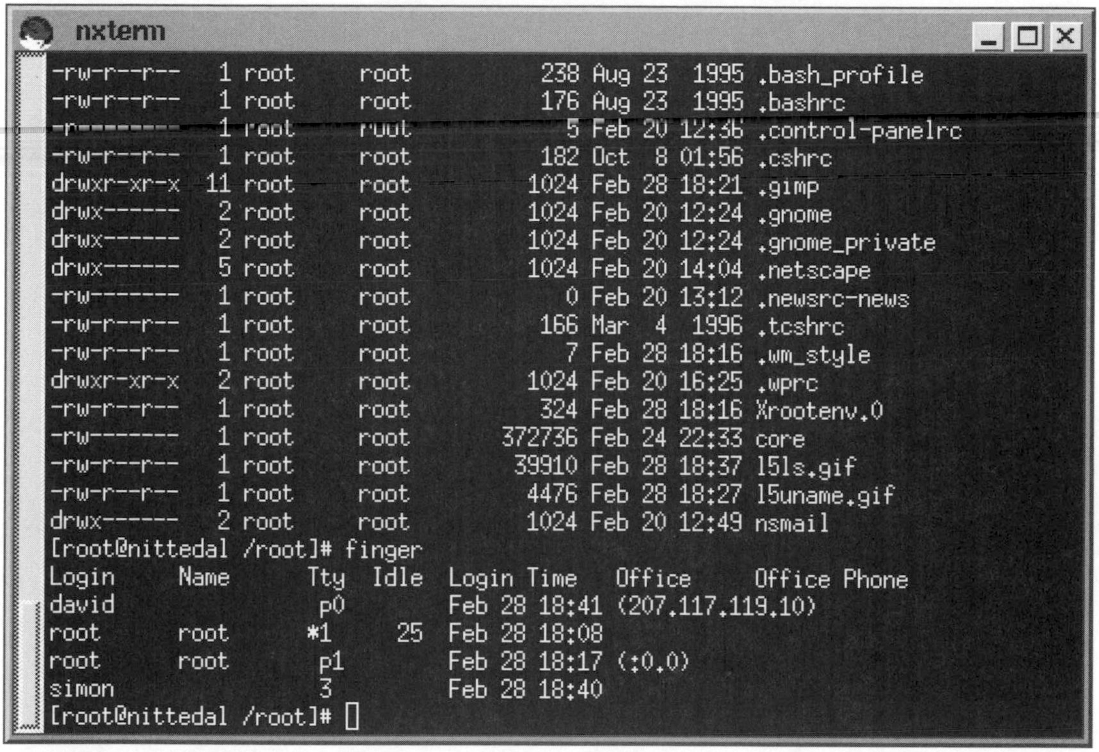

```
nxterm
-rw-r--r--   1 root     root          238 Aug 23  1995 .bash_profile
-rw-r--r--   1 root     root          176 Aug 23  1995 .bashrc
-r--------   1 root     root            5 Feb 20 12:36 .control-panelrc
-rw-r--r--   1 root     root          182 Oct  8 01:56 .cshrc
drwxr-xr-x  11 root     root         1024 Feb 28 18:21 .gimp
drwx------   2 root     root         1024 Feb 20 12:24 .gnome
drwx------   2 root     root         1024 Feb 20 12:24 .gnome_private
drwx------   5 root     root         1024 Feb 20 14:04 .netscape
-rw-------   1 root     root            0 Feb 20 13:12 .newsrc-news
-rw-r--r--   1 root     root          166 Mar  4  1996 .tcshrc
-rw-r--r--   1 root     root            7 Feb 28 18:16 .wm_style
drwxr-xr-x   2 root     root         1024 Feb 20 16:25 .wprc
-rw-r--r--   1 root     root          324 Feb 28 18:16 Xrootenv.0
-rw-------   1 root     root       372736 Feb 24 22:33 core
-rw-r--r--   1 root     root        39910 Feb 28 18:37 15ls.gif
-rw-r--r--   1 root     root         4476 Feb 28 18:27 15uname.gif
drwx------   2 root     root         1024 Feb 20 12:49 nsmail
[root@nittedal /root]# finger
Login     Name       Tty  Idle  Login Time   Office     Office Phone
david                 p0        Feb 28 18:41 (207.117.119.10)
root      root       *1     25  Feb 28 18:08
root      root        p1        Feb 28 18:17 (:0.0)
simon                 3         Feb 28 18:40
[root@nittedal /root]#
```

**Figure 5-2**
*Example with the Linux command* `finger`.

```
Office:  Nittedal,  22777696
On since Fri Nov 27 12:21 (CET) on tty6    1 hour 29
minutes idle
On since Fri Nov 27 11:00 (CET) on ttyp0 from
207.117.119.220
   1 second idle
No mail.
No Plan.
```

See also: `date`, `who`, `whoami`, `ps`

## 5.9 Determine current file type - file

If you don't know the type of a given file, you can use the `file` command (see Figure 5-3) to determine its type. `file` executes a series of tests. If you are handling an ASCII file, the first block will be tested to determine which language the file is written in. If the test finds an 8-bit character, the file will be classified as 8-bit text. Numerous formats are recognized.

**file Command – What Is the File Type?**

| | |
|---|---|
| Command | `file [-f] file/directory [filename]` |
| Function | Gives information on files/directories. |
| Argument | The `file` command requires an argument, i.e., a filename or wildcard (see Chapter 16 for information on using wildcards). If you use the option `-f`, the file is a list of filenames. |
| Options | See the Linux man pages. |
| `-f` | The next argument is a file with a list of filenames. |

File types:

| | | |
|---|---|---|
| ascii text | — | Text files where less than 20% of the commands are separated by a space or a line feed. |
| cannot open | — | No read access. |
| c program text | — | C source code program. |
| commands text | — | The file is a bash shell program (script). |
| directory | — | A directory. |
| empty | — | An empty file. |
| data | — | A standard data file. |

Example:

```
[david@nittedal david]$ file *
batch:          commands text
c-files:        directory
cls.bat:        commands text
cls.c:          c program text
convert.c:      c program text
fil:            empty
ifs:            commands text
test:           directory
uni.c:          c program text
uniconv.c:      c program text
```

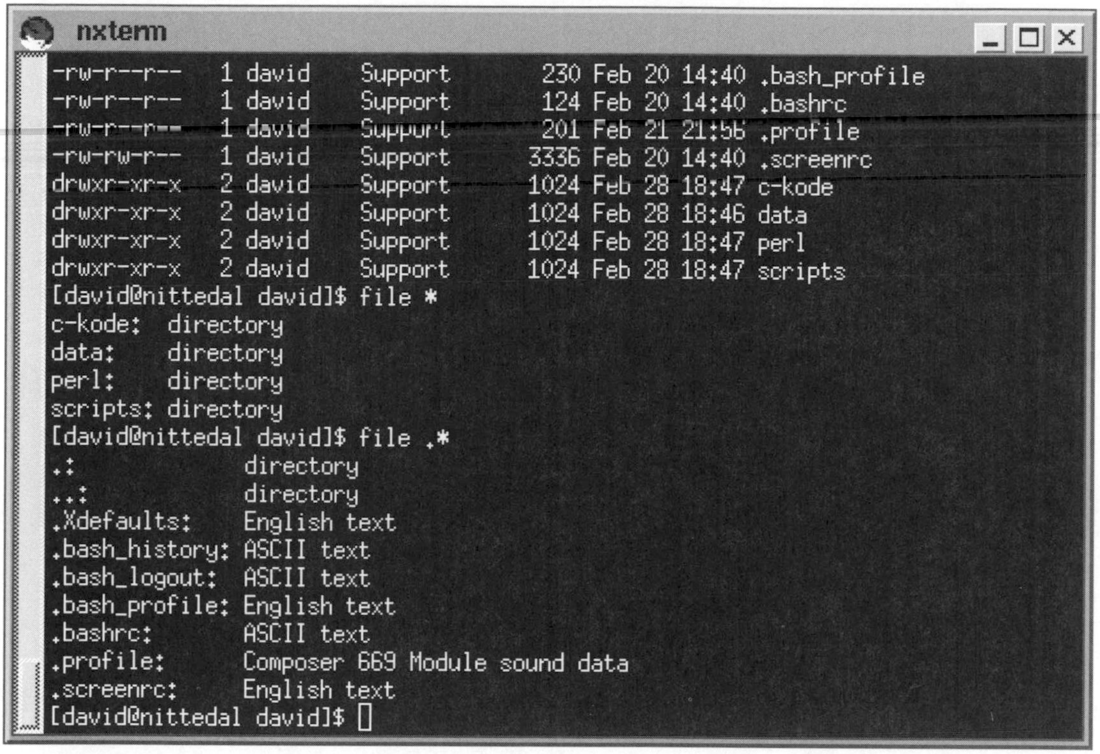

```
nxterm
-rw-r--r--   1 david    Support       230 Feb 20 14:40 .bash_profile
-rw-r--r--   1 david    Support       124 Feb 20 14:40 .bashrc
-rw-r--r--   1 david    Support       201 Feb 21 21:56 .profile
-rw-rw-r--   1 david    Support      3336 Feb 20 14:40 .screenrc
drwxr-xr-x   2 david    Support      1024 Feb 28 18:47 c-kode
drwxr-xr-x   2 david    Support      1024 Feb 28 18:46 data
drwxr-xr-x   2 david    Support      1024 Feb 28 18:47 perl
drwxr-xr-x   2 david    Support      1024 Feb 28 18:47 scripts
[david@nittedal david]$ file *
c-kode:  directory
data:    directory
perl:    directory
scripts: directory
[david@nittedal david]$ file .*
.:             directory
..:            directory
.Xdefaults:    English text
.bash_history: ASCII text
.bash_logout:  ASCII text
.bash_profile: English text
.bashrc:       ASCII text
.profile:      Composer 669 Module sound data
.screenrc:     English text
[david@nittedal david]$ 
```

**Figure 5-3**
*Example with the Linux command* `file`.

## 5.10 Terminal name - tty

The terminal controls all the processes that are started by a user. A control program controls each connected unit. Standard I/O (input/output) and errors are automatically connected to the user's terminal. If you want to know the name of your terminal and its device driver, you can use the `tty` command.

**tty Command – Which Terminal Device Driver?**

| | |
|---|---|
| Command | `tty [option]` |
| Function | Displays the name of the current device driver. |
| Argument | None. |
| Options | See the Linux man pages. |

Example:

```
[david@nittedal david]$ tty
/dev/tty1
```

## 5.11 Disk space usage - du

The du command (disk usage) gives you an overview of the amount of disk space a user or the whole system consumes (in 512- or 1024-byte blocks). As root, you can use this command to find out which users or programs consume the most space on the system's hard disk drives.

**du Command – Disk Usage per File/Directory**

| | |
|---|---|
| Command | du [-as] [argument] |
| Function | Displays disk usage by file, directory, and total usage for the current directory (filesystem). |
| Argument | File or directory. |
| Options | See the Linux man pages. |
| -a | Number of blocks used by each file and directory. |
| -s | Displays total usage for the specified directory only. |

Providing no option gives you the number of blocks, directories, and total block usage summarized for the hard disk drive.

Example:

```
[root@nittedal /usr/bin]# du -a /root
1       /root/.prognet/RealServer50
2       /root/.prognet
2       /root/.Xdefaults
?
1       /root/.seyon/startup
14      /root/.seyon
3       /root/.bash_history
1       /root/Xrootenv.0
1       /root/.FVWM2-errors
29      /root
[root@nittedal /usr/bin]#
```

The numbers represent block usage for each file and directory. The last number represents total usage.

```
[root@nittedal /usr/bin]# du -s /root
29      /root
[root@nittedal /usr/bin]#
```

This number represents the total number of blocks used by the directory /root.

## 5.12 Linux version/name - uname

The `uname` command gives information about the Linux (or Unix) system you are working on. This is useful in system-to-system communication.

**uname Command – Linux Operating System/System Name**

| | |
|---|---|
| Command | `uname [-snrvma]` |
| Function | Displays hardware architecture, Linux system name, and the node name of your Linux machine (Unix). |
| Argument | None. |
| Options | See the Linux man pages. |
| `-s` | Displays the name of the system. |
| `-n` | Displays the node/domain name. This name is used as a reference when using network communication. |
| `-r` | Displays the release number of your OS. |
| `-v` | Displays the version of your OS. |
| `-m` | Displays the hardware in use, e.g., Pentium, MC68XXX, Alpha, etc. |
| `-a` | Displays all information. |

If you don't use options, you will get the Linux system name on the terminal. Examples:

```
[david@nittedal david]$ uname -s
Linux
```

meaning that the system name is `Linux`.

```
[david@nittedal david]$ uname -a
Linux nittedal.c2i.net 2.4.14-5.0 #1 Fri Mar 8 21:07:39
EST 2001 i686 unknown
```

This contains the system name (`Linux`), the node/domain name (`nittedal.c2i.net`), the release number (`2.4.14-5.0`), the version number of the OS (`#1 Fri Mar 8 21:07:39 EST 2001`), and the hardware architecture (`i686 unknown`).

## Exercises for Chapter 5

1. Display a calendar for next year.
2. Type your name on the screen by means of the `echo` command.
3. Try more than one variation of the `ls` command.
4. Is your system time correct? Log in as root and set the time and date correctly.
5. Check users and virtual terminals with the `who` command. Has anyone fallen asleep at his or her terminal? Try different options with the `who` command.
6. What kinds of files are in the directories `/usr/bin` and `/usr/doc`?
7. Which two methods can be used to determine which device driver your terminal uses? Try both!
8. What is the total amount of disk space in use on your Linux system (number of blocks)? What kind of Linux system do you use and what is your hardware architecture?

CHAPTER
6

# File Management

## 6.1 File manager

The Linux commands you will learn in this chapter are used for managing files. All these commands are easy to use. Most of them can also be executed from the file manager GNU Midnight Commander in GNOME (see Figure 6-1) (*[david@nittedal david]$* **gmc &**) or from the file manager kfm in KDE (*[david@nittedal david]$* **kfm &**).

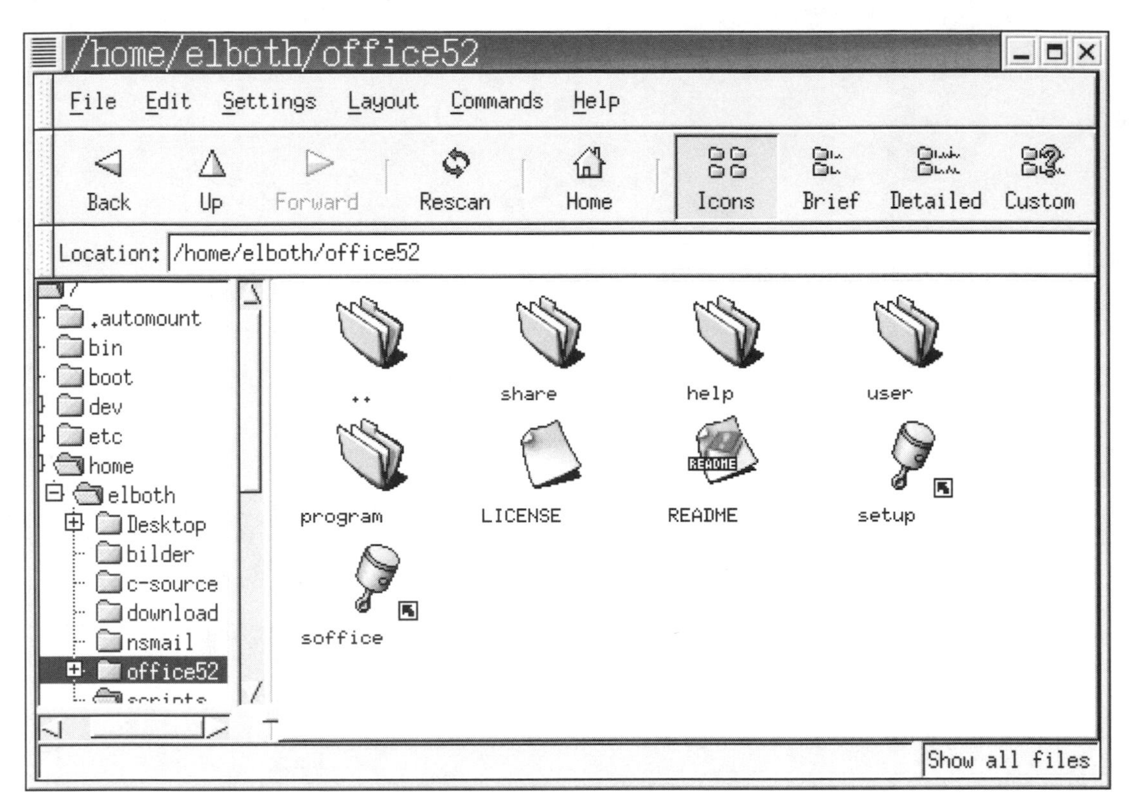


**Figure 6-1**
*The GNU Midnight Commander in GNOME.*

## 6.2 Linux filenames

Linux supports filenames up to 256 characters long, but only the first 64 characters are significant. Some Unix variants handle only 14 characters. If you are an experienced DOS or Windows user, you are used to three characters after a dot at the end of the filename describing the file type. In Linux, it is customary to use one character prefixed by a dot. Examples: `program.c` or `program.o`. You can use more than one dot in a filename.

I must emphasize that there are no limits to how you specify filenames; Linux leaves it all up to you. As opposed to DOS or Windows, there is nothing in the filename that indicates whether the file can be executed (`exe`, `com`, etc.). The file must be defined as executable in the filesystem.

In the Linux world, it is also normal to use standard 3-4 character descriptions for file types like `gif`, `jpg`, `pdf`, `html`, etc. (see Chapter 7).

Linux has these rules for filenames:

- Filenames can be up to 256 characters long.
- These special characters are used in Linux commands and cannot be used in filenames:

  ( ) { } ? [ ] < > ; | ‘ ` “ \ &

  For the same reason, neither spaces nor control characters can be used in filenames.
- Linux is case-sensitive, although most filenames are lower-case. It is important to use meaningful filenames as this makes it easier to retrieve them later. For example, using the filename `letter.elboth.xmas` is better than just `letter`.
- All login files start with a dot. Examples: `.bash_profile`, `.bashrc`, `.profile`, `.login`, `.cshrc`, `.tcshrc`, and `.kshrc`. To hide a file, prefix the filename with a dot, for example `.letteranne`. Hiding a file means that it will be listed only when you include `-a` as an option in the `ls` command.

## 6.3 Linux file types

Linux supports several file types (see Figure 6-2). When using GNOME `gmc` or the `ls` command, information about the file will be listed.

The first column contains a description of the file type. The other columns list access codes. These are the various file types:

- (hyphen) — Standard Linux file.<br>
`d` — Directory.<br>
`b` — Block device driver.<br>
`c` — Character device driver.

For file types like `gif`, `jpg`, `pdf`, `html`, etc., see Chapter 7.

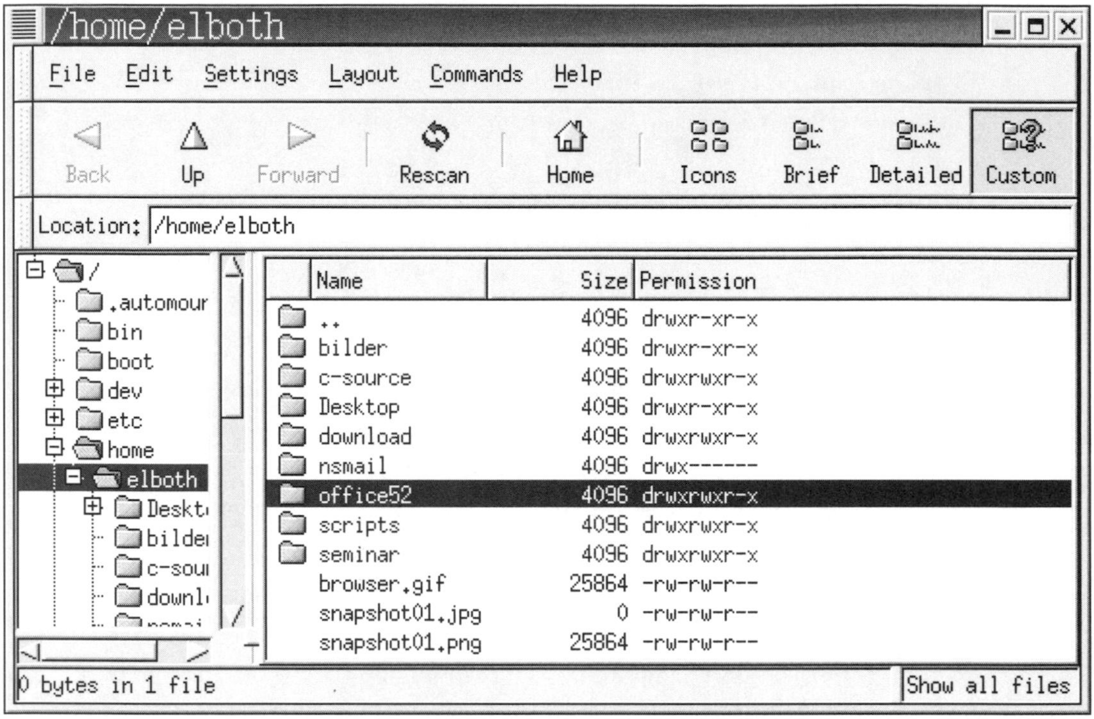

**Figure 6-2**
*From the GNU Midnight Commander in GNOME you will see file types.*

## 6.4 Access to files and directories

The creator of a file/directory automatically becomes the owner of the file or directory. The owner of a file or directory sets his or her own access privileges in addition to privileges for the other members of his/her user group and for everyone else.

When creating a file or directory, you apply codes that decide read access, write access, and execute access. Chapter 8 is all about these codes and how to set and alter them, etc.

### *6.4.1 Using wildcards*

Linux uses the following special characters as wildcards in the names of files and directories:

* ? [ ]

When you type a wildcard, Linux will replace it with other characters according to the rules shown below. By using wildcards, you may specify names for files and directories and groups of files/directories.

The following rules apply to the use of wildcards:

| | | |
|---|---|---|
| ? | — | Each question mark is one single character. |
| * | — | Represents a group of characters (any number). |
| [ ] | — | Represents characters or intervals (when using a hyphen). |

Wildcards can be combined with other wildcards and regular characters.

| Wildcard | Description |
|---|---|
| * | All files in specified directory. |
| f* | All files starting with "f". |
| *.o | All files ending with "o". |
| ???? | All files with four characters. |
| Linux? | All files beginning with "Linux" and including one more character, e.g., Linuxa, Linuxb, Linuxc, etc. |
| Linux[1-4] | Similarly, Linux1, Linux2, Linux3, etc. |
| [LU]inux | Either Linux or Uinux. |

You can use wildcards in connection with most of the file management commands in Linux. The commands will manage files with filenames that fit the pattern you have given.

Use wildcards with caution! For example, the command `rm *` will remove all files in the current directory.

Some examples of commands that include wildcards:

| | |
|---|---|
| `cat *` | `ls -la t*` |
| `cat /usr/u*` | `rm '-!?*-'` (removes the file `-!?*-`) |
| `lp chap[1-20]` | `ls -la chap???` |
| `ls -la.*` | `rm del?.test` |
| `ls ???S*` | `ls f??g` |

If you use single apostrophes (' ') or quotation marks (" "), wildcards have no effect. Any wildcard will be interpreted as plain text.

## 6.5 Print files to the screen - cat

The `cat` command prints your text files to screen. "`cat`" means concatenate and was originally designed to combine several files into one. If you use `cat` without any options or arguments, it expects data from the standard input channel, i.e., the keyboard. You can always finish with <Ctrl-d>.

**cat Command - Prints Files to the Screen**

| | |
|---|---|
| Command | `cat [-s] [-v] [arguments ...]` |
| Function | Displays the contents of a text file on the screen or copies one or more files to the screen/file. |
| Arguments | File, directory, and/or wildcards. |
| Options | See the Linux man pages. |
| `-s` | No message about nonexisting files. |
| `-v` | Control characters are displayed, e.g., ^X, ^? |

When using the `cat` command without options (see Figure 6-3), only the file(s) are listed on the screen. You can specify an argument of one or more files, but arguments are not required. With the `cat` command, you can also write directly to the screen.

Example:

```
[david@nittedal david]$ cat
I write some text
I write some text
using the cat-command
using the cat-command
I quit with Control d.
I quit with Control d.
<Ctrl-d>
```

Each line is printed twice—first when you type it, then as an echo from the OS.

Example:

```
[david@nittedal david]$ cat -v davidtext
```

Prints the text file `davidtext` to the screen, including all control characters. See also Chapters 7 and 8.

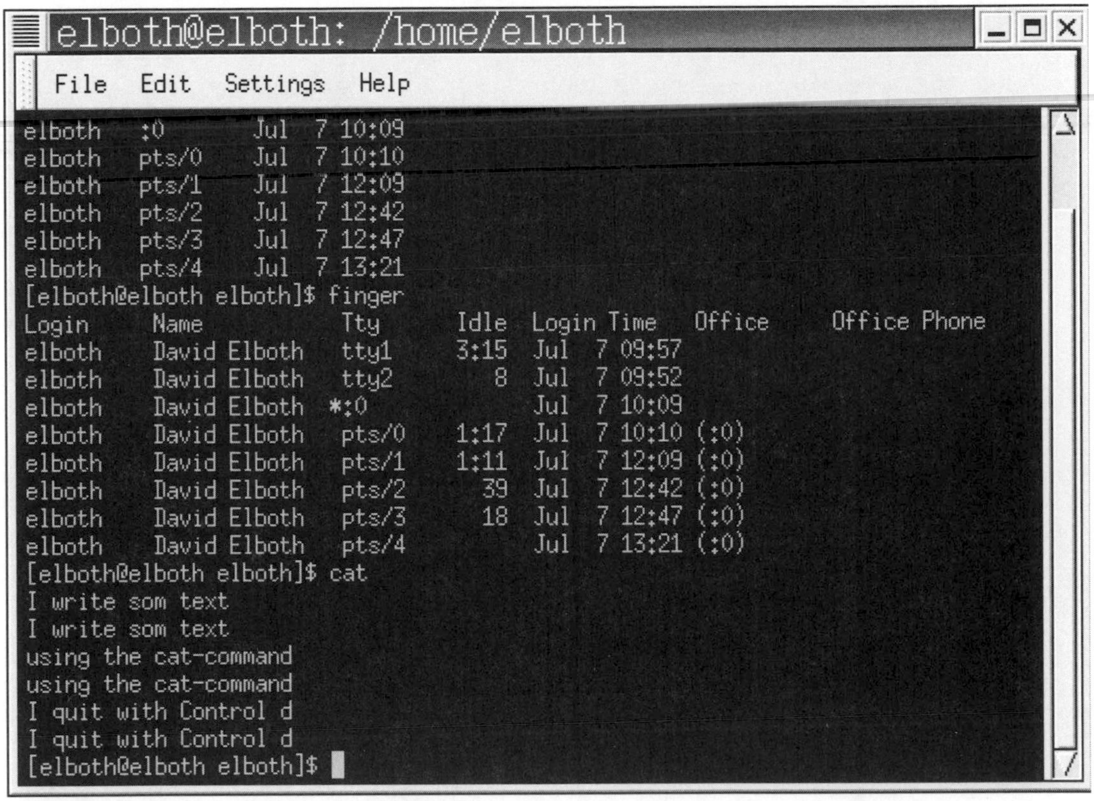

```
elbOth@elboth: /home/elboth
File  Edit  Settings  Help
elboth   :0       Jul  7 10:09
elboth   pts/0    Jul  7 10:10
elboth   pts/1    Jul  7 12:09
elboth   pts/2    Jul  7 12:42
elboth   pts/3    Jul  7 12:47
elboth   pts/4    Jul  7 13:21
[elboth@elboth elboth]$ finger
Login     Name           Tty      Idle  Login Time   Office     Office Phone
elboth    David Elboth   tty1     3:15  Jul  7 09:57
elboth    David Elboth   tty2        8  Jul  7 09:52
elboth    David Elboth  *:0             Jul  7 10:09
elboth    David Elboth   pts/0    1:17  Jul  7 10:10 (:0)
elboth    David Elboth   pts/1    1:11  Jul  7 12:09 (:0)
elboth    David Elboth   pts/2      39  Jul  7 12:42 (:0)
elboth    David Elboth   pts/3      18  Jul  7 12:47 (:0)
elboth    David Elboth   pts/4          Jul  7 13:21 (:0)
[elboth@elboth elboth]$ cat
I write som text
I write som text
using the cat-command
using the cat-command
I quit with Control d
I quit with Control d
[elboth@elboth elboth]$
```

**Figure 6-3**
*Example using the Linux command* `cat`.

## 6.6 Copy files - cp

With the `cp` command, you can copy single files or groups of files inside a directory or to/from a directory. If you want to copy a file, you need read access to the file and write access to the directory you are copying to.

**cp Command – Copies Files**

| | |
|---|---|
| Command | `cp fil1 fil2`<br>or<br>`cp files directory` |
| Function | Copies single files and groups of files. |
| Arguments | File, directory, and/or wildcards. |
| Options | See the Linux man pages. |

**cp Command – Copies Files (*Continued*)**

| | |
|---|---|
| -f | Forces replacement of destination file(s). |
| -i | Requests before replacing files. |
| -p | Preserves the original attributes, e.g., owner, access rights, and time of last modification. |
| -r | Also copies subdirectories. |
| -v | Verbose modes=show; displays the name of each file that is copied. |
| fil1 | Name of the file to be copied (source). |
| fil2 | Name of the new file (destination). |

Examples:

```
[david@nittedal david]$ cp report report1
```

The file `report` will be copied to a new file named `report1`.

```
[david@nittedal david]$ cp *nrf text/
```

Copies all files ending with `nrf` to the directory `text/`. The new files have the same filename, `user-id`, group ID, etc. See Chapter 7 for more information about directories.

```
[david@nittedal david]$ cp letter1 letter2 /usr/letterdir
```

Copies the files `letter1` and `letter2` to the directory `/usr/letterdir`.

See also: `cpio`, `ln`, `mv`, `rm`, `chmod`

## 6.7 Move/change filenames - mv

The `mv` command lets you move files from one directory to another. You can rename the file in the same operation. If the file has the same name as the destination file, the old destination file will be deleted before the file is moved. You can also change the name of directories.

**mv Command – Changes Names of Files/Directories**

| | |
|---|---|
| Command | `mv [-f] fil1 fil2`<br>or<br>`mv [-f] directory1 directory2`<br>or<br>`mv [-f] fil ... directory` |
| Function | Renames and/or moves files; directories can only be renamed. |
| Arguments | File, directory, and/or wildcards. |
| Options | See the Linux man pages. |
| `-f` | You can move a file even when there is another file with the same name as the destination file, and also if this file is write-protected. |
| `fil1` | Name of the file to be moved or changed (source). |
| `fil2` | The new name of the file. |

Examples:

```
[david@nittedal david]$ mv smb.conf smb
```

The file `smb.conf` is renamed `smb`.

```
[david@nittedal david]$ mv linux* linuxbook
```

All files with names starting with `linux` are moved to the directory `linuxbook`.

```
[david@nittedal david]$ mv /tmp/letter
/home/david/letter-copy
```

This moves the file `letter` in the `/tmp` directory to the `/home/david` directory. The file is renamed `letter-copy`.

```
[david@nittedal david]$ mv /home/david/wp
/home/david/corel
```

This renames the directory `wp` to `corel`.

If `fil1` and `fil2` are in different filesystems, the `mv` command must first copy and remove the source. The owner of the copied file and the original link references will be lost.

See also: `cp`, `chmod`

## 6.9 Delete files and directories - rm

The `rm` command deletes single files or groups of files. You can delete one or more files or a whole directory tree. Removing files requires that you have write access to the directory. If you are the owner of the file, no other privileges are required.

**rm Command – Deletes One or More Files/Directories**

| | |
|---|---|
| Command | `rm [-fri] [argument]` |
| Function | Deletes one or more files/directories. |
| Arguments | File, directory, and/or wildcards. |
| Options | See the Linux man pages. |
| `-f` | Deletes unwritable files without warning. |
| `-r` | Deletes all files/directories and subdirectories. Use this option with care! |
| `-i` | If you choose to delete interactively, each file name to be deleted is shown on screen. To delete, you must confirm with y, otherwise you must press n. |

Note: You should delete unnecessary files.

Examples:

```
[david@nittedal david]$ rm linux.fil
```

Deletes the file `linux.fil`.

```
[david@nittedal david]$ rm /bin/test
```

Deletes the file `test` in the `/bin` directory.

```
[david@nittedal david]$ rm -f mess*
```

Removes, without warning, all files beginning with `mess`.

[david@nittedal david]$ **rm -i testdir**

I will be asked (see Figure 6-4) to confirm whether I want to delete the file testdir.

[david@nittedal david]$ **rm -r /home/david**

Removes the /home/david directory and all its subdirectories.

[david@nittedal david]$ **rm -r ***

Removes all files in the current directory and all its subdirectories.

The -r option is risky to use. It can remove up to 17 levels of subdirectories (see Chapter 7).

See also: rmdir

```
elboth@elboth: /home/elboth
File  Edit  Settings  Help
-rw-r--r--    1 elboth   elboth       435 jul  4 13:37 .kderc
drwxrwxr-x    2 elboth   elboth      4096 jul  7 13:14 .mc
drwxrwxr-x    5 elboth   elboth      4096 jul  7 12:50 .netscape
drwxrwxr-x    3 elboth   elboth      4096 jul  6 10:00 .sane
drwxrwxr-x    3 elboth   elboth      4096 jul  6 10:30 .sawfish
-rw-r--r--    1 elboth   elboth      3394 jul  4 13:37 .screenrc
-rw-rw-r--    1 elboth   elboth        52 jul  4 13:41 .sversionrc
-rw-rw-r--    1 elboth   elboth      8192 jul  6 10:29 .user52.rdb
drwx------    3 elboth   elboth      4096 jul  6 11:28 .xauth
-rw-------    1 elboth   elboth      2033 jul  7 13:18 .xsession-errors
drwxr-xr-x    2 elboth   elboth      4096 jul  4 13:09 .xvpics
drwxr-xr-x    5 elboth   elboth      4096 jul  4 13:37 Desktop
drwxr-xr-x    2 elboth   elboth      4096 jul  7 13:27 bilder
-rw-rw-r--    1 elboth   elboth     25864 jul  6 14:01 browser.gif
drwxrwxr-x    2 elboth   elboth      4096 jul  4 14:12 c-source
drwxrwxr-x    2 elboth   elboth      4096 jul  7 13:01 download
drwx------    2 elboth   elboth      4096 jul  4 12:36 nsmail
drwxrwxr-x    6 elboth   elboth      4096 jul  4 13:41 office52
drwxrwxr-x    2 elboth   elboth      4096 jul  7 13:13 scripts
drwxrwxr-x    2 elboth   elboth      4096 jul  4 14:13 seminar
-rw-rw-r--    1 elboth   elboth         0 jul  7 12:07 snapshot01.jpg
-rw-rw-r--    1 elboth   elboth     25864 jul  6 10:03 snapshot01.png
[elboth@elboth elboth]$ rm -i download/*
rm: slette «download/so-5_2-ga-bin-linux-en.bin»?
```

**Figure 6-4**
*Example using the Linux command* rm.

## 6.10 Assign multiple filenames - ln

It is sometimes useful to have multiple names for one file. One of the names may show which project the file belongs to, while another shows information about the contents of the file. This is called linking several references (filenames) to one single file.

**ln Command – Links Files/Directories**

| | |
|---|---|
| Command | `ln [option] fil1 fil2`<br>or<br>`ln [option] fil1 ... directory` |
| Function | Creates a link to a file, i.e., makes it possible to give one single file several different filenames. The file `fil1` is also given the filename `fil2`. The logical process is that you define two filenames that have the same inode number as a reference. It is possible to link files in different filesystems. The same applies to directories. |
| Arguments | File, directory, and/or wildcards. |
| Options | See the Linux man pages. |
| `-f` | Makes a link even if the new filename already exists. |
| `-s` | Makes a symbolic link, which can link via different filesystems. The default is a hard link, which cannot link across filesystems. |

When using the `rm` command, a file will not be deleted until you delete the last reference (filename) to the file.

Examples:

```
[david@nittedal david]$ ln sford textsf
```

Now the files `sford` and `textsf` belong to the same inode (see Chapters 7 and 8).

```
[david@nittedal david]$ ln .profile /home/anne/.profile
```

Here, two users have access to the same system file (see Figure 6-5). The link goes via a different directory.

```
[david@nittedal root]# ln /dev/fd0H1440 /dev/A
```

Device drivers sometimes have long names. Here, I define a short name that is simple to remember. In this example, you must be root.

**Figure 6-5**
*Example using the Linux command* `ln`.

You remove a link with the `rm` command, i.e., you remove one of the filenames.

```
[david@nittedal david]$ rm sford
```

Removes the linked filename `sford` and removes the link.

The `ln` command has a variety of uses that aren't that obvious to users familiar with Microsoft DOS or Windows. I'll give two practical examples.

All new programs created with gtk (a tool for creating GUIs in Linux (http://www.gtk.org)) use a file called `gtkrc` to decide the appearance of a program (see http://gtk.themes.org). This file normally is created in a subdirectory (`.program name`) in your home directory. If you have several of these programs, it is not effective to edit each of them when you want to change the programs' appearance. The solution is to use `ln` to make sure that you have the same file in all directories. When you change the file in one directory, it will be updated all over.

Another example illustrates the efficiency of the `ln` command. I was installing Linux on a laptop PC without a CD-ROM drive. The laptop had a docking station with a built-in Ethernet adapter, which made it possible to connect it to my desktop unit that runs as an FTP server. With the `ln` command, I set up a link from the desktop's CD-ROM drive to the FTP server. This made the CD-ROM drive (with a Linux CD installation disk) accessible via FTP without having to copy the whole contents to the hard disk drive. I could run the installation of Linux to the laptop via FTP.

See also: `cp`, `rm`, `mv`, `inodenumber`

## Exercises for Chapter 6

1. Use the `ls` command and wildcards to find out the following about your system:

   a) How many filenames have exactly 14 characters?

   b) Which filenames have exactly five characters?

   c) Which filenames end with "sss"?

   d) Which four-character filenames start with "d" and ends with "e"?

   e) Which three-character filenames end with a character in the interval "e-k"?

   f) List all filenames ending with "?" (illegal).

   g) List all filenames starting with "*" (illegal).
2. Can you make illegal filenames? How can you use these files later?
3. What are your file types?
4. How can you represent the files mentioned below with wildcards?

   a) abc abd abe b) rapp1 rapp2 rapp3

   c) x1s xes d) All files starting with the characters "s" or "d".
5. Print your entire text file to screen with and without control characters.
6. Make backups of all your system files.
7. Rename your backup files.
8. Try and remove a text file with the option `-f`.
9. Make several names (links) for your backup files.

CHAPTER
7

# Directories and Filesystems

## 7.1 Introduction

In this chapter, you will learn about directories and filesystems. You will also see how the Linux filesystem is designed and what each directory contains. Finally, you will learn how to move around in the directory structure and how to make and remove directories.

## 7.2 Directories and filesystems

A directory is a list of files. The OS interprets a directory as a file, but unprivileged programs cannot write to it. A filename is specified with a pathname, e.g., `/home/david/perl-test`. The path consists of the root filesystem, then the directories `home` and `david`. If the path does not start with a /, the system will start to search from the directory where the user is situated (the working directory). Every directory has at least two addresses:

- **.** **Points at the working directory.**
- **..** **Points at the parent directory of the working directory.**

The filesystem in Linux consists of files and directories plus the information necessary to find and access them. Each filesystem is an independent entity that contains a number of files and directories. Directories are handled exactly like other files with one exception: In Linux you cannot write directly to a directory. Directories contain filenames. Each reference in the directory consists of two separate parts:

- **A filename up to 256 characters long (variable).**
- **A pointer called a link.**

The link points at the inode, which is the most important part of a file in the OS. The inode holds all the information about the file, e.g., length, creation date, ownership, etc. The file does not physically exist in a directory. The directory only consists of filenames and pointers (links). When Linux attempts to open a file, it first finds the inode number of the file where the filename is listed. The next step is reading the inode to establish which file type it is and determining its access properties. If it is a standard file or a directory, the first block pointer will be used to find the beginning of the data.

## 7.3 Inodes

All files have only one inode. There is no fixed, one-to-one relationship between filenames and physical data files. Two or more directories can have filenames that point at the same file. When you have a physical file with several different names, the filenames are linked. (Refer to the section regarding the `ln` command in Chapter 6.) Linux also supports symbolic linking that allows linking different filesystems and directories. A symbolic link gets its own inode and inode number.

When using the `rm` command, the file (and its inode) will not be removed before you delete the last reference to the file.

Inodes are the descriptions of files in the Linux system, while directory references allow direct references to a physical file with a filename. The inode system lets the Linux system find blocks of data very fast.

These are the main contents of an inode:

- **Inode number.**
- **Length of file.**
- **The file's creation date.**
- **Time of last access to the file.**
- **Time of last change to the file.**
- **Time of last change to the inode.**
- **Owner and group.**
- **Size of file.**
- **Access properties.**
- **Direct pointers to blocks of data.**
- **Indirect pointers to blocks of data.**
- **Double indirect pointers to blocks of data.**
- **Triple indirect pointers to blocks of data.**

If you use different options with the `ls` command, you will get nearly all the information about the inode. For example, the option `-i` will give you the inode number of a file.

## 7.4 The physical filesystem

Linux handles all files as a sequence of 1KB blocks (some Unix systems use 512-byte, 1KB, 2KB, 4KB, or 8KB blocks) numbered 0, 1, 2, etc. The first block on your hard disk drive is the boot block (LILO), also called the primary block.

### *7.4.1 Super Block*

The second block on your drive is the super block of the filesystem. This contains the size of the filesystem in number of blocks; **`fsize`**, which gives the number of blocks reserved for inodes; and **`isize`**, which points at the first free block. The super block also contains general status information like the number of free inodes in the system, the number of inodes and data blocks, etc. All status information comes from the super block. The super block is updated approximately every 30 seconds.

The blocks from `2+isize` to `fsize` are reserved for data storage. The free data blocks are chained together to form a free list.

Isize is a pointer that points to the beginning of the list of free blocks. The blocks from isize+2 to fsize are reserved for data storage (see Figure 7-1).

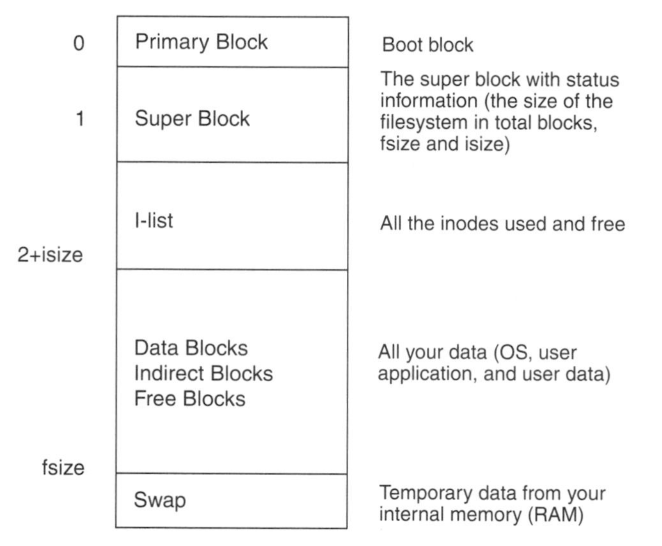


**Figure 7-1**
*The physical organization of the Linux filesystem.*

### 7.4.2 Paging

The rest of the space in the physical system is used for swapping and paging. Paging and swapping are described in Chapters 2 and 3.

### 7.4.3 Indirect Addressing

Inodes have a limited number of block pointers, depending on the size of the file. If the file is large, the inode uses three pointers to indirect blocks (see Figure 7-2).

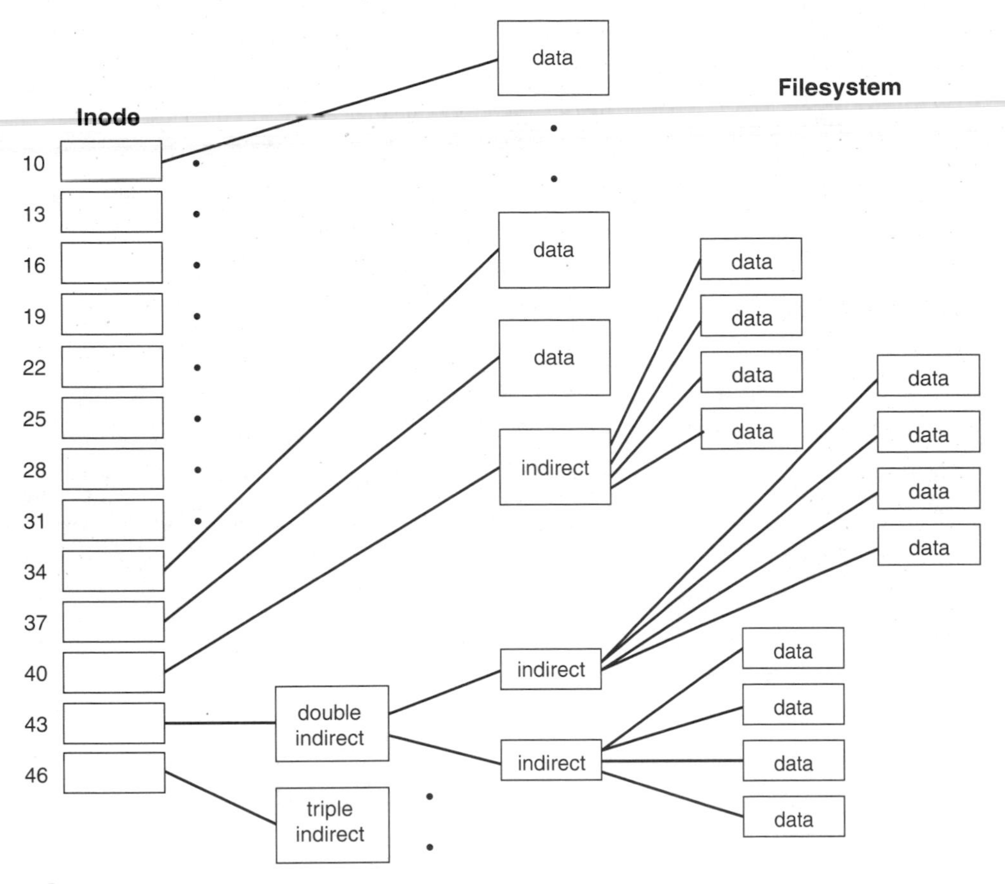


**Figure 7-2**
*The Linux filesystem.*

### 7.4.4 Maximum File Size

One inode can address a maximum of 10 data blocks consisting of 1KB (some systems have blocks of 2, 4, or 8KB, or 512 bytes). If the file is larger, the inode will use three pointers to indirect blocks that each contain 256 pointers to data blocks. The maximum size of a file under Linux is accordingly:

1024 bytes * (10+256+256**2+256**3)=17 247 250 432 bytes

This is valid when the disk blocks are allocated with a fixed size of 1024 bytes. If each disk block is 4KB, the maximum file size will be 68GB. If each disk block is 8KB, the maximum file size will be 136GB.

The Linux filesystem Ext2 uses a different allocation structure. Ext2 with

1KB blocks has a maximum size of 4TB. Each file under filesystem Ext2 can have a maximum size of 2GB.

If you are running a Linux filesystem with blocks of 1KB, you should never have more than 286 files in each directory. If you have less than 30 files, searching a disk will be very efficient because you only use one disk block.

## 7.5 Different filesystems

All Linux systems have at least one filesystem on the first hard disk drive. This filesystem, called the root filesystem, is represented with the symbol /. The root filesystem consists of programs and directories that form the OS.

It is possible to have up to 16 filesystems on each physical hard disk drive (valid for a PC system). The most usual names of filesystems are: /home, /usr, /bin, /var, /usr2, etc.

The system administrator's (root) maintenance job will be simplified if several filesystems are in use. If you have a separate filesystem for users (`/home`), the process of backing up in connection with mounting and unmounting will be simplified (see Figure 7-3). If you have free capacity on your hard disk drive (with one filesystem), you can mount a new filesystem with the `mount` command. The Linux `df` command gives you an overview of your filesystems. Figure 7-4 shows the mounted filesystems from `linuxconf`.

```
root@nittedal /root # linuxconf &
```

Linux supports a variety of filesystems. These are the most important of them:

- **Linux.**
- **XENIX.**
- **Unix.**
- **DOS (16/32 bits).**
- **Mac.**

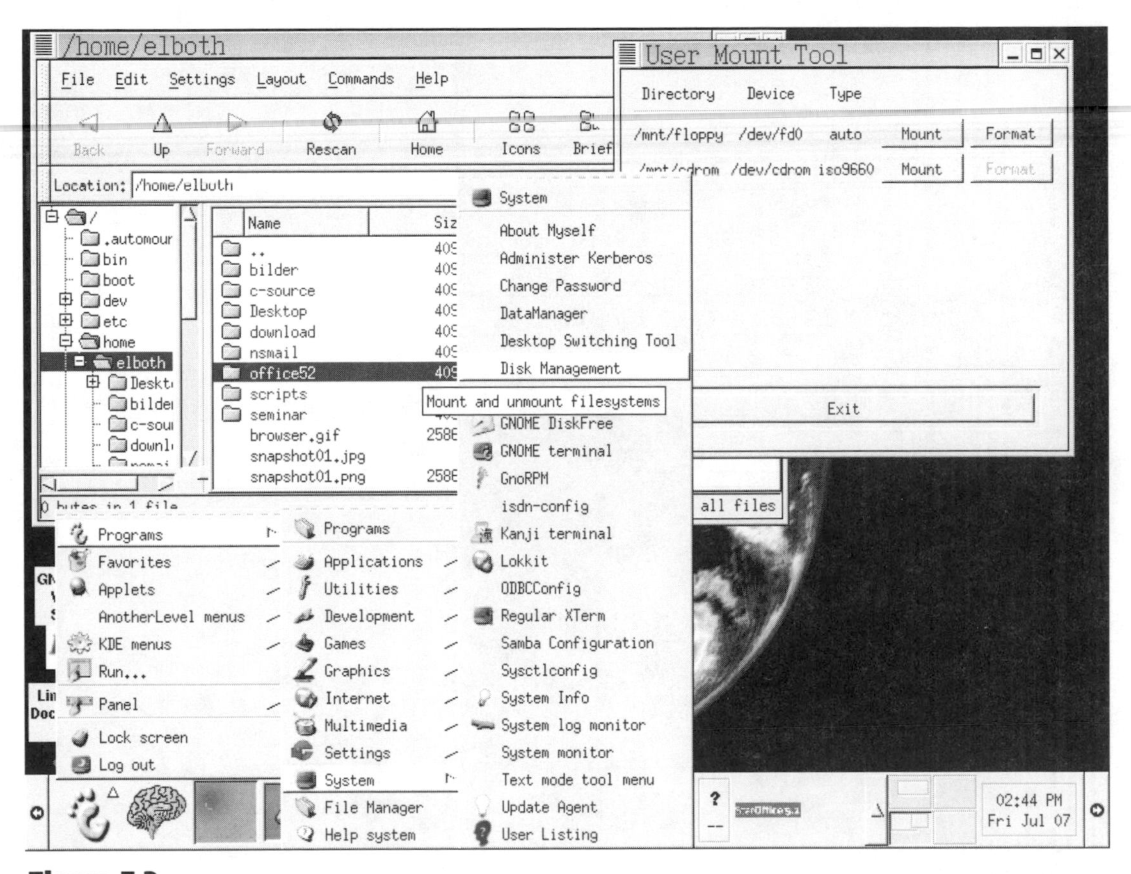


**Figure 7-3**
*User mount tool (mounting filesystems).*

The internal structure of Linux and Unix filesystems is slightly different. One of the most used filesystems for Unix operating systems is AFS, which is a lot faster than Unix and XENIX. SCO UnixWare supports AFS. For Solaris 2.8 from Sun, the UFS filesystem is the default.

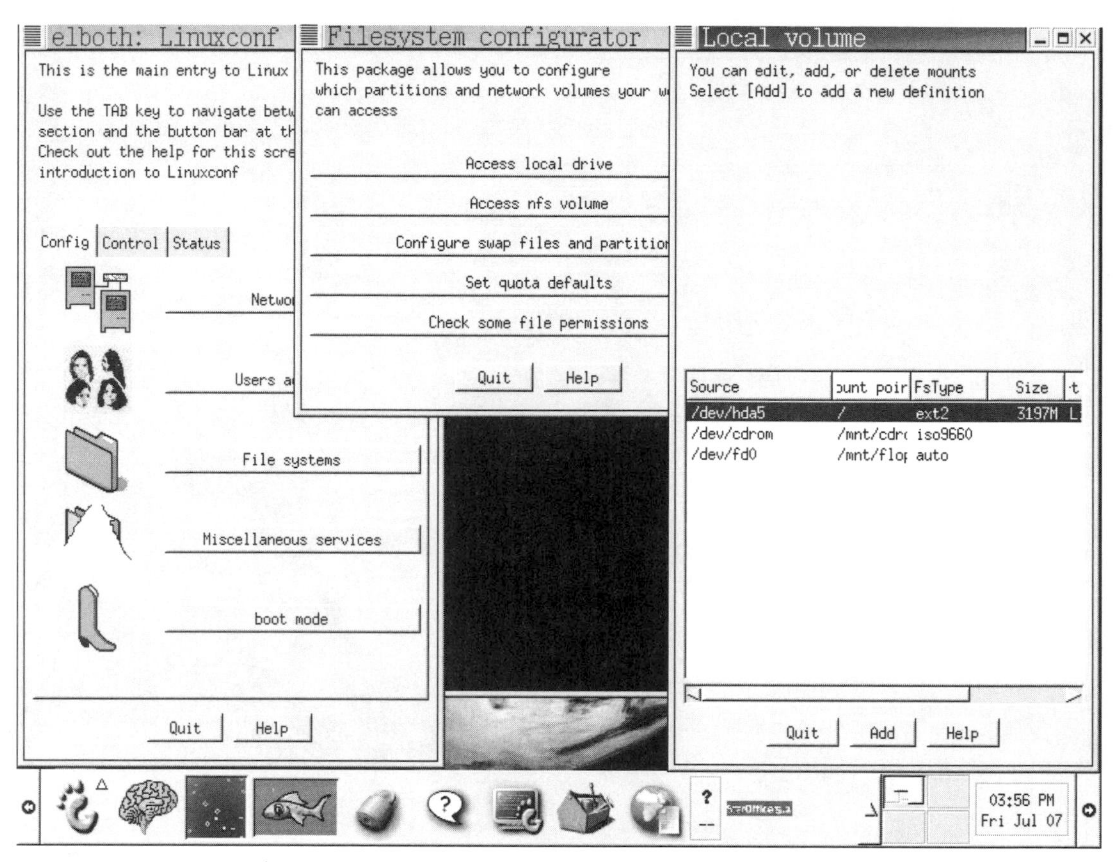


**Figure 7-4**
*Mounting devices from the Linux-utility* `linuxconf`.

## 7.6 Directory structure in the filesystem

Linux uses a hierarchical filesystem (file tree structure) to organize its system files. Each system directory stores various parts of the Linux system (see Figure 7-5).

The Linux kernel is always stored in the boot directory. The name of the kernel normally starts with `vmlinuz-xxxx`, for example, `vmlinuz-2.4.36-0.7`.

Each user has a disk area for storing user files and directories. These user areas are usually set up as directories below `/home`, `/home1`, `/usr`, etc. These directories may be organized as separate filesystems. For example, the user `david`'s files are placed in `/home/david` or `/usr/david`, and user `anne`'s files are placed in `/home/anne` or `/usr/anne`.

A directory can contain one or more subdirectories or files. Root has the fol-

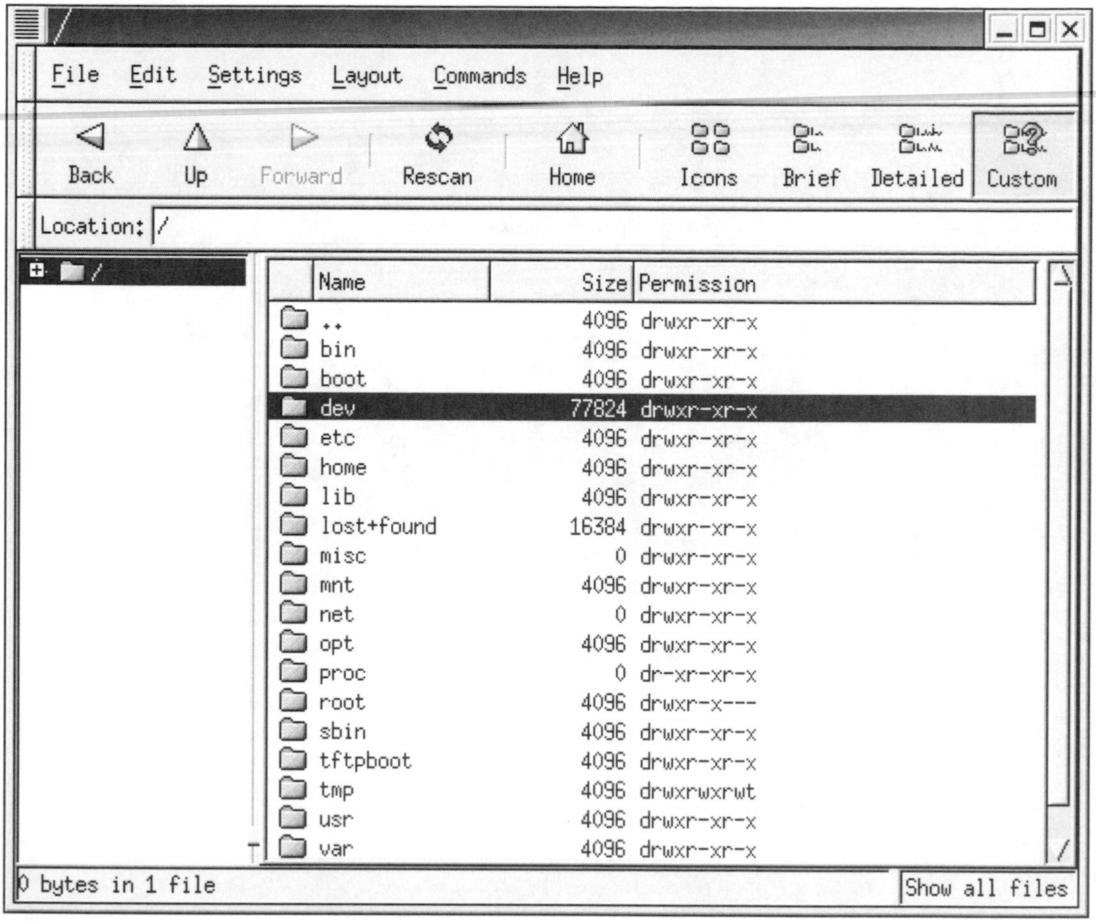

**Figure 7-5**
*Linux directory structure from GNOME GUI.*

lowing system directories (see Figure 7-6):

- `/home` — Linux user's user directory.
- `/bin` — Linux commands.
- `/dev` — Device drivers.
- `/etc` — Administration directory.
- `/lib` — Libraries used by the Linux OS.
- `/mnt` — Mount directory (more later).
- `/sbin` — System programs started at boot.
- `/usr` — User routines and user area.
- `/tmp` — Temporary files.

```
nxterm
[root@nittedal /boot]# cd ..
[root@nittedal /]# ls -la
total 57
drwxr-xr-x  20 root     root        1024 Feb 21 21:45 .
drwxr-xr-x  20 root     root        1024 Feb 21 21:45 ..
drwxr-xr-x   2 root     root        1024 Oct 11 08:25 .automount
drwxr-xr-x   2 root     root        2048 Feb 20 01:36 bin
drwxr-xr-x   2 root     root        1024 Mar 25 08:45 boot
drwxr-xr-x   3 root     root       21504 Mar 25 07:48 dev
drwxr-xr-x  30 root     root        3072 Mar 25 07:50 etc
drwxr-xr-x   9 root     root        1024 Feb 25 09:33 home
drwxr-xr-x   4 root     root        2048 Feb 20 00:45 lib
drwxr-xr-x   2 root     root       12288 Feb 19 22:41 lost+found
drwxr-xr-x   2 root     root        1024 Oct  7 02:16 misc
drwxr-xr-x   4 root     root        1024 Feb 19 22:42 mnt
dr-xr-xr-x   2 root     root        1024 Feb 21 21:45 net
drwxr-xr-x   3 root     root        1024 Feb 20 14:19 opt
dr-xr-xr-x   5 root     root           0 Mar 25 08:45 proc
drwxr-x---   9 root     root        2048 Mar 25 11:23 root
drwxr-xr-x   3 root     root        2048 Feb 20 01:35 sbin
drwxrwxrwt   5 root     root        1024 Mar 25 11:23 tmp
drwxr-xr-x  22 root     root        1024 Mar  4 16:34 usr
drwxr-xr-x  19 root     root        1024 Feb 20 01:35 var
[root@nittedal /]# 
```

**Figure 7-6**
*Linux directory structure from a terminal window.*

All of these directories are necessary for the Linux system.

- **The /bin Directory**—This directory contains the Linux system com mands. These may be Linux commands or Linux shell script routines. These are some of the familiar programs:

```
basename      echo        passwd      su
cp            expr        rm          sync
date          fsck        sh          tar
dump          login       sleep       restore
```

- **The /dev Directory**—The `/dev` directory contains device drivers for hard disk drives, floppy drives, tape drives, displays, etc. Most of the files in this directory are in use and cannot be removed. Below `/dev` you will find sub-directories for certain devices like tape streamers, hard disk drives, etc.
- **The /etc Directory**—The `/etc` directory contains the files and tables used by the system administrator. No files can be removed from this directory.

- **The /lib Directory**—The `/lib` directory contains library files for a variety of programming tools like GNU C, C++, FORTRAN, etc.
- **The /mnt Directory**—The `/mnt` directory is an empty directory reserved for connecting a temporary, external filesystem like a CD-ROM, floppy disk, network disk (NFS=Network Filesystem), etc.
- **The /tmp Directory**—The `/tmp` directory stores temporary files, i.e., files with short life spans. A file's life span usually is the same as the life span of the connected program. If the program is aborted, the temporary file may still exist. Temporary files should be removed if they are not connected to a running program.
- **The /usr Directory**—The `/usr` directory contains user directories and several other directories and user commands. Some of the important ones are:

| Directory | Description |
|---|---|
| `/usr/X11` | Linux X Window. |
| `/usr/iP5-linux` | Linux libraries. |
| `/usr/docs` | Linux documentation. |
| `/usr/man` | Linux man pages. |
| `/usr/games` | Linux games. |

## 7.7 Linux file types

| File Suffix | Description |
|---|---|
| `.Z` | Compressed file. |
| `tar` | Archived file (`tar` format). |
| `.gz` | Compressed (`gzipped`) file. |
| `.tgz` | `tar` and `gzipped` file. |
| `.txt` | Pure text file. |
| `.html/htm` | HTML file. |
| `.ps` | PostScript file. |
| `.au` | Audio file. |

| File Suffix | Description (*Continued*) |
|---|---|
| `.wav` | Audio file. |
| `.xpm` | Graphical file. |
| `.jpg` | Graphical file. |
| `.gif` | Graphical file. |
| `.png` | Graphical file. |
| `.rpm` | Red Hat packet file. |
| `.conf` | Configuration file. |
| `.a` | Archive file. |
| `.lock` | Locking file. |
| `.h` | C or C++ header file. |
| `.c` | C source code file. |
| `.cpp` | C++ source code file. |
| `.o` | Object file. |
| `.pl` | Perl script file. |

## 7.8 Working directory - pwd

The `pwd` command gives information about the directory you currently are working in. This command displays the complete path from root down through the entire directory structure (see Figure 7-7).

**pwd Command – Shows Working Directory**

| | |
|---|---|
| Command | `pwd` |
| Function | Shows the complete path. |
| Argument | None. |
| Options | None. |

Examples:

```
[david@nittedal david]$ pwd
/home/david
```

```
nxterm
lrwxrwxrwx   1 root     root         5 Feb 19 22:48 X386 -> X11R6
drwxr-xr-x  10 root     root      1024 Mar  4 16:52 applix
drwxr-xr-x   2 root     root     22528 Feb 20 01:36 bin
drwxr-xr-x   2 root     root      1024 Feb 20 01:19 dict
drwxr-xr-x 247 root     root      6144 Feb 20 01:36 doc
drwxr-xr-x   2 root     root      1024 Feb 20 00:10 etc
drwxr-xr-x   2 root     root      2048 Feb 20 01:35 games
drwxr-xr-x   4 root     root      1024 Feb 19 23:02 i386-redhat-linux
drwxr-xr-x   3 root     root      1024 Feb 20 00:21 i486-linux-libc5
drwxr-xr-x   3 root     root      1024 Feb 19 22:48 i486-linuxaout
drwxr-xr-x  44 root     root      6144 Feb 20 01:36 include
drwxr-xr-x   2 root     root      9216 Feb 20 01:36 info
drwxr-xr-x  64 root     root      9216 Feb 20 01:36 lib
drwxr-xr-x   3 root     root      1024 Feb 19 22:53 libexec
drwxr-xr-x  11 root     root      1024 Feb 19 22:42 local
drwxr-xr-x   2 root     root     12288 Feb 19 22:41 lost+found
drwxr-xr-x  13 root     root      1024 Feb 20 00:45 man
drwxr-xr-x   2 root     root      4096 Feb 20 01:35 sbin
drwxr-xr-x  34 root     root      1024 Feb 20 01:19 share
drwxr-xr-x   4 root     root      1024 Feb 20 00:49 src
lrwxrwxrwx   1 root     root        10 Feb 19 22:42 tmp -> ../var/tmp
[root@nittedal /usr]# pwd
/usr
[root@nittedal /usr]# 
```

**Figure 7-7**
*Example with the Linux command* pwd.

The user is working in the directory `/home/david`.

```
[david@nittedal david]$ pwd
/u/hansen
```

The user is working in the directory `/u/hansen`.

```
[david@nittedal david]$ pwd
/usr/spool/lp/interface
```

The user is working in the directory `/usr/spool/lp/interface`.

See also: `cd`, `mkdir`, `rmdir`, `Linux dos`

## 7.9 Change directory – cd

The Linux `cd` command is used to change from one directory to another unless you are set up in restricted shell or you have a Linux system with a high degree

**cd Command – Changes Working Directory**

| | |
|---|---|
| Command | `cd [directory]` |
| Function | Changes working directory. |
| Argument | Path/working directory. |
| Options | None. |

of security based on Orange Book.

If you enter `cd` without arguments, you are automatically brought to your user directory, e.g., `/home/david`.

- `cd /directory1` — Changes to `directory1`.
- `cd ..` — Moves one directory (node) up.
- `cd ../../` — Moves two directories (nodes) up.
- `cd /` — Moves to the top level (root), whatever your starting point.
- `cd ../directory2` — Moves one node up and then down to `directory2`.

Examples:

```
[david@nittedal david]$ cd /
```

Moves you to root, i.e., the top of the file tree structure. Try the `pwd` command to confirm that you are in root. The command `ls -la` will list files and directories in root.

```
[david@nittedal david]$ cd ../david
```

Moves one node up and then down to `david`.

```
[david@nittedal david]$ cd ../../etc
```

Moves two nodes up and then down to `/etc`. An easier way is to enter:

```
[david@nittedal david]$ cd /etc
```

In the next example, you start from the directory `/usr/david`:

```
[david@nittedal david]$ cd wp
```

This moves you down to /home/david/wp. Alternatively, you can enter the full pathname.

```
[david@nittedal david]$ cd /home/david/wp
```

If you want to move from /home/david/wp/txt to the neighboring data directory, enter:

```
[david@nittedal david]$ cd ../data
```

To move two directory levels up to /home/david, enter:

```
[david@nittedal david]$ cd ../../
```

You can enter cd without arguments. This always brings you to your home directory ($HOME).

See also: pwd, mkdir, rmdir

## 7.10 Make directory – mkdir

When logging in to a Linux terminal, you always get to your user area. This means that you are placed in your user directory, e.g., /home/david or /usr/david. Your user directory is where you will do most of your work. From your user directory and its subdirectories, you can use the mkdir command to create subdirectories.

**mkdir Command – Makes Directory**

| | |
|---|---|
| Command | mkdir [argument] ... |
| Function | Makes a directory. |
| Argument | Directory name. |
| Options | See the Linux man pages. |

In the directory /home/david, I want to make four directories: wp, linux, c, and bin. The mkdir command is a tool I can use to make directories and create my own tree structure. This is how I make directories:

```
[david@nittedal david]$ mkdir wp
```

This makes the wp directory. The other directories are made in the same way.

```
[david@nittedal david]$ mkdir linux

[david@nittedal david]$ mkdir c

[david@nittedal david]$ mkdir bin
```

You can also make directories by specifying the full pathname (syntax).

```
[david@nittedal david]$ mkdir /home/david/wp
```

It is only necessary to use the full pathname syntax if you are not in the parent directory of the new directories.

Note that you must have write access to the parent directory when making a new directory.

See also: `rmdir`, `umask`

## 7.11 Remove directory – rmdir

Removing empty directories is as simple as deleting a file. These conditions must be met to remove a directory:

- The directory cannot contain any files.
- The directory cannot contain any subdirectories.
- The directory cannot be the current working directory.

**rmdir Command – Removes Directory**

| | |
|---|---|
| Command | `rmdir [argument]` |
| Function | Removes directory. |
| Argument | Directory name. |
| Options | See the Linux man pages. |

Examples:

To remove the directory `/home/david/corel/wp`, enter:

```
[david@nittedal david]$ rmdir wp
```

If you are not in the parent directory of wp, enter:

```
[david@nittedal david]$ rmdir /home/david/corel/wp
```

See also: mkdir, rm

## 7.12 Free space per filesystem - df

The Linux command `df` lists the filesystems you have and how much free space each filesystem has. The GNOME and KDE user interfaces can give you information about available filesystems. You can use the "User Mount Tool" or `linuxconf`. These tools can also be used to mount and unmount filesystems.

**df Command - Free Space per Filesystem**

| | |
|---|---|
| Command | `df [-a] [-i] [-k]` |
| Function | Lists information about mounted filesystems and free space. |
| Argument | See the Linux man pages. |
| Options | See the Linux man pages. |
| `-a` | Lists all filesystems, including those with zero blocks. |
| `-i` | Lists used inodes. |
| `-k` | Displays used space in kilobytes (KB). |

If you enter `df` without options, all mounted filesystems are listed (see Figure 7-8). The total size of the filesystems' used and free space is reported in 1KB blocks. Used space as a percentage and the location where each filesystem is mounted is also reported.

Example:

```
[elboth@elboth elboth]$ df -iak
```

## Exercises for Chapter 7

1. What is an inode?
2. What is the function of the super block?

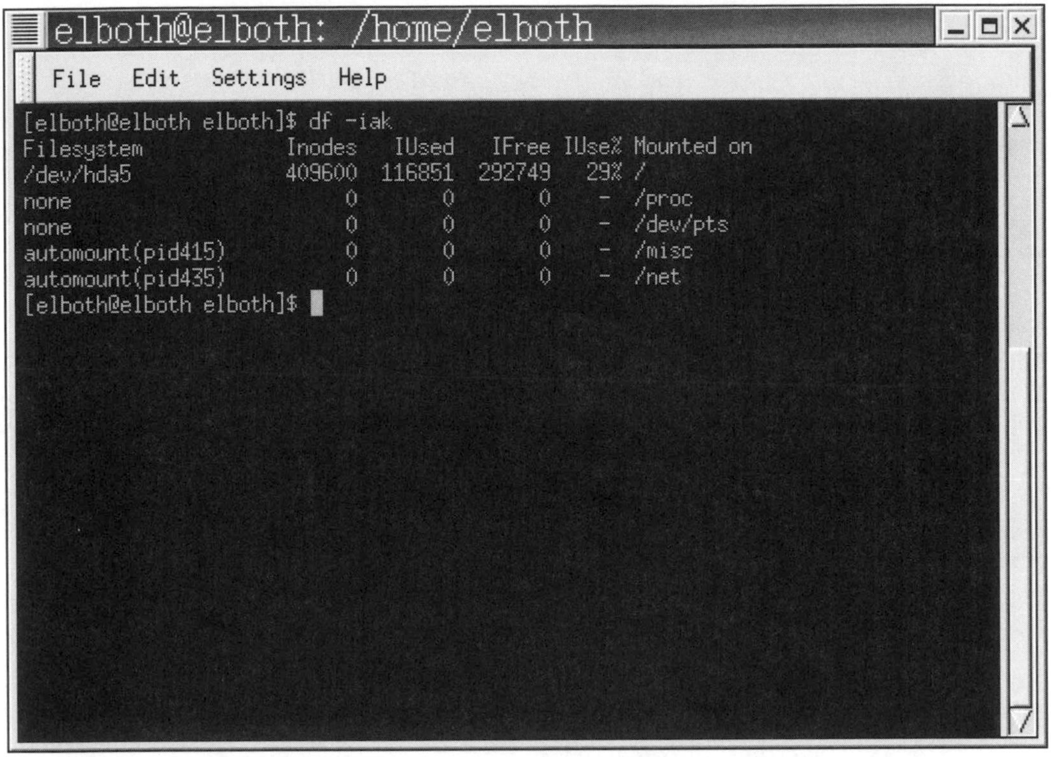

```
elboth@elboth: /home/elboth
File  Edit  Settings  Help
[elboth@elboth elboth]$ df -iak
Filesystem            Inodes   IUsed   IFree IUse% Mounted on
/dev/hda5             409600  116851  292749   29% /
none                       0       0       0     - /proc
none                       0       0       0     - /dev/pts
automount(pid415)          0       0       0     - /misc
automount(pid435)          0       0       0     - /net
[elboth@elboth elboth]$
```

**Figure 7-8**
*Example with the Linux command* `df`.

3. Describe the Linux directory structure.
4. What does indirect addressing mean?
5. What is the maximum size of a file with the Ext2 filesystem?
6. Set your working directory to your home directory. Use the complete path description. List the files in root; use the complete path description. Look at the contents of your Linux directory tree (`ls` command). How many directories are there under root in your system? Where are all the users? List everything in root, this time with relative pathnames.
7. Make the following directories in your user area: `bin`, `doc`, `c-file`, `tcl`, `bash`, and `copy`. Below the `doc` directory, `$HOME/doc`, make the directories `text`, `data`, and `calc`.
8. Remove the directories `$HOME/c-file` and `$HOME/doc/data`.

CHAPTER
8

# Passwords and Access Permissions

## 8.1 Introduction

The Linux commands described in this chapter are all about passwords and access permissions to files and directories. If you make mistakes here, you can lose access to your Linux system.

## 8.2 Changing the Linux password

To stop intruders from entering your system, you should change your password frequently.

**passwd Command – Changes Password**

| | |
|---|---|
| Command | `Passwd [-u user name]` |
| Function | Changes yours or someone else's password. |
| Options | See the Linux man pages. |
| `-u user` | Changing a user's password; only the system administrator can change another user's password. |

If you just enter `passwd` (see Figure 8-1), you can change your own password to the system.

Input
Changing password for elboth
(current) UNIX password:
OK Cancel

**Figure 8-1**
*Changing password under GNOME GUI.*

Example:
To change your own password (`david`):

```
[david@nittedal david]$ passwd
Changing password for david
(current) UNIX password: dfhg657ui
New UNIX password: nmjklo9897
Retype new UNIX password: nmjklo9897
passwd: all authentication tokens updated successfully
```

Passwords are not displayed on the screen.

Remember to press ENTER after typing a password. For security reasons, passwords are not shown on-screen. If you enter your new password twice, the new password is valid. It is important to remember your password. Without the password, you will not be able to log in to the system. If you have the system administrator (root) password, you can change or remove any other password. If you do not have the root password, you must boot the Linux system from a floppy disk and mount the root filesystem. It is then relatively simple to change the key files /etc/passwd and /etc/group.

Your authorization level in Linux depends on what you specified when installing the system. The alternatives are shadow password, MD5 password, LDAP authentication, or Kerberos 5. Your user information configuration can be NIS, LDAP or Hesiod. If you are part of an NIS-based network, passwords can be controlled from a central point. Ask your system administrator about network permissions. If you selected shadow passwords, the security level in your Linux system is a bit higher. The encrypted password is placed in the file /etc/shadow instead of in /etc/password. If you chose an MD5 password, it can have up to 256 characters. If you did not choose MD5, your password must have at least 8 characters. It can have more than 14 characters, but only the first 14 characters (in some Unix dialects, it is 5 or 8 characters) are significant. The password cannot begin with a number or a special character.

If you are root, you can decide the number of days users must wait before they are allowed to change their passwords. You can also force users to change their passwords at certain intervals. A password must contain at least one special character (not a control character) or number. You may not choose a password that has been used before.

Password parameters may change. There are no password limitations on the system administrator; root may change the password for any user. Root is also the only user that can define passwords for any user.

To remove someone's password, use the option -u together with the passwd command:

```
[root@nittedal root]# passwd -u nils
```

When the system asks for the new password, just press ENTER. Under Linux, the new password is stored in the file /etc/passwd. If the security level is shadow password or C2 or B1, the coded password is placed in the encryption file /etc/shadow. This is also the default in Unix V.4.

The password parameters in Linux are set in these files:

- /etc/passwd
- /etc/shadow
- /etc/pam.conf (Linux PAM file).

See also: su, mask, chgrp, chown

## 8.3 Change the active user-id – su

The command `su` changes `user-id`. If you want to have a different ID with different user privileges, access rights, and a different user directory, you must know the other user's user name and password. You will find `su` a useful command if you temporarily want to be root.

**su Command – Changes Active user-id**

| | |
|---|---|
| Command | `su [-] [-c command] [-l] [user [argument]]` |
| Function | Changes active `user-id`. |
| Options | See the Linux man pages. |
| - | Makes a new shell that acts as a login shell; all parameters except the variables `TERM`, `HOME`, and `SHELL` are changed. The shell reads the user's login files `(.profile, .bashrc)` and executes their command, e.g., moves `user-id` to the home directory. |
| `-c command` | Executes `command` only as the specified user. |
| `-l` | The same function as `-` ; you may operate as a different user with certain shell arguments. |
| `user` | The `user-id` you want to change to. Check the user ID from the file `/etc/passwd`. |
| Arguments | You may set shell variables, etc. |

Examples:

```
[david@nittedal david]$ su anne
```

Changes the `user-id` to anne without reading anne's shell environment.

```
[david@nittedal david]$ su -
```

Changes the `user-id` to system administrator (root). I also read root's shell environment.

```
[david@nittedal david]$ su -c "init 2"
```

In this example, I change to system administrator (root). The `init 2` command takes the Linux system down to level 2.

Password parameters in Linux are set up in these files:

- `/etc/passwd`
- `/etc/pam.conf` (Linux PAM file).

See also: `passwd, mask, chgrp, chown`

## 8.4 Linux access codes

Linux has three types of access rights to files and directories:

- **Read access.**
- **Write access.**
- **Execute access (search a directory).**

All access rights are set independently for each of the four user categories: u, g, o, and a.

The user categories are:

| | | |
|---|---|---|
| u | — | User. |
| g | — | Group. |
| o | — | Other. |
| a | — | All. |

The user that creates a file normally is the owner of the file. The group consists of everyone belonging to the same group as the owner of the file. The system administrator defines all groups. Users that don't belong to the owner's group are defined as other.

A file may have three levels of protection. There are separate access levels for the owner, for members of the group, and for everyone else.

If you want to allow full access for all users, you must set read, write, and execute access for owner (u), group (g), and other (o).

The `ls` command lists the access rights that are set.

```
[david@nittedal david]$ ls -la text
total 20
```

```
-rw-r—r—   1 david   Support      544 Oct 22 23:21 text
```

This list gives the following information:

| | | |
|---|---|---|
| `total 20` | — | The total number of blocks used by the directory. |
| `-rw-r—r—` | — | File type and access codes. |
| `1` | — | The total number of links to the file (i.e., a physical file may have several names). |
| `david` | — | The name of the owner of the file. |
| `Support` | — | The name of the group that the file belongs to. |
| `544` | — | Size of the file in bytes. |
| `Oct 22 23:21` | — | Time of last change to the file. |
| `text` | — | Name of file. |

As mentioned in Chapter 6, the first character refers to the type of file. The next nine characters (access codes) hold information about rights for the user, group, and other to the file or directory.

These access codes can be used:

- r, read—The right to print the contents of the file to the screen or a printer. Gives read access to directories.
- w, write—The right to change the contents of a file. In a directory, you can change or delete files and create new ones.
- x, execute—The permission to execute or open a file and search the directory.

You can use any combination of these access codes.

After the first character, the next three characters give you access codes for the owner's permissions (u-user). The next three characters show the group's permissions, and the three last characters show everyone else's permissions (o-other).

To execute a program or command file, you need permission. To read or write to a file, you need an access code to the directory and read or write rights to the file. To change the access code to a file, you must have write access to the directory that contains the file.

Here are some access permission examples:

`-rwxrw-r--`

The access codes normally are:

| | | |
|---|---|---|
| `rw` | — | For user. |
| `r` | — | For group. |
| `r` | — | For other. |

Accordingly, if you create a command file (see Chapter 16) with vi or emacs (see Chapter 12), you must add x to execute the program. You can use the `chmod` command to change the access code.

## 8.5 Change access codes - chmod

The `chmod` command changes access codes. With this command you can change the different access codes for files and directories. As a rule only the owner of the file and the system administrator can change the access codes.

**chmod Command - Changes Access Codes**

| | |
|---|---|
| Command | `chmod [-R] [modus] [argument]`<br>or<br>`chmod [who] + - =[permission ...] file/directory ...` |
| Function | Changes access codes to files and directories; changes read, write, and execute rights of files and directories. |
| Arguments | File, directory, and/or wildcards. |
| Options | See the Linux man pages. |
| `-R` | With option `-R`, the command will be executed recursively, i.e., from a specified directory and all its subdirectories. |
| Mode | The mode consists of who gets access permission, how to change the access code, and which access code to change. The codes can be set with octal syntax or in ASCII code (see the `umask` command also). |

**Permissions are valid for:**

u — User (owner).

g — Group (the same group as owner).

o — Other (everyone other than owner/group).

a — All (all, including owner).

If you don't specify whose access you are changing, the `chmod` command is valid for all users.

**The following characters change access rights:**

+ adds right.

- removes right.

= sets right.

**Access codes that can be changed:**

r — Read.

w — Write.

x — Execute.

- (hyphen) — No access.

**Special access codes:**

`s` — Sets owner or group ID when file is executed.

`t` — Sets the sticky bit on a directory.

`l` — Locks file at access; only one user can access the file.

Access code `s` enables defining owner and group at the time of execution. `chmod u+s` sets the file username and `chmod g+s` sets the file group name. Other combinations have no effect. When the sticky bit is set, the program is automatically placed in RAM. (The program "sticks" to RAM). Only `chmod u+t` sets the sticky bit. Other combinations have no effect. The execution of these programs is very fast. How useful it is to have sticky bits on some programs will depend on the size of your RAM, the size of your hard disk drive, the size of the program, and your hardware setup. Only the system administrator can set sticky bits on certain programs.

There is no point in setting sticky bits on text files.

Access code l locks the file for everyone else at access, meaning that only one user at a time can access the file.

The option characters must be entered in this order:

**Who How Which**

For example: `g-r`

An alternative to the access codes r, w, x, and - is using a three-digit octal number as follows:

| Code | Permission | Maps to |
|---|---|---|
| 7 | Read, write, and access | rwx |
| 6 | Read and write | rw |
| 5 | Read and execute | rx |
| 4 | Read | r |
| 3 | Write and execute | wx |
| 2 | Write | w |
| 1 | Execute | x |
| 0 | None | - |

The first digit refers to owner, the second refers to group, and the third to other users.

Examples:

```
[david@nittedal david]$ chmod u+x program
```

The user gets permission to execute the file `program`.

```
[david@nittedal david]$ chmod o+xw program
```

Other users get permissions to execute and write to the file `program`. If `program` is a directory, the user gets write permission to the directory `program`.

```
[david@nittedal david]$ chmod a+rwx batch
```

Everybody is allowed permissions to read, write, and execute the file `batch`.

```
[david@nittedal david]$ chmod g-r letter.txt
```

Everyone in your group is denied the right to read the file `letter.txt`.

```
[david@nittedal david]$ chmod ug=rwx report.sdw
```

You and everyone else in your group are given all rights to the file `report.sdw` (StarOffice file).

```
[david@nittedal david]$ chmod g+r, o+r text.sdw
```

Allows everyone in the group as well as everyone else to read the file `text`.

```
[david@nittedal david]$ chmod +x not.important
```

Gives all users the right to execute the file `not.important`.

```
[david@nittedal david]$ chmod 777 not.important
```

Gives all users the rights to read, write, and execute the file not.important.

```
[david@nittedal david]$ chmod +l datafile
```

Locks the file `datafile;` only one user can access the file.

```
[root@nittedal root]# chmod u+t calc
```

The system administrator sets the sticky bit to the program `calc`.
See also: `ls, chgrp, chown`

## 8.6 Change owner – chown

The `chown` command changes the owner of a file or directory. Changing ownership does not actually move the file or directory.

**chown Command – Changes Owner**

| | |
|---|---|
| Command | `chown [-R] [owner] [group] [argument] ...` |
| Function | Changes ownership of files and directories. |
| Owner | Can be user number or username. |
| Group | Can be group number or group name. |
| Arguments | File, directory, and/or wildcards. |
| Options | See the Linux man pages. |
| `-R` | When using the `-R` option, the command will be executed recursively, i.e.,from a specified directory and all its subdirectories. |

The owner can be defined by user number or username. Normally, only the owner or system administrator can change a file or directory owner or group.

Examples:

```
[david@nittedal david]$ chown erik *
```

`erik` becomes the owner of all the files in the current directory (except system files, e.g., `.profile`).

```
[david@nittedal david]$ chown david /usr/david/*
```

`david` becomes the owner of all files (not system files) in the `/usr/david` directory.

```
[david@nittedal david]$ chown 555 annes.fil
```

Changes the owner of the file `annes.fil` to the user with ID number 555.

System files: `/etc/passwd`, `/etc/group`

See also: `chgrp` and `chown`

## 8.7 Change group ID – chgrp

The owner of a file or directory can change its group identification (ID). The members of the new group will have access in accordance with the set group access rights.

**chgrp Command – Changes Group ID**

| | |
|---|---|
| Command | `chgrp [-R] [group] [argument] ...` |
| Function | Changes the group ID of files and directories. |
| Group | Group name or group number. |
| Arguments | File, directory, and/or wildcards. |
| Options | See the Linux man pages. |
| `-R` | When using the `-R` option, the command will be executed recursively, i.e., from a specified directory and all its subdirectories. |

Group may be a group name or group number. Normally, only the owner or system administrator can change a file or directory group.

Examples:

```
[david@nittedal david]$ chgrp technical *
```

Changes the group for all files in the current directory to `technical`.

```
[david@nittedal david]$ chgrp technical .*
```

Changes the group for all system files.

```
[david@nittedal david]$ chgrp Support *
```

Changes the group for all files in the current directory to `Support`.

```
[david@nittedal david]$ chgrp Support .*
```

Changes the group for all system files to `Support`.

```
[david@nittedal david]$ chgrp 540 text file
```

Changes the group to `540`. The file `/etc/group` will tell you which group `540` is.

See also: `chown, chmod, mask`

## 8.8 Change active group - newgrp

A user may be a member of several groups. The `newgrp` command temporarily switches to another group that you are a member of. All new files that you create will get the name of the new group.

**newgrp Command - Changes Active Group**

| | |
|---|---|
| Command | `newgrp [argument]` |
| Function | Changes the users active group. |
| Group | Group name or group number. |
| Arguments | Any group that you belong to (defined in `/etc/group`). |
| Options | See the Linux man pages. |

When changing the group, a new shell starts. When a user is set up in the bash shell, shell parameters will be zeroed when the user changes group, e.g., when changing the group in the tcsh-shell, the history table will be zeroed, and you must enter <Ctrl-d> to log off. The command `newgrp` without any arguments changes the user back to the default group defined in `/etc/passwd`. You must be defined in one or more groups in the file `/etc/group` to change to another group. After changing the group, you can access files and directories that are members of the new group.

Example:

```
[david@nittedal david]$ newgrp Support
```

After this command, all files created by this user will have the group name `Support`. The user now has all the rights included with the group `Support`.

See also: `chgrp` and `chown`

## 8.9 Default permission - umask

Every file and directory you create gets specific rights. These rights are controlled by the `umask` command. The `umask` command is defined with a specified value. The most used value is 022, which gives read access to all users. The first digit sets the access code for the user, the second digit sets the access code for the group, and the third digit sets the access code for all other users

If you are in the bash shell, the `umask` command is set in the `.profile` (`/etc/profile` for the whole Linux system) file, which is executed by all bash users at login. You can also create a `HOME/.bash_profile` for each user. This file will be executed when logging in as a bash user. It is a good idea to have a `$HOME/.bashrc`. All non-login copies of bash will execute this file. If you have no `.bash_profile`, the `.profile` will be used instead.

When using tcsh-shell, the `umask` command may be set either in `$HOME/.tcshrc` (which is executed at login and by all new copies of tcsh), or in `$HOME/.login`, which is executed only at login followed by `.tcshrc`. If you have no `.tcshrc` file, the `.cshrc` file will be used instead if it exists.

When using the Korn shell, the `umask` command may be set either in `.profile` or in `.kshrc`.

**umask Command – Default Permissions**

| | |
|---|---|
| Command | `umask [argument]` |
| Function | Sets default permissions to the files and directories that you create. |
| Arguments | Three numbers; the maximum value for each digit is 7. |
| Options | See the Linux man pages. |

Entering `umask` without specifying arguments will display the current `umask` value. Octal values are used. The relationship between these and decimal values and binaries is shown here:

| Decimal Value | Octal Value | Binaries |
|---|---|---|
| 0 | 0 | 000 |
| 1 | 1 | 001 |
| 2 | 2 | 010 |
| 3 | 3 | 011 |
| 4 | 4 | 100 |
| 5 | 5 | 101 |

| Decimal Value | Octal Value | Binaries (*Continued*) |
|---|---|---|
| 6 | 6 | 110 |
| 7 | 7 | 111 |

0 = The access code is switched on.
1 = The access code is switched off.

If the `umask` value is set to 073 (see Figure 8-2), all files that you create will have rwx (read, write, and execute) access codes for the owner, no access for members of your group, and read access for everyone else. Entering `umask` without any arguments will display the default `umask` value.

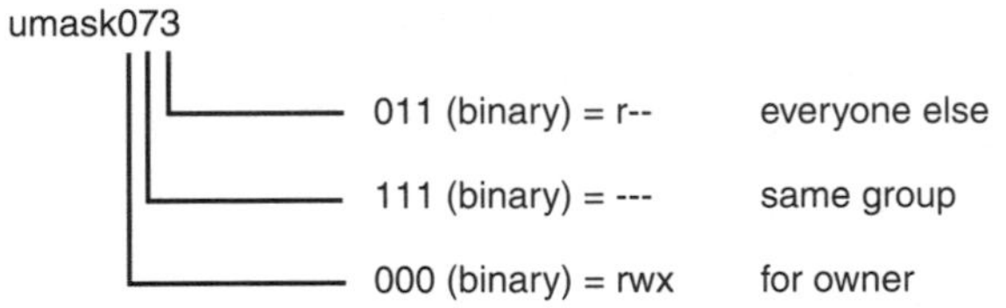

```
umask073
 |||
 ||└──── 011 (binary) = r--    everyone else
 |└───── 111 (binary) = ---    same group
 └────── 000 (binary) = rwx    for owner
```

**Figure 8-2**
*Access code under the different notation (number systems).*

Examples:

```
[david@nittedal david]$ umask
022
```

The owner has read and write access. The group and everyone else have read access only. If you want to have execute permission on text files (owner), you will have to define that manually with the `chgrp` command.

```
[david@nittedal david]$ umask
042
```

Group members have write access; everyone else has read access. The owner has read and write access.

See also: `chmod`, `csh`, `sh`

## Exercises for Chapter 8

1. Who owns the file `/usr/bin/who`? Describe how to find the owner.
2. What protection level does the file `/boot/vmlinux` have? Describe how to find out.
3. Set the protection of the file `test` so that no one from your group can change it. Do you need to change anything in the directory?
4. Does anyone in addition to the owner have access to changing the owner's files?
5. Describe the difference between o (other) and a (all).
6. What happens if you take away all your access permissions?
7. Make the following text files with access codes:

| Filename | Access Codes |
|---|---|
| `datafile1` | `rwx rwx rwx` |
| `datafile2` | `r– –– ––` |
| `datafile3` | `rwx –x –x` |
| `datafile4` | `rw- r– ––` |

CHAPTER
9

# Redirection and Pipes under Linux

## 9.1 The Linux shell

The shell is the most used utility program under a Linux system. It is the Linux system command interpreter. It handles the interaction with the user through the keyboard and terminal display (xterm). The shell manages the dialogue between the computer user and the Linux system. In this chapter, I will discuss the Linux system shell features, redirection, and pipes. Linux programs designed to interact with a user can easily be instructed to take their input from any other source, such as a file, and send their output to another destination, such as a printer or tape streamer. Any program can easily be connected together (pipes) to perform complex functions, thus minimizing the need to develop new programs.

## 9.2 Standard input, output, and error

Data for a program or command is fetched from standard input. The keyboard is usually the standard input (0). This means that if nothing else is decided, data is fetched from the keyboard.

Standard output (1) is usually the screen. A program or command may, for example, send data to a screen, hard disk, printer, diskette, or tape. But if nothing else is specified, data is sent to the screen.

When an error occurs, an error message is sent to the standard error device (2).

To differentiate between the standard input, output, and error devices, Linux has three different file indicators (see Figure 9-1 and 9-2).

**I/O Redirection with the linux shell**

**File indicators:**

| | |
|---|---|
| 0 | Standard input (`stdin`). |
| 1 | Standard output (`stout`). |
| 2 | Standard error device (`stderr`). |

The names `stdin`, `stout` and `stderr` are also part of the C language. They are defined as pointers of type FILE in the C language.

A file indicator may be looked at as a number, through which it is possible to connect to a data file. Both the input and the output may be redirected. As an example, output may be redirected to a file, a printer, or another terminal.

I can redirect data to various physical units. I perform this by redirecting the data to certain files associated with the various units (devices). These files are named device drivers. They are situated in the `/dev` directory. For example, `/dev/tty5` represents a terminal and `/dev/lp0` represents the parallel port of your Linux computer.

Both the standard input and standard error devices can be redirected to various units. Redirection may also change the file indicators belonging to a process.

| Example of I/O Redirection and pipes with the linux shell | |
|---|---|
| `command > file` | Sends standard output to `file`. |
| `command >> file` | Adds standard output to `file`. |
| `command 2> file` | Sends standard error to `file`. |
| `command 2>> file` | Adds standard error to `file`. |
| `command > file 2 >&1` | Sends standard output and error to `file`. |
| `command < file` | Reads standard input from `file`. |
| `command << word` | The program reads the text from standard input until it finds the first occurrence of the text "`word`" (see Chapter 16). |
| `command.1 \| command.2` | The result of `command.1` is further executed by `command.2` (see Chapter 2). |
| `command.1 2 >&1 \| command.2` | The result of `command.1` and standard error is further executed by `command.2` (see Chapter 2). |

With the help of a pipe, data from a process is sent directly over to another process for further processing. More of this will be discussed in Chapters 11 and 16.

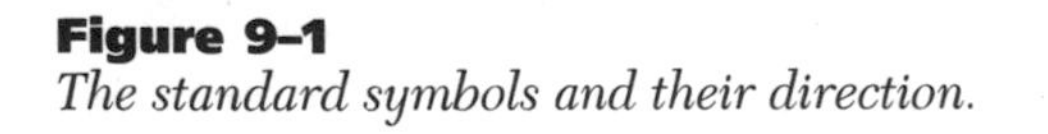

**Figure 9-1**
*The standard symbols and their direction.*

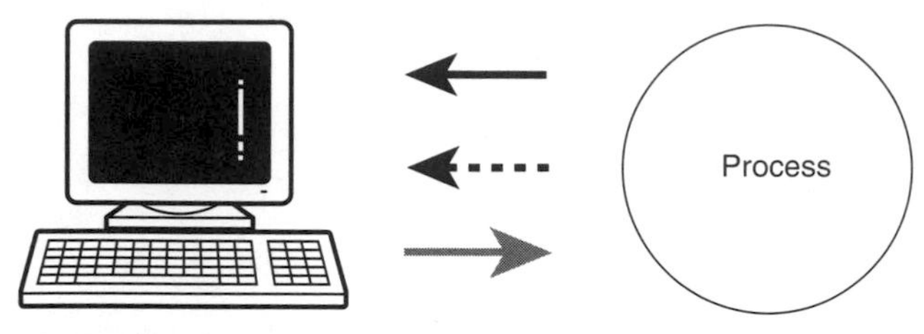


**Figure 9-2**
*Standard direction of data. By default, the standard input is the keyboard, and the standard output and standard error are the screen.*

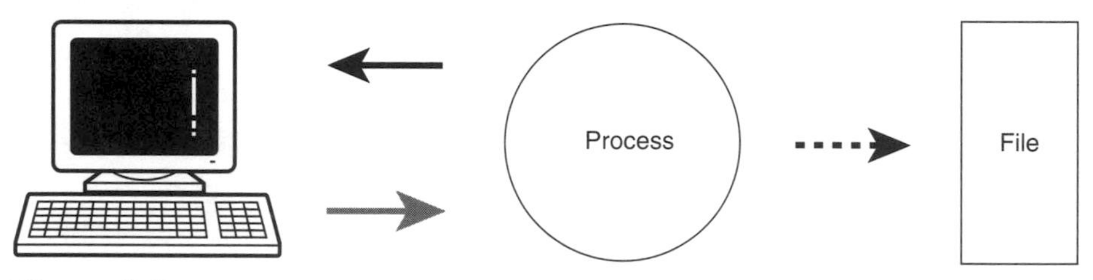


**Figure 9-3**
*Redirection of output. Here, I redirect the Linux output from the standard output (usually the screen) into a specified file.*

## 9.3 Output redirection – >

The greater than symbol (>) redirects the result of a program into a specified file instead of the terminal screen (see Figure 9-3). The specified file may be a device driver, thus sending the result further into a printer, terminal, tape streamer, or floppy disk.

Syntax: `command/program [argument] > file`

Example with `cat`:

```
[david@nittedal david]$ cat >textfile
```

This is an example of a text file written with the help of the `cat` command. You can do the same thing in MS-DOS by writing `COPY CON` and the filename. In MS-DOS, you terminate with <Ctrl-z>; here, you terminate with <Ctrl-d>.

The `cat` command receives the message for sending the result to `textfile` instead of to the screen (the standard output (1)).

With the `ls` command, I can see the new file I created:

```
[david@nittedal david]$ ls -la textfile
-rw-r—r—    1 david     Support       1639 Oct 27 04:18
textfile
```

To look at the contents of `textfile`, you may again use the command `cat textfile`.

```
[david@nittedal david]$ cat part1 part2 part3 >report
```

The files `part1`, `part2`, and `part3` are concatenated into a new file, named `report`.

```
[david@nittedal david]$ ls > data
```

The directory contents are put into the file `data`. The command `cat data` now gives you a list of files.

## 9.4 Input Redirection - <

The less than symbol (<) redirects a program's input data from a specified file instead of from the terminal. The specified file can be a device driver for the printer, terminal, tape station, or floppy disk.

Syntax: *command/program [argument]< file*

Example with `cat` and command control:

```
[david@nittedal david]$ cat < textfile
```

This is an example of a text file written with the help of the `cat` command. You can do the same in MS-DOS by writing `COPY CON` and the filename. In MS-DOS, you terminate with <Ctrl-z>; here, you terminate with <Ctrl-d>.

`cat` reads the file `textfile` instead of reading the standard input (0), which is the keyboard. The contents of `textfile` are displayed on the screen.

## 9.5 Adding to a file - >>

The >> symbol adds information to the end of a file. The existing data in the file is untouched.

Syntax: *command/program [argument] >> file*

Example:

```
[david@nittedal david]$ who >> data
```

The result of the `who` command is now added to the end of the file `data`.

## 9.6 Redirection and error messages

When standard input is redirected to a file, the error messages are still displayed on the screen. To redirect standard error messages, I must include the file indicator in the command.

To register the error messages to specified files, you can use the notation `2>` to redirect the error messages. `1>` or only `>` is used to indicate where the standard output will be redirected.

Example:

I have two files, `myfile` and `superuser`. I made `myfile` myself, while the system administrator (root) is the owner of the file `/root/superuser`. I have no read or write access to this file. The contents of `myfile` consist of the text: `Here is the textfile myfile`. I will try the following:

```
[david@nittedal david]$ cat myfile /root/superuser 1>
fileout 2> filerror
```

The result is placed into the file `fileout` and error messages into the file `filerror`.

I have no read rights to file `superuser`. Therefore, for example, the error message:

```
cat: cannot open /root/superuser
```

is placed into the file `filerror`. The file `myfile` is placed into `fileout`.

Also, try the following command:

```
[david@nittedal david]$ cat /root/superuser
```

If you would like both to have the standard output and error messages sent to the same file, you would write `2>&1`.

Examples:

```
[david@nittedal david]$ cat myfile /root/superuser 1>
alldata 2>&1


[david@nittedal david]$ cat alldata
Here we have the textfile myfile
cat: cannot open /root/superuser
```

## 9.7 Redirection in tcsh shell

In the bash shell (bash), standard units are specified with numbers. In the tcsh shell (tcsh), this is not necessary.

If you write `> textfile` as part of the command line, the shell itself performs:

1. Opening the file.
2. Removing earlier content.
3. Sending data into standard output.

If you write `>> textfile`, the data is added to `textfile`, and no previous data will disappear. This is equal to the procedure in the bash shell.

If you are going to redirect standard input, you can do this with `< textfile`. Instead of reading from the keyboard, the program will now read from the file `textfile`. This is similar to the procedure in the bash shell.

If you write `<< end`, the program reads the text you are writing until it finds the first occurrence of the text `end`. This is equal to the procedure in the bash shell.

If it is preferable that not only the standard output, but also the standard error messages should be redirected, you write this as either a `>& textfile` or `>>& textfile`. Here, the procedure differs between the bash shell and the tcsh shell.

## 9.8 Combining several commands - pipes

With the help of pipes, you can combine several programs. The results from one program will be sent into another program for further processing (see Figure 9-4). By using pipes, you may combine several small commands into one powerful command. In this way, you may construct combinations of commands and create your own programs.

A pipe has the same effect as if I redirected standard output from one program into a file and afterwards used the file as standard input into another program. Linux uses the | symbol for a pipe. Piping is the same in all Linux shells.

Syntax: *program.1 [arguments] | program.2 [arguments]*

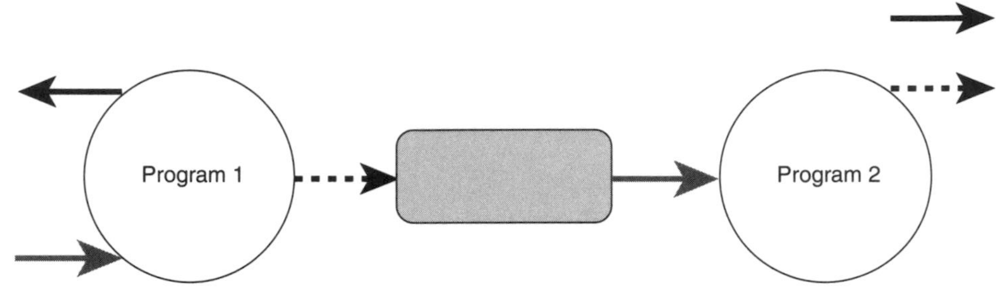


**Figure 9-4**
*Combining several commands. Standard output from* `program1` *acts as the standard input to* `program2` *(pipe).*

Examples:

```
[david@nittedal david]$ ls | lpr -P postlaser
```

`ls` lists the files in the home directory. Output from `ls` is then sent to the program `lpr`, which prints the list on the printer. In this example, the alternatives to pipes are the following tree commands.

```
[david@nittedal david]$ ls > list; lpr -P postlaser
list; rm list
```

```
[david@nittedal david]$ ls -la | wc -l
```

At first, I get the directory contents listed; afterwards, the `wc` command counts the number of lines.

```
[david@nittedal david]$ cal | lpr
```

The calender list is sent to the printer.

```
[david@nittedal david]$ lf | wc -w
```

The number of words from the `lf` command is counted by the command `wc`. At last, I include some examples of redirecting and combining various commands.

```
[david@nittedal david]$ ls -la | more
```

I use a filter showing one full screen at a time.

```
[david@nittedal david]$ sort listing | uniq | lpr
```

Here, I sort a file named `listing`. All unique lines are selected and sent to the printer. The different commands are described in Chapters 12, 13, and 14.

```
[david@nittedal david]$ ls -l /dev | sort -n +3
```

I sort the result from the `ls` command.

```
[david@nittedal david]$ cat /etc/passwd | wc -l > num-
ber.users
```

I count the number of lines in the `/etc/passwd` file, and place the result into the file `number.users`. Alternatively you can write:

```
[david@nittedal david]$ wc -l </etc/passwd >number.users
```

Here, the `wc -l` command is read from standard input (0), which is `/etc/passwd`. The result is sent to standard output (1), which is the file `number.users`.

You may also write:

```
[david@nittedal david]$ wc -l >number.users </etc/passwd
```

Pipes are so important and so valuable in Linux that some programs are designed mainly with a view to being a component of a pipe, rather than being used by themselves. Such programs are known as filters (see Chapter 13).

## Exercises for Chapter 9

1. What happens if you just give the command `cat`?
2. Create a file with the help of the `cat` command and redirect standard output (>).
3. Try some simple Linux commands, including redirecting standard input and output.
4. Try redirecting data and error messages into different files.
5. Combine the commands `ls` and `wc` with pipes. What actually happens when we use pipes (|)?
6. Why don't the two following examples give the same result?

   a.
   ```
   ls > tmpfil
   wc -l tmpfil
   rm tmpfil
   ```
   b.
   ```
   ls | wc -l
   ```
7. Make a small change to Exercise 9.6 to make both examples give the same result.
8. How can you redirect both the standard output and standard error when you are in the tcsh shell?
9. How many normal files exist in the `/dev` directory?
   (Hint: See Chapter 13: `ls -l /dev | grep ^- | wc -l`)

CHAPTER
10

# X Window

## 10.1 X Window

The design of the GUI in Linux may seem confusing and fragmented to people with experience from the Windows and Mac environments. But most people who use Linux for a while come to appreciate the flexibility of the Linux GUI. Most of the components are found in Microsoft Windows and Apple Mac OS, but as these operating systems are marketed as complete packages, most people aren't used to thinking of the separate processes and systems they are composed of. GUIs in Linux and Unix are based on a system called X Window. The X Consortium, controlled from the Massachusetts Institute of Technology (MIT), is behind X Window. X (X Window) is written as a system that is independent of the hardware and CPU platform.

This means that the software is completely independent from the hardware architecture. It is possible to download a version of X from the X Consortium, but this only serves as an implementation example, and lacks elements like display card support. It is up to others to use this example implementation in their own solutions. This is exactly what all the commercial Unix producers do. Most Linux distributions come with an implementation of X called Xfree86. This is a version of X that is free like the rest of the Linux system. There are also commercial versions of X for Linux, such as those from MetroLink and Xi.

X Window is based on a simple client/server architecture, where the X client is running the application itself while the server simply is a graphical display server that generates the graphical picture.

If you are running Linux on a PC, the PC will work both as the X client and the X server. But there is nothing stopping you from setting up your PC as an X server (display server) for other Linux/Unix workstations.

Under X, the physical resolution of the workstation (the PC) or the X terminal limits the display resolution. Each terminal session can be either a standard character-based terminal image or the graphical pictures and applications of X Window.

But X is only the foundation of the GUI. The next layer is the window manager. Whereas X takes care of the connection to the hardware and some basic graphical libraries, the window manager looks after things like the looks and behavior of the windows in your system. Several window managers are available for Linux. For example:

- OSF/Motif—A commercial implementation which is the default in most Unix versions.
- Fvwm—A fast and configurable window manager that for a long time was the de facto standard under Linux.
- Qvwm—A window manager that tries to be a Windows look-alike visually as well as practically.
- Enlightenment—A window manager that aims at being as adaptable as possible and at the same time look trendy.
- WindowMaker—A window manager that tries to look like NextStep, which many users regard as one of the most attractive GUIs ever made.
- Sawmill—A window manager that is easy to integrate and has lean resource consumption.

The third layer in the GUI consists of libraries, i.e., standards and protocols for program development purposes. In the Unix world, this is centered on a set of libraries called Motif. The problem with Motif as seen from the Linux point of view was that it was commercially available only, in addition to having a poor design. Additionally, it was lacking some functionality. As a result of this, there were a number of free libraries developed in the Linux environment, including a free Motif clone called Lesstif. Consequently, Linux programs don't have the same standardized look that the Mac and Windows worlds offer.

This initiated two ambitious projects that aimed at developing an integrated Linux GUI with as good or, preferably, better features than those offered by Mac and Windows. The first of these projects was KDE (K Desktop Environment). KDE was developed with a set of commercial C++ libraries (Qt) from the Norwegian company Troll Tech. This connection to a commercial product and some disagreements over technical solutions were reasons why the GNOME (Gnu Network Object Model Environment) project started. GNOME quickly gained support from important Linux groups like GNU ("GNU is Not Unix"), Debian, and Red Hat. GNOME is based on the C library Gtk, but has threads for development under a number of languages.

KDE as well as GNOME are available for free download, and are supplied together with most Linux distributions, including Red Hat 7.x. KDE was completed first and has built up a considerable number of users in the Linux community. However, GNOME seems to have the greatest momentum and developer support, and my guess is that GNOME will probably be the de facto standard user interface in the future. Even though the licensing rules for the Qt library (the Qt library is now GPL – GNU Public License) have been modified in an attempt to accommodate the critical Linux users, the chunk of them still feel that using the "dedicated" Linux library license (LGPL) is the only acceptable solution for such a central part of the OS.

## 10.2 Configuring X

When you want to configure X, it is important to know as much as possible about your video card. The important details are the make, model, and which chipset your card uses. X Window can be set up by running Xconfigurator (Red

Hat Linux), which I went through in the installation chapter, or you can run `xf86config`, which updates the `XF86Config` file. (You can read more about this in the `/usr/X11R6/lib/X11/doc/README.Config` file.) You can also start Xconfigurator (see Figure 10-1) from the setup program. You must be a system administrator (root) to use setup and Xconfigurator.

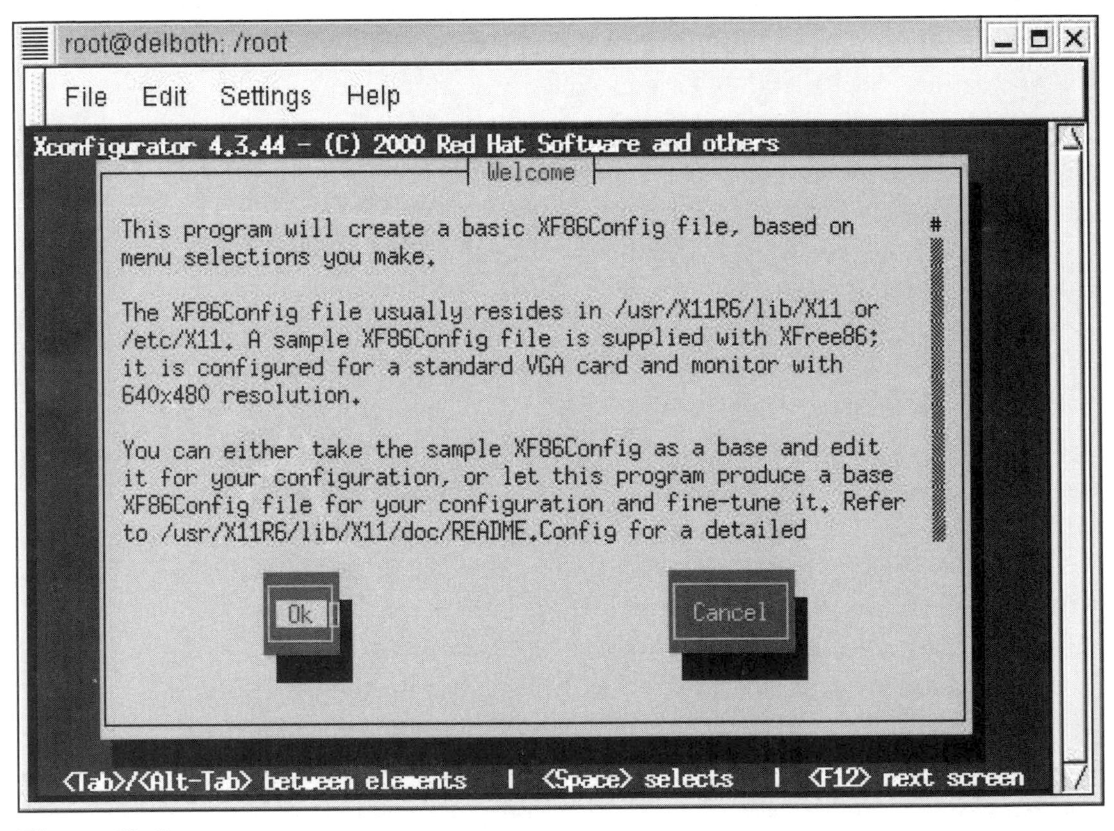


**Figure 10-1**
*The startup screen from the Xconfigurator program.*

If you don't know which parameters to enter when running `XF86config`, the SuperProbe program can help you find out which video card you are using. You must obtain the specifications of your display, for instance, its sync frequency. To run X, your machine must have at least an Intel 80386 CPU, a minimum of 16 megabytes of RAM, and 16 megabytes of swap. A faster CPU and more memory will give faster processing.

The table below lists some of the video cards supported by Linux. If you don't know anything about your card, choose VGA 16 to get started. VGA 16 uses the 4-bit VGA server on your machine. This server uses the lowest common denominator (640x480 resolution, 16 colors) that almost all video cards will support.

Linux also supports accelerated video cards; for example: ATI Mach8, Mach32; Cirrus CLGD5420, CLGD5422, CLGD5424, CLGD6205, CLGD6215, CLGD6225, CLGD6235; S3 86C911, 86C924, 86C801, 86C805, 86C805i, 86C928, 86C864, 86C964; Western Digital WD90C31, WD90C33; Weitek P9000; IIT AGX-014, AGX-015, AGX-016; and Tseng ET4000/W3X.

| **Server** | **Supported Chipset** |
|---|---|
| 8514 | IBM 8514/A card and clones. |
| AGX | All XGA cards. |
| I128 | #9 Imagine 128 card. |
| Mach32 | All ATI cards with Mach32 chipset. |
| Mach64 | All ATI cards with Mach64 chipset. |
| Mach8 | All ATI cards with Mach8 chipset. |
| Mono | All monochrome VGA cards. |
| P9000 | Diamond Viper (not the 9100 series) chipset. |
| S3 | All cards with S3 chipset, most #9, Diamond and Orchids cards. |
| S3V | All cards with S3 ViRGE chipset. |
| SVGA | Trident TVGA8800CS, TVGA8900B, TVGA8900C, TVGA8900CL, TVGA9000, TVGA9000i, TVGA9100B, TVGA9200CX, TVGA9320, TVGA9400CX, VGA9420; Cirrus Logic CLGD5420, CLGD5422, CLGD5424, CLGD5426, CLGD5428, CLGD5429, CLGD5430, CLGD5434, CLGD6205, CLGD6215, ET4000, and others. |
| VGA16 | All VGA cards that support 16 colors only. |
| W32 | All ET4000 and W32 cards. |

By running the SuperProbe program that comes with the Xfree86 distribution, you can get more information about your video card's chipset. You will find it useful to check Xfree's Web page (http://www.xfree86.org) for more information about new, available drivers.

All standard bus types, including VLB and PCI, are supported. The most usual color configuration is 8 bits, or 16 bits per pixel. If you don't find your Linux video card after installation, you have several device driver options. Video software with a device driver (video card) can, for example, be downloaded from:

- www.xfree.com.
- www.redhat.com.
- Linux CD.

After downloading, the X Window device driver must be connected to the X directory. Below you'll find an example describing how to retrieve the device drivers from the Linux CD:

```
[root@nittedal /root]# mount /mnt/cdrom
[root@nittedal /root]# cd /mnt/cdrom/RedHat/RPMS
[root@nittedal /root]# rpm -i Xfree86-AGX*
```

(Here's an example with a device driver from the Internet: If you download files from the Internet you must also unzip them. Check if you have the `/usr/X11R6` directory. If you haven't got this directory, make it.)

```
[root@nittedal /root]# mkdir /usr/X11R6
```

Unzip the files from `/usr/X11R6` with the `gzip` command:

```
[root@nittedal /root]# gzip --dc XF86_AGX.tar.gz | tar
xfB --
```

Remember that these `tar` files are zipped relative to `/usr/X11R6`, which is why it is important to unzip them in that directory.

Next, link `/usr/X11R6/bin/X` to the server that you intend to use.

```
[root@nittedal /root]# ln -sf /usr/X11R6/bin/XF86_AGX
/etc/X11/X
```

You must apply exactly the same commands when using other servers.

## 10.3 Starting X

When the XF86Config file has been configured, you can start X by entering startx (see Figure 10-2), which starts the xinit process. If X doesn't start, you must check that the search path ($PATH) to /usr/X11R6/bin has been set.

```
[david@nittedal david]$ startx
```

When the X server is started, it will search for the initialization file (.xinitrc) in your home directory. If there is no local .xinitrc file, the system will read the default file, which is located in /usr/X11R6/lib/X11/xinit/xinitrc.

If you want to use 16-bit color depth with 65,000 different colors, enter:

```
[david@nittedal david]$ startx -- -bpp 16
```

With the double dashes (--), I pass the arguments directly to xinit. In this way, I can start up X in the resolution I need. If you want this automatically, place exec X :0 -bpp 16 in your Xservers file (.xserverrc). This will only work if you have the following in the screen section of your XF86Config with DefaultColorDepth 16.

```
[david@nittedal david]$ startx -- -bpp 8
```

Here, I start X in 256-color mode.

```
[david@nittedal david]$ startx -- -bpp 32
```

Here, I start X in true color mode.

After a short while, an interface similar to Microsoft Windows will appear. Use the mouse to navigate and activate windows and menus. The graphical appearance can be adjusted to your needs. When you want to exit X, enter the combination [Ctrl]-[Alt]-[Backspace]. The X server will immediately stop and the window system will terminate.

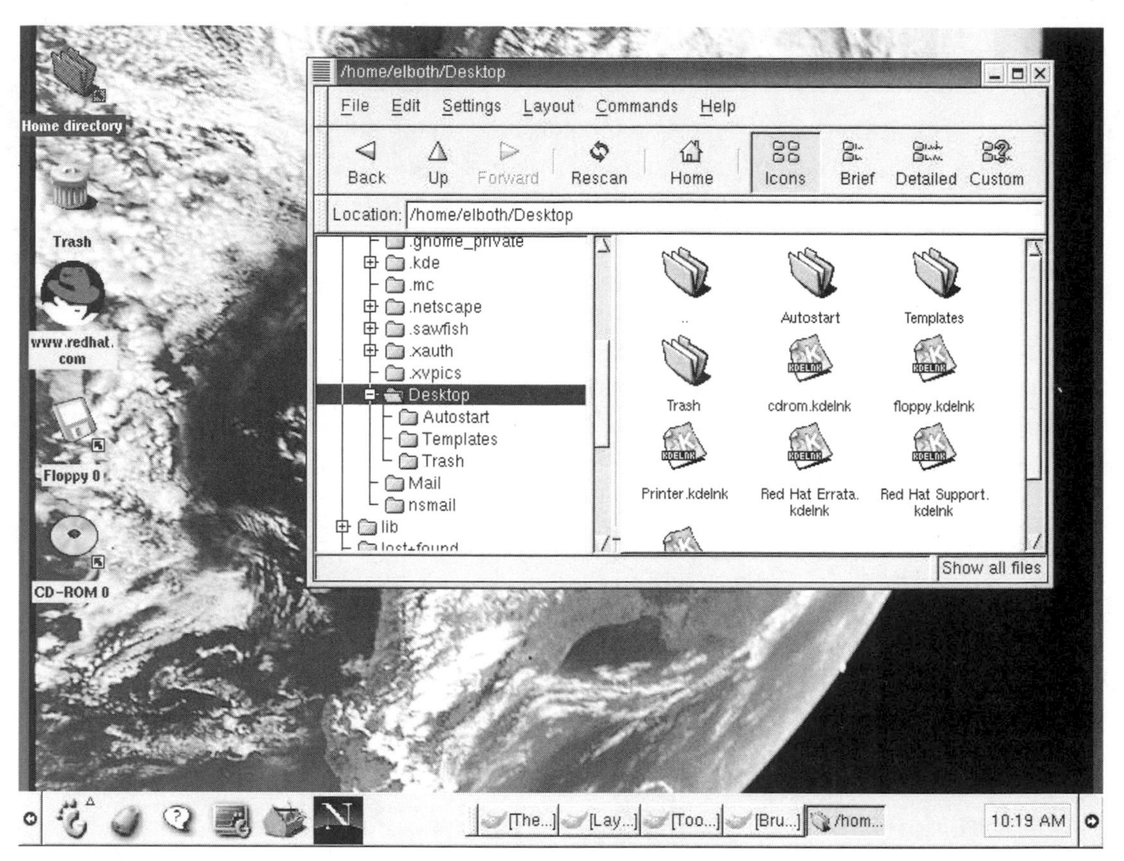


**Figure 10–2**
*An example of a GNOME environment under Red Hat Linux (the screen has 1024 x 768-pixel resolution).*

## 10.4 GNOME or KDE user interface

The illustrations in this chapter show either the GNOME or KDE user interface (see Figure 10-3). Under Red Hat Linux, you can choose from several window managers. It is possible to run X Window directly from a window manager without GNOME or KDE, but you'll lose the additional functionality offered by these interfaces. Most Linux distributions use GNOME or KDE as the basis of their GUI. It is therefore important to choose a window manager that supports both the GNOME and KDE interfaces.

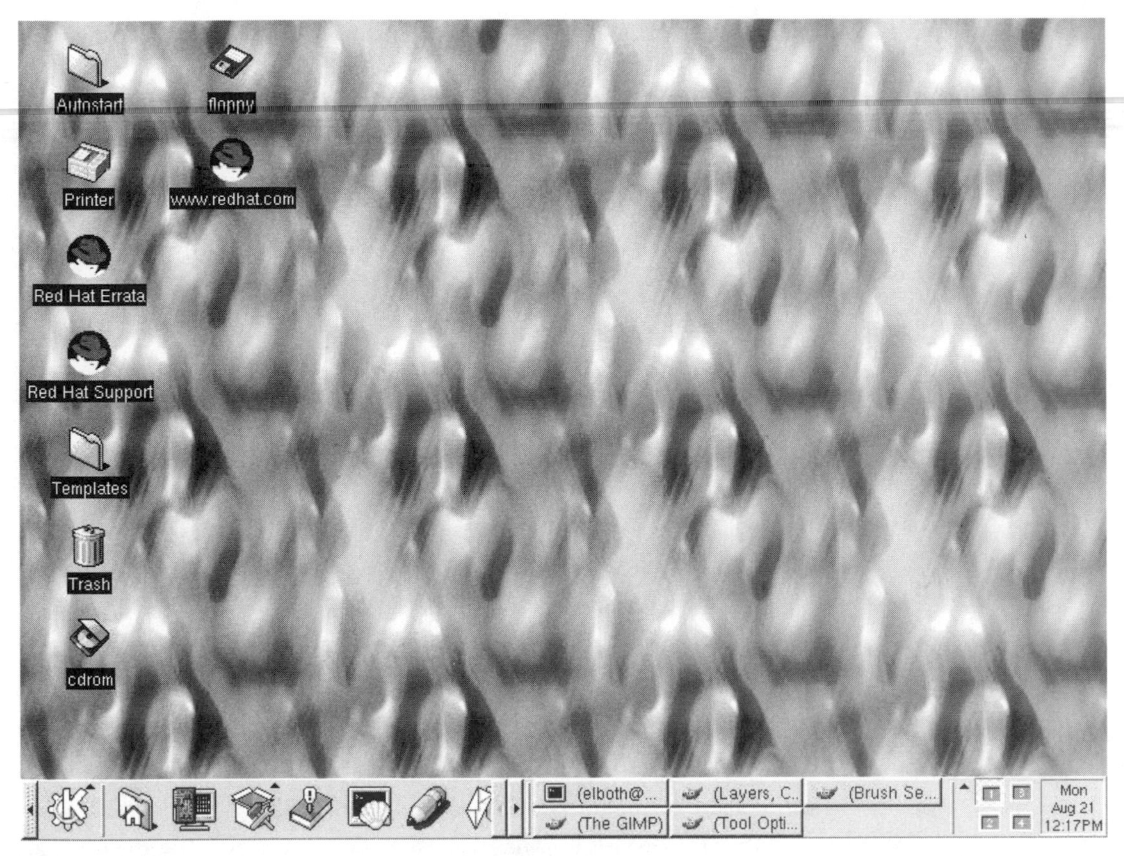


**Figure 10-3**
*An example with KDE environment under Red Hat Linux.*

KDE is by default equipped with its own window manager, KWM, but also Blackbox and WindowMaker support KDE to some extent. GNOME has always tried to remain more independent from window managers; up to now, Enlightenment has been the default. In addition, WindowMaker, Qvwm, Afterstep, Icewm, Fvwm, Sawmill, and Flwm support GNOME. In the new version of GNOME, Sawmill is now the default due to its better integration and lean resource consumption.

In the future, most window managers will work with both systems because of a project that aims at establishing a new, common standard for window managers.

GNOME offers functionality on a level with what you are used to from Windows 98 and Windows 2000. This includes copying to intermediate storage, drag-and-drop, etc. GNOME 1.x is now available in more than 18 languages.

In addition to Linux, GNOME can be run under BSD, Solaris, HP-UX, and Digital Unix. Several Linux distributors, including Red Hat, Debian GNU/Linux, LinuxPPC, and SuSE, offer GNOME with their systems.

As mentioned before, there is tough competition between GNOME and KDE. Debian, Red Hat, Linux PPC, and TurboLinux go for GNOME, while Caldera, Corel, and SuSE are some of the Linux distributors that prefer KDE. KDE 2.x is now available in more than 30 languages.

If you want to download a newer version of KDE for your Red Hat Linux, visit www.kde.org for further advice.

GNOME and KDE are different in many ways. The technical differences are mainly different choices of components and architecture for CORBA (Common Object Request Broker Architecture). GNOME has developed an architecture called Bonobo, and KDE has KOM/OpenParts. GNOME is better suited for developers that use languages other than C++; for example, Ada, C, Objective-C, TOM, Perl, Python, and Guile.

Some 350 programmers all over the world develop GNOME. Miguel de Icaza leads this mostly voluntary work. Red Hat has supported the process. The project is connected to the Free Software Foundation (FSF), which is conducted by Richard Stallman, who founded GNU. GNU means "GNU is Not Unix," and was initiated to promote the idea of free software. The FSF has established a license known as the "General Public License" (GPL). This gives full freedom to run, copy, distribute, study, and improve any GPL-licensed program.

Visit www.gnome.org for information when you wish to download a newer version of GNOME for your Linux.

## 10.5 GNOME with Red Hat Linux

There are several alternative GUIs in Red Hat Linux; for example, GNOME, KDE, FVWM, Enlightenment, WindowMaker, and TWM. When installing Red Hat Linux, GNOME is by default set up as the GUI. From this user interface, you'll see the GNOME taskbar at the bottom of your screen. At the left side of the screen, there are icons with references to Red Hat and Linux documentation. There are also icons for handling peripherals, including a CD-ROM player (see Figure 10-4) and floppy drive (see Figure 10-5).

When you want to look at the contents of a floppy or CD-ROM, click the

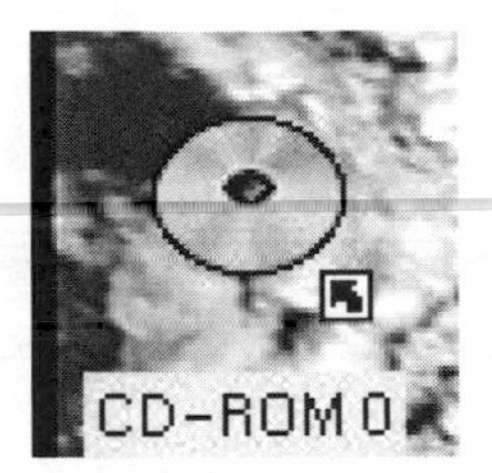


**Figure 10-4**
*The CD-ROM player icon under GNOME.*

**Figure 10-5**
*The floppy drive icon under GNOME.*

appropriate icon. If you are using an MS-DOS or Windows floppy, you must use the Linux Mtools; for example, `[david@nittedal david]$` **`mdir a:`**

The bottom bar in GNOME is the taskbar (see Figure 10-6), similar to the Windows 2000 taskbar. All operative applications are displayed as application buttons. A clock is displayed at the far right. When you move the cursor across the clock, today's date is displayed.

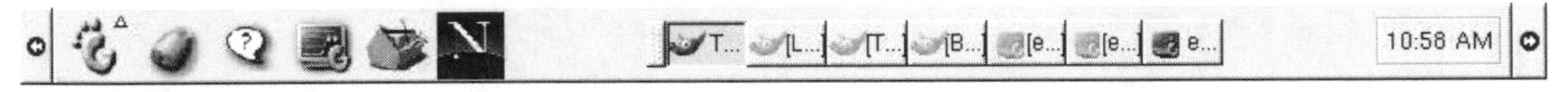


**Figure 10-6**
*The GNOME taskbar.*

Counting from the center of the taskbar to the left, there are buttons for Netscape, the toolbox (the GNOME configuration tool), terminal emulation, help, and lock screen. The GNOME foot button is at the far left (see Figure 10-7).

**Figure 10-7**
*The GNOME foot (button).*

This is the same as the Start button; you click it whenever you want to start a function in GNOME.

When you click the Start button, a Start menu appears at the left corner (see Figure 10-8). These are the program folders: Programs, Favorites, Applets, KDE menus, Run, Panel, Lock screen, and Log out.

Pull up the Programs folder by pointing the mouse at the folder. When you touch the folder, a new Programs folder with programs opens. These are the program folders: Applications, Utilities, Development, Games, Graphics,

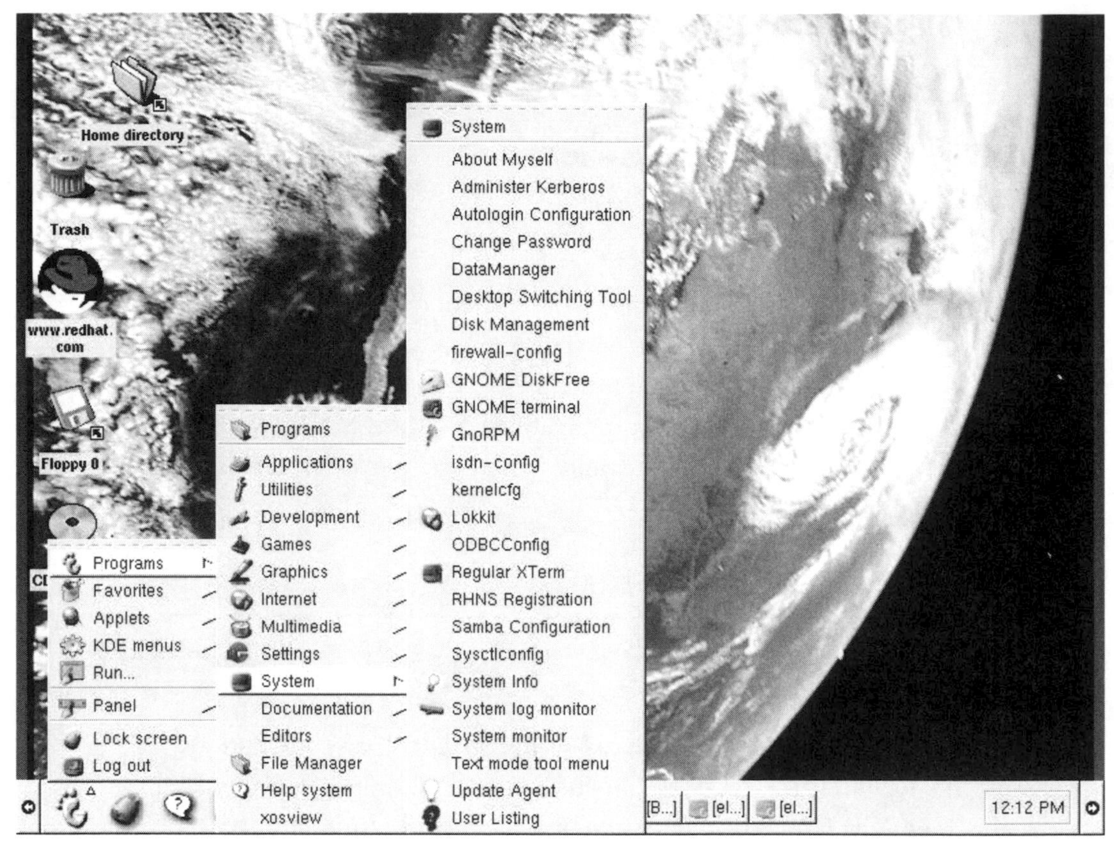


**Figure 10-8**
*Example with the start menu under GNOME.*

Internet, Multimedia, Settings, System, Documentation Editors, File Manager, Help system, and xosview (system load).

When making a selection, move the mouse pointer to the desired program and click the left mouse button. The most important folders for system administration are Programs and System.

A graphical interface of your files is found in the folders Programs and File Manager. File Manager is also defined as an icon (see Figure 10-9), so the alternative is to click the icon for the home directory (File Manager).

The File Manager application (see Figure 10-10) lets you manipulate your files. At the left-hand side of the window, you can view the directories, and at the right-hand side, you can see the contents of the selected directories. If you want to move a file or a directory, you simply drag and drop.

To copy a file, select the file while pressing the Ctrl key. To run a program or

**Figure 10-9**
*The File Manager icon under GNOME.*

edit, double-click the icon. If you want to execute other operations like deleting or renaming a file, first mark the file by clicking the right mouse button, then make the appropriate choice. When marking multiple files, press the Shift key at the same time.

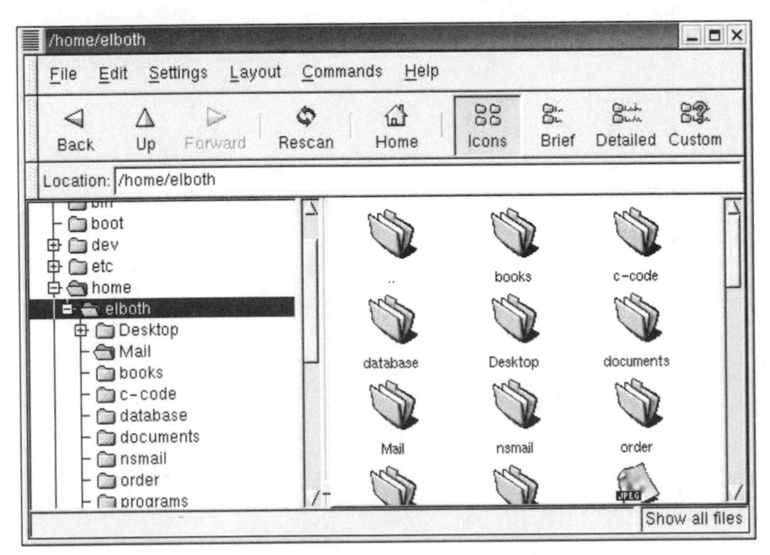


**Figure 10-10**
*The File Manager application under GNOME.*

When you want to run several operations between multiple directories, just start more instances of File Manager. You can drag files from File Manager to File Manager or to the GNOME desktop.

When you need help for the GNOME user interface, press the GNOME button, then Programs and Help system.

All Linux programs can be run directly from Run (see Figure 10-11). Just enter the name of the program; for example type `xboard` if you like to play chess.

If you are familiar with the menus in the KDE interface, you will find them under KDE menus. If you need a new program button, select the Panel button

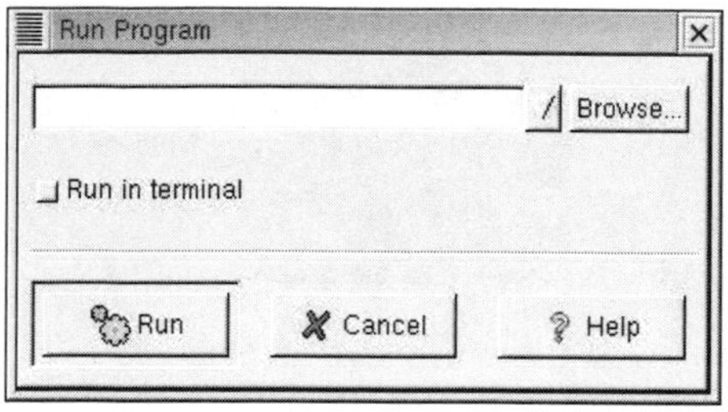

**Figure 10-11**
*The Run Program under GNOME.*

(see Figure 10-12). Here you can make your own buttons or update new programs under the Programs directory.

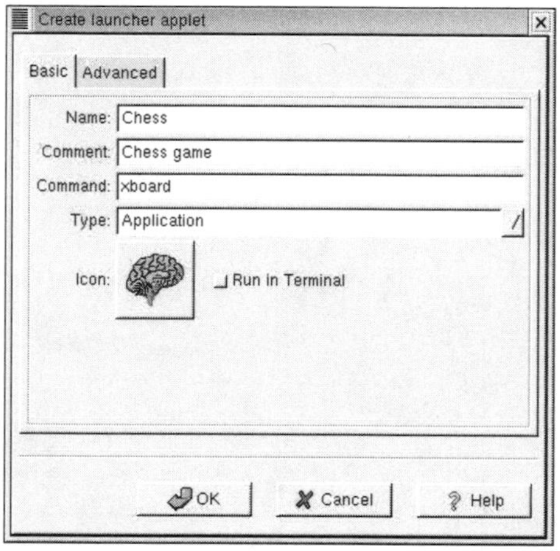

**Figure 10-12**
*Creating a launcher applet under GNOME.*

The last, but possibly the most important button, is Log out; here you can log out as well as shut the system down (see Figure 10-13).

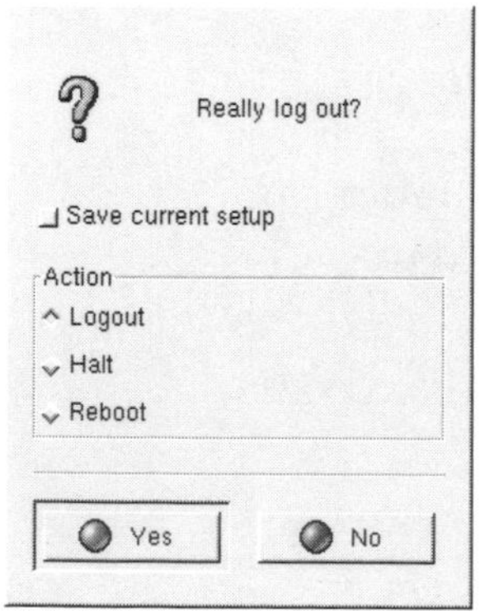

**Figure 10-13**
*Here you can choose if you want to logout, halt the system, or reboot.*

When the background image is visible, you can change your desktop at any time by clicking the right mouse button. The right mouse button gives you access to the program window, in which you can change the position of icons, create new windows, update your desktop (directories, devices, icons), configure your background image, start a new terminal emulation window, make a new directory, make a URL reference, define an application/directory icon, or run programs like, for example, GIMP (image processing), Gnumeric (spreadsheet), etc.

To create your own fancy desktop with different X applications, just make your own `.xinitrc` file in your home directory. GNOME can generate this file automatically. When doing it manually, check the syntax of the `/usr/X11R6/lib/X11/xinit/xinitrc` file. Additional information is available on the man pages under the commands `xterm`, `xclock`, and `twm`.

## 10.6 From GNOME to KDE

As Red Hat Linux supports both GNOME and KDE, you always have the option to switch between the two. When you want to change your desktop, you can run the `switchdesk` command (see Figure 10-14) from the terminal prompt; for example:

```
[david@nittedal david]$ switchdesk
```

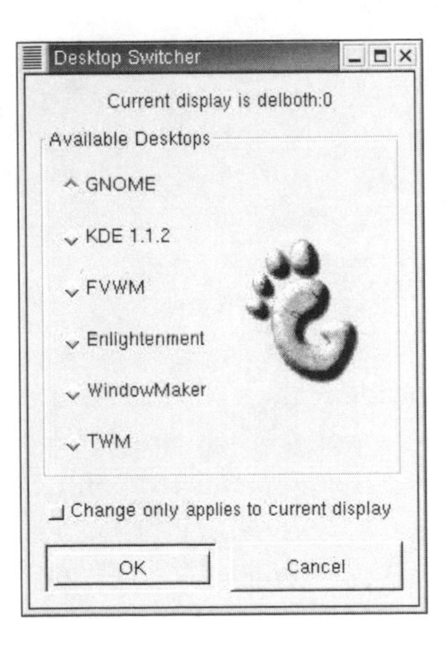


**Figure 10-14**
*From the Desktop Switcher you can change the desktop.*

When selecting KDE instead of GNOME, you will have the KDE interface the next time you log in (see Figure 10-15). From the desktop switcher, you will also see that Red Hat Linux support the desktops fvwm, Enlightenment, WindowMaker, and TWM.

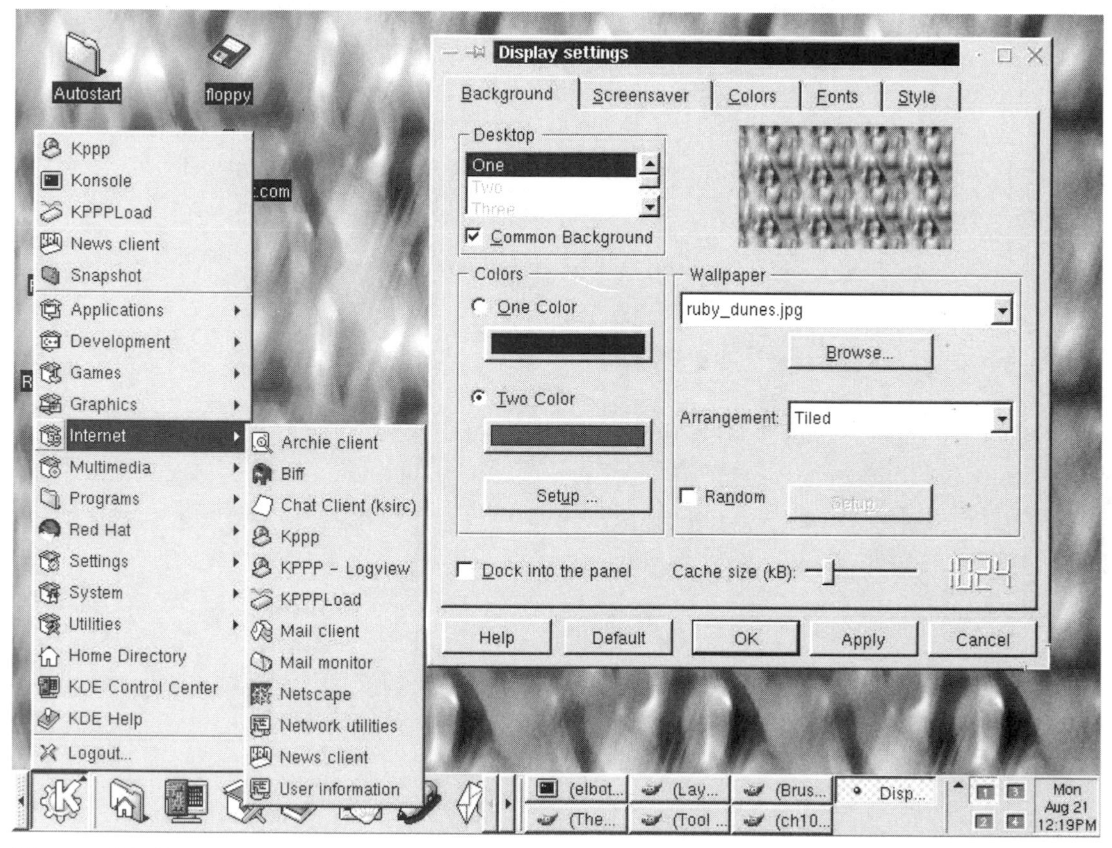


**Figure 10–15**
*An example KDE environment under Red Hat Linux.*

At the left side of the screen, there are icons with references to Red Hat and Linux documentation. There are also icons for handling the peripheral floppy disk drive (see Figure 10-16) and CD-ROM drive (see Figure 10-17). Additionally, there are separate icons for Autostart (see Figure 10-18), Printer (see Figure 10-19), Templates (see Figure 10-20), and Trash (see Figure 10-21).

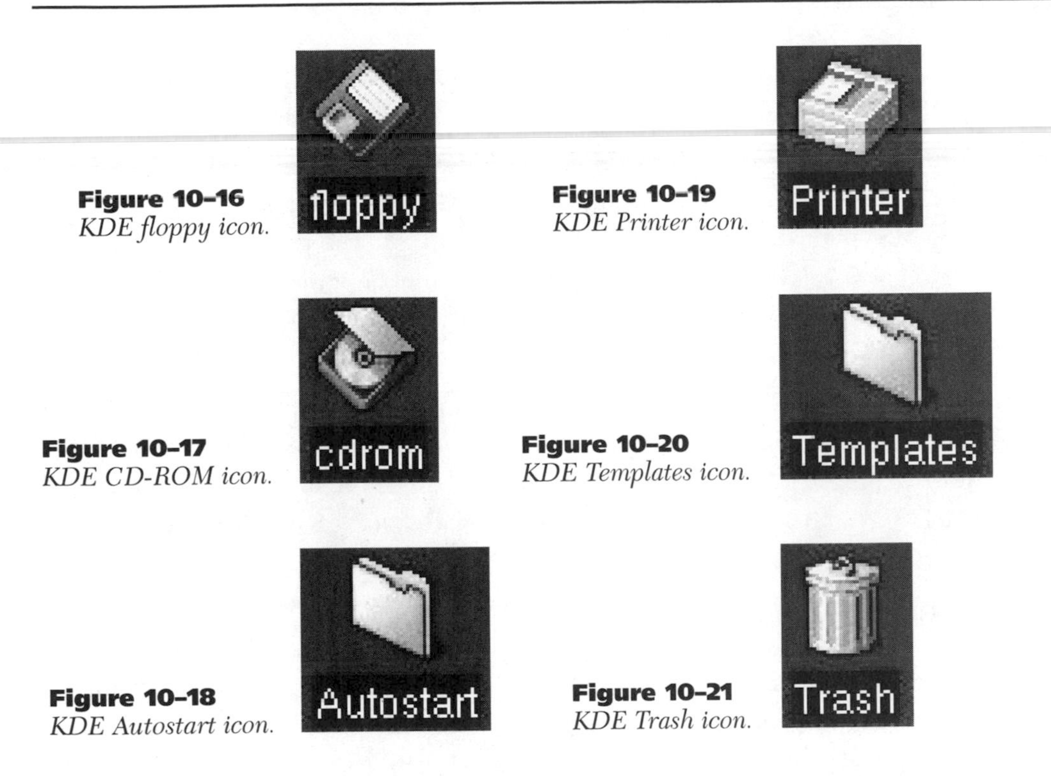


**Figure 10-16**
*KDE floppy icon.*

**Figure 10-17**
*KDE CD-ROM icon.*

**Figure 10-18**
*KDE Autostart icon.*

**Figure 10-19**
*KDE Printer icon.*

**Figure 10-20**
*KDE Templates icon.*

**Figure 10-21**
*KDE Trash icon.*

In KDE, the taskbar (see Figure 10-22) differs a bit from the one in GNOME. At the right of today's date and the clock, there is an overview of your virtual graphical displays. The screen is divided in four logical parts. Your physical screen only overlaps parts of the other screens. You can jump to the desired screen by clicking on the display icon in the center of the taskbar.

**Figure 10-22**
*KDE taskbar.*

In the center of the taskbar, all active applications are shown as application buttons. From the center and toward the left of the taskbar, there are buttons for the home directory, KDE Control Center, utilities, KDE Help, a terminal console, an editor (advanced editor), mail client, CD player, sound mixer panel, and Netscape Web client.

The KDE feet at the far left work like the GNOME Start button; you can click the button whenever you want to start something in KDE.

## 10.7 Changing the window manager in GNOME

When starting an application under GNOME, the application will open in a separate window. You will find dedicated buttons in the right window that manage each window. There are buttons for minimizing, maximizing, and closing windows. The appearance of the windows can be controlled with a window manager. The default window manager for 7.x versions of Red Hat is Sawfish. You can change your GNOME interface by reconfiguring your window manager. This is done by first clicking the toolbox button (the GNOME configuration tool) at the bottom left position on the taskbar. Then, click Window Manager. Select the active window manager. As this by default is Sawfish for Red Hat 7.x, run the configuration tool for Sawfish.

Now you can configure the appearance of your user interface.

The default window manager for Red Hat versions 6.x is Enlightenment. As with Sawfish, you can use various styles, e.g., Clean and ICE. When using the Clean border style (see Figure 10-23), underline means minimize, square means maximize, and the x key closes the window.

**Figure 10–23**
*Example with Clean board style.*

ICE (see Figure 10-24), on the other hand, only has an x button and an arrow key. Clicking the x button closes the window. Clicking the arrow with the left mouse button minimizes the window. Clicking the arrow with the right mouse button brings up a menu.

**Figure 10–24**
*Example with ICE board style.*

## 10.8 GNOME/KDE Control center

You can adjust your desktop in the GNOME Control Center or in the KDE Control Center (`[david@nittedal david]$` **`kcontrol &`** ). When you want to access the GNOME Control Center, you click the toolbox icon (the GNOME configuration tool) directly or you press the GNOME foot (button), then Settings, and then GNOME Control Center (see Figure 10-25).

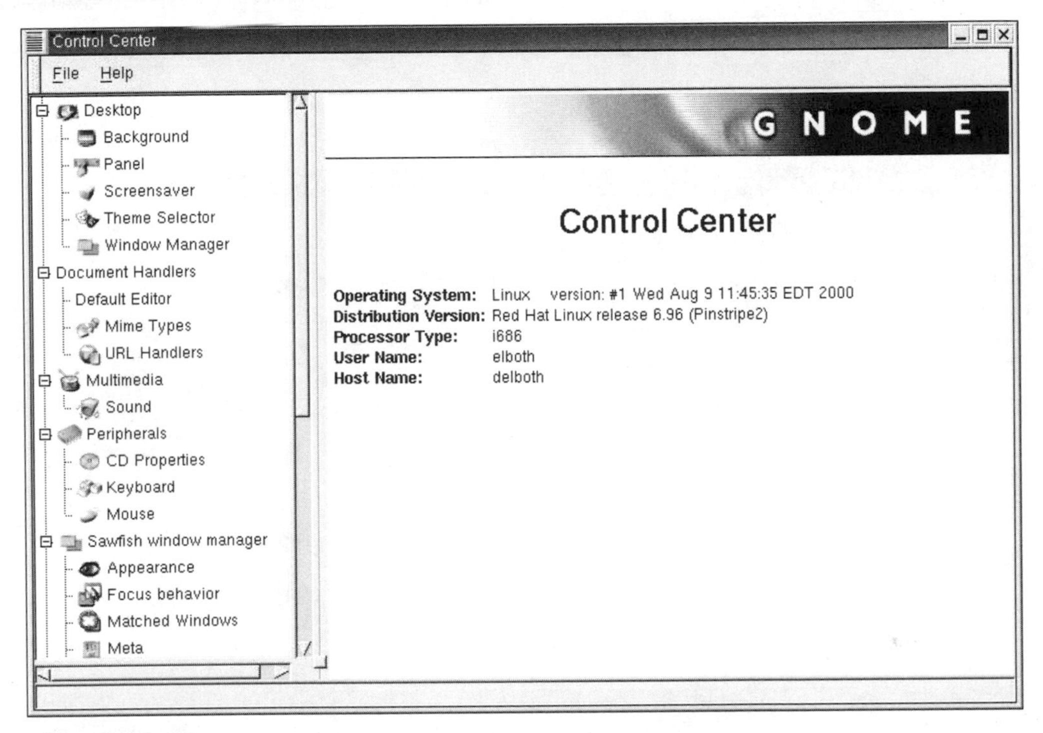


**Figure 10-25**
*The main menu in the GNOME Control Center.*

From the GNOME Control Center, you can fine-tune your desktop setup by:

- Defining your default editor.
- Defining application handling, particularly login handling, a Web browser, and panel setup.
- Defining your desktop (Background, Screensaver, Theme Selector, active Window Manager (in Red Hat Linux, 7.X Sawfish is the default)).
- Defining file types (MIME) based on file suffixes.
- Defining the setup of the keyboard and system sound.
- Reading information about most I/O units like a CD-ROM drive (mount, automount), keyboard (sound and sensitivity), and mouse (acceleration, left, right).

- Defining programs to start at login.
- Defining the URLs of help texts.
- Defining the user interface setup with regard to applications (icons, moving, status), dialogs (buttons, boxes), and MDI.

From the KDE Control Center (see Figure 10-26), you can fine-tune your desktop setup by:

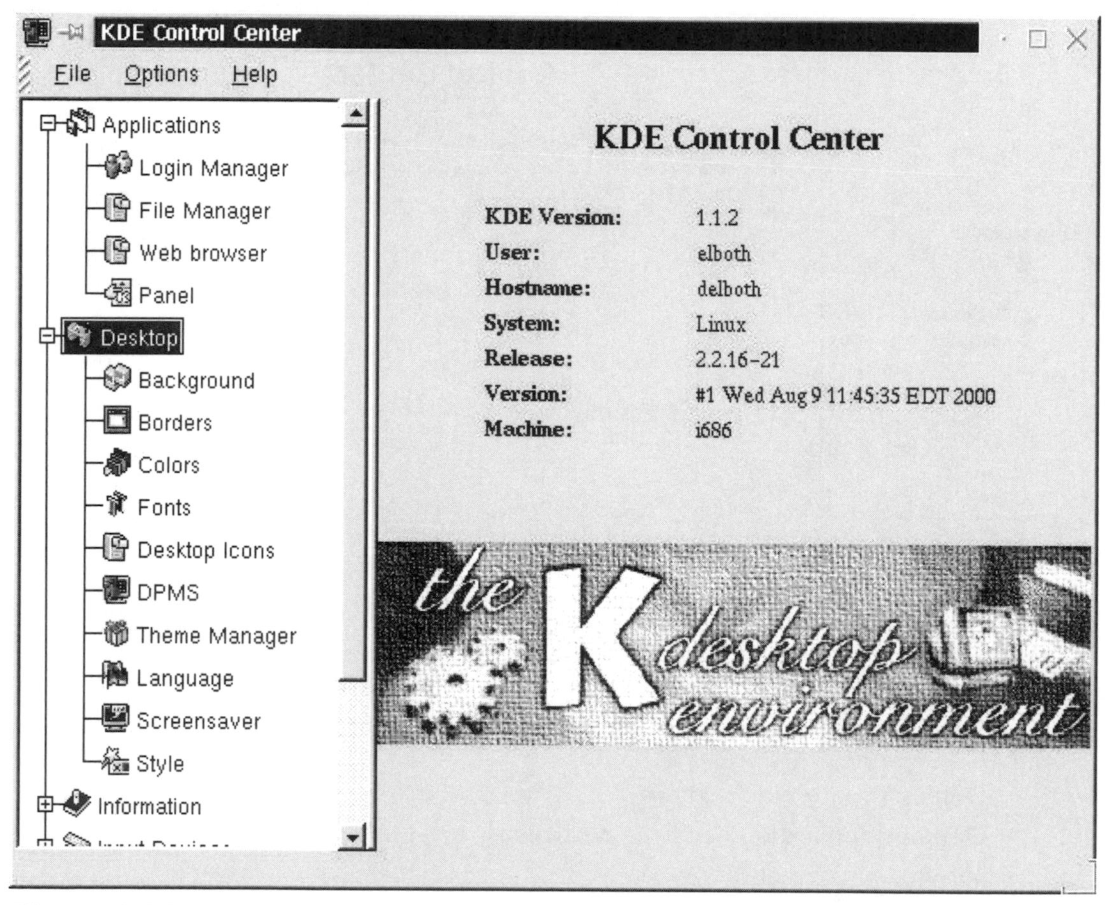


**Figure 10-26**
*The main menu in the KDE Control Center.*

- Defining application handling, particularly login handling, a Web browser, and panel setup.
- Defining a desktop setup (Background, Borders, Colors, Fonts, Desktop Icons, DPMS, Theme Manager, plus your choice of

Language, Screensaver, and Style).

- Reading information about most I/O units like DMA, I/O ports, interrupt, etc.
- Defining input devices like setting the keyboard language and adapting the mouse.
- Defining global keys and ordinary keys.
- Defining various network configurations.
- Defining alarms and system sounds.
- Defining the window setup (buttons, title line, and mouse handling).

## 10.9 Using a mouse with GNOME/KDE

Note that the left mouse button is used for marking and moving files and directories. The right mouse button is used for starting a menu for the selected option. This, of course, works only when there is a menu for the selected option. Most Unix systems are based on a three-button mouse. The middle button is normally used for pasting text or graphics. If you have a two-button mouse, you get the same function by pressing both buttons at the same time.

If you have a two-button mouse that emulates a three-button mouse, you have a function similar to the GNOME/KDE Start button. When only the background picture is displayed on your screen, just press both mouse buttons at the same time.

## 10.10 The XFCE3 alternative

If you are used to commercial Unix versions, you probably know and feel comfortable with the CDE user interface. CDE is also quite similar to OS/2. XFCE3 (see Figure 10-27) is a user interface for Linux that looks and feels a lot like CDE. The most recent versions offer compatibility with GNOME, which makes this a good alternative. So far, XFCE3 is not included in Red Hat Linux, but you can download it for free from http://www.xfce.org.

**Figure 10–27**
*Example with the XFCE3 GUI.*

## 10.11 Standard X applications

You'll find a lot of Linux applications that are intended to run under X. I have included a collection of programs that I think will be useful to you. Any X application may be started directly from a window manager or from the terminal prompt by entering the name of the program and an ampersand (&). The & character makes the program run in the background.

| X Program (Tool) | Description |
|---|---|
| gimp | Graphics program like Adobe Photoshop. |
| gv | Viewer for PostScript files. |
| ical | Simple appointment calendar. |
| userinfo | User information. |
| userpasswd | Changes password. |
| usermount | Mounts and unmounts filesystems. |
| usernet | Checks network interfaces. |
| linuxconf | Lets you set most parameters; compares to the Control Panel and Registry of Microsoft Windows 98. |
| xcalc | A simple calculator. |
| xclock | A standard clock. |
| xdos | DOS emulator (runs DOS programs). |
| xeyes | Eyes that follow your cursor. |
| xmag | Magnifier for people with poor eyesight. |
| xman | Gives you the man pages (GUI front for man). |
| xpdf | Makes it possible to view documents in various formats; uses Adobe's standard format. |
| xterm | Lets you run several terminal sessions. |
| gdm (xdm) | Controls login (X terminal). |
| xv | A simple graphics program. |
| xwd | A tool for making X11 screen dumps in connection with documentation. |

The most important X applications are xterm and gdm. There are many other X applications for Linux, but I have only included the most popular ones.

## 10.12 X games

Here is a table of interest to gamers:

| X Game | Description |
|---|---|
| acm | Simple flight simulator. |
| paradise | Net-based combat game. |
| xbill | Game where the purpose is to stop a virus attack from "Microsoft." |
| xboard | Very good chess game (see Figure 10-28) that can be played via the Internet. |
| xchomp | Classic Pac-man game. |
| xdemineuer | Simple mine sweeper game. |
| xjewel | Traditional Tetris game with many variations. |
| xlander | Simple moon landing game. |
| xpilot | Network-based combat game. |
| xpuzzles | Bundle of puzzle games. |

There are many other X-based Linux games; this is just a selection of some of the most popular ones.

**Figure 10–28**
*Xboard is a popular game.*

## 10.13 X commands

Most X Window preferences can be set from GNOME in a similar way to the Control Panel in Windows. An alternative is to enter the X commands directly.

Examples:

If you need information on how to set up X Window, try the `xwininfo` command:

```
[david@nittedal david]$ xwininfo
```

With X Window, it is in principle possible to log in to any machine (host) in the network and send a GUI image (X Window) to any desired screen. To do this, you must have the required access rights and the `DISPLAY` parameter must be set correctly.

```
[david@nittedal david]$ xhost ftpnode.c2i.no
```

This gives `ftpnode` access to the screen at `nittedal`.

```
[david@nittedal david]$ rlogin ftpnode.c2i.no
```

I log in to the host's `ftpnode`.

```
[ftpnode]$ export DISPLAY=david.nittedal.no:0
```

This defines the use of the screen at host `david.nittedal.no`. If you are running the tcsh shell instead of the bash shell, use the `setenv` command: `[ftpnode]$ setenv DISPLAY david.nittedal.no:0`

```
[ftpnode]$ xboard
```

Finally, I start the chess game xboard on the `ftpnode` machine. The screen image is sent to my display (`nittedal`). All CPU processing generated by the chess game is left to the `ftpnode` machine.

You must request permission from the X server every time you want to write to a screen. You'll find the `.Xauthority` file in your home directory. If you keep a copy of this file at a remote host like, for example, `ftpnode`, you may send screens to this host. You will then not need to use the `xhosts` command.

In the example below, I swap functions between the left and right mouse buttons:

```
[david@nittedal david]$ xmodmap -e  "pointer 3 2 1"
```

This increases the mouse acceleration.

```
[david@nittedal david]$ xset m "50 5"
```

This slows the acceleration.

```
[david@nittedal david]$ xset m "4 8"
```

To make some screen dumps, try xwd:

```
[david@nittedal david]$ xwd > printer_image
```

This dumps the screen to the `printer_image` file. You can continue working with this file in the xv or GIMP programs.

```
[david@nittedal david]$ xsetroot -solid blue
```

This sets a blue background.

```
[david@nittedal david]$ xclock &
```

This starts xclock, which is running in the background.

## 10.14 Starting gdm

When you are running Red Hat Linux 7.x, you will by default start up in X Window. When running other Linux variants, you don't necessary automatically start in X Window. If you want gdm (the X Display Manager) to start by default whenever you start your Linux box, you just need to change one line in the `/etc/inittab` file as follows:

```
[root@nittedal /root]# vi /etc/inittab
```

Find the line with the text `initdefault`. Sometimes, this is what you find:

```
id:3:initdefault:
```

Change the second field, which is the system level, from 3 to 5.

```
id:5:initdefault:
```

Update the changes you have made in `/etc/inittab`. Reboot the system with, for example, init 0, reboot, shutdown, or force `init` to read `/etc/inittab` by entering:

```
[root@nittedal /root]# /sbin/telinit q
```

You must be absolutely sure that X Window starts in a normal way before changing /etc/inittab. Test this by entering startx from the terminal prompt. If you make changes to /etc/inittab other than those I have specified, there is a chance that you will never again get contact with your Linux box!

When starting the machine, you can also select the desired Linux system level from the LILO prompt. Linux 3 (LILO: linux 3) gets you to text mode even if the system is set to start in graphical mode. This is a good option if you are experiencing problems with the X server settings. Linux 5 will start you in graphical mode.

## 10.15 3D acceleration and Linux

For a long time, Linux has lagged a bit behind in supporting 3D acceleration, although Linux supported 3dfx for a while. This is the reason why a project supported by, among others, Red Hat and Silicon Graphics was initiated. The project is administrated by a third company, Precision Insight, which aims at combining the Silicon Graphics GLXtechnology with MesaGL, the free implementation of OpenGL.

The results of this work can be studied in Xfree 4.0. Companies like 3dfx, Nvidia, Elsa, and Matrox support the project and supply drivers.

Several new 3D games are now available for Linux; for example, Quake III Arena and Unreal Tournament.

## 10.16 X Window references

There are many references for X Window on the Internet. A general description of how to set up X Window is also available on the Linux CD under XFree86-HOWTO.

XFree86's home page contains nearly everything you need: http://www.Xfree86.org

For commercially available drivers, you can check:

http://www.xi.com

http://www.metrolink.com

Try these sites for information about 3dfx cards and 3D under Linux:

http://glide.xxedgexx.com

http://www.mesa3d.org

http://www.precisioninsight.com

For information about commercial and free games, etc. for Linux and X Window:

http://www.linuxgames.com

http://www.happypenguin.org

http://www.lokigames.com

For more information about GNOME: http://www.gnome.org
For more information about KDE: http://www.kde.org
For more information about XFCE3: http://www.xfce.org

## Exercises for Chapter 10

1. What is X Window?
2. Which GUIs are available for Linux?
3. Which tools can be used for configuring X under Linux?
4. Log in as root and try different setups for your graphics card and display. Notice the changes. Do you have the optimal setup?
5. Set up GNOME or KDE for your own purposes.
6. Make the necessary changes in `/etc/inittab` for gdm to start automatically when you load Linux.

CHAPTER
11

# Linux Processes

## 11.1 Parent and child processes

A process is a program being executed. One process may start other processes. The initial process is called the parent process, while the new process is called the child process. When a program has been executed, the process belonging to it will be terminated. A parent process may stop before its child process. The child process will inherit the process ID number (PID) 1 (`/sbin/init` under Linux and `/etc/init` under standard Unix V.4).

Every process has a dedicated process number (PID), which is a value between 0 and 65565. All Linux systems have limits for the number of processes that can be active in the system at one time, and the number of processes each user may have. These limitations are set in the Linux kernel.

If you have a Linux kernel with a version number lower than 2.4 (# **`uname`**

**-a**), your Linux system has a limit of 1024 processes. Linux kernels with a version number of 2.4 or higher have a process limitation dependent on the system memory, which can be a maximum of 64GB (Intel).

The owner of a process can terminate it with the Linux command `kill`. The system administrator can remove all processes. It is the Linux shell that reads and executes the commands that are entered. The shell initiates the execution, submits arguments, and waits until they are done before displaying a new prompt.

This is what happens when executing a simple command like `echo`:

```
[david@nittedal david]$ echo "Hello"
Hello
```

The shell (bash) reads the line `echo "Hello"` and parses the `echo` command from the argument. Then the following happens:

- The process is divided into two exact copies.
- The parent process waits for the child to terminate.
- The child swaps the old program (bash) for the new command (`echo "Hello"`).
- The child executes the program.
- The child terminates.
- The parent process goes on and you get your shell prompt back.

The process is divided into two identical copies. In order that a process copies itself, the **fork** function call must be started. After `fork`, you have two processes: one parent process and one child process. The difference between them is their PID number. The two processes share open files, and each process knows that there is a parent/child relationship to the other. In this example, the parent says that it will wait for the child to finish by starting the function call **wait**. The child then determines that it will execute a new program and uses the function call **execute**. (With `execute`, you can transform the process that was created by `fork` into a new program.) The child gives a new list of arguments to the new program. The Linux kernel frees memory that was committed to the old program and starts the new program. The new program (`echo`) writes its arguments to standard output (the terminal). Finally, `echo` executes the system call **exit** and terminates. After the termination of the child, the waiting shell is activated. The parent process returns and you get the prompt back.

## 11.2 Foreground and background processes

Linux is a multi-user, multiprocessing OS. You may run a process in the foreground or in the background. If a process is running in the foreground, all messages are displayed on the screen. Accordingly, it is only possible to run one process in the foreground.

You may run several simultaneous background processes. However, it is important to note that all output should be redirected to a file. If the program runs in the foreground, the shell waits for the child process to terminate (see Figure 11-1). The program may be a menu-based application with or without expected user input. When the child process is terminated, the Linux prompt is returned.

When the user starts a background process, the shell does not wait for the child process to terminate. Instead, it displays the PID belonging to the child process and returns your prompt (see Figure 11-2).

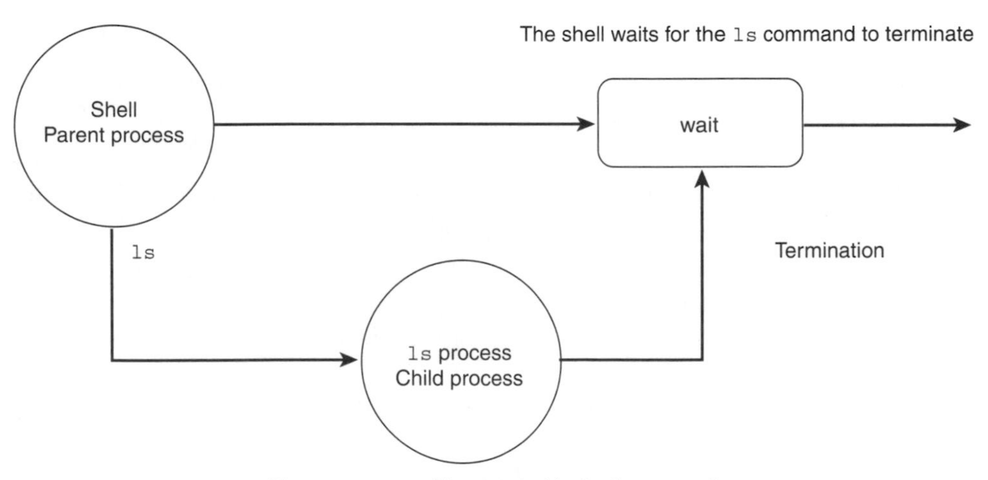


**Figure 11-1**
*Example with a foreground process.*

To start a foreground process, just enter the name of the program. The display and keyboard will be associated with the foreground program.
If you instead want background processing, you must include the `&` character at the end, after the command or program. After starting a background process, the prompt is immediately returned and the shell is ready for new commands

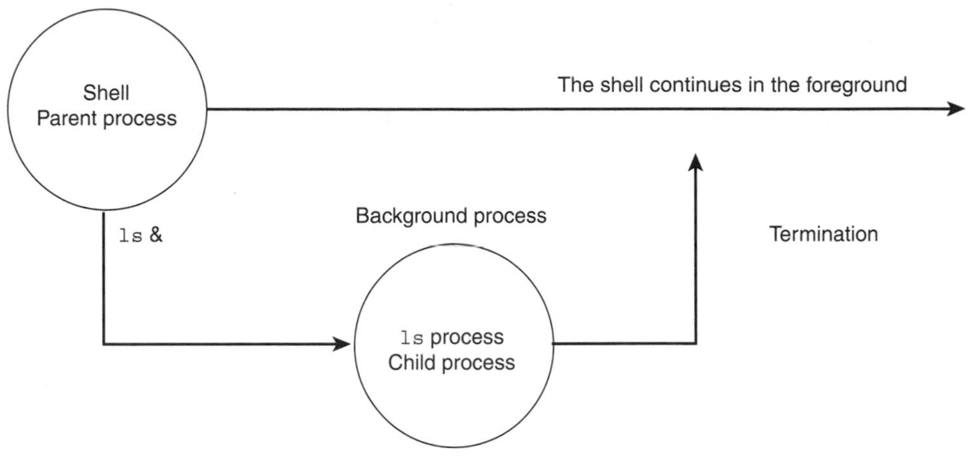


**Figure 11-2**
*Example with a background process.*

or programs. The background and foreground processes are running at the same time. A background process cannot be run interactively.

Example:

```
[david@nittedal david]$ who > datafile &
```

I start the who command and send the result to the text file datafile. An & is included so the process runs in the background.

Example:

```
[david@nittedal david]$ linuxprogram &
```

I start the program linuxprogram, which will run in the background.

Example:

```
[david@nittedal david]$ gcc corelfilter.c &
```

This runs a compilation of C source code in the background.

```
[david@nittedal david]$ who | wc -l > user.list &
```

The result of who | wc -l is sent to the file user.list. The process runs in the background. A process that runs in the background gets a unique PID. The number is displayed on-screen after you enter your command.

## 11.3 Display process table – ps

A process is usually associated with a command or program. Each process gets a unique PID when it is started. The `ps` command is used by system administrators, etc. to determine information about certain processes or about all processes in the system.

Figure 11-3 shows the GNOME System Monitor. This displays all running processes.

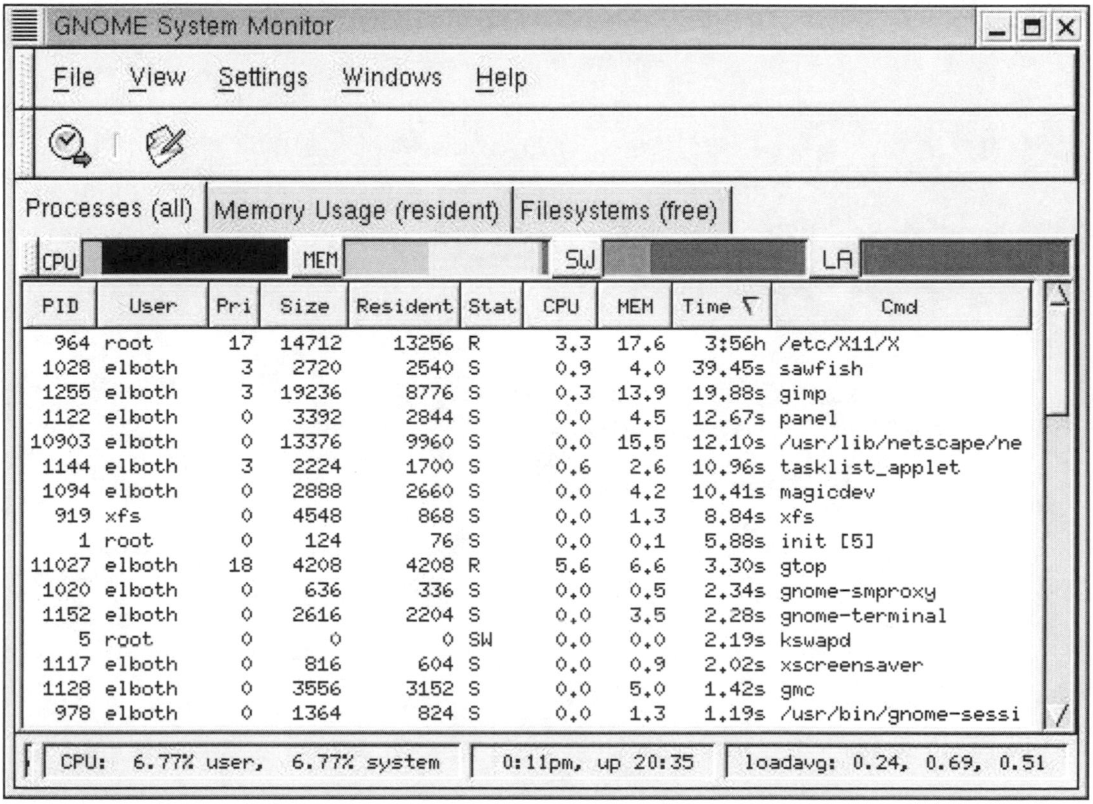

GNOME System Monitor

File View Settings Windows Help

Processes (all) | Memory Usage (resident) | Filesystems (free)

CPU MEM SW LA

| PID | User | Pri | Size | Resident | Stat | CPU | MEM | Time | Cmd |
|---|---|---|---|---|---|---|---|---|---|
| 964 | root | 17 | 14712 | 13256 | R | 3.3 | 17.6 | 3:56h | /etc/X11/X |
| 1028 | elboth | 3 | 2720 | 2540 | S | 0.9 | 4.0 | 39.45s | sawfish |
| 1255 | elboth | 3 | 19236 | 8776 | S | 0.3 | 13.9 | 19.88s | gimp |
| 1122 | elboth | 0 | 3392 | 2844 | S | 0.0 | 4.5 | 12.67s | panel |
| 10903 | elboth | 0 | 13376 | 9960 | S | 0.0 | 15.5 | 12.10s | /usr/lib/netscape/ne |
| 1144 | elboth | 3 | 2224 | 1700 | S | 0.6 | 2.6 | 10.96s | tasklist_applet |
| 1094 | elboth | 0 | 2888 | 2660 | S | 0.0 | 4.2 | 10.41s | magicdev |
| 919 | xfs | 0 | 4548 | 868 | S | 0.0 | 1.3 | 8.84s | xfs |
| 1 | root | 0 | 124 | 76 | S | 0.0 | 0.1 | 5.88s | init [5] |
| 11027 | elboth | 18 | 4208 | 4208 | R | 5.6 | 6.6 | 3.30s | gtop |
| 1020 | elboth | 0 | 636 | 336 | S | 0.0 | 0.5 | 2.34s | gnome-smproxy |
| 1152 | elboth | 0 | 2616 | 2204 | S | 0.0 | 3.5 | 2.28s | gnome-terminal |
| 5 | root | 0 | 0 | 0 | SW | 0.0 | 0.0 | 2.19s | kswapd |
| 1117 | elboth | 0 | 816 | 604 | S | 0.0 | 0.9 | 2.02s | xscreensaver |
| 1128 | elboth | 0 | 3556 | 3152 | S | 0.0 | 5.0 | 1.42s | gmc |
| 978 | elboth | 0 | 1364 | 824 | S | 0.0 | 1.3 | 1.19s | /usr/bin/gnome-sessi |

CPU: 6.77% user, 6.77% system | 0:11pm, up 20:35 | loadavg: 0.24, 0.69, 0.51

**Figure 11-3**
*GNOME System Monitor.*

All processes have a status that may change during the process. As long as the process is active, it will keep the same PID number and run from the same login shell. Redundant processes can be removed with the `kill` command. The `ps` command displays active processes.

**ps Command – Displays Process Table**

| | |
|---|---|
| Command | `ps [t] [a] [e] [f] [l] [m] [u]`<br>`ps help` |
| Function | Lists processes. |
| Arguments | None. |
| Options | See the Linux man pages. |
| `a` | Displays all processes (not only your own). |
| `e` | Adds environmental parameters (environment). |
| `f` | Displays family tree relations. |
| `l` | Displays a long list, which contains more information. |
| `t` | Selects by terminal device, TTY (`ps t5` checks `tty5`). |
| `x` | Selects processes without controlling TTYs (terminal devices). |

Example:

```
[david@nittedal david]$ ps a
  PID TTY STAT TIME COMMAND
  420    1 S     0:02 /bin/login – root
  421    2 S     0:02 /bin/login – root
  422    3 S     0:00 /sbin/mingetty tty3
  426    5 S     0:00 /sbin/mingetty tty5
  427    6 S     0:00 /sbin/mingetty tty6
…
425    4 S     0:02 /bin/login – david
  685    4 S     0:00 -bash
  696    4 S     0:00 sleep 10000
  726   p0 S     0:02 /bin/login -h 207.117.119.10 -p
  727   p0 S     0:00 -bash
[david@nittedal david]$
```

| ps Column | Description |
|---|---|
| UID | Owner of process. |
| PID | The PID of the current process; if you know the PID, you may stop the process with the `kill` command. |
| PPID | Parent PID. |
| TIME | System time spent by the process. |
| STAT | Shows process status (S=sleeping/R=running). |
| TTY | Controlling terminal (terminal device name). |
| COMMAND | Name of command/program. |

The structure of processes is hierarchical with parents and children. Process #0 is the swapper and belongs to root. This is the first process that is started by the OS. The next process is `/sbin/init` (#1). This process is the parent of several processes like `portmap`. When looking at process #0, you will see that this is the parent of most other processes like `kflushd`, `kswapd`, `syslogd`, `crond`, `inetd`, `named`, `lpd`, etc.

Example:

```
[vigdis@nittedal david]$ ps ax
  PID TTY STAT TIME COMMAND
    1  ?  S     0:03 init [3]
    2  ?  SW    0:00 (kflushd)
    3  ?  SW<   0:00 (kswapd)
...
421    2 S     0:02 /bin/login – root
  422    3 S     0:00 /sbin/mingetty tty3
743   p0 S     0:02 su - anne
  744   p0 S     0:01 -bash
  822   p0 R     0:01 ps ax
  823   p0 S     0:00 more
  425    4 S     0:02 /bin/login – david
  685    4 S     0:00 -bash
  696    4 S     0:00 sleep 10000
  726   p0 S     0:02 /bin/login -h 207.117.119.10 -p
```

The `su - anne` process is tied to the terminal `ttyp0`. The `ps alx` command is useful if you want a full overview of parent processes and associated child processes on the entire system.

| | | |
|---|---|---|
| System files: | /dev/mem | memory |
| | /dev/ttxx | terminal name |
| See also: | kill and nice | |

## 11.4 Continue processes after logout – nohup

Processes that are started from a terminal (background as well as foreground processes) are automatically stopped when you log out. If you have jobs that must continue after logout, they must be started with the nohup command.

**nohup Command – Continues Processes after Logout**

| | |
|---|---|
| Command | nohup [argument] |
| Function | Prevents processes from stopping after logout. |
| Command | The program that you want to run in the background. |
| Arguments | Any program/command argument. |

Unless the result of the command is redirected, it will be sent to the file nohup.out. If the user doesn't have write access to the directory, the result will be sent to $HOME/nohup.out. $HOME refers to the user's home directory, e.g., /home/david.

Example:

```
[david@nittedal david]$ nohup account 2001 > result &
```

Runs the program account. The number 2001 is an argument to account. All messages from the program account will be sent to the file result.

Example:

```
[david@nittedal david]$ nohup ps axl | grep httpd >
/tmp/number.httpd &
```

The grep command searches for the text string httpd in the output from the ps command. The output is placed in the file /tmp/number.httpd. You can log out directly, without waiting for the result of the command.

Commands that are started with the `nohup` command can be stopped with the `kill` command.

See also: `nice` and `kill`

## 11.5 Stop a process – kill

A program that has been started from the terminal as a foreground process can always be stopped by pressing the terminal's interrupt key Delete or <Ctrl-C> (PC console).

For background processes, pressing <Ctrl-C> is not sufficient; you must know the PID and stop the process with the `kill` command. Only the system administrator can stop processes owned by other users.

**kill Command – Stops Processes**

| | |
|---|---|
| Command | `kill [-s signal] pid`<br>`kill -l [signal]` |
| Function | Stops processes. |
| Options | See the Linux man pages. |
| `-s` signal | Specifies `signal`; `signal` may be a number or name. |
| `-l` | Displays a list of signal names. |
| `pid` | PID. |

The PID identifies the process. The `ps` command displays the various process numbers. The signal number depends on the architecture of your system (processor).

Example:

```
[david@nittedal david]$ kill -l
 1) SIGHUP       2) SIGINT     3) SIGQUIT      4) SIGILL
 5) SIGTRAP      6) SIGIOT     7) SIGBUS       8) SIGFPE
 9) SIGKILL     10) SIGUSR1   11) SIGSEGV     12) SIGUSR2
13) SIGPIPE     14) SIGALRM   15) SIGTERM     17) SIGCHLD
18) SIGCONT     19) SIGSTOP   20) SIGTSTP     21) SIGTTIN
22) SIGTTOU     23) SIGURG    24) SIGXCPU     25) SIGXFSZ
26) SIGVTALRM   27) SIGPROF   28) SIGWINCH    29) SIGIO
30) SIGPWR
```

Alternatively, you can check the file `/usr/include/linux/signal.h`. This explains some of the signal numbers:

| Signal Number | Description | Signal Number | Description |
|---|---|---|---|
| 1 | Hangup. | 2 | Interrupt. |
| 3 | Quit. | 4 | Illegal instruction. |
| 5 | Trace trap. | 6 | IOT instruction. |
| 7 | EMT instruction. | 8 | Floating point exception. |
| 9 | Kill. | 10 | Bus error. |
| 11 | Segmentation violation. | 12 | Bad argument to system call. |
| 13 | Write on a pipe with no one to read it. | 14 | Alarm clock. |
| 15 | Software (soft kill). | 6 | User-defined signal. |
| 17 | Death of a child. | 19 | Power fail restart. |

Quite frequently, you will need to terminate a process. For example, at some time, you will have to stop a background process that was started with & and won't finish.

The most usual situation is that you have a terminal that "hangs up." When a terminal hangs up, it does not respond to any commands that you enter.

Terminals often hang up as a result of an undefined control sequence in connection with complicated screen handling. If you have a hung terminal, you can log on to another terminal (Ctrl, Alt, and Function key <n>= a new terminal window) with the same `user-id` and execute the `ps` command from there. If you know the terminal name of the hung terminal, you can, for example, enter:

```
[david@nittedal david]$ ps t4
  PID TTY STAT TIME COMMAND
  425   4 S    0:02 /bin/login — david
  685   4 S    0:00 -bash
[david@nittedal david]$
```

Or, you can get a full status by entering:

```
[david@nittedal david]$ ps axl
```

Both methods will give you the PID of the hanging process. Then you can stop the hanging process with the `kill` command.

Examples:

```
[david@nittedal david]$ kill -9 425
```

Terminates process `425`. You may also terminate the user's shell:

```
[david@nittedal david]$ kill -9 685
```

When you terminate the user's shell, the user has to log on again.

```
[david@nittedal david]$ kill -15 789
```

Interrupts process `789` with signal number `15`. If signal number `15` doesn't work, try signal number `9`:

```
[david@nittedal david]$ kill -9 1
```

Not even the system administrator (root) can kill the `init` process. Linux does not report errors in this command; nothing at all happens.

If you want to terminate the `init` process, you can write *[root@nittedal root]$* # **init 0** instead.

See also: `ps` and `bash`

## 11.6 Change priority of processes – nice

By increasing the priority of a process, the process will allocate a larger part of the CPU power to this process, and thereby increase the speed of the process. Decreasing the priority will allocate less CPU power and slow down the process.

The higher the priority number, the lower the priority. The priority of a command is specified with a number between -20 (highest) and 19 in all Linux-based systems. In larger Unix systems, the priority is specified with numbers between -120 and 120. The default priority is 0.

Ordinary users can only decrease the priority of a program, and cannot increase it. To decrease priority, a value is added to the priority number; to increase priority, a value is subtracted from the priority number. The system administrator can run programs with a higher than normal priority by using two minus signs (hyphens). For example, entering--10 will give a `nice` value of 10, which is higher than the default value, 0.

**nice Command - Changes Priority of Processes**

| | |
|---|---|
| Command | `nice [-n adjust] [-adjust] [--adjust] command [argument]` |
| Function | Changes the priority of a process by adding a value to its priority number. |
| Options | See the Linux man pages. |
| adjust | Enter a difference value or a positive or negative adjustment [-20..19]. –20 is the highest priority, 19 is the lowest. |
| Command | Enter the name of the program that you want to give a different priority. |
| Arguments | Any program/command argument. |

Examples:

```
[david@nittedal david]$ nice -15 /usr/bin/linux_machine
```

The system will add 15 to the original value of the priority number. The new priority number of the program `linux_machine` is 0+15=15.

```
[david@nittedal david]$ nice /bin/calc/numeric
```

No number is entered; the value increases by 10. The new value is 0+10=10.

```
[root@nittedal root]$ nice --10 /bin/c-make
```

The system administrator starts a program that subtracts 10 from the original value, 0. Accordingly, the new priority number is 0-10=-10. The program `/bin/c-make` will run at a higher priority than normal.

See also: `nohup` and `ps`

## 11.7 Determine time used on process – time

The `time` command displays the amount of time that Linux uses for various Linux commands and the time elapsed when executing programs.

**time Command – Shows Time Elapsed**

| | |
|---|---|
| Command | `time [argument]` |
| Function | Displays the amount of time used to execute a command. |
| Arguments | The program to be run. |
| Options | See the Linux man pages. |

When the command has been executed, the elapsed time for the command itself is displayed, i.e., the time from the moment you started the command until the prompt returns to your screen. You get the following information:

- Time in seconds used by the program in the Linux system.
- User load (overhead) CPU usage in seconds.
- System load (overhead) CPU usage in seconds.

Example:

```
[david@nittedal david]$ time du /home/david
1        /home/david/.tin/.mailidx
1        /home/david/.tin/.index
4        /home/david/.tin
10       /home/david
 ...
  real      0m0.901s
  user     0m0.010s
  sys      0m0.060s
```

## 11.8 Schedule work – crontab

In Linux, different types of jobs can be run in the background at certain scheduled times. The `crontab` command can be used to manipulate scheduled jobs. Scheduled jobs may update log files, delete temporary files, run certain mailing lists, etc.

Scheduled jobs are stored in your directory under `/var/spool/cron/crontabs`. The `cron` processes read these scheduled jobs and start the programs as scheduled.

**crontab Command – Updates Job File**

| | |
|---|---|
| Command | `crontab [-u user] file`<br>`crontab [-u user] [-l] [-r] [-e]` |
| Function | Updates job file (scheduled jobs). |
| Options | See the Linux man pages. |
| file | Name of job file being installed. |
| -l | Lists `crontab` file. |
| -r | Deletes `crontab` file. |
| -e | Edits `crontab` file by starting the standard editor. |
| -u user | Specifies the name of the user whose `crontab` is to be tweaked. |

Each job line in the `crontab` file has six fields. A space, a tab, or both separate each field.

| **Field** | **Description** |
|---|---|
| 1 | Minute of execution. |
| 2 | Hour of execution. |
| 3 | Day of the month of execution. |
| 4 | Month of execution. |
| 5 | Day of the week of execution (Sunday is 0, Monday is 1, etc.). |
| 6 | Program to be executed. |

The time fields may consist of a comma-separated list or * to indicate each period, e.g., each hour, each week, each month, etc. You may add comments to your crontab file after #.

As an example, say you have a program (ftp_data_homepage) that updates your home page with pictures, sound, etc. four times a day on weekdays. If you have made a script for this, crontab can easily be configured to execute the scheduled job.

Example:

```
55   6,   12,   18,   23    *   *   1-5 ftp_data_homepage
```

Now, say you want to run a tape backup of your Linux system every weekday night. This is your crontab file:

```
55   23   *   *   0-6     backup_everyday
```

If the program in crontab results in text to the screen and you haven't redirected this to a file or printer, you will automatically get the result as mail.

All crontab files are stored in the directory /var/spool/cron/crontabs. If your username is frank, you will find your crontab files in /var/spool/cron/crontabs/frank.

Root is /var/spool/cron/crontabs/root. If you are logged on as root, you can easily add, edit, or delete user-ids in the crontab command list.

See also: /etc/cron.allow, /etc/cron.deny, cron

## Exercises for Chapter 11

1. What is the difference between a foreground process and a background process?
2. Which processes are running right now? Which processes do you own, and which processes are parent processes?
3. Start a background process with the **sleep 500 &** command, log out, and then log in again. Is the process still running? Do the same with the nohup **sleep 500 &** command.

CHAPTER
12

# Linux and Editors

## 12.1 Text editor or word processor?

We use text editors to write and edit messages and other text files. But there is a big difference between text editors and word processors. The only common thing between them is that you can use them to edit text files. A word processor is also capable of formatting your text and showing you the text on the screen with the same font size and type as will appear on the printer. These word processors are normally called WYSIWYG (What You See Is What You Get). In this category, you will find Corel Office Suite (WordPerfect), ApplixWare, StarOffice, Koffice, and Abiword. If you are not writing a book or an article and just want to change your system files, make a bash shell script, or make your own C program, you only need a text editor. With your Linux distribution, you will find basic text editors like joe, pico, emacs, vim, and vi.

Joseph H. Allen originally developed joe. You will find the text editor in five different versions: jmacs, joe, jpico, jstar, and rjoe. The different versions emulate different keyboard commands. For example, jstar uses the old WordStar keyboard commands. joe is a powerful editor with on-screen help. It is a good choice for many beginners. joe is easier to use than vi since you don't have the different modes which you find under vi.

You will find the pico editor included with the University of Washington's pine electronic mail program. pico offers nothing over joe. Today, it is the default editor for pine (e-mail).

One popular choice today is emacs, which was originally developed by Richard Stallman, who founded the Free Software Foundation, or FSF. emacs is the most widely available, full-featured, free editor today. You will find that many emacs users just live in emacs all day.

Bram Moolenaar originally developed vim. vim is a text editor that is compatible with vi. You will often find that the vim editor is used as a replacement for the ex, vi, and view editors. On many Linux implementations, you will find vi replaced with vim.

The simplest solution is vi. Bill Joy originally developed vi. You will find that vi has the best integration with other Linux tools. You will also find that regular expressions like `sed` and `grep` work in vi. Since vi is included in nearly all distributions, this chapter is focused on this text editor. The vi editor is sufficient in most cases. If you want to write a Linux book, however, use a word processor like StarOffice.

## 12.2 The vi editor

### *12.2.1 Text, Program, and Command Files*

vi is a simple editor; it is able to write, correct, and edit text. It can also be used for making command (batch) files. Lots of people are frustrated by the different modes of vi. However, you can generally do more work with fewer keystrokes in vi than with other editors. The commands in vi can be divided into three groups: commands for screen mode, text mode, and command mode (see Figure 12-1).

### 12.2.2 Screen Mode

When starting vi, you will always enter the screen mode. If you are unsure of which mode you are in, press ESC. ESC will always bring you back to the screen mode. When you press ESC while in the screen mode, nothing will happen. Just a beep will sound.

In this mode, you can move around in a document, search for words, and replace words. You can also store a document or terminate vi.

### 12.2.3 Text Mode (Insert Mode)

To be able to write text or make changes in a file, you have to be in text mode. Text mode is also called write mode or insert mode. You can move from screen mode to text mode by the following commands:

| | |
|---|---|
| `a` | Append after cursor. |
| `A` | Append at end of line. |
| `i` | Insert before cursor. |
| `I` | Insert before first non-blank line. |
| `o` | Open line below. |
| `O` | Open line above. |
| `r` | Replace one character with single-byte character. |
| `R` | Replace characters. |

### 12.2.4 Command Mode

To go from screen mode to command mode, press : (colon). A : (colon) will appear at the left bottom of the screen. This is a sign to show that you are in command mode. In command mode, you may execute the following commands:

| | |
|---|---|
| `x` | Update file and exit from vi. |
| `q` | Quit; exit from file without any update. |
| `q!` | Quit; exit from file without any update, even if file was changed. |
| `n` | move to line number n. |

| | |
|---|---|
| `dn` | Remove n lines from where cursor was placed. |
| `e filename` | Edit filename. |
| `e!` | Re-edit; discard changes. |
| `e + filename` | Edit, starting at end of file. |
| `r filename` | Read filename. |
| `w filename` | Write filename. |
| `w` | Write back changes. |
| `w!` | Forced write, if permission originally not valid. |
| `wq` | Store file and exit from vi. |

If you are going to add text from other files, this can be done while in command mode.

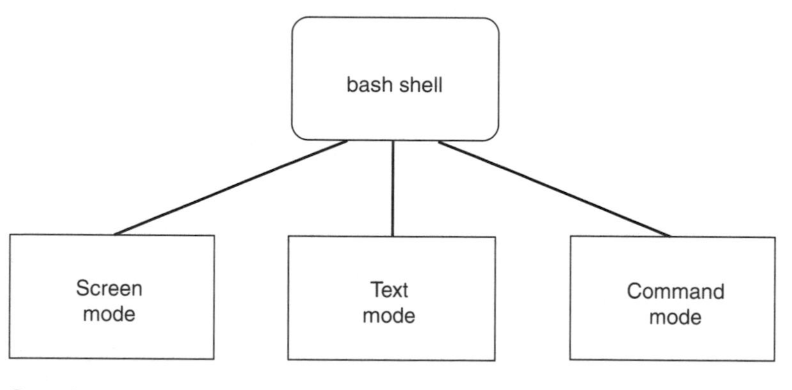


Start vi : vi filename
Save and exit vi : ZZ

**Figure 12-1**
*The different modes of the vi editor.*

## 12.3 Write a text file

### *12.3.1 Start vi (Simple)*

You start vi by giving the command `vi` together with a filename as an argument. To create a text file named `text1`, enter the command:

```
[david@nittedal david]$ vi text1
```

You now get an empty screen with the ~ (tilde) character at the left side of the screen. You are now in screen mode.

### 12.3.2 Write Text

Enter insert mode by giving the command:

```
i
```

You may now enter new text. For example, write:

```
Linux contains the text editor vi.....
```

### 12.3.3 Store the File

To store the file and terminate vi:

1. Go to screen mode by pressing **ESC**.
2. Terminate vi by pressing **ZZ** (remember to use upper-case "Z").

The file will now be stored under the name `text1` and vi will be terminated. You are put back into the shell and the shell prompt is displayed on the screen.

When you are in command mode, you alternatively can store the file with the `x` and `w` commands. If you do not wish to store, you can use the `q!` command while in command mode.

## 12.4 Start vi

vi can be started in several different ways.

**vi Command – Screen Editor**

| | |
|---|---|
| Command | `vi [option] [argument]` |
| Function | Screen editor. |
| Options | See examples and the Linux `man` pages. |
| Arguments | Name of the file to be stored or edited. |

Without any options or arguments, the `vi` command enables you to create a new document. The entered text is stored in memory. After writing the text, you can store it with a name while giving the command to store.

Examples:

```
[david@nittedal david]$ vi letterPeter
```

Fetches the file `letterPeter` in a mode for editing. If no file exists with this name, a new file named `letterPeter` will be created when the entered text is stored.

```
[david@nittedal david]$ vi +20 note1
```

The file `note1` is fetched for editing and the cursor is placed at line number `20`.

```
[david@nittedal david]$ vi + note2
```

The file `note2` is fetched for editing and the cursor is placed at the last line.

```
[david@nittedal david]$ vi +/food note3
```

The file `note3` is fetched for editing. The cursor is placed at the first line containing the text `food`.

```
[david@nittedal david]$ vi -r note4
```

The file `note4` is fetched for editing. The `-r` option is used when an earlier editing exited in an unregular way, for example, by power failure.

## 12.5 Move the cursor in a text file

There are three command groups for moving a cursor in a text file.

- Commands for line positioning.
- Commands for character positioning.
- Commands for words, sentences, and paragraphs.

### *12.5.1 Commands for Line Positioning*

To be able to use the commands for line positioning, you first have to be in screen mode (press ESC).

You have the following commands for line positioning:

| | |
|---|---|
| `H` | Top line on screen. |
| `L` | Last line on screen. |
| `M` | Middle line on screen. |
| `+` | Next line, at first non-white character. |
| hyphen (`-`) | Previous line, at first non-white character. |
| CR | Return; same as `+`. |
| `j` | Next line, same column. |
| `k` | Previous line, same column. |

### 12.5.2 Commands for Character Positioning

To be able to use the commands for character positioning, you first have to be in screen mode (press ESC).

You have the following commands for character positioning:

| | |
|---|---|
| `0` | Beginning of line. |
| `$` | End of line. |
| `l` | Forward. |
| `h` | Backward. |
| `^H` | Same as backspace (^ is the same as the Ctrl key). |
| space | Spacebar. |
| `fx` | Find next single-byte character `x`. |
| `Fx` | Find previous single-byte character `x`. |
| `tx` | Move to character prior to next single-byte character `x`. |
| `Tx` | Move to character following previous single-byte character `x`. |

### 12.5.3 Commands for Words, Sentences, and Paragraphs

To be able to use the commands for words, sentences, and paragraphs, you first have to be in screen mode (press ESC).

You have the following commands for words, sentences, and paragraphs:

| | |
|---|---|
| `w` | Forward a word. |
| `b` | Back a word. |
| `e` | End of word. |
| `)` | To next sentence. |
| `}` | To next paragraph. |
| `(` | Back a sentence. |
| `{` | Back a paragraph. |

## 12.6 Commands for positioning within a file

To be able to quickly change your position within a file, you first have to be in screen mode (press ESC).

You have the following commands for positioning within a file:

| | |
|---|---|
| `^F` | Forward a screen (^ is the same as the Ctrl key). |
| `^B` | Back a screen. |
| `^D` | Scroll down half a screen. |
| `^U` | Scroll up half a screen. |
| `nG` | Go to the beginning of the specified line (end default), where `n` is a line number. |
| `/string` | Next line matching string. |
| `?string` | Previous line matching string. |
| `N` | Reverse last / or ? command. |
| `]]` | Next section/function. |
| `[[` | Previous section/function. |

## 12.7 Commands for adjusting the screen

To be able to adjust the screen, you first have to be in screen mode (press ESC).
You have the following commands for adjusting the screen:

| | |
|---|---|
| `^L` | Clear and redraw window. |
| `^R` | Clear and redraw window if ^L is keyed. |
| `zCR` | Redraw screen with current line at top of window. |
| `z-` | Redraw screen with current line at bottom of window. |
| `z.` | Redraw screen with current line at center of window. |
| `/pat/z-CR` | Move `pat` line to bottom of window. |
| `zn.` | Use `n`-line window. |
| `^E` | Scroll window down one line. |
| `^Y` | Scroll window up one line. |

## 12.8 Commands for yank and put

To be able to yank or put, you first have to be in screen mode (press ESC).
You have the following commands for yank and put:

| | |
|---|---|
| `4yy` | Yank four lines to the default buffer. |
| `4yl` | Yank three characters to the default buffer. |
| `p` | Put back text from the default buffer after cursor position. |
| `P` | Put back text from the default buffer before cursor position. |

You can also yank and put to memory buffer with a name. For example:

| | |
|---|---|
| `"xy` | Yank text from buffer `x`. |
| `"xp` | Put text into buffer `x`. |
| `"xd` | Delete text from buffer `x`. |

See also the example with yank and put in section 12.12 and 12.13.

## 12.9 Commands for deleting text

To delete text, you must be in screen mode (press ESC). You first place the cursor in the position where you wish to start the deleting action.

You have the following commands available to delete text:

| | |
|---|---|
| `x` | The character in the position to the cursor. |
| `2x` | The character in the position to the cursor, plus the next character to the right. |
| `xxxx` | The character under the cursor plus three characters to the left. |
| `dw` | The word pointed to by the cursor. |
| `4dw` | The word pointed to by the cursor and four words to the right. |
| `dd` | The line pointed to by the cursor. |
| `3dd` | The line pointed to by the cursor and two lines. |
| `D` | From the position of the cursor to the end of the line. |

Three of the commands include numbers (2, 4, and 3). By inserting different numbers, you can delete different numbers of characters, words, or lines.

## 12.10 Command for undelete text

You can undo your last delete action with the command:

```
u
```

If more than one delete action is performed, you can undo all of them with one command (works for one line only):

```
U
```

## 12.11 Write more text

To be able to add more text to a file, you have to be in text mode. When you move from screen mode to text mode, you can, at the same time, place the cursor in a chosen position. The commands for moving into text mode are explained in section 12.2.3.

You now may enter new text. The entered text is placed in the position of the cursor. The text to the right of the cursor is moved rightwards. To change the line, press RETURN. To leave text mode, press ESC.

## 12.12 Move text

The easiest way to move text is to delete the text and then paste it from the default buffer. You can use the following commands for restoring deleted text:

| | |
|---|---|
| `p` | Place the last deleted text after cursor. |
| `P` | Place the last deleted text in front of cursor. |

You can use all the commands for deleting from section 12.9. As an example, you can move five lines, including the line pointed to by the cursor, like this:

1. Move into screen mode by pressing **ESC**.
2. Move the cursor to the first of the five lines to be moved.
3. Delete the five lines by pressing **`5dd`**.
4. Move the cursor to the position where the five lines should be inserted.
5. Insert the five lines by pressing **`p`**.
6. The lines are placed after the earlier cursor position.

If you instead wanted to move three words, you should have used the delete command `3dw` in step 3.

## 12.13 Copy text

You copy text by first copying the text into a buffer (intermediate storage). You then move the cursor to the target position and fetch the text (from the buffer) by the command `p` or `P`.

You have the following commands available to copy text into the buffer:

| | |
|---|---|
| `y` | Copies the line pointed to by the cursor. |
| `3y` | Copies the line pointed to by the cursor, plus the following two lines. |

In the same way, you may also copy a different number of lines by inserting a different number instead of 3.

The following example shows how to copy two lines.

1. Move into screen mode by pressing ESC.
2. Move the cursor to the beginning of the lines to be copied.
3. Store the two lines in the buffer by pressing `2y`.
4. Move the cursor to the target position.
5. Insert the lines by pressing `p`.
6. The two lines are inserted in the position after the cursor.

## 12.14 Search for text

The command to search for text is:

```
/argument or ?argument
```

where `argument` is the text to be searched for. You can search for text forward or backward from the cursor's document position. Remember to be in screen mode.

### 12.14.1 Search Forward

To search for text data.

1. Move into screen mode by pressing ESC.
2. Type **/data**.
3. Press **RETURN**.
4. The cursor moves to the first occurrence of the word `data`.

If you need to search several times for the same text, you can repeat the last search by pressing `n`.

### 12.14.2 Search Backward

To search backward, use the command `?` instead of `/`. The remaining actions are done in the same way as when searching forward.

## 12.15 Search and replace

In command mode, you can search for a certain string of text and replace it with another by using the following command:

```
g/s1/s//s2/g
```

The first `g` is the command itself, telling us that text will be replaced. `s1` is the text to be replaced. `s` (substitute) tells us that the text `s1` will be replaced by the text `s2`. `s2` is the new text. The last `g` means that text `s1` is going to be globally replaced throughout the whole document. If you do not include the last `g`, only the first string of text `s1` in the document will be replaced by `s2`. As an example, replace the word `data` with the word `edp` like this:

1. Move into screen mode by pressing **ESC**.
2. Move into command mode by pressing **:** (colon).
3. Enter **g/data/s//edp/g**.
4. Press **RETURN**.
5. Search and replacement are both executed and all occurrences of `data` are replaced by `edp`.

To see where text in the document is replaced, you can type:

**g/data/s//edp/gp**
(p=page)

Remember, you must be in command mode.

## 12.16 Read and write a file

The following commands are available to read, store a file, and/or terminate the edit of a file:

| | |
|---|---|
| `x` | Update file and exit from vi. |
| `q` | Quit; exit from file without any update. |
| `q!` | Quit; exit from file without any update, even if the file was changed. |
| `r filename` | Read `filename`. |
| `w filename` | Write `filename`. |
| `w` | Write back changes. |
| `w!` | Forced write, if permission originally not valid. |
| `wq` | Store file and exit from vi. |

After starting vi, you can read a file and edit it like this:

1. Move into screen mode by pressing **ESC**.
2. Enter **`:e note7`**.
3. Press **RETURN**.
4. The file `note7` is fetched and you can proceed to edit it.

You can also read a file by using the command `r` instead of `e`. With `r`, you insert a whole file into the current text. The file, which is read, is placed from the position of the cursor forward. The text behind the cursor is moved back.

In the above example, the command in step 2 would look like:

**:r note7**

To be able to store or exit from a file, you have to be in command mode. You change from screen mode to command mode by:

1. Enter **:x**.
2. Press **RETURN**.

You have just updated the file `note7` and exited from vi.

Note that the `ZZ` command can only be given from screen mode.

## 12.17 Print

You can print a file created in vi as explained in Chapter 14. vi contains no commands for printing.

## 12.18 Macro definitions

To ease the work of editing in vi, you can store macros in a startup file named `.exrc`. The macro definitions, called `map` commands, make it possible to redefine a key into a sequence of commands or a string of text. The startup file, `.exrc`, must be placed in the user's home directory or in the directory where the vi program was started from. The `map` commands can also be defined directly when you are in vi's command mode.

To redefine keys, use the `map` command. The syntax is:

```
map [key] [command/textstring]
```

Examples of use within the vi editor:

```
:map #0 Life is wonderful
```

Each time you press F1 (while in text mode), the text `Life is wonderful` is included in the document.

```
:map q & w! temp<Ctrl>v <Enter>
```

Each time you press `q`, the edited file is stored in the file `temp`.

To reset a key while in the vi editor, you can use the `unmap` command. For example:

```
:unmap #0
```

Resets the function key F1.

```
:unmap *
```

resets the key `*`.

Example of a `.exrc` file:

| Function Key | Comments |
|---|---|
| `map #0 l` | F1 moves cursor to the right. |
| `map #1 j` | F2 moves cursor one line down. |
| `map #2 k` | F3 moves cursor one line up. |
| `map #3 dd` | F4 deletes the line pointed to by the cursor. |
| `map #4 x` | F5 deletes the character pointed to by the cursor. |
| `map #5 R` | F6 overwrites text. |
| `map #6 i` | F7 enters text mode. |
| `map #7 u` | F8 is the undo key. |

To try the above example, just enter the text in the left-most column. The right-most column contains comments.

The first position after the `map` command points to the key to be defined. #1 to #8 refer to function keys F1 to F8 on a PC or PS/2 keyboard.

For example, when you press function key F1 while in screen mode, you move the cursor to the right. If you are in text mode while pressing function key F1, you will get a small "l" displayed on-screen. If you press function key F2 while in screen mode, the cursor will move one line down, etc.

If you develop programs in the C programming language, the following `.exrc` file may be suitable to include in your `$HOME/C` directory:

```
map #0 #include <stdio.h>
map #1 #include <curses.h>
map #2 #include <signal.h>
map #3 main()
```

While pressing F1, the text `#include <stdio.h>` will be included in the line where the cursor is placed. The assumption for this is that you are in text mode. Using different function keys will result in different text strings.

## 12.19 Set parameters

Various environment parameters may also be placed in the `.exrc` file. The most important parameters are:

| | |
|---|---|
| `set bf` | (beautify) Neglects certain control characters. |
| `set nobf` | (no beautify) Accepts all control characters. |
| `set dir` | (directory) Specifies the directory in which vi will place the editing buffer file. |
| `set nu` | (number) Shows line numbers for all lines. |
| `set nonu` | (no number) Does not show line numbers. |
| `set window=30` | Sets window size to 30 lines. |
| `set wm=8` | Sets right margin to 8 characters. |
| `set wm=0` | Sets right margin to 0 characters (standard). |

All these `set` parameters may also be directly defined while in vi's command mode; for example:

```
:set nu
```

You get the numbers of all lines in the file. This is a particularly useful function when developing programs.

Example of `.exrc` with `map` and `set`:

```
set nu
set wm=4
map #0 l
map #1 j
map #2 #include <signal.h>
map #3 main()
map #4 The book comes from Prentice Hall
```

In this last example, vi defines line numbers on all lines. Afterward, vi defines the right margin to four characters. The function keys F1-F2 are associated with various commands in vi. F4 and F5 result in various text strings. These may be useful while programming in C. The last line (F5) gives us the text string "The book comes from Prentice Hall."

## Exercises for Chapter 12

1. Use the `man helping` function to find out more about vi.
2. What are the three modes in vi?
3. Start vi. Enter the following text:

   **This is my first try using the text editor vi.**
   **After writing this text, I want to store it.**

   Store this text in a file named `Ex12.3` and exit from vi.
4. Fetch the text stored in the previous exercise.
   Train yourself to move the cursor, delete text, and insert new text.
   Then try to move and copy text.
5. Name three ways to store a document in vi.
6. Name three ways of exiting from vi, without storing.
7. Write a long text file with vi. Then try:
   a) A global search, both forward and backward in the file.
   b) A global search and replacement of various words.
8. Create an `.exrc` file, assigning your six most used vi commands to function keys F1 to F6. Then add the following `set` commands into `.exrc`:

   set window=10
   set nu

   Check if the `.exrc` file is initiated.

CHAPTER
13

# Linux Tools

## 13.1 The Linux shell

Programs that produce results are tools. There are two types of tools:

- **Specific tools.**
- **Flexible tools.**

Later in this chapter, we will take a closer look at the flexible tools that can perform a number of similar tasks. Tool programs offer a wide variety of options and may be used in different combinations. By combining various tool programs, you can solve many complicated tasks.

Most tool programs work with text. A significant tool program feature is that they can be used as filters.

This chapter includes some examples of the most popular Linux tool programs.

## 13.2 Display file contents – more

The Linux more command functions nearly like the cat command, except that more stops at each new screen and waits for a command before continuing. The more command is not a flexible tool program, but is frequently used together with various other tool programs.

**more Command – Displays File Contents**

| | |
|---|---|
| Command | `more [-n.l] [option] [+line number] [+/<pattern>] file ...` |
| Function | Displays the contents of one or more files. |
| `-n.l` | (`n.l` = number of lines) sets number of lines to be displayed; equals size of window. |
| line number | Defines from which line screen display starts. |
| File | May be files or directories. |
| Options | See the Linux man pages. |
| -c | Prevents scrolling; clears old line when displaying new line. |

When using more, the text "more" is displayed at the bottom of your screen. This means that the more command is waiting for a new user command. If you want to scroll to the next screen, press the Spacebar.

These are the most frequently used commands in more:

| **more Commands** | **Description** |
|---|---|
| `h` | Displays help. |
| Spacebar | Displays next screen. |
| RETURN | Displays next line. |
| `<n>f` | Jumps n screens forward. |
| `<n>s` | Jumps n lines forward. |
| `/<pattern>` | Searches for the text pattern. |
| `!<command>` | Executes Linux command (starts a shell). |
| `q` | Quits more. |

Examples:

```
[david@nittedal david]$ more /etc/termcap
```

Displays the contents of the file `/etc/termcap`, one screen at a time. Pressing the Spacebar displays the next screen.

```
[david@nittedal david]$ more *.c
```

Displays all files ending with `.c`.

```
[david@nittedal david]$ ps ex | more
```

Displays a process overview, one screen at a time.

```
[david@nittedal david]$ more -12 /etc/passwd
```

Displays the contents of the file `/etc/passwd`. The display is set to a window size of 12 lines.

```
[david@nittedal david]$ more +15 /etc/hosts
```

Displays the file `/etc/host` from line 15.

```
[david@nittedal david]$ more -12 +25 datafile
```

The display starts at line 25 of the file `datafile`, and the window size of each screen is set at 12 lines.

```
[david@nittedal david]$ more +/vt220 /etc/termcap
```

Display will start two lines before the line containing the text `vt220` first appears in the file `/etc/termcap`.

## 13.3 Display file contents – less

`less` is a Linux filter that is a variation of `more`. `less` has the same functions as `more`, but offers some additional options.

**less Command – Displays File Contents**

| | |
|---|---|
| Command | `less -h [-p text pattern] file ...` |
| Function | Displays the contents of one or more files. |
| File | May be one or more files. |
| Options | See the Linux man pages. |
| `--help` | Show `less` help. |
| `-p text pattern` | Displays the file from the specified `text pattern`. |

Examples:

```
[david@nittedal david]$ less -p Linux
operatingsystem_report
```

Displays the pages where the first reference to the text string `Linux` in the file `operatingsystem_report` is found.

```
[david@nittedal david]$ less –help
```

Displays an overview of all options.

## 13.4 Sort data – sort

Each line to be sorted can contain numbers, single words, or a string of numbers and words. The line is divided into fields that are separated by spaces or other characters of your choice.

`sort` results can be displayed in ascending or descending order. You can choose between numerical and alphabetical sorting. You can specify which fields you want sorted and which fields the sort should be based on. The `sort` command has many options, so you will need some experience to master it fully.

**sort Command – Sorts Text and Data**

| | |
|---|---|
| Command | `sort [-m] [-o file] [-dfrnu] [-t separator] [+position.1] [-position.2] [file list]`<br>or simplified<br>`sort [option] file name` |
| Function | Sorts the contents of one or more files. |

**sort Command – Sorts Text and Data (*Continued*)**

| Options | See the Linux man pages. |
|---|---|
| `-m` | Sorts multiple incoming files. |
| `-d` | Only characters, numbers, spaces, and tabs are significant; alphanumerical sort. |
| `-f` | Ignores case; with this option set, there is no difference between LINUX and linux. |
| `-n` | Sorts the specified fields in numerical order. |
| `-r` | Sorts in descending order. |
| `-t` | Redefines the field separator into another character, e.g., `-t:` means the field separator is a colon. |
| `-u` | Ignores repeated lines. |
| `-o file` | To be used when you want to define an output file. |

Examples:

```
[david@nittedal david]$ who | sort
david         tty1       Jul 11 06:15
vigdis        tty2       Jul 11 06:16
root          ttyp0      Jul 11 06:15
```

The output from the `who` command is sorted alphabetically by username. The order of characters and numbers will depend on the character set used by your computer.

Here is a data file that shows further use of the `sort` command:

```
[david@nittedal david]$ cat > datafile
John Paul:22071959:Boy:6072.55.34567:Union Bank
Anne:04051945:Girl:9190.10.34566:Industry Bank
Peter David:01019356:Boy:9190.10.56543:Industry Bank
Roger:01041941:Boy:2234.12.34569:Super Bank
<Ctrl-d>
```

The file `datafile` consists of first name, family name, date of birth, gender, account number, and bank. The contents are to be sorted, and the separator is : (colon).

```
[david@nittedal david]$ sort -t: datafile
```

```
Anne:04051945:Girl:9190.10.34566:Industry Bank
John Paul:22071959:Boy:6072.55.34567:Union Bank
Peter David:01019356:Boy:9190.10.56543:Industry Bank
Roger:01041941:Boy:2234.12.34569:Super Bank
```

The file was sorted by the first field with : (colon) as the field separator.

```
[david@nittedal david]$ sort -f -t: datafile
Anne:04051945:Girl:9190.10.34566:Industry Bank
John Paul:22071959:Boy:6072.55.34567:Union Bank
Peter David:01019356:Boy:9190.10.56543:Industry Bank
Roger:01041941:Boy:2234.12.34569:Super Bank
```

The contents of the file `namelist` are sorted on the basis of the first column with the : (colon) as the field separator. The sorting is not case-sensitive.

### *13.4.1 Position Parameters*

The notations `+position.1` and `-position.2` limit the sort key from the beginning of position 1 to the end of position 2. The characters in positions 1 and 2 are included in the sort key. If you do not include the end position (position 2), the sort field is limited to the field between position 1 and the end of the line to be sorted.

```
[david@nittedal david]$ sort -t: +2 datafile
Roger:01041941:Boy:2234.12.34569:Super Bank
John Paul:22071959:Boy:6072.55.34567:Union Bank
Peter David:01019356:Boy:9190.10.56543:Industry Bank
Anne:04051945:Girl:9190.10.34566:Industry Bank
```

The third field (gender) sorts the file.

```
[david@nittedal david]$ sort +1 -o sortdata datafile
[david@nittedal david]$ cat sortdata
Anne:04051945:Girl:9190.10.34566:Industry Bank
Roger:01041941:Boy:2234.12.34569:Super Bank
Peter David:01019356:Boy:9190.10.56543:Industry Bank
John Paul:22071959:Boy:6072.55.34567:Union Bank
```

The file is sorted by the second field. The field with a second name becomes field number 2 because no field separator is specified. The result is placed in the file `sortdata`.

```
[david@nittedal david]$ sort -n +1 -t: -o sortdata datafile
Peter David:01019356:Boy:9190.10.56543:Industry Bank
Roger:01041941:Boy:2234.12.34569:Super Bank
Anne:04051945:Girl:9190.10.34566:Industry Bank
John Paul:22071959:Boy:6072.55.34567:Union Bank
```

The second field sorts the file. The specified field separator is : (colon). Since the option `n-` is specified, the sort is based on the numerical content of column number 2. The result is placed in the file `sortdata`.

```
[david@nittedal david]$ sort -t: +1 -2 datafile
Peter David:01019356:Boy:9190.10.56543:Industry Bank
Roger:01041941:Boy:2234.12.34569:Super Bank
Anne:04051945:Girl:9190.10.34566:Industry Bank
John Paul:22071959:Boy:6072.55.34567:Union Bank
```

The second field is used to sort the file `namelist`. The option `+1` indicates that the sort field is the start of the second line. If the end position (position 2) is not included, the sort field will be limited to the field between position 1 and the end of the line to be sorted.

```
[david@nittedal david]$ sort -t: +2n -3 /etc/passwd
```

This sorts the password list. Example of output:

```
root:x:0:0:root:/root:/bin/bash
bin:x:1:1:bin:/bin:
daemon:x:2:2:daemon:/sbin:
adm:x:3:4:adm:/var/adm:
lp:x:4:7:lp:/var/spool/lpd:
sync:x:5:0:sync:/sbin:/bin/sync
shutdown:x:6:0:shutdown:/sbin:/sbin/shutdown
halt:x:7:0:halt:/sbin:/sbin/halt
mail:x:8:12:mail:/var/spool/mail:
news:x:9:13:news:/var/spool/news:
uucp:x:10:14:uucp:/var/spool/uucp:
operator:x:11:0:operator:/root:
games:x:12:100:games:/usr/games:
gopher:x:13:30:gopher:/usr/lib/gopher-data:
ftp:x:14:50:FTP User:/var/ftp:
named:x:25:25:Named:/var/named:/bin/false
postgres:x:26:26:PostgreSQL
Server:/var/lib/pgsql:/bin/bash
```

```
gdm:x:42:42::/home/gdm:/bin/bash
xfs:x:43:43:X Font Server:/etc/X11/fs:/bin/false
mailnull:x:47:47::/var/spool/mqueue:/dev/null
apache:x:48:48::/home/apache:/bin/bash
nobody:x:99:99:Nobody:/:
elboth:x:500:500:David Elboth:/home/elboth:/bin/bash
```

The password file is sorted by numerical usernames; this is the third column. The field separator is : (colon).

## 13.5 Find character data – grep

The `grep` command finds character data in one or more files. Unless otherwise specified, the result is displayed on-screen. The `grep` command (global regular expression print) is part of a family of commands, including `grep`, `fgrep`, and `egrep`. Each of the three commands has its advantages and disadvantages. `egrep` means extended `grep`; this is a more advanced command that can handle more complicated expressions.

You will need some practice before mastering the `grep` command. The `grep` command uses less memory than the `egrep` command, but is usually slower. `fgrep` means fixed `grep`. This command only finds fixed strings and no wildcards.

**grep Command – Finds a String of Data in One or More Files**

| | |
|---|---|
| Command | `grep [-vcln] expression [file1 ...]` |
| Function | Finds a string of data in one or more files. |
| Options | See the Linux man pages. |
| `-c` | Specifies the number of lines that contain the text string. |
| `-i` | Ignores difference between upper- and lower-case. |
| `-l` | Prints the names of files containing matching lines. |
| `-n` | Displays all line numbers that contain the text string. |
| `-v` | Displays all lines that do not contain the text string |
| `expression` | Text string you are looking for. |
| `file1` | One or more filenames with or without wildcards (*, ?, [ ]). |

If you enter a text string and a filename with no options specified, `grep` will find and display all lines containing the text string.

Note: If the string contains more than one word, the text string must be placed inside quotation marks.

Examples:

```
[david@nittedal david]$ grep david filename
```

All lines in the file `filename` containing the word `david` are printed to the screen.

```
[david@nittedal david]$ grep -n Peter datafile
```

The `grep` command finds the number of the line containing the text string `Peter`.

```
[david@nittedal david]$ grep -c Peter datafile
```

Displays the number of lines in the file `datafile` containing the pattern `Peter`.

```
[david@nittedal david]$ grep -v Peter datafile
```

Displays all lines that do not contain the pattern `Peter`.

```
[david@nittedal david]$ grep -i Peter datafile
```

Because the option `-i` is specified, case distinctions are ignored.

```
[david@nittedal david]$ grep -l ansi
/etc/termcap /etc/termcap.old /usr/lib/terminfo/a/ansi
```

All files containing the pattern `ansi` are printed to the screen.

```
[david@nittedal david]$ grep -n set *
```

All files are searched for the text string `set`. If you are searching for expressions containing the special characters [, ], }, {, \, |, $, etc., the special function may be turned off with ' (single quote) before and after the special character.

```
[david@nittedal david]$ grep 'Jim' file1
```

Displays all lines containing only the text string `Jim`.

```
[david@nittedal david]$ grep 'O..' file1
```

Displays all lines consisting of three characters, where the first character is `O`.

```
[david@nittedal david]$ grep '[Jj]im' file1
```

Displays all lines consisting of Jim and `jim`.

```
[david@nittedal david]$ grep '[^o-z]le' file1
```

Displays words containing three characters that do not start with characters `o` to `z`, but end with `le`.

```
[david@nittedal david]$ grep ',$' file1
```

Displays all lines ending with comma (`,`).

```
[david@nittedal david]$ grep -n '^$' file1
```

Displays all empty lines.

```
[david@nittedal david]$ fgrep "david" datafile
```

Searches for the text string `david` in the file `datafile`. As this is a fixed text string, `fgrep` is used rather than `grep`.

The following regular expressions may be used with `egrep`:

| Text String | Explanation |
|---|---|
| `textstring +` | One or more text strings connected. |
| `textstring ?` | Text string plus one character. |
| `expression1 \| expression2` | Searches for either `expression1` or `expression2`. |

```
[david@nittedal david]$ egrep 'An+e' namelist
```

Searches the file `namelist` for the text string `Ane`, `Anne`, `Annne`, etc.

```
[david@nittedal david]$ egrep 'david | dave' namelist
```

Searches for the text string `david` or `dave` in the file `namelist`.

## 13.6 Find files – find

`find` is a tool for finding a specified file or directory anywhere in the filesystem (see Figure 13-1). `find` allows several search criteria: filename, inode number, file owner, group, size, or date of file, etc. Unless otherwise specified, the result is printed to the screen.

**find Command – Finds One or More Files (Directories)**

| | |
|---|---|
| Command | `find directory criteria [file name] command`<br>or simplified<br>`find where what what-are-we-doing` |
| Function | Finds one or more files that measure two criteria as defined by the expressions you enter. |
| Description | See the Linux man pages. |
| `-name file` | True if the files are identical to `filename`. |
| `-user user` | True if the files belong to `user`. |
| `-group group` | True if the files belong to `group`. |
| `-size n` | True if the size of the file is `n`; `n` being the number of blocks (one block=512 bytes). |
| `-atime n` | True if file was in use `n` days ago. |
| `-exec cmd` | Executes shell command `cmd`. |
| `-print` | Displays search path on-screen. |

If no criteria are specified, the `find` command will not produce any result. Examples:

```
[david@nittedal david]$ find . -name letter -print
```

A period (.) is used to search in the current directory. The command **`-name`** `letter` specifies a search for the file named `letter`. The command `print`

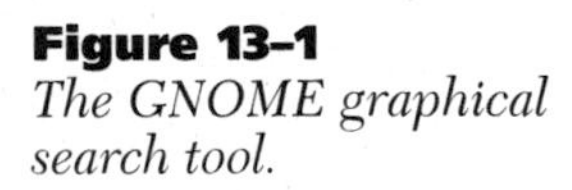


**Figure 13–1**
*The GNOME graphical search tool.*

sends the result to the screen.

```
[david@nittedal david]$ find / -name Linuxbook -print
```

Searches for the file `Linuxbook` from root / and down through the entire file structure. If the file `Linuxbook` is found, the result is displayed on-screen.

```
[david@nittedal david]$ find / -user david -print
```

Searches for all files belonging to `david`.

```
[david@nittedal david]$ find / -atime +2 -print
```

Searches for all files that have been used during the last two days.

```
[david@nittedal david]$ find . -size 0 -print
```

Searches for all files in the current directory with zero size.

```
[david@nittedal david]$ find / -name wp -exec ls -l {} \;
```

Searches for all files with the name `wp`. If a file with the name `wp` is found, this will be shown with the `ls -l` command. `exec` executes the `ls -l` command. {} indicates the searched file. `\;` indicates the end of the command. (You will find more on these operators in Chapter 16.)

Finally, a more complicated example:

```
[david@nittedal david]$ find / \( -name core -o -name
"*.out" \) -atime +7 -exec rm {} \;
```

This deletes all files with the name `core` and all files ending with `.out`. Only files that have not been read or written to during the last seven days are deleted.

## 13.7 Cut data in a file – cut

The `cut` command is used to cut vertical fields in a file. The command manipulates input files and sends the results to the terminal. `cut` is most useful when handling data in a tabulated format. The `cut` command is not standard in version 7 or Berkeley-based Unix systems.

To use `cut`, you must know how the columns are separated. The simplest field separator is a tab, but you may also use other characters like : (colon) or space.

**cut Command – Cuts Vertical Fields in a Text File**

| | |
|---|---|
| Command | `cut -c list [file1 file2 ...]`<br>`cut -f list [file1 file2 ...]`<br>or<br>`cut -f list [-d field separator] [file1 file2 ...]` |
| Function | Cuts vertically in a text file. |
| Description | See also Linux man pages. |
| `-c list` | The list after -c specifies a character position. For example means -c1-72 that there only will be copied from character position 1 to 72. |
| `-f list` | Field, for example -f1,7, means that only the first and the seventh column is copied. |
| `-d separator character` | The character after `-d` is the field separator. |

Examples:

```
[david@nittedal david]$ cut -f2,5 -d":" datafile
```

Extracts fields `2` and `5` in the file `datafile`. The field separator is : (colon). The output is:

```
22071959:Union Bank
04051945:Industry Bank
01019356:Industry Bank
01041941:Super Bank
```

```
[david@nittedal david]$ cut -c1-3 datafile
```

Gives the first three characters in the first column of the file `datafile`.

```
Joh
Ann
Pet
Rog
```

```
[david@nittedal david]$ cut -d: -f1,5 /etc/passwd
root:root
bin:bin
daemon:daemon
adm:adm
lp:lp
sync:sync
shutdown:shutdown
halt:halt
mail:mail
news:news
uucp:uucp
operator:operator
games:games
gopher:gopher
ftp:FTP User
nobody:Nobody
apache:
named:Named
xfs:X Font Server
gdm:
postgres:PostgreSQL Server
mailnull:
elboth:David Elboth
```

Extracts the username and user description (process) from the file `/etc/passwd`.

```
[david@nittedal david]$ name=`who am i | cut -f1 -d" "'
```

Extracts my username.

## 13.8 Paste data in a file – paste

The `paste` command manipulates vertical sections of text files. `paste` is mostly used to handle data in a tabulated format. The `paste` command is used to vertically merge several files into one file. `paste` manipulates files and sends the results to the terminal.

The `paste` command is not standard in version 7 or Berkeley-based Unix systems.

To use `paste`, you must know how the columns are separated. The simplest field separator is a tab, but you may use any other character.

**paste Command – Merges Files**

| | |
|---|---|
| Command | `paste [-s] [-d field separator] file1 file2 ...` |
| Function | Merges several files vertically. |
| Description | See the Linux man pages. |
| `-d field separator` | The character after `-d` is the field separator. |
| `-s` | Transforms single lines from one file. |

Examples of cut and paste:
Separating first names from the telephone list telephone.
First I create the list:

```
[david@nittedal david]$ cat >telephone
david      02453449
nick       02834896
owen       05749845
vicky      07374758
gus        02549474
oliver     02653433
```

The –f option specifies the first field. After cutting the first field (first names) from the file telephone, I put them into the file `firstname`:

```
[david@nittedal david]$ cut -f1 telephone >firstname
```

I use the `cat` command to see the content:

```
[david@nittedal david]$ cat firstname
david
nick
owen
vicky
gus
oliver
```

Now `paste` can be used to combine the two vertical tables. I create a new file and name it `newlist`, in which the telephone numbers are listed in the first column and first names in the second. The `paste` command automatically separates the two columns with a tab character.

```
[david@nittedal david]$ cut -f1 telephone >name
[david@nittedal david]$ cut -f2 telephone >number
[david@nittedal david]$ paste number name >newlist
[david@nittedal david]$ cat newlist
02453449   david
02834896   nick
05749845   own
07374758   vicky
02549474   gus
02653433   oliver
```

```
[david@nittedal david]$ rm number name
```

Removes the file's `number` and `name`.

Examples with the `paste` command:

```
[david@nittedal david]$ paste -d":" data1 data2 > data
```

Combines the columns of the file `data1` with the columns in the file `data2`. The new file is named `data`. : (colon) is defined as the column separator.

```
[david@nittedal david]$ ls | paste -d" " -
```

Lists the index in one column.

```
[david@nittedal david]$ ls | paste - - - -
```

Lists the index in four columns.

```
[david@nittedal david]$ paste -s -d"\t\n" namefile
```

Combines two lines in the file `namefile` into one single line.

See also: `cut`, `grep`, `ls`, `rm`

## 13.9 Remove duplicate lines of text – uniq

The `uniq` command is used to remove duplicate lines from a file. The command reads from the input file and compares adjacent lines. When two lines are repeated, one is removed. This is true only when lines are adjacent to each other. Sometimes duplicate lines are scattered in a file. When this is the case, you must sort the file to remove duplicate lines.

**uniq Command – Finds Unique Lines in a File**

| | |
|---|---|
| Command | `uniq [-udc] [-field] [+character] [input] [output]` |
| Function | Removes adjacent duplicate lines from a file. |
| Options | See the Linux man pages. |
| `-field` | Defines the first field to be skipped before starting to compare adjacent lines. |
| `+character` | The first characters of each line are skipped before the comparison of adjacent lines starts. If a field is already specified, `uniq` will skip the field before skipping characters. |
| `-u` | All non-duplicate lines are displayed. |
| `-d` | All duplicate lines are displayed. |
| `-c` | Ignores the `-u` and `-o` options and displays the number of duplicate lines. |

uniq without any options will display the same results as when using both -u and -d.

Examples:

```
[david@nittedal david]$ sort datafile | uniq
```

The file datafile is first sorted, then all duplicate lines are removed.

```
[david@nittedal david]$ sort datafile | uniq -c
```

Displays the number of duplicate lines.

See also: sort

## 13.10 Convert text – tr

The tr command converts a text from one form to another. The text is read from standard input or from a file. The result is sent to standard output unless otherwise specified.

**tr Command – Converts Text**

| | |
|---|---|
| Command | tr [-cds] [string1] [string2] |
| Function | Swaps or removes selected characters. |
| Options | See the Linux man pages. |
| -c | Inverts characters specified at string1 (complement). |
| -d | Deletes characters specified at string1. |
| -s | Reduces (squeezes) a specified number of adjacent characters into one character. |

Input is specified by string1 and output is string2.

Examples:

```
[david@nittedal david]$ tr -s "\012" < datafile
```

Removes all empty lines from the file datafile.

```
[david@nittedal david]$ tr "[A-Z] [a-z]" < datafile
```

All upper-case characters in the file `datafile` are converted to lower-case.

```
[david@nittedal david]$ echo "This is the Linux world" |
tr L U
```

This is the Uinix world

The `tr` command swaps the character `L` for the character `U` in the text string "`This is the Linux world`".

```
[david@nittedal david]$ tr -cs "[A-Z][a-z]" "[\012*]" <
datafile.1 >output.file
```

In this example, a list is created from the words in the file `datafile1`. Each of these words forms one single line in `output.file`. Each word contains the characters `A-Z` or `a-z`. `012`, meaning RETURN, has been included to specify a carriage return after each word in `output.file`.

See also: `echo` and `codes`

## 13.11 Format page – pr

The `pr` command formats text. The `pr` command may be used to format text to be displayed on-screen or sent to a printer. The `pr` command does not send the document directly to a printer, only to standard output, the screen.

**pr Command – Formats Page**

| | |
|---|---|
| Command | `pr [option] [file ...]` |
| Function | Formats one or more files. |
| Options | See the Linux man pages. |
| `-(n)` | Files are displayed in `n` columns. |
| `-h` | Uses the next argument as a headline on each page. |
| `-m` | Merges specified files into one file. Each file is printed as one column; file 1 is placed in column 1, file 2 is placed in column 2, etc. |
| `-t` | Does not print the first and last five lines of the file(s). |
| `-w(n)` | Sets line width to `n` characters. |

The options selected affect how the files are displayed. The original file is not changed.

Examples:

```
[david@nittedal david]$ pr -3 datafile
```

Displays the file `datafile` in 3 columns.

```
[david@nittedal david]$ pr -w70 letter-offer
```

Line width is set at `70` characters instead of the default value, 72.

```
[david@nittedal david]$ pr -h "Budget 2002" bud1 -h
"Budget 2003" bud2 bud3
```

Prints the file `bud1` with the header `Budget 2002`, and prints the files `bud2` and `bud3` with the header `Budget 2003`.

```
[david@nittedal david]$ pr -h "Budget 2005" bud1 bud2
bud3  |  lpr -P laser-III
```

Merges the files `bud1`, `bud2`, and `bud3`. The header `Budget 2005` is placed on top of each page. Finally, the document is sent to the printer `laser-III`. The original file is not changed.

```
[david@nittedal david]$ pr -m -t  -h "PH Publishing"
Calc2002 Calc2003
```

`Calc2002` and `Calc2003` are merged and displayed in two columns. `Calc2002` is placed in column 1 and `Calc2003` is placed in column 2. The first five and last five lines are not included in the files. The header "`PH Publishing`" is included at the top of each page.

```
[david@nittedal david]$ ls /usr/ole | pr -8 -w132 | lpr
-P laser-III
```

The output from the `ls` command is formatted into `8` columns and the width is set at `132` characters. Finally, the document is sent to the printer queue `laser-III`.

See also: `cat`

## 13.10 Packing data and programs

Like Microsoft DOS and Windows, Linux can use a variety of file compression programs. Each program has a variety of options (see the Linux man pages). Here are some examples:

```
[david@nittedal david]$ gzip -v *
```

Gives an overview of space saved by compressing (zipping) selected files in the current directory.

```
[david@nittedal david]$ gzip Linuxbook
```

Zips the file `Linuxbook`. The old file is removed. The new zipfile is named `Linuxbook.gz`.

```
[david@nittedal david]$ gzip -d Linuxbook
```

Unzips the file `Linuxbook`. The new filename is `Linuxbook`.

The table below gives an overview of the most frequently used compression software programs for Linux.

| **Command** | **Description** |
|---|---|
| `compress` | Used to be a popular zip software. Files compressed with `compress` have the suffix `.Z`. The file `Linux.Z` is a result of `compress`, whereas `Linux.gz` is a result of `gzip`. |
| `uncompress` | Uncompresses files that were created with `compress`; `gunzip` is an alternative. |
| `gzip` | Compression program that uses Lempel-Zip code; can compress and uncompress. |
| `gunzip` | Uncompression software for `.gz` files (`gzip`). |
| `zcmp` | Unzips files and compares them with the Linux command `cmp`. |
| `zdiff` | Unzips files and compares them with the Linux command `diff`. |
| `zgrep` | Unzips files and searches for text patterns with the Linux command `grep`. |

| Command | Description (*Continued*) |
|---|---|
| `zless` | Unzips files and prints to the screen. |
| `zip` | Linux relative of `pkzip` and `winzip` for Microsoft DOS and Windows. |
| `unzip` | Linux relative of `pkunzip` for Microsoft DOS and Windows. |

The `gunzip` command can be used to unzip a file that has been zipped with `gzip`. This has the same effect as `gzip -d`.

```
[david@nittedal david]$ gunzip Linuxbook
```

Unzips the file `Linuxbook` with `gunzip`. The new filename is `Linuxbook`.

```
[david@nittedal david]$ zgrep  Gnome  *.gz
```

Gives an overview of all zipped text files containing the text string "`Gnome`".

```
[david@nittedal david]$ unzip Linux.zip chap1 chap2
```

Unzips the files `chap1` and `chap2` from the zipped file `Linux.zip`.

## Exercises for Chapter 13

1. What is the difference between the tools `more` and `less`?
2. Make a list in alphabetical order of all files in your user area.
3. Use the `grep` command to check whether you have been defined in the file `/etc/passwd`.
4. Find out how many subdirectories `/usr` has. (Hint: `ls -F / | grep '/' | wc`)
5. Which files in your user area have been in use in the last week? (Hint: `find $HOME -name -atime +7 -print`) Select all files larger than 750KB. (Hint: `find` and `-size`.) Select all files belonging to you. (Hint: `find` and `-user`)

6. How can you display all files in the `/usr` directory with the name `test.data`? Use the `find` command. (Hint: `find /etc -name 'test.data' -exec ls -la {} \;`)
7. Use the `cut` command to select the users defined in `/etc/passwd`. Place the list in a new text file.
8. Use the `cut` and `paste` commands in `/etc/passwd` and make a list consisting of usernames and the text describing the fields in `/etc/passwd`.
9. A file contains the following data:

   david 123456

   nick 565467

   anne 435674

   peter 233453

   vicky 221209

   Sort the file in alphabetical order. Place the telephone numbers in column 1. Use the `cut` and `paste` commands.
10. Explain the function of the following commands:

    a) `grep id number < namebase >> result`

    b) `ls /etc | grep hosts | wc -l`

    c) `find / -name core -print`

    d) `pr -m -t test1 test2 test3`

    e) `tr a g < testfile`
11. Compress all files in your home directory. Use `gzip`. Uncompress the files in a different location in the Linux system. Do the same with the `zip/unzip` commands.

CHAPTER
14

# Printing from Linux

## 14.1 Linux and printing

This chapter describes how to set up the Linux spooling system, how to start and stop the spooling system, how to print text files, and how to stop printing.

## 14.2 The Linux spooling system

When sending a file to a printer in Linux, the file is sent to a spooling area. The spooling system handles all print jobs. Spool means simultaneous peripheral operations on-line. Each file is processed in sequence. The spooling system makes it possible to send multiple jobs to a printer at the same time and allows you to continue with other tasks after you have sent a job to a printer.

Linux is based on the BSD (Berkeley) spooling system. The Unix world uses two different spooling systems: AT&T and BSD. The systems are somewhat different, but work more or less the same for the user. The AT&T system is a more flexible spooling system. BSD is simpler to use and comes as a default in Linux. As it is the standard Linux spooling system, this chapter will focus on BSD.

## 14.3 Defining a printer queue

You can define your spooling system by running the graphical X Window program `printtool` (`/etc/X11/wmconfig/printtool`) (see Figure 14-1), which can also be run from the GNOME GUI interface or from `linuxconf`.

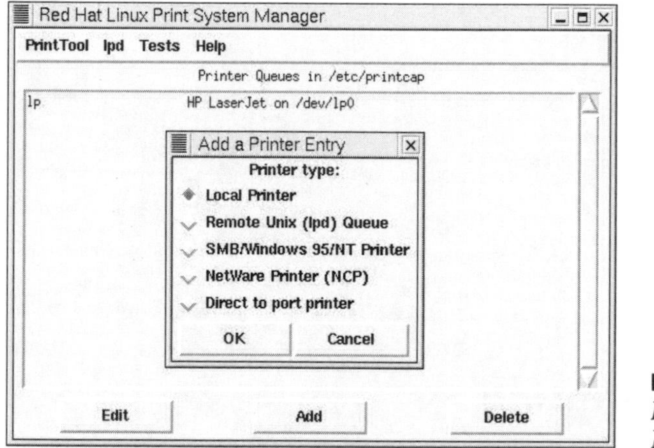


**Figure 14-1**
*Red Hat Linux Print System Manager.*

These are the main points to define when setting up a printer queue under Linux:

- **Port control program (serial or parallel).**
- **Printer definitions (drivers).**
- **Filters (character conversion).**
- **Access control.**
- **Starting/stopping the spooling system.**

Under Linux, you can define local or remote printer queues. Linux supports the following remote printer queues:

- **Unix printer (`lpd`).**
- **LAN Manager (SMB/Windows 95/NT).**
- **Novell NetWare.**

All of this can be controlled and configured from `/etc/X11/wmconfig/-printtool`. Local printers can be connected to the parallel port or serial ports. You only need to define the name of the printer queue, spooling area, port, and print emulation. Here is a list of printer ports that may be used:

| Unit | Device Name | Address | IRQ | DMA |
|---|---|---|---|---|
| `/dev/ttyS0` | COM1 | 3F8 | 4 | n/a |
| `/dev/ttyS1` | COM2 | 2F8 | 3 | n/a |
| `/dev/ttyS2` | COM3 | 3E8 | 4 | n/a |
| `/dev/ttyS3` | COM4 | 2E8 | 3 | n/a |
| `/dev/lp0` | LPT1 | 378-37F | 7 | n/a |
| `/dev/lp1` | LPT2 | 278-27F | 5 | n/a |

| Parameters | Input Example |
|---|---|
| Printer type | LOCAL |
| Queue | `hplaser` |
| Spool directory | `/var/spool/lpd/hplaser` |
| Printer device | `/dev/lp0` |
| Printer driver | HP LaserJet Plus |
| Paper size | Letter (8.5 x 11 in.) |
| Resolution | 300x300 |
| Bits per pixel | Default |

The table above exemplifies a local printer setup. If you want to use a remote printer via `lpd`, the setup is even simpler; you only need to specify the name of the computer that the printer is connected to (as defined in the `/etc/hosts` file or in the DNS) and the name of the queue, which is already defined on the remote computer.

| Printer Parameters | Input Example |
|---|---|
| Remote hostname | `ftp.powertech.com` |
| Remote queue | `hplaser` |

If you have one or more printers that are controlled by LAN Manager (Windows 98, Windows NT, or Samba), choosing LAN Manager to connect to a printer is reasonable. You need to know the LAN Manager hostname, IP address, share name, username, and password. The setup may look like this:

| Printer Parameters | Input Example |
|---|---|
| LAN Manager host | `calculate.c2i.net` |
| LAN Manager IP | `207.117.119.40` |
| Share name | windows |
| Username | guest |
| Password | guest0 |

If the printer queue is controlled by the Novell spooling system, you may choose NetWare.

If you have a standard printer, setting up printer queues is simpler on a PC with Linux than with Windows 98 or Windows NT. The manual technical updates mentioned below will, in most cases, not be required.

## 14.4 Key files

The username `lp` must be defined in `/etc/passwd` and `/etc/group` for the spooling system to work. Here is an example of a definition in `/etc/passwd`:

```
[root@nittedal /etc]# more passwd
root:tQ8pfxCWkCWA.:0:0:root, Nittedal,
67078944:/root:/bin/bash

..
lp:*:4:7:lp:/var/spool/lpd:
..
```

And here is an example of a definition in /etc/group:

```
[root@nittedal /etc]# more group
..
lp::7:daemon,lp
..
```

The files used by lpr are set by values in the different printer configuration files. The following are commonly used and have a set of default values:

| Configuration Files | Description |
|---|---|
| /etc/printcap | Definition file for different printer queues. |
| /etc/lpd.conf | lpr configuration file. |
| /etc/lpd.perms | Printer permissions file. |
| /var/spool/printer* | Spool directories. |
| /var/spool/printer*/printer | Lock file for queue control. |
| /var/spool/printer*/control.printer | Queue control. |
| /var/spool/printer*/active.printer | Active print job. |
| /var/spool/printer*/log.printer | Printer log file. |
| /var/spool/*/minfree | The number of free blocks reserved for a specified spool directory. |
| /dev/printer | Printer control program (device driver). |
| /etc/hosts.equiv | Lists machines (hosts) that may use the printer connected to this machine. |
| /etc/hosts.lpd | Lists machines (hosts) that may use the printer connected to this machine, but that are not controlled by this machine. |

If your spooling system is not working, check the following additional command files: lpc, lpd, lpq, checkpc, lpr, lprm, and pr.

If you have special requirements, you must manually update various key files like: /etc/printcap, /etc/lpd.conf, /etc/lpd.perms, /var/spool/-*/minfree, /etc/hosts.lpd, and /etc/hosts.equiv.

You will find that /etc/printcap is an important key file. In this file, printer emulation, filters, and remote host (if the printer is connected to a remote host) are defined. Only the system administrator (root) may change this key file. I'll give some examples that show various setups.

The screen dump shown in Figure 14-2 describes a printer connected to the local parallel port of the PC. The printer uses HP LaserJet emulation. The device driver for the parallel port is /dev/lp1 (/dev/lp0, /dev/lp1, /dev/lp2). On most PCs, this is the first parallel port.

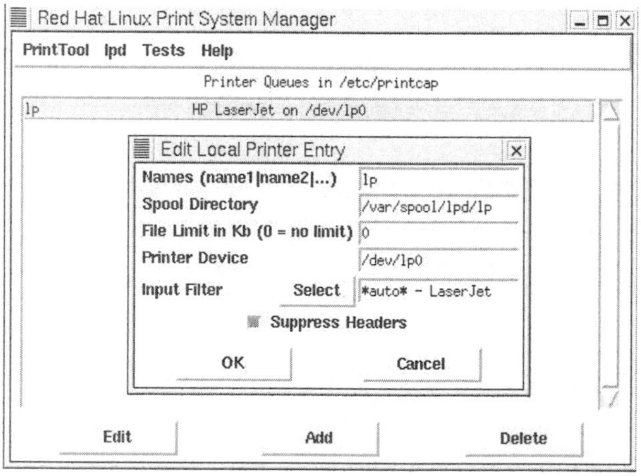

**Figure 14-2**
*Editing local printer in the Red Hat Linux Print System Manager.*

Example:

```
[root@nittedal /etc]#  more /etc/printcap
# /etc/printcap
#
# This file can be edited with the printtool in the con-
trol-panel.
##PRINTTOOL3## LOCAL laserjet 300x300 a4 {} LaserJet
Default {}
lp:\
        :sd=/var/spool/lpd/lp:\
        :mx#0:\
        :sh:\
```

```
        :lp=/dev/lp1:\
        :if=/var/spool/lpd/lp/filter:
[root@nittedal /etc]#
```

| Key | Description of /etc/printcap Options |
|---|---|
| lp | Control program (device driver) or destination file. |
| ms | Certain print features like XON/XOFF (see stty). |
| sd | Location of spooling directory. |
| lf | Location of error messages. |
| rm | Name of remote machine to which you spool, e.g., rm=pluto. |
| mx | Buffering data (size). |
| if | Location of spooling filter. |

The simplest method is defining a standard PostScript or HP LaserJet printer in /etc/printcap. If many of your text files are in PostScript format, you'll find a PostScript printer a convenient alternative. A substitute is using GhostScript. You'll find out more about this in the printing HOWTO.

To learn more about the printer queue definitions in your Linux system, you may check the /etc/termcap file. This file contains a number of terminal and printer definitions. The compressed terminal and printer definitions directory, /usr/share/terminfo, is simpler to read as the definitions are listed in alphabetical order; for example, all the HP definitions on the system are located in the /usr/share/terminfo/h directory.

If you need certain filters to handle emulations, character sets, and fonts, try this FTP site:

ftp://ftp.nvg.ntnu.no/pub/Linux/sunsite/system/Printing

## 14.5 Print access and disk use

After setting up the Linux printer queue system, you can control the access to this system over the LAN either with the /etc/hosts.equiv file or the /etc/hosts.lpd file. The hosts.equiv file will only be used if the computers are connected via r (remote) commands in BSD. You'll find out more about this in Chapter 22. The files /etc/hosts.equiv and /etc/hosts.lpd should only contain lists of the names of the hosts that are allowed access to your printers.

Example:

```
[root@nittedal /etc]# cat /etc/hosts.lpd
pluto
nittedal
boulder
```

If you run into disk space problems in the spooling area, you can set up the `minfree` file in each spool directory. In `minfree`, you simply set the number of disk blocks you want to be available for each spool area. The `minfree` file can be edited with the vi or emacs editors.

## 14.6 Remote print to a Unix queue

If you need to access printers that are connected to other Unix hosts, you may use the remote print function from Linux. The table below shows the shell programs that must be initiated in each system to set up the spooling system.

| Unix System | Administration Shell |
|---|---|
| HP-UX | `sam` |
| IBM AIX | `smit` |
| NCR Unix V.4 | `sysadm` |
| Solaris | `hosts.lpd` and `hosts.equiv` |
| SCO XENIX | `sysadm`, `lpinit`, or `mkdev lpr` |
| SCO Unix | `sysadmsh` |
| SCO UnixWare | `sysadmsh` |

During the installation procedure in most Unix systems, Linux included, most directories and key files will be updated automatically by the shell interfaces (`sysadm..sam`). In most Unix systems and Linux, `/etc/printcap` is one of the most important files when the spooling systems are based on BSD.

Below you'll find an example that describes how to access a remote printer that is connected to a different Linux or Unix computer. It is indifferent whether the printer is connected via the parallel or the serial port. All you need to know is the IP address of the machine and the type of printer emulation.

```
[root@davelin /etc]# more /etc/printcap
# /etc/printcap
#
# This file can be edited with the printtool in the con-
trol-panel.
##PRINTTOOL3## REMOTE POSTSCRIPT 300x300 a4 {} PostScript
Default {}
lp:\
        :sd=/var/spool/lpd/lp:\
        :mx#500:\
        :sh:\
        :rm=pluto:\
        :rp=hplaser:\
        :if=/var/spool/lpd/lp/filter:
[root@davelin /etc]#
```

## 14.7 Control printer – lpc

Under Linux, general print services can be controlled with the Linux command `lpc`. This command allows a number of options and arguments. If you type `lpc` only, you enter command mode.

**lpc Command – Configures Printer Services**

| | |
|---|---|
| Command | `lpc [command] [argument...]` |
| Function | Configures printer queues and general print services. |
| Commands | See table below. |
| Argument | See the Linux man pages. |

**lpc Commands**

| | | | |
|---|---|---|---|
| abort | disable | restart | topq |
| clean | down | start | up |
| enable | help | status | ? |
| exit | quit | stop | |

Example:

```
[root@nittedal /root]# lpc
lpc> down all
lp:
        printer and queuing disabled
lpc> start all
lp:
        printing enabled
        daemon started
lpc> status
lp:
        queuing is disabled
        printing is enabled
        no entries
        no daemon present
lpc> quit
[root@nittedal /root]#
```

From `lpc` you can:

- **Start/stop a printer.**
- **Start/stop the related spooling queue.**
- **Change the order of print jobs in a printer queue.**
- **Obtain the status of printers and related spooling queues and processes.**

If you are running X Window, many of these services are easier to administer from GNOME or KDE.

## 14.8 Start/stop the spooling system – lpd

Under Linux, the spooling system can be started with the `lpd` command. Alternatively, you can use X Window (`printtool`) or restart the spooling system from `/etc/rc.d/rc2.d/S60lpd`.

**lpd Command – Controls Spooling System**

| | |
|---|---|
| Command | `lpd [-Llogfile] [-F] [-V]` |
| Function | Starts the spooling system (printer daemon). |

**lpd Command – Controls Spooling System** ***(Continued)***

| | |
|---|---|
| Argument | None. |
| Options | See the Linux man pages. |
| `-Llogfile` | Makes a log (logfile) containing print jobs received from the network. |
| `-F` | In standard mode, the `lpd` server will run in background mode. The `-F` flag forces it to run in foreground mode, where you can more, easily debug. |
| `-V` | Prints the program's version information. |

Example:

```
[root@nittedal /root]# /usr/sbin/lpd -Ldatafile
```

Starts the spooling system. The tidiest way is to run the start script, `/etc/rc.d/rc2.d/S60lpd`.

Example:

```
[root@nittedal /root]# ./S60lpd start
```

There are several options if you want to stop the spooling system.

You can kill the `lpd` process. You find the PID with the `ps ax | grep lpd` command. When you know the PID, you can use `kill -9` PID.

You can also stop the system from X Window's `printtool`. Additionally, you can use the `stop` option in the script `/etc/rc.d/rc2.d/S60lpd`; for example:

```
[root@nittedal /root]# ./S60lpd stop
```

## 14.9 Remove a spool lock

If you are unable to print, try and remove a spool lock. The lock file, `/var/spool/printer*/printer`, is created automatically to control the queue. You may need to remove a spool lock after a power outage or as a result of an overload in the spooling system. The file lock is automatically deleted when the computer is restarted. This is normally done in the start file, `/etc/rc.d/rc2.d`. (More details on this can be found in Chapter 17.)

## 14.10 Print – lpr

Use the `lpr` command to print. If there are multiple printers in the system, the `P` option (similar to the `d` option in Unix spooling) specifies the desired printer. When no printer is specified, the standard printer is selected. Normally the first page contains the date, time, name of printer, name of print job, etc. This is called the banner. You can skip it by specifying `nobanner`.

**lpr Command – Prints to a Queue**

| | |
|---|---|
| Command | `lpr [option] argument` |
| Function | Places the file in a printer queue. |
| Argument | One or multiple files. |
| Options | See the Linux man pages. |
| `-#copies` | Prints number of copies. |
| `-h` | Prints no banner or front page. |
| `-m` | Sends mail to user when print job is finished. |
| `-p` | Formats document with the `pr` command. |
| `-P printer` | Allocates print job to "printer." |

Examples:

```
[david@nittedal david]$ lpr letter1 letter2 letter3
```

Sends the files `letter1`, `letter2`, and `letter3` to the default printer.

```
[david@nittedal david]$ lpr -P hpprinter2 .profile
```

Sends the `.profile` file to the printer `hpprinter`.

```
[david@nittedal david]$ lpr -P printer1 -m doc1.ps
doc2.ps summary.ps
```

The files `doc1.ps`, `doc2.ps`, and `summary.ps` are sent to printer `printer1`. When the files have been printed, mail is sent to inform the user that the printer has received the print job.

```
[david@nittedal david]$ lpr -#3 order.txt
```

Three copies of the file `order.txt` are printed. The print job is sent to the default printer.

## 14.11 Check a printer queue – lpq

The `lpq` command allows for checking the status of your own and other users' print jobs. Under standard Unix V.4, you can use the `lpstat` command.

**lpq Command – Checks a Printer Queue**

| | |
|---|---|
| Command | `lpq [-l][-P printer][user-id]` |
| Function | Displays status of print jobs. |
| Options | See the Linux man pages. |
| `-L` | Prints detailed information about each file that is placed in a printer queue. |
| `-P printer` | Displays information about each file in a specified printer queue. |
| `user-id` | Displays print jobs for specified users only (when no user option is specified, all print jobs are displayed). |

Examples:

```
[david@nittedal david]$ lpq -L
```

Gives detailed information about all files sent to all printer queues under Linux.

```
[david@nittedal david]$ lpq -P hplaser
```

Gives detailed information about all files sent to printer queue `hplaser`.

```
[david@nittedal david]$ lpq davide
```

Gives detailed information about all files that user `davide` has sent to printer queues under Linux.

## 14.12 Cancel a print job – lprm

Any print job that you have started can be cancelled with the `lprm` command under Linux. (Under standard Unix V.4, use the `cancel` command.) Only the system administrator (root) can cancel print jobs that other users have started.

**lprm Command – Cancels Print Jobs**

| | |
|---|---|
| Command | `lprm [-P printer] [job number] [user-id]` |
| Function | Deletes a print job from the printer queue. |
| Options | See the Linux man pages. |
| `-P printer` | Deletes jobs from the specified queue. |
| `job number` | Lists job numbers to be deleted (use `lpq` to display job number). |
| `user-id` | Displays print jobs for specified users only (without the `user` option, all print jobs are displayed). |

Examples:

```
[david@nittedal david]$ lprm  printer-233
```

Cancels print job `printer-233` from the printer queue (printer).

```
[david@nittedal david]$ lprm -P hplaser hplaser-22
hplaser-24
```

Cancels print jobs `hplaser-22` and `hplaser-24` from printer queue `hplaser`.

```
[david@nittedal david]$ lprm  david
```

Cancels all printer queues associated with the user `david`. If additional jobs are to be removed, remove them from the `/var/spool/printer* requests` directories.

## Exercises for Chapter 14

1. What does spool mean?
2. Print to different print queues (printers).
3. Print two copies of a document without printing a banner.
4. Which option must be selected with the `lpr` if you want to get a message when the print job is finished?
5. Which option must be selected if you don't want a banner?
6. Send a print job to a printer that is turned off. Check the status with the `lpq` command.
7. How can you find the printer that is set as the standard printer (default)?
8. Cancel your own print jobs. Can you stop other users' print jobs?
9. Name a simple way to check that the printer port in a Linux system functions correctly. (Hint: `cat fil > /dev/lp0`)
10. Define two printers in your Linux system. Connect one through the serial port, and connect the other one to the parallel port. If you are running Red Hat Linux, you may use the X Window application `printtool`.
11. How do you start and stop a Linux spooling system?
12. How can you remove a spool lock?

CHAPTER

15

# Integration with DOS, Windows, and Mac

## 15.1 Tools for accessing MS-DOS filesystems

There are many tools available for accessing MS-DOS filesystems under Linux. You may use Mtools, mount MS-DOS filesystems, or use an MS-DOS or Windows emulator for Linux. Linux is easily integrated into Windows with the server software Samba, which makes the Linux box (PC) look like a traditional Windows NT (SMB) file server. As Linux supports the network protocol IPX/SPX, there is also good integration with file and print services in Novell NetWare.

If you have a Mac environment, you will find tools that compare to the Linux Mtools (MS-DOS). These Mac tools are called H-tools ("H" for HFS volumes).

## 15.2 Mounting MS-DOS filesystems

Mounting MS-DOS filesystems is just like mounting Linux systems. This is the procedure:

1. Log on as root (*[root@nittedal /root]#*).
2. Make an empty directory from / (root) with the `mkdir` command.
3. Update the file `/etc/fstab` (device driver program and mount point).
4. Enter the command:

```
[root@nittedal /root]#  mount -a
```

so that the `/etc/fstab` file is read.

Here, I assume that the second partition on your first hard disk drive (`/dev/hda2`) is an MS-DOS filesystem. If you want the filesystem to mount automatically in the `/msdos-c` directory, update your `/etc/fstab` file like this:

| Device Driver Program | Mount Point | Filesystem | Option | DF | flevel |
|---|---|---|---|---|---|
| /dev/hda2 | /msdos-c | msdos | default | 0 | 0 |

Use the vi or emacs editor to make the necessary changes. The first column gives the name of the device driver. The second column contains the directory in which the filesystem will be mounted. The next column gives the type of the filesystem (`msdos`, `linux`). The Option column gives you the freedom to choose how to mount the filesystem. The dump frequency (see the `dump` command) is set in the DF column. This value sets the backup level. When zero is selected, full backup runs the first time the dump program is run. The last column sets the time when the Linux program `fsck` cleans up the new filesystem. The default is 0 (see the `fsck` command).

On my workstation (PC), I have the following `/etc/fstab` file:

```
[root@nittedal /root]#  cat /etc/fstab
/dev/hda5    /            ext2     defaults                 1 1
/dev/cdrom /mnt/cdrom   iso9660 noauto,owner,ro          0 0
/dev/hda6    /usr         ext2     defaults                 1 2
```

```
/dev/hda1    /msdos-c      msdos    uid=0,gid=100,umask=007  0 0
/dev/hda7    swap          swap     defaults                 0 0
/dev/fd0     /mnt/floppy   ext2     noauto,owner             0 0
none         /proc         proc     defaults                 0 0
none         /dev/pts      devpts   gid=5,mode=620           0 0
```

If your Linux system is connected to a backup unit (e.g., tape streamer), this unit can also back up your MS-DOS filesystems when they are mounted. If you have an MS-DOS backup system, you must copy your Linux filesystems to your MS-DOS volume (partition) to back them up.

It is also possible to mount an MS-DOS hard disk or floppy disk volume directly under Linux. For example, if you have an MS-DOS floppy with the control program `/dev/fd0`, you can mount it with this command:

Example:

```
[root@nittedal /root]#  mount -t msdos /dev/fd0 /msdos-a
```

The floppy drive (A) will be mounted under `/msdos-a`.

Example:

```
[root@nittedal /root]#  mount -t msdos /dev/hda2 /msdos-c
```

This mounts the MS-DOS volume (C) under `/msdos-c`.

It is important to unmount partitions (volumes under MS-DOS and filesystems under Linux) when they are not in use.

Example:

```
[root@nittedal /root]#  umount  /msdos-a
[root@nittedal /root]#  umount  /msdos-c
```

This unmounts the MS-DOS volumes. Never be in a filesystem that you want to unmount. No processes must access the filesystems that you are unmounting.

## 15.3 Accessing MS-DOS volumes (partitions)

Mtools is a set of commands that functions like traditional MS-DOS commands. The difference is only the "`m`" preceding the MS-DOS command.

For example, the `mcd`, `mdir`, and `mcopy` commands will function exactly like the equivalent MS-DOS commands, `cd`, `dir`, and `copy`. When installing Mtools, you also install the user manual for these commands.

All Mtools support long filenames (VFAT). The Mtools access the MS-DOS filesystems with the same drive names as MS-DOS. For example, floppy drives are A and B, and hard disk drives are C, D, etc. In Mtools, wildcards function like they do in Linux, i.e., `*.*` under MS-DOS is the same as `*` under Linux. The Mtools will access an MS-DOS file or an MS-DOS directory with the syntax *MS-DOS [drive]* and a colon. The Mtools support low- as well as high-density floppies.

You will find that all Mtools programs use the configuration files `/etc/mtools.conf` and `$HOME/.mtoolsrc`. Check the Linux man pages for a complete description of configuration files on the various Mtools commands.

## 15.4 Change directory – mcd

The `mcd` command changes a directory in the MS-DOS volume. The information will be stored in your home directory, `$HOME/.mcwd`.

**mcd Command – Changes an MS-DOS Directory**

| | |
|---|---|
| Command | `mcd [dos directory]` |
| Function | Moves you to the specified MS-DOS directory. |
| Argument | The name of an MS-DOS directory or an MS-DOS volume. |
| Options | None. |

Example:

```
[david@nittedal david]$ mcd  a:\win32
```

This moves me to the MS-DOS volume A and down to the `\win32` directory.

## 15.5 Copy files – mcopy

The `mcopy` command copies from one MS-DOS volume to another.

**mcopy Command – Copies MS-DOS Files**

| | |
|---|---|
| Command | `mcopy [-m] [-n] [-t] argument1 argument2`<br>or<br>`mcopy [-m] [-n] MS-DOS source file` |
| Function | Copies MS-DOS or Linux files. |
| Argument | Name of an MS-DOS directory/MS-DOS volume. |
| `Argument1` | One or more source files. If using wildcards or multiple files, `Argument2` must be a directory. |
| `Argument2` | Destination file when only one file is copied. Directory when copying multiple files. |
| MS-DOS source file | A file in an MS-DOS volume. `mcopy` copies the file to the current Linux directory. |
| Options | See the Linux man pages. |
| `-m` | Preserves the original date and time attributes of the file. |
| `-n` | Overwrites without asking. |
| -t | Copying text with automatic conversion between MS-DOS and Linux formats. Converts RETURN/newline sequence to newline only. |

Example:

```
[david@nittedal david]$ mcopy a:partno.txt.
```

Copies the file `partno.txt` from the MS-DOS volume (A, or floppy drive) to the current Linux directory.

## 15.6 Delete files – mdel

The `mdel` command deletes one or more files from an MS-DOS volume.

**mdel Command – Deletes Files**

| | |
|---|---|
| Command | `mdel [-v] argument` |
| Function | Deletes one or more files on a MS-DOS media. |

**mdel Command – Deletes Files (*Continued*)**

| | |
|---|---|
| Argument | Name of one or more MS-DOS files. |
| Options | See the Linux man pages. |
| -v | Verbose mode; Linux displays what it does. |

Example:

```
[david@nittedal david]$ mdel c:license.txt
```

Deletes the file `license.txt` from the MS-DOS volume C (hard disk drive).

```
[david@nittedal david]$ mcd a:\codes
```

Moves to the MS-DOS volume A and down to the `\codes` directory.

```
[david@nittedal david]$ mdel a:read.me
```

Deletes the MS-DOS file `read.me` (`A:\codes\read.me`) from the MS-DOS volume A.

## 15.7 Show Directory information – mdir

The `mdir` command works like the MS-DOS command `DIR`, i.e., it gives information about a specified MS-DOS directory.

**mdir Command – Displays MS-DOS Directory**

| | |
|---|---|
| Command | `mdir [-w] argument1`<br>or<br>`mdir [-a] [-w] argument2` |
| Function | Gives information about a specified MS-DOS directory. |
| Argument | Name of an MS-DOS directory or a MS-DOS volume. |
| `Argument1` | Name of an MS-DOS directory. |
| `Argument2` | MS-DOS filenames with or without wildcards. |
| Options | See the Linux man pages. |
| -a | Includes hidden files in the list. |

**mdir Command – Displays MS-DOS Directory (*Continued*)**

| | |
|---|---|
| -w | Multiple columns; lists all filenames without size and date information. |

Example:

```
[david@nittedal david]$ mdir a:
```

Displays information about the floppy drive (A).

## 15.8 Display information about boot sector – minfo

The `minfo` command displays boot sector information about the MS-DOS volume on the hard disk drive or floppy disk.

**minfo Command – Shows Information about MS-DOS Boot Sector**

| | |
|---|---|
| Command | `minfo [-v] argument` |
| Function | Gives boot sector information. |
| Argument | Any logical MS-DOS drive (A-Z). |
| Options | See the Linux man pages. |
| -v | Gives a complete hexadecimal dump of the boot sector. |

Example:

```
[david@nittedal david]$ minfo a:
```

Gives boot sector information for the floppy volume on A.

## 15.9 Make MS-DOS directories – mmd

With the `mmd` command, you can make MS-DOS directories on an MS-DOS volume.

**mmd Command – Makes MS-DOS Directories**

| | |
|---|---|
| Command | `mmd argument` |
| Function | Makes an MS-DOS directory. |
| Argument | Name of directory. |
| Options | See the Linux man pages. |

Example:

```
[david@nittedal david]$ mmd a:data-dir
```

This makes the directory `data-dir` in volume A (floppy drive).

## 15.10 File to screen – mtype

The `mtype` command displays the contents of a text file on-screen. You may use options to convert data.

**mtype Command – Displays Files On-Screen**

| | |
|---|---|
| Command | `mtype [-t] argument` |
| Function | Displays contents of a text file. |
| Argument | Any MS-DOS text file. |
| Options | See the Linux man pages. |
| -t | Converts return/newline sequence to newline only. |

Example:

```
[david@nittedal david]$ mtype -t c:read.me | more
```

Displays the contents of the MS-DOS file `read.me`. The file is converted from MS-DOS format to Linux (Unix) format.

## 15.11 Different Mtools

Here you'll find other popular Mtools:

| Command | Function |
|---|---|
| `matttrib` | Sets or removes attribute bits. |
| `mbadblocks` | Scans for bad blocks. |
| `mdeltree` | Deletes a directory tree structure. |
| `mformat` | Formats an MS-DOS volume (partition). |
| `mkmanifest` | Makes a Linux script to handle problems with name conventions in MS-DOS. (8-character filenames and 3-character suffixes) |
| `mlabel` | Defines the volume label on an MS-DOS partition. |
| `mmount` | Mounts an MS-DOS filesystem. |
| `mmove` | Changes the name of a file or directory. |
| `mpartition` | Makes an MS-DOS partition. |
| `mrd` | Removes an MS-DOS directory. |
| `mren` | Changes the name of an MS-DOS file or directory. |
| `mtoolstest` | Tests your Mtools configuration. |

## 15.12 Accessing Mac volumes

As a parallel to the "`m`"commands for accessing MS-DOS volumes, Linux uses "`h`" commands to access Mac "partions," i.e., HFS volumes. The difference is that you must mount Mac media with the `hmount` command. Afterward, the volume is unmounted with the `hunmount` command.

In the Mac world, RETURN is used to separate the lines of a text file. Linux and Unix use the newline character. If you get into trouble with the file formats, you may use the Linux command `sed` or `tr` to replace characters. When converting a Mac file to Linux, do the following:

Example:

```
[david@nittedal david]$ tr '\015' '\012' < mac_text >
linux_text
```

This replaces the return code (`015;octal`) with newline (`012;octal`) throughout the document.

## 15.13 Mount Mac volumes – hmount

With the `hmount` command, Mac volumes can be mounted. The mounted volumes can be accessed with the "`h`" commands.

**hmount Command – Mounts Mac Volumes**

| | |
|---|---|
| Command | `hmount argument volume (partition)` |
| Function | Mounts Mac volumes. |
| Argument | Linux search path to a block control program or a regular file that represents the HFS volume. |
| Partition | Represents the part of the volume (partition) that you want to mount. |
| Options | See the Linux man pages. |

## 15.14 Unmount Mac volumes – hunmount

The `hunmount` command unmounts Mac volumes.

**hunmount Command – Unmounts Mac Volumes**

| | |
|---|---|
| Command | `humount argument` |
| Function | Unmounts Mac volumes. |
| Argument | Volume name or path to HFS volume to be unmounted. |
| Options | See the Linux man pages. |

## 15.15 Different "h" commands – HFS

After mounting the Mac volumes that you want access to, you can use many different "h" commands. Below you'll find a list of the most important ones:

| Command | Function |
|---|---|
| hcd | Changes active directory in Mac volume. |
| hcopy | Copies files between Mac volumes and Linux system. |
| hdel | Deletes one or more files from a Mac directory |
| hdir | Lists files in a Mac directory. |
| hmkdir | Makes new directory in current Mac volume. |
| hattrib | Changes file or directory attributes. |
| hformat | Makes a new HFS filesystem. |
| hfs | Gives a shell for accessing HFS volumes. |
| hls | Lists all files in the HFS directory. |
| hpwd | Displays the working directory in the HFS volume. |
| hrename | Changes the names of files or directories in the HFS volume. |
| hrmdir | Removes an empty directory in the HFS volume. |
| hvol | Displays changes in an active HFS volume. |
| xhfs | Gives a GUI to HFS commands. |

## 15.16 MS-DOS and Windows emulators

When using an MS-DOS emulator under Linux, you will find that not all MS-DOS applications will run. The MS-DOS emulator is primarily a solution for anyone who only needs access to MS-DOS occasionally. The performance of an MS-DOS emulator under Linux is far too limited, in particular when only native 8088 mode is supported.

MS-DOS applications that run with the MS-DOS-emulator under Linux include Microsoft Windows 3.0 (in real mode), cc-mail (DOS-based), Foxpro 2.0, Harvard Graphics, MathCad, Turbo Pascal, and WordPerfect 5.1, MS-DOS commands, and standard DOS tools. The following MS-DOS emulator tools are available for Linux:

- **dos** or **dosemu.**
- **xdos.**
- **dosexec.**
- **dosdebug.**

Only xdos (see Figure 15-1) is X Window-based; the other emulators are run directly from the character-based terminal prompt. If you want to run the DOS emulator under Red Hat Linux, you will have to install the Red Hat PowerTools CD.

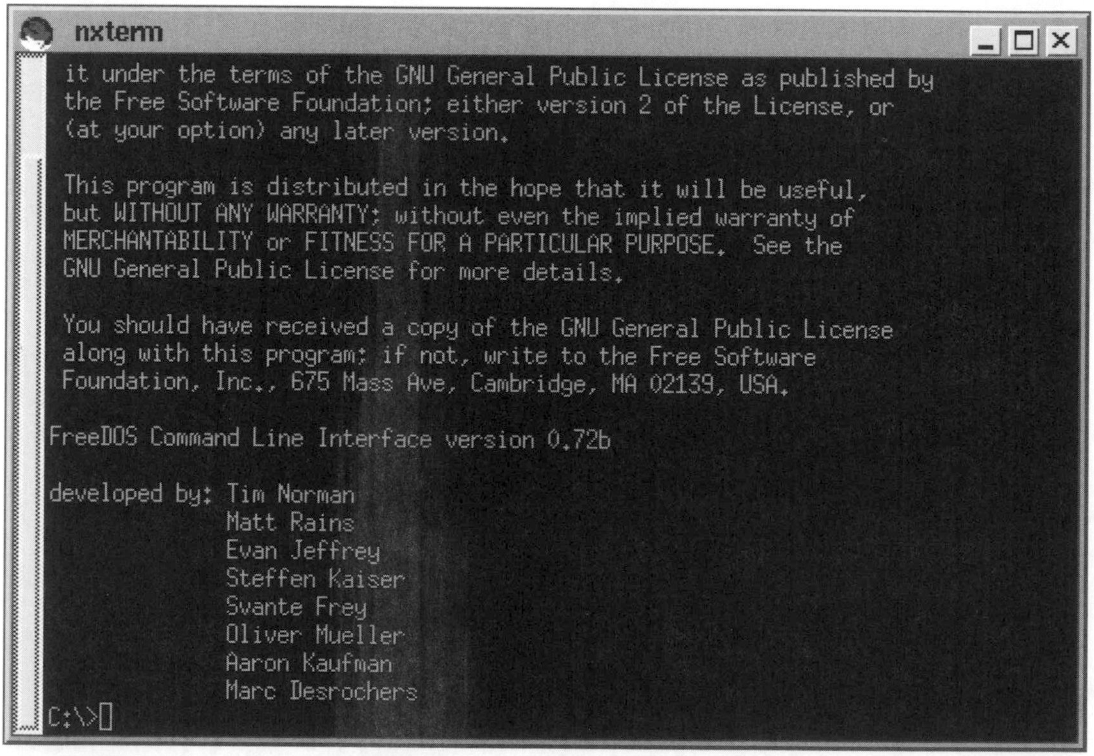

**Figure 15-1**
*Running an MS-DOS emulator under Linux.*

The WINE program, which is a Microsoft Windows API emulator for the X Window system, is based on the same technology as Sunsoft's WABI emulator. WINE will make it possible to run Windows applications directly from Linux.

You can download WINE from http://www.winehq.com.

An alternative Windows emulator is WABI, which can be downloaded from http://wabiapps.psgroup.com.

To run WINE and WABI, the system must have a minimum of 48MB RAM ( 64MB RAM is recommended) and a swap area of at least 20MB. You should reserve 25MB of hard disk space for the WABI application.

WINE as well as WABI make it possible to run many Windows 3.1 applications and some 32-bit applications for Windows 95/98/2000. But that's enough about MS-DOS and Windows; this is a Linux book!

## Exercises for Chapter 15

1. What are the names of the device drivers for accessing filesystems (hard disk and floppy) that are used under MS-DOS and Linux?
2. How can you make your Linux machine automatically mount your MS-DOS partitions as you boot your machine?
3. How do you manually mount and unmount MS-DOS filesystems?
4. Which Linux command would you use to look at the contents of a text file on an MS-DOS floppy?
5. Copy the Linux system files `/etc/passwd` and `/etc/group` to an MS-DOS floppy.
6. Copy the MS-DOS files `CONFIG.SYS` and `AUTOEXEC.BAT` from an MS-DOS floppy to your Linux user area.
7. Name two ways of looking at the directory information in an MS-DOS partition. What is the difference between the two methods?
8. Is it possible to make and remove subdirectories in an MS-DOS partition from Linux?
9. Try and remove a file from a MS-DOS partition by using an "`m`" command (Mtools).

CHAPTER
16

# Bash Shell Programming

## 16.1 Command files

The shell is a command interpreter that interprets all commands that you enter at the system prompt. The commands are executed interactively, i.e., command by command.

It is also possible to execute programs that consist of several commands in sequence. A command file consisting of multiple Linux commands is used for this purpose. You can use the vi or emacs text editors to make command files (see Chapter 12).

Command files are also called batch files. In addition to the normal Linux commands, a batch file may contain control structures, variables, and arguments. There is little difference between using traditional programming languages and making command files. Like programming tools, shells have different control structures, variables, and arguments.

The most widely used shells under Linux are:

- Bourne Again shell (bash).
- T shell (tcsh).
- Z shell (zsh).

But Linux also supports these shells:

- Bourne shell (sh).
- C shell (csh).
- Korn shell (ksh).

These three shells are standard parts of Unix V.4. Under most Unix systems, the Bourne shell is called `/bin/sh`. This shell has a BASIC-like syntax. The C shell uses a different syntax that is a bit similar to the C programming language. In most Unix systems, the name is `/bin/csh`. The korn and bash shells are extensions of the Bourne shell and have many of the advanced features that are found in zsh. The korn and bash shells support a superset of the Bourne shell syntax. Z shell is a superset of ksh with many improved functions. For those who prefer using C shell syntax, it is useful to know that Linux supports tcsh, which is an extended version of the original C shell.

The Bourne and C shells are not included in Linux by default, but can be downloaded for free from several web sites (see Chapter 26).

Tcsh and zsh should be preferred if you want an interactive shell. Tcsh and zsh accept most of the Bourne syntax. Most of the control structures like `if`, `for`, `while`, and `case` have their own syntax under these shells.

The following factors will affect your choice of shell:

- Should the script be portable (to other Unix systems)?
- What needs to be done? Program development or pure batch jobs?
- What is simplest for you?
- Personal preferences.

Most users prefer the Bourne shell syntax with advanced features from bash or ksh. As both support a superset of the Bourne syntax, most shell scripts that are written with the standard Bourne shell will work with bash or ksh.

The Bourne shell is the most widely used, and is recommended if you are developing command files (batch files) to be used in other Unix systems. In Linux, the system administrator (root) is set up with the bash shell.

This chapter focuses on Bourne shell (sh) syntax, as bash as well as ksh are downward-compatible with this. In the rest of this chapter, I'll write "bash" rather than "bash shell," as this is the name used in the Linux world. All command files described in this chapter will work under bash. Command files that use the option -n with the echo command will not work under Bourne shell (sh). You will find that the screen handling is somewhat different between sh and bash. But most of the command files in this chapter also will work under sh.

## 16.2 Making simple command files

I have created a command file named `test`. It contains several shell commands which I could execute statement after statement from the command prompt.

```
#!/bin/bash
# Cake program
food="cakes"
echo "Do you eat $food"
echo 'Do you eat $food'
```

The first line means that we have a bash command file.

# is used to include comments in your command file. Be aware of the following: When a file starts with #, it is considered a tcsh command file. We therefore include `!/bin/bash` after the # character. With this included, there is no doubt that this is a bash command file.

In the third line, we assign the variable `cakes` to the text string `food`. We may, at any time in the program, assign a variable. If you are going to use the variables later on, specify `$` prefixed to the variable.

In the fourth and fifth lines, we use the `echo` command. `echo` sends strings of text to the screen. At the fourth line, we use double quotation marks, both at the left and the right side of a text string. This means that the contents of the variable are displayed on the screen. At the fifth line, we use single quotation marks. All of it then is interpreted as a string of text, and the contents of the variable are not displayed on the screen. This is also used in connection with wildcards (Chapter 6).

### 16.2.1 Writing a Command File

To be able to create a command (batch) file, you have to know how to create a text file. You may do this by using the `cat` command.

```
[david@nittedal david]$ cat > file
```

If you are going to create larger command files, it is best to use an editor. You may use vi (Chapter 12) or any word processing system that is able to store files in pure text formats (ASCII), without any text or control codes.

### 16.2.2 Executing Command Files

Here, we are going to show examples of command files and their results. The first batch file, `textsend`, sends a message to another user (terminal):

```
#!/bin/bash
echo "Hello there" > /dev/pts/0
```

The text string "`Hello there`" is sent to the terminal using the device driver `/dev/pts/0`.

I make the file an executable by:

```
[david@nittedal david]$ chmod u+x textsend
```

I then start execution of the command file by:

```
[david@nittedal david]$ textsend
```

The command file `diskuse`:

```
#!/bin/bash
echo " Utilisation of disk"
du /home/delboth
```

Here, you get the utilization of blocks in the directory `/home/delboth`.

The command file `sendterm`:

```
#!/bin/bash
sh | tee /dev/pts/1
```

Here, I send the picture of my terminal to the terminal using the device `/dev/pts/1` (virtual terminal on the PC). You can find out more about the `tee` command by using the Linux `man` command (*[david@nittedal david]$* **man tee**).

The command file `sendout`:

```
#!/bin/bash
cu   -ltty1a   -s9600 dir
```

Sends out a terminal polling to the serial port. You can find out more about the `cu` command by using the Linux `man` command (*[david@nittedal david]$* **man cu**).

The command file `listsort`:

```
#!/bin/bash
ls /bin | sort
```

The command file checks the files in the directory `/bin` and sorts the content (more about the `sort` command in Chapter 13).

The command file `fcount`:

```
#!/bin/bash
ls   -l | sed 1d | wc   -l
```

Here, I count the number of files in the local directory.

## 16.3 Variables

Variables are storage areas for data. The content (data) of a variable can be changed.

There are four ways of defining shell variables:

- Normal allocation.
- Position parameters.
- Allocation of position parameters.
- Reading with the read command.

You can decide for yourself which contents the variables are going to get.

The name of a variable cannot start with a digit, nor can it include any special characters (see Chapters 6 and 7).

### 16.3.1 Normal Definition of Variables

We can allocate temporary variables and environment variables. Environment variables are permanent, but the values may be changed.

Temporary variables become created when needed. With the help of the equals sign, we can do an allocation.

Examples of temporary variables:

```
computer=DellPentum
number=3.14
food=cheese
price=12
directory=/home/delboth/c-files
homedirectory='pwd'
```

(See Section 16.6.5, "Commands in Variables.")

If a zero value is wanted, enter:

```
[david@nittedal david]$ percentage=
```

You may use a variable by prefixing $ it. If you wish to know the contents of a variable, you only write to the screen with the echo command; for example:

```
[david@nittedal david]$ echo $price
[david@nittedal david]$ echo $homedirectory
[david@nittedal david]$ cp prog.c $directory
```

Here, we used a variable in connection with a command for copying.

Variables consisting of control characters or shell commands must be ringed in with single quotations; for example:

```
[david@nittedal david]$ todaysdate='date'

[david@nittedal david]$ user='who | wc  -l'
```

If a variable contains an apostrophe, it must be ringed in with double quotations; for example:

```
[david@nittedal david]$ text="Several PC's are sold"
```

If a variable contains quotations, it must be ringed with extra quotations; for example:

```
[david@nittedal david]$ text=""Hello there""
```

Environment variables (system variables) are always written with capital letters. They are recognized because they are associated with your own environment.

Examples of bash environment variables are `HOME`, `PATH`, and `PS1`. The special shell variable `PATH` controls which of the programs are being executed. `PATH` tells something about the search path for the shell interpreter. Without the `PATH` command, it will only be possible for you to run those programs and commands placed within your local directory. The environment variables can be used in the same way as the temporary variables. Try with `$HOME`:

```
[david@nittedal david]$ echo $HOME
```

You now get your home directory displayed on the screen.

#### Important Bash System (also Bourne Shell) Variables

| | |
|---|---|
| `PATH` | A list of directories which may be searched by the command interpreter. The directories are searched in the sequence set up in `PATH`. |
| `LOGNAME` | Your username (login name). |
| `TERM` | When you see the terminal type displayed on the screen, Linux has used the TERM variable to define the terminal type. Several types of terminals exist. The most used ones are `ansi`, `at386`, `vt52`, `vt100`, `vt220`, and `xterm`. Most programs have to know which type of terminal is being used. |
| `HOME` | The name of the user's home directory |
| `MAIL` | The name of the user's electronic mailbox, usually placed under `/usr/spool/mail`. The `MAIL` variable is normally used to change the path and filename for the mailbox. |
| `MAILCHECK` | This parameter specifies how often (in seconds) the mail should be checked. |

**Important Bash System (also Bourne Shell) Variables (*Continued*)**

| | |
|---|---|
| `PS1` | In bash, this variable defines your prompt. The standard value for the prompt of a bash user is the `$` character. For a tcsh user, it is `%`. |
| `PS2` | A secondary prompt. You will see this prompt when your shell is expecting more input. The `PS2` prompt is also used in connection with command lines larger than 80 characters. The `PS1` prompt is shown at the first line, while the `PS2` prompt shows the continuation of the line. |
| `IFS` | Decides which variable is going to be the field separator. |

**Important tcsh System Variables**

| | |
|---|---|
| `alias` | Definition of aliases, i.e., you may define different names of commands. |
| `history` | Remembers all the commands. If you simply enter `history`, you will get a list of already executed commands. |
| `rehash` | Builds a new hash table, i.e., makes an update of the files that are contained in your tree structure. |
| `cdpath` | Search path for a user. |
| `ignoreof` | Prohibits logout by <Ctrl>-d. |
| `noclobber` | Prohibits overwriting existing files. |
| `home` | Name of the user's home directory. |

### *16.3.2 Allocation of Position Parameters*

When a command file is executed, the shell allocates position parameters. `$0` contains the name of the command; `$1` is the first argument, `$2` the second, etc. up to `$9`.

If you are starting a batch file with an argument, the name of the command file becomes position parameter `$0`, and the argument becomes `$1`. If you have different arguments each time you run a command file, the content in `$1` will be different.

An example of a batch file with four arguments:

```
[david@nittedal david]$ start a b c d
```

Here, `$0` is assigned to the batch file `start`, `$1` is assigned to `a`, `$2` to `b`, `$3` to `c`, and `$4` to `d`.

You may also assign values of position parameters directly by using the `set` command; for example:

```
[david@nittedal david]$ set Prentice Hall Best on IT
```

Here, `$1` will be assigned to the text string `Prentice`, `$2` to the text string `Hall`, `$3` to the text string `Best`, `$4` to the text string `on`, and `$5` to the text string `IT`.

If you try with:

```
[david@nittedal david]$ echo "$3, $4, $5, $1, $2"
```

You get:

```
Best on IT Prentice Hall
```

If you try with:

```
[david@nittedal david]$ set A B C
```

You get the parameters by writing:

```
[david@nittedal david]$ echo "$1 $2 $3"
A B C
```

### 16.3.3 Predefined Variables

We also have predefined variables. These may be included in command files to construct various tests in different control structures.

**Predefined Variables**

| | |
|---|---|
| `$#` | Gives the number of arguments included in a command line. If we have the command `test A B C`, `$#` gets the value `3`. |
| `$?` | Gives the status for the last command executed. If the command was free of syntax errors, the value is set to zero. |
| `$n` | The argument of the command. May have values from 1 to 9 (see Section 16.3.2). |
| `$*` | Gives all the arguments. |
| `$$` | Gives the process number of the current process. |
| `$!` | Gives the process number of the last background process. |
| `$` | Gives a list of execution flags being used. |

Predefined variables come as an addition to position parameters.

Here is a simple bash script, which prints out all its arguments:

```
#!/bin/bash
for arg in $*
do
  echo Argument $arg
done
```

The total number of arguments is `$#`. The `$*` symbol gives us the entire list of arguments.

The following is a two-line command file, `number`:

```
#!/bin/bash
echo $#
```

The command file starts with `#!/bin/bash` to indicate that it is a bash shell. The character `$#` gives us the `number` of arguments. Try to run the command file, `number`, using the arguments `a`, `b`, `c`, and `d`:

```
[david@nittedal david]$ number a b c d
4
```

$0 is now the name of the command (number). $1 is a, $2 is b, etc. $1 to $9 vary for each time number is run.

The command file where:

```
#!/bin/bash
who | grep $1
```

An example using the where script:

```
[david@nittedal david]$ where jane
```

jane must be a defined user working on the Linux system.

The command file variable:

```
#!/bin/bash
echo Number of arguments is $#.
date &
echo Process id from the date command was $!.
wait
echo Process id for this shell is $$.
grep vt100 /etc/ttytype
echo The return-code from grep was $?.
echo I had the following set options $-.
```

Here, I have a command file where all the predefined variables are used. Note that there is no use of double quotations. If you write echo with double quotations, the result will be the same. You may write echo The number of arguments is $#, or you could write echo "Number of arguments is $#.".

An example using the command file variable:

```
[david@nittedal david]$ bash  x variable A B > testfile
+ Number of arguments is 2.
+ date
+ echo Process id from the date command was 1155.
+ wait
+ echo Process id for this shell is 1154.
+ grep vt100 /etc/ttytype
+ echo The return-code from grep was 1.
+ echo We had the following set of options x.
```

More information about execution flags can be found in Section 16.8.2.

### *16.3.4 Variables with the read Command*

With the help of the `read` command, we can read a whole line. If you are using `read` in a program file, the shell will be reading from the default input and placing it into the variable.

Example:

```
#!/bin/bash
clear
echo "Hello!"
echo "What is your name? "
read answer
echo "Fine to meet you $answer"
```

In this example, the shell will place input from the user into the variable `answer` and display the text.

## 16.4 Handling screen output

While redirecting default output, you can decide where to place the results from a command file. The default output may be sent to a terminal, a printer, or a file. You can find out more information about redirecting default input and output in Chapter 8.

If you are using the `echo` command, the argument is separated by a space and terminated by a line feed. The `echo` command under bash also understands special codes, including the following:

`-n` Does not output a trailing newline.

`-e` Enables interpretation of the Backslash-escaped characters, which are listed below. `-E` disables interpretation of these sequences in strings. Without `-E`, the following sequences are recognized and interpolated:

`'\a'` Alert (bell).

`'\b'` Backspace.

`'\c'` Suppress trailing newline.

| | |
|---|---|
| `'\f'` | Form feed. |
| `'\n'` | Newline. |
| `'\r'` | Carriage return. |
| `'\t'` | Horizontal tab. |
| `'\v'` | Vertical tab. |
| `'\\'` | Backslash. |
| `'\NNN'` | A character whose ASCII code is NNN (octal). |

Example:

```
[david@nittedal david]$ echo -e '\a'
```

Sounds a bell from the terminal.

```
[david@nittedal david]$ echo -e '\v'
```

Gives a vertical tab.

```
[david@nittedal david]$ echo -e '\111'
```

Gives you a big "I" on the screen.

If you wish to have a larger number of terminal codes, use the `tput` command:
Syntax: ***tput termcode***

| termcode | Function |
|---|---|
| clear | Clears the screen for the current terminal. |
| cols | Prints the number of columns for the current terminal. |
| bel | Gives bell sound from the terminal. |
| blink | Blinks. |
| dim | Dims the terminal screen. |
| smul | Starts underline. |
| rmul | Stops underline. |
| sgr0 | Turns off all codes. |

Example:

```
[david@nittedal david]$ tput dim
```

Reduces the power of the light on the screen.

```
[david@nittedal david]$ tput clear
```

Clears the screen.

```
[david@nittedal david]$ tput sqr0
```

Turns off all the codes.

```
[david@nittedal david]$  echo "`tput smul` "This is a
text with underline `tput rmul`"
```

Displays text with underline.
See also Chapter 5 (echo).

### 16.4.1 Examples of Variables and Screen Handling

The command file info:

```
#!/bin/bash
echo -n "Todays date and time     :  "
date
echo  -n "Number of users          :  "
who | wc  -l
echo  -n "My personal status       :  "
whoami
```

First, the command file info gives today's date and time, the number of users, and my personal status. Text is first displayed on the screen with the echo command. The option -n prohibits a line feed. The result of the date command is placed on the same line.

The command file `info1`:

```
#!/bin/bash
TIME="Todays date and time  :  "
USER="Number of users       :  "
ME="Personal status         :  "
echo -n "$TIME"
date
echo -n "$USER"
who | wc  -l
echo -n "$ME"
whoami
```

The command file `info1` does exactly the same as `info`, but now we first define three text variables. These variables are reused later by the `echo` commands.

## 16.5 Conditional commands

The Linux programming language has logical control structures. We will go through the most important ones here. Syntax is based on the bash shell. In tcsh, the principles are similar, but the syntax is somewhat different. If you want to program under tcsh, refer to a Linux reference book or handbook.

The shell often makes use of arguments in a loop and executes conditional commands for each argument. Bash has effective aids for controlling flow. For example, `for`, `case`, and `while` may be used.

Commands can either be written directly to the screen or executed in a command file.

### *16.5.1 The test Command*

The `test` command returns an initial status. This value may be used in connection with conditional commands. The `test` command is only to be used from command files.

Example:

```
test  -f file
```

Returns an initial status of zero (true) if the file exists, and an initial status other than zero (false) if the file does not exist. Here are some of the arguments you may use:

| | |
|---|---|
| `test -s file` | True if file is created and not empty. |
| `test -f file` | True if file exists and is normal. |
| `test -r file` | True if file can be read. |
| `test -w file` | True if file can be written to. |
| `test -x file` | True if file exists and can be executed. |
| `test -d file` | True if file is a directory. |
| `test -n s1` | True if length of the string (`s1`) is other than zero. |
| `test -z s1` | True if length of the string (`s1`) is equal to zero. |
| `test s1 = s2` | True if `string1` and `string2` are equal. |
| `test s1! = s2` | True if `string1` and `string2` are unequal. |
| `test s1` | True if `s1` is not a zero string. |
| `test n1 -eq n2` | True if integers `n1` and `n2` are equal. |
| `test n1 -ne n2` | True if integers `n1` and `n2` are unequal. |
| `test n1 -gt n2` | True if integer `n1` is bigger than `n2`. |
| `test n1 -ge n2` | True if integer `n1` is bigger than or equal to `n2`. |
| `test n1 -lt n2` | True if integer `n1` is less than `n2` . |
| `test n1 -le n2` | True if integer `n1` is less than or equal to `n2` . |

We can also combine `test` with other operators; for example, position parameters (Section 6.3.2) and/or the `expr` function (Section 16.7.1).

Try the example `checkpass`:

```
#!/bin/bash
if test $#=0
then echo "You have to write a username!"
else grep $1 /etc/passwd
fi
```

We have, in our example, used the `if` structure. Read more about this in Section 16.5.4. We have also used `test` and the position parameter **`$#`**. **`checkpass`** examines if any arguments are specified. If no arguments are specified, the echo string is sent to the screen. If an argument is specified, it will be searched for in /etc/passwd.

### 16.5.2 for Looping

With the for command, you can execute many operations on each file, or you can execute a command with several arguments. The general notation for a for loop is:

```
for variable in word-list
do
command-list
done
```

Here, word-list may be a list of variables separated by blanks. The command-list is executed once for each word in word-list. Try the example printoutnumber:

```
#!/bin/bash
for i in `ls`
do
pr  -f $i | lpr;
done
```

Here, we do a printout of all the files in the current directory. word-list here is the ls command, giving us all the files in the directory where the command file is started. Each single file is placed in $i, formatted by the pr command, and then sent to the printer. pr is a formatting command for Linux.

If word-list is left out, you can use the same command for all arguments. If you do not use word-list, certain position parameters are utilized as arguments.

The command file checkif:

```
#!/bin/bash
for i
do grep $i *.c
done
```

Now try:

```
[david@nittedal david]$ checkif `hash(`insert`
```

All C files ending with .c in the current directory are checked for the text string hash(`insert.

### 16.5.3 The case Condition

The case notation makes it possible to jump to various locations in a program. You will find a similar command in all modern programming languages. The general syntax is:

```
case word in
pattern1) commandlist1;;
pattern2) commandlist2;;
...
...
esac
```

The command file tries to compare word against all the patterns in the case statement. This is done until it finds a word identical to a pattern. If word is identical to pattern1, commandlist1 will be executed. If word is identical to pattern2, commandlist2 will be executed, etc. If word is not identical to any of the patterns, no commandlist will be executed.

;; Functions as a terminator of the case loop.

;; Terminates each commandlist.

Only one single pattern needs to be identical to word. We then jump out of the loop and check for patterns that are not executed. esac marks the end of the case block.

We call the following example casechoice:

```
#!/bin/bash
case $1 in
      1) who;;
      2) finger;;
      3) whoami;;
      0) exit;;
esac
```

Here, the case loop uses the first position parameter ($1) as a variable. To try this, you may, for example, write:

```
[david@nittedal david]$ casechoice 3
```

The whoami command is executed.

The word variable can only be identical to one single pattern. If * is the first pattern, the string hits exactly there, and nowhere else.

```
case $i in
       *.c) cc $i
            ;;
       *.h | *.sh)
            echo "Please, relax"
            ;;
       *)   echo "$i unknown type"
            ;;
esac
```

Here, we have an example of several alternative patterns.

The various alternatives are separated by the connecting command. Read more about this in Section 16.7.

### 16.5.4 The if Condition

The shell provides a structured conditional capability with the if command. The simplest if command has the following syntax:

```
if command-list
then command-list
fi
```

The command or list of commands following if is executed. In most cases, this will be a test. If the result is true (0=true), the command or list of commands following will then be executed. fi is the end of the if test.

If you want to execute commands when an if test is untrue, make use of the else statement.

```
if commandolist
then commandolist
else commandolist
fi
```

Here's an example called checkpass:

```
#!/bin/bash
for i
do
      if grep $i /etc/passwd
      then
            echo "$i is defined in /etc/passwd"
      else
            echo "$i is not defined in /etc/passwd"
      fi
done
```

Example:

```
[david@nittedal david]$ checkpass david
david:*:200:100:Tech. Writer:/home/david:/bin/bash
david is defined in /etc/passwd
```

The command file filex:

```
#!/bin/bash
for FILE
do
echo $FILE is:
if test  -r "$FILE"; then
      echo " readable,"
fi
if test  -w "$FILE"; then
      echo " writeable,"
fi
if test  -f "$FILE"; then
      echo " a normal file,"
fi
if test  -d "$FILE"; then
      echo " a directory,"
fi
if test  -s "$FILE"; then
      echo " and consists of more than 0 characters."
else
      echo " and consists of 0 characters."
fi
done
exit 0
```

filex checks which type of file you have. The example also illustrates how important the test routine is.

The command file passgroup:

```
#!/bin/bash
BB=/dev/null
for NAME in $@; do
      if grep $NAME /etc/passwd > $BB 2>$BB; then
            echo $NAME is found in file password
      else
            if grep $NAME /etc/group >$BB 2>$BB; then
                              echo $NAME is found in file
group
            else
                              echo $NAME is either found in
                              echo file password or group
            fi
      fi
done
```

The command file passgroup expects a username. If the username is found in /etc/passwd or /etc/group, it will display a message about it. The BB variable is first defined as /dev/null. This means that BB is the same as a device driver sending data to nothing. Several if structures are used to find out if the username only exists in /etc/passwd, /etc/group, or in both files.

### 16.5.5 The while Loop

while is used to make loops. It has the following syntax:

```
while command-list1
do
      command-list2
done
```

The commands in the command list (command-list1) are executed as long as the command list is true (status=0). If the exit status of the last command in the command list is zero (status=0), then the commands in the second command list (command-list2) are executed. This sequence is repeated as long as the exit status of the first command list is zero (status=0). A loop will only be executed as long as the first command-list returns a nonzero status.

The command file `readable`:

```
#!/bin/bash
while test  -r *
do
      ls  -la *
done
```

Lists all the readable files.

The following example is named `copypair`:

```
#!/bin/bash
while test "$2" != ""; do
      cp $1 $2
      shift; shift
done
if test "$1" != ""; then
      echo "$0: unequal number of arguments!"
fi
```

The command file `copypair` copies to pairs of files. This command file uses the shell command `shift`, which is described in Section 16.6.1.

Example:

```
[david@nittedal david]$ copypair file1 file2 file3 file4
```

Copies `file1` to `file2`, and `file3` to `file4`.

### *16.5.6 The until Loop*

A `while` loop loops as long as the command list is true (status=0). An `until` loop only executes as long as the command list is untrue. When the command list is true (status=0), the program jumps out of the loop.

The following example is named `until.test`:

```
until test  -f datafil
do
      sleep 1000
done
```

The structure goes in a loop until a data file is created. We do a test for each 1000 units of time, which is about once every 500 seconds.

## 16.6 More commands

### 16.6.1 Position Parameters and the shift Command

When a command file is started, the shell automatically creates the position parameters. The name of the command file itself gets the variable `$0`, while the first argument is set to `$1`, the next to `$2`, etc., until `$9`. We have a limitation of nine position parameters. With the `shift` command, we can overcome this limitation. The `shift` command moves the arguments one position to the left.

The value belonging to `$1` is then thrown away. `$1` gets the contents that were placed in `$2` earlier, and `$2` gets the contents earlier placed in `$3`, etc.

The command file `echoshift`:

```
#!/bin/bash
while test $# !=0
do
        echo $1 $2 $3 $4 $5 $6 $7 $8 $9
        shift
done
```

Each time we loop one more time in the `while` loop, we also move one position to the left. Example with the command file `echoshift`:

*[david@nittedal david]$* **echoshift a b c**

```
a b c
b c
c
```

The following command file may be used to read 12 names:

```
#!/bin/bash
countvar=1
while test $countvar  -le 12
do
        echo "Name : $1"
        shift
done
```

Note: You can force the position parameters into variables `$1` to `$9` by using the `set` command.

### 16.6.2 The break and continue Commands

With the help of the `break` command, you can interrupt a `for` or `while` loop. To jump out of a loop, only for the present turn, you can use the `continue` command. Both `break` and `continue` are used between the `do` and `done` commands.

If you have several loops inside each other, `break` will only terminate the innermost loop. To exit from more than this loop, you can use `break n`, where `n` is the level of the loop. Because `continue` only has influence in the innermost loop, you must use `continue n` to interrupt several loops.

```
while true
do
        echo "Enter data"
        read indata
        case "$indata" in
        "done")    break
                ;;
        "")
                continue
                ;;
        *)
                echo "Hello"
                ;;
        esac
done
```

`while true` is a loop that is going on forever. If you enter the text `break`, the program exits the loop structure. If you press the RETURN key only, the program jumps to the beginning of the loop and `indata` is read again. If you enter your name or anything else, the text `hello` is displayed.

### 16.6.3 The exit Command

With the `exit` command, it is possible to send positive or negative messages. The status value 0 (zero) is given after the error-free execution of a command. Otherwise, the status value becomes a number other than zero.

Exit codes can be used for communication between the shells. The `exit` command simulates the termination of a command file. Therefore, a command file can be terminated normally by placing `exit 0` as the last statement in the file.

Description of exit codes:

0—Error-free execution.

1—Error in the command.

2—Error in the syntax.

3—Does not contact the interrupting signal.

Examples:

```
if test $#  -lt 2
then
      echo "We need two or more arguments";exit 0
fi
```

We make a test of the number of arguments the user has written. If the user has specified less than two arguments, the program jumps out with `exit`.

```
if grep $var orderlist
then
      exit 0
else
      echo "Was not inside the orderlist"
      exit 1
fi
```

We have a test which gives either a positive or negative message.

### 16.6.4 Grouping Commands

Within a shell, there are two different ways to group commands:

- By the use of normal parentheses, ( and ). With these, you create a sub-shell that reads the group of commands. The left and right parentheses can be placed freely at the line.
- With the help of { and }. No sub-shell is created, but the commands are read directly from the shell. We use grouping with { and } when default output is going to be used as default input to a command. { and } are only accepted if { is placed as the first character of the command line.

Example:

```
[david@nittedal david]$ (date; who | wc  -l) >> datafile
```

At first, the date command is executed. Thereafter, we count the number of users who are logged on. Both of these results are added to datafile.

```
[david@nittedal david]$ (gcc  o calc calc.c; strip calc;
mv calc calculate) &
```

We perform a compilation and a stripping of the file. We change the name of the file calc to calculate. All operations are executed in the background.

```
[david@nittedal david]$ cp /etc/passwd /usr/david/passwd
[david@nittedal david]$ (cd /etc; cp passwd)
```

At the first statement, the file /etc/passwd is copied to /usr/david/-passwd. In the second example, we first change to the directory /etc; then, the file is copied. Both command lines have equal effects.

```
[david@nittedal david]$ {ls /dev; ls /dev/dsk} | tr [a-
z] [A-Z]
```

All the files in /dev and /dev/dsk become default input to the tr command.

### 16.6.5 Commands in Variables

All commands can be defined in a variable. The only thing to remember is to ring in the content with quotations. We call this command substitution. The shell executes a command limited by quotations. Then the shell replaces the command's expression. For example:

```
[david@nittedal david]$ todaysdate='date'
```

The date command is placed in the shell variable todaysdate. To display the variable todaysdate, write:

```
[david@nittedal david]$ echo $todaysdate
```

We can limit several commands by quotations; for example:

```
[david@nittedal david]$ numberofiles='ls | wc -l'
```

The number of files is placed into the variable `numberofiles`. See also Section 16.3.

### 16.6.6 Reserved Characters in Commands and Expressions

Below is a list of the operators and expressions you can use inside a command file. There are some new reserved words. For repetition, read Chapter 8 concerning redirection, pipes, and filters. For information about wildcards, read Chapter 6.

**Metacharacters and Reserved Words**

<table>
<tr><td>|</td><td>Pipe symbol.</td></tr>
<tr><td>&&</td><td>And-if symbol. If you write two commands with && in between, only the last command is executed if the first is terminated after a successful execution.</td></tr>
<tr><td>||</td><td>Or-if symbol. If you write two commands with || in between, only the last command is executed if the first was terminated after a non-successful execution.</td></tr>
<tr><td>;</td><td>Separates commands.</td></tr>
<tr><td>;;</td><td>Terminates a case condition.</td></tr>
<tr><td>&</td><td>Background processing.</td></tr>
<tr><td>()</td><td>Groups commands by using sub-shells.</td></tr>
<tr><td><</td><td>Redirects default input.</td></tr>
<tr><td><<</td><td>here document (see also Section 16.6.7).</td></tr>
<tr><td>></td><td>Redirects default output.</td></tr>
<tr><td>>></td><td>Adds to default output.</td></tr>
<tr><td>#</td><td>Comments in bash shell command files.</td></tr>
</table>

**Patterns (Wildcards)**

<table>
<tr><td>*</td><td>Replaces one or several characters.</td></tr>
<tr><td>?</td><td>Replaces one character.</td></tr>
<tr><td>[...]</td><td>Match any of the enclosed characters.</td></tr>
</table>

| Substitution | |
|---|---|
| `$n` | Substitutes shell variable. |
| `` `...` `` | Substitutes command output. |

| Quoting | |
|---|---|
| `\` | Quotes next character as literal with no special meaning. |
| `'...'` | Quotes enclose characters. |
| `"..."` | Quotes enclose characters, except: `$ ` \ "`. |

Definition of Variables:

```
name="string"   $name has the string value.
```

Reserved words

```
if              esac
then            for
else            while
elif            until
fi              do
case            done
in              {}
```

### 16.6.7 here Document

Instead of having your own data files, you can collect data in a command file. This is used in connection with `here` documents.

```
for i
do
      grep $i <<s
      123.45     Oslo
      124.50     Copenhagen
      156.60     Stockholm
      124.56     Helsinki
      125.76     London
      s
done
```

In the example, the shell takes the text between `<<` and `s` as standard input for the `grep` command. We have chosen the `s` character for the termination of the file. You can choose any termination character. More information about `here` and redirecting is found in Section 16.6.6 and Chapter 9.

## 16.7 Functions and procedures

All programming languages have internal functions and the possibility to define functions. The possibility to make procedures gives us the possibility to divide a program into smaller parts. Groups of commands, repeated in several different places, do not need to be redefined.

### *16.7.1 Internal Function expr*

We have a built-in command named `expr`. It is for calculations. With `expr`, we can execute mathematical calculations of shell variables.

The following operators can be used in `expr`:

+ Addition

- Subtraction

* Multiplication

/ Division

% Remainder

The operators and the operand may have several different arguments to `expr`. Therefore, we must place a space between the various variables.

The command file `multi`:

```
[david@nittedal david]$ expr $1 * $2
multi 8 4
32
```

The command file `plus`:

```
#!/bin/bash
expr $1 + $2 + $3 + $4
```

```
[david@nittedal david]$ plus 2 3 6 7
18
```

### 16.7.2 Defined Functions

In the shell, we can define functions. Defined functions are similar to procedures, with one exception. Functions are found in computer memory, while procedures are stored on the disk as separate command files (programs). The shell process therefore executes functions, while procedures are executed as separate processes.

The syntax of a defined function is:

```
name () {
commandlist;
}
```

We have to define a name for the function and to make a command list. The start of the command list begins with { and ends with }. A function can be called as often as you like.

This is an example of a simple function:

```
standard_text ()
{
echo "**********************************************"
echo "              Prentice Hall                   "
echo "**********************************************"
}
```

You may use this function wherever you want, including in the command file. You call the function by writing the name of the function. In this case, the name is `standard_text`.

This is an example of a function reading a text and finding out if you have written yes or no.

```
fetch_yes_no ()
     while echo -n "$* (y/n)?" >& 2
     do
          read yes_no
          case $yes_no in
          [yY]) return 0;;
          [nN]) return 1;;
```

```
            *)      echo "Answer yes or no" >& 2;;
            esac
        done
}
```

The function adds the text (y/n) to the default output. The function only accepts Y, y, and N, n as input and returns a code of 0 or 1. If the input from the user is anything else, the function sends the text "Answer yes or no". It will loop forever if the user does not answer Y, y, N, or n.

Example of calling the function fetch_yes_no:

```
fetch_yes_no "Should we break the program" || exit
```

### 16.7.3 Procedures

You make a procedure as a separate command file and set the x bit. Thereafter, you call the procedure from the main command file. The procedure is therefore a normal command file only.

Remember that the main program and procedures should be placed in the same directory. If not, the path must be correctly specified.

Example:

Here, we create a procedure named letter_to_all:

```
letter=$1
shift
for i in $*
do mail $i < $letter
done
```

In the main program, we may call the procedure; for example:

*[david@nittedal david]$* **letter_to_all report david john peter**

If you are able to make a command file, it is simple to make procedures.

## 16.8 The shell environment

The type of environment you have is dependent on your shell definition. The system administrator defines this. Earlier we mentioned the bash and tcsh shells. Under Linux, you will find that the bash shell is the most widely used.

If you are defined as a bash shell user, the files `.profile` and `.bash_profile` are read each time you log in. Included in these files are system and user variables that are exported to all children of the main shell.

If you wish to change the environment parameters, you must change your `.profile` or `.bash_profile` file, provided you are defined as a bash shell user.

It is not necessary to log in and out when you make changes to `.profile` or `.bash_profile`. Just enter `.profile` or `.bash_profile` after the system prompt.

### 16.8.1 Changing the bash Shell's Execution Flag

With the `set` command, we can also change the shells execution flag (options) by setting various flags. The flags most often used are `x` and `v`. They are used when searching for errors in command files. For example:

```
[david@nittedal david]$ set  -x
```

and

```
[david@nittedal david]$ set  -v
```

The two flags have the following meaning:

**-v**

Default inputs are displayed as fast as the shell reads them. This flag is mostly used to isolate errors.

**-x**

Commands and their arguments are displayed as fast as they become executed. The shell commands as, `for`, `while`, etc. are not displayed. It is important to note that `x` only makes a trace of the executed commands, while `v` displays each line. To turn these flags off, write **`set +x`** or only **`set`**.

You may also use the flags directly without using the `set` command first. To do this, put the option in front of the bash shell; for example:

```
[david@nittedal david]$ bash  x batchfile
```

### 16.8.2 The shell's Environment

All variables, with belonging values given while executing a command/command file, represent the shells environment (`env`). The environment includes variables, which the command file inherits from the parent process. Key parameters initiating a command file are a part of the environment for the command file.

The variables placed by the shell into a child process are those exported by the `export` command. The `export` command places the specified variables both into the mother shell and into other child processes belonging to the mother shell.

A procedure can access any variable defined in its environment. If a command file changes an environment parameter, the change is only valid locally for this procedure, and not globally for the shell. If the change is going to be made globally for the shell, the variable has to be exported. Writing `export` and the variable name exports the variable.

If you want a list of variables set globally for the shell, you can write `env`. Example:

```
[david@nittedal david]$ env
BROWSER=/usr/bin/netscape
HISTSIZE=1000
HOSTNAME=nittedal.c2i.net
LOGNAME=david
HISTFILESIZE=1000
MAIL=/var/spool/mail/david
MACHTYPE=i386
TERMCAP=xterm|vs100|xterm terminal emulator (X11R6 Window
System):am:km:mi:ms:xn
:xo:co#80:it#8:li#24:AL=\E[%dL:DC=\E[%dP:DL=\E[%dM:DO...
WINDOWID=20971533
PWD=/tmp
SHLVL=5
_=/usr/bin/env
[root@nittedal /tmp]#
```

Example with `set`:

```
 [david@nittedal david]$ set
BASH=/bin/bash
BASH_VERSION=1.14.7(1)
BROWSER=/usr/bin/netscape
...
[root@nittedal /tmp]#
```

With the `set` command, you will also get your special bash, sh, zsh, or tcsh variables.

## 16.9 Bash script

To summarize this chapter, I have made the following universal bash script (see Figure 16-1). Note that you will find different logical control structures at work in this menu-based bash script.

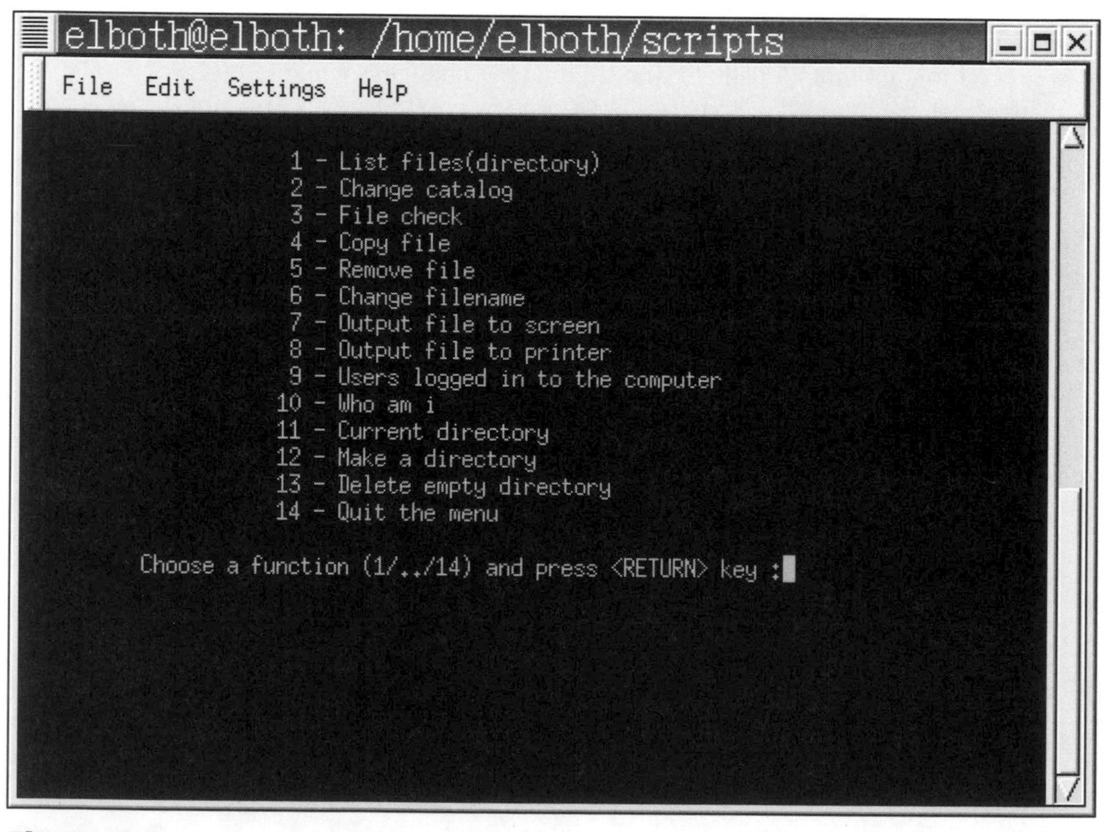


**Figure 16-1**
*Main menu in our universal bash script.*

```
#!/bin/bash
clear
while test "$answer" != "0"
do
```

```
clear
echo ""
echo "                              1 - List files(directory)  "
echo "                              2 - Change catalog           "
echo "                              3 - File check              "
echo "                              4 - Copy file               "
echo "                              5 - Remove file              "
echo "                              6 - Change filename          "
echo "                              7 - Output file to screen "
echo "                              8 - Output file to printer"
echo "                              9 - Users logged in to the
                              computer"
echo "                             10 - Who am i"
echo "                             11 - Current directory"
echo "                             12 - Make a directory"
echo "                             13 - Delete empty directory"
echo "                             14 - Quit the menu"
echo ""
echo -n "          Choose a function (1/../14) and press
                   <RETURN> key :"
read answer
cd $home
#
#         1 - List files(directory)
#
if test "$answer" = "1";then
        clear
        echo ""
        echo "Current/working directory is :"
        pwd
        echo ""
        echo "List files and directories"
        ls -la | more
        echo ""
        echo -n "Press <RETURN> to continue :"
        read stop
fi
#
#        2 - Change directory
#
if test "$answer" = "2";then
        clear
        echo ""
        echo -n "Current/working directory :"
        pwd
```

```
          echo ""
          echo "To continue in current/working directory
answer with
'.'(period) and press <RETURN>"
          echo "If you want to move one level up, answer
with
'..'(two periods) and press <RETURN>"
          echo ""
          echo "If you want to move back to your own
home-directory you only need to press <RETURN>"
          echo ""
          echo "If you want to move to a child-directory
just write the name of the directory and press <RETURN>"
          echo ""
          echo -n "Which directory would you like to use :"
          read dir
          cd $dir
          echo ""
          echo -n "New active directory is :"
          pwd
          echo ""
          echo -n "Press <RETURN> to continue :"
          read stop
fi
#
#         3 - File check
#
if test "$answer" = "3";then
          clear
          echo ""
          echo -n "Which file do you wish to check :"
          read file
          if test -d "$file";then
             echo ""
             echo "   "$file" is a directory"
             echo ""
             echo  -n "Press <RETURN> to continue :"
             read stop
          fi
          if test -r "$file";then
             echo ""
             echo "We can read the file"
          fi
          if test -w "$file";then
             echo ""
```

```
            echo "We can write to the file"
        fi
        if test ! -f "$file";then
            echo ""
            echo ""$file" is not a sub-directory or a
file in the specified directory"
        fi
        echo ""
        echo -n "Press <RETURN> to continue :"
        read stop
fi
#
#       4 - Copy file
#
if test "$answer" = "4";then
        clear
        echo ""
        echo ""
        echo -n "You are now placed in directory :"
        pwd
        echo ""
        echo -n "Which file do you want to copy :"
        read fromfile
        echo ""
        if test  -s "$fromfile";then
            echo -n "Which directory/file would you like
to copy to :"
            read tofile
            if test ! -s "$tofile";then
                cp "$fromfile" "$tofile"
            else
                echo ""
                echo -n ""$tofile" exist do you want
overwrite (y/n) :"
                read yes
                if test "$yes" = "y";then
                    cp "$fromfile" "$tofile"
                fi
            fi
        else
            echo ""
            echo -n ""$fromfile" do not exist - press
<RETURN> :"
            read stop
        fi
```

```
fi
#
#       5 - Delete file
#
if test "$answer" = "5";then
        clear
        echo ""
        echo -n "Which file do you want to delete :"
        read file
        if test -f "$file";then
           clear
           echo ""
           echo -n ""$file" exists. Do you really want
to delete the file (y/n) :"
           read yes
           if test "$yes" = "y";then
              rm $file
           fi
       else echo ""
             echo -n ""$file" do not exists - press
<RETURN>"
             read stop
        fi
fi
#
#     6 - Change name on file
#
if test "$answer" = "6";then
        clear
        echo ""
        echo -n "You are now in directory :"
        pwd
        echo ""
        echo  -n "Which filename would you like to
change :"
        read file
        if test -f "$file";then
           clear
           echo ""
           echo -n ""$file" exists. Please give a new
name :"
           read newname
           if test ! -f "$newname";then
              mv "$file" "$newname"
           else
```

```
                echo ""
                echo  -n ""$newname" exists - press
<RETURN> :"
                read stop
             fi
         else
             echo ""
             echo -n ""$file" do not exists - press
<RETURN> :"
             read stop
         fi
fi
#
#        7 - Output file to monitor screen
#
if test "$answer" = "7";then
         clear
         echo ""
         echo "If the file is more than one page you may
continue by pressing the <RETURN> key"
         echo ""
         echo -n "Which file would you like to see on
your monitor screen :"
         read file
         if test  -s "$file";then
             more "$file"
             echo ""
             echo -n "Press <RETURN> to continue :"
             read stop
         else
             echo ""
             echo "The file do not exists or is empty"
         echo ""
             echo -n "Press <RETURN> to continue :"
             read stop
         fi
fi
#
#        8 - Output file to printer
#
if test "$answer" = "8";then
         clear
         echo ""
         echo -n "Which file would you like to print :"
         read file
```

```
          echo ""
          lpr $file
      echo ""
fi
#
#       9  - Users logged on the system
#
if test "$answer" = "9";then
      clear
      echo ""
      echo -n "Please, wait....."
          who > /tmp/who-list
          clear
          echo ""
          echo "Active users logged on the system :"
          echo ""
      cat /tmp/who-list
      echo ""
          echo -n "Number of users logged on the system :"
      cat /tmp/who-list | wc -l
      echo ""
          echo -n "Press <RETURN> to continue:"
          read stop
fi
#
#       10 - Who am I
#
if test "$answer" = "10";then
          clear
          echo ""
          echo -n "I am user :"
          whoami
          echo ""
          echo -n "Press <RETURN> to continue :"
          read stop
fi
#
#      11 - Current directory
#
if test "$answer" = "11";then
          clear
          echo ""
          echo -n "Current directory is :"
          pwd
      echo ""
```

```
        echo -n "Press <RETURN> to continue :"
        read stop
fi
#
#    12 - Make a directory
#
if test "$answer" = "12";then
        clear
        echo ""
        echo -n "Current directory is :"
        pwd
        echo "  "
        echo -n "Is this the right directory - would
you like to continue (y/n) :"
        read yes
        if test "$yes" = "y";then
           echo ""
           echo -n "What is the name of the new sub-
directory :"
           read subdir
           if test ! -d  "$subdir";then
              mkdir "$subdir"
              if test ! -d "$subdir";then
                 echo ""
                 echo -n ""$subdir" this directory do
not exists :"
                 read stop
              fi
           else
              echo ""
              echo -n ""$subdir" this directory do
already exists - press <RETURN> :"
              read stop
           fi
        fi
fi
#
#      13 - Delete empty directory
#
if test "$answer" = "13";then
        clear
        echo ""
        echo -n "Current directory is :"
        pwd
        echo ""
```

```
        echo -n "Which empty directory would you like to
delete :"
        read file
        if test  -d "$file";then
           cd $file
           echo ""
           echo "Checking directory"
           ls -la
           cd ..
           echo ""
           echo -n "Any files in that directory? -
(y/n)  :"
           read yes
           if test "$yes" = "y";then
              rmdir "$file"
              if test ! -d "$file";then
                 echo ""
                 echo -n ""$file" is deleted - press
<RETURN> :"
                 read stop
              fi
           fi
        else
           echo ""
           echo -n ""$file" is not a directory - press
<RETURN> :"
           read stop
        fi
fi
#
#      14 - Quit the menu
#
if test "$answer" = "14";then
     exit;
fi
done
```

## Exercises for Chapter 16

1. Create a command file named `shell.1`.

   The command file should contain these three lines:

   ```
   echo "What is your name?"
   ```

```
read name
echo "Hello $name"
```

Execute the file in three possible ways.

2. Create a command file that reads the first name, family name, sex, height, and weight from the command line. After the data is registered, the program should display the information preceded by background texts. Name the command file `shell.2`

3. What do these command lines do:

```
data='ls  -la | grep "*.txt"'
(echo "What is your name"; read name) || exit
{who; whoami; you;} | wc  -l
```

4. Create a command file displaying:

   Today's date and time

   Number of users

   My status

   My home directory

   Placed in directory

   My files

   Hints:

```
date
who
whoami
$home
pwd
ls  -la | more
```

5. What does the following command file do?

```
:
for i in L I N U X
do
   echo "Enter the capital letters $i"
   echo -n "$i  "
done
```

CHAPTER
17

# Booting the Linux System

## 17.1 Booting Linux from a PC

This chapter explains how to boot Linux on a PC. The details are slightly different from one system to another. Booting a Linux system is comparable to the similar processes in Unix and Windows. I also explain the different init levels in the Linux OS. This is more or less the same in both Linux and Unix.

Booting Linux on a PC is a simple operation. You start by doing what you do with other operating systems: Switch the computer on!

## 17.2 Booting Windows 98

As this book is focused on PC architecture, we'll start with a look at what happens when a PC with the Windows 98 OS is booted.

Booting Windows has the following sequences:

- **ROM (BIOS).**

  Self-test.

  Motherboard test.

  I/O test.

  Reads the first sector/track from drive A, then (if applicable) from drive C or the CD-ROM drive.

- **Hidden files, e.g., *.SYS, are loaded.**
- **CONFIG.SYS.**
- **COMMAND.COM (Windows' COMMAND.COM).**
- **[AUTOEXEC.BAT].**
- **Windows 98.**

The first thing that happens when you switch a PC on is that a program in ROM (Read Only Memory) starts. This program runs a self test on the machine. The self test checks the main board and I/O units like the serial ports (RS-232), printer ports (parallel ports), video card, floppy drives, hard disk drives, etc.

After completing the self test, the system looks for a boot block on the floppy disk in the first floppy drive (which is A under DOS). If no floppy is found or no start block is found on the floppy, the system seeks the hard disk drive (C under DOS/Windows) or the CD-ROM.

Thus far, booting under Window 98 is identical to booting under Linux, as the hardware architectures are identical. The first part of the booting procedure follows this sequence in most micro/mini machines.

After loading the boot block, some invisible files, e.g., *.SYS, are loaded. These files in turn load the text file CONFIG.SYS. The Windows 98 command interpreter, COMMAND.COM, is then loaded; this in turn loads the batch file AUTOEXEC.BAT. Finally, the last part of Windows 98 is loaded, and the PC is up and running with the Microsoft Windows 98 OS.

## 17.3 Booting Unix and Linux

Booting Unix and Linux is a process very similar to booting Windows 98. The sequence is as follows:

- **ROM (BIOS)**

  Self-test.

  Motherboard test.

  I/O test.

Reads the first sector/track from drive A, then (if applicable) from drive C (or the CD-ROM). The Unix environment uses a program named `boot`. In Linux, the boot program is called `LILO boot`. The boot programs are placed in the boot block of sector 0 and track 0. The programs give the following prompt:

| **Unix System V** | **Linux** |
|---|---|
| `boot:` | `LILO boot:` |

You may specify other Unix or Linux kernels or options to the kernel; for example:

```
unix.old   unix.SCSI   linux       linux single (option)
unix.tape  unix.clean  linux.clean linux mem=256M (option)
```

If you have a Windows 98 partition on your hard disk drive, you may specify that you want the Windows 98 OS to boot by entering `dos` after the `boot:` prompt.

Example:

```
LILO boot: dos
```

It is also possible to boot the Linux OS or Unix system from a floppy disk or CD-ROM. After loading the Linux kernel, the system reads various system files. The changes that you have made to the boot files will decide which system files the system reads. The init process starts when you boot any Linux system. This process is also found in standard Unix V.4. Init starts all other standard, necessary processes like `smtp`, `ftp`, `news`, `http`, `nfs`, or specific routines that you have created.

Linux used to be based on the booting procedure of BSD inits, but it is increasingly being based on System V. The result is that standard Unix V.4 and Linux are quite similar. Most distributors have switched to the System V booting method because it is simpler, more powerful, and more adaptable than, for example, the traditional BSD procedure. A standard System V boot sequence locates all configuration files in directories under `/etc/rc.d` (see Figure 17-1), as opposed to BSD, which stores most configuration files in the `/etc` directory.

| **Booting Unix** | **Booting Linux** |
|---|---|
| `unix` | `linux` |
| `init` | `/etc/rc.d/init.d` |
| `/etc/rc` | `/etc/rc.d/rc` |
| `/etc/rc2` | `/etc/rc.d/rc.local` |
| `/etc/rc3` | `/etc/rc.d/rc.local` |
| `/etc/rc.d` | `/etc/rc.d/rc.sysinit` |
| `/etc/rc.d/0..9` | `/etc/rc.d/rcn(n=0,,6).d` |

Linux seeks for init in several locations and runs the first occurrence it finds. Init reads `/etc/init.d/bcheckrc` or `/etc/rc.d/rc.sysinit` (valid for Red Hat Linux), then all scripts required for the specified run level (1,2,3,4,5,6).

These system init files contain commands and data that are set for the various run levels. You will find that the Linux structure is not consistent.

Under Red Hat Linux, the `/etc/rc.d/init.d` directory holds most of the init scripts that are read at various run levels (1,2,3,4,5,6). The run level for each script can be found in the related directories, `/etc/rc.d/rc1.d`, `/etc/rc.d/rc2.d`, `/etc/rc.d/rc3.d`, etc. Each file is linked to `/etc/rc.d/init.d`. At run level 2, you'll find `cron`, `lpd`, etc. In run level 3, you'll find `sendmail`, `rwalld`, `postgresql`, `sound`, `httpd`, etc. In the `/etc/rc.d/rc2.d` and `/etc/rc.d/rc3.d` directories, you'll find the scripts that are initiated at run levels 2 and 3.

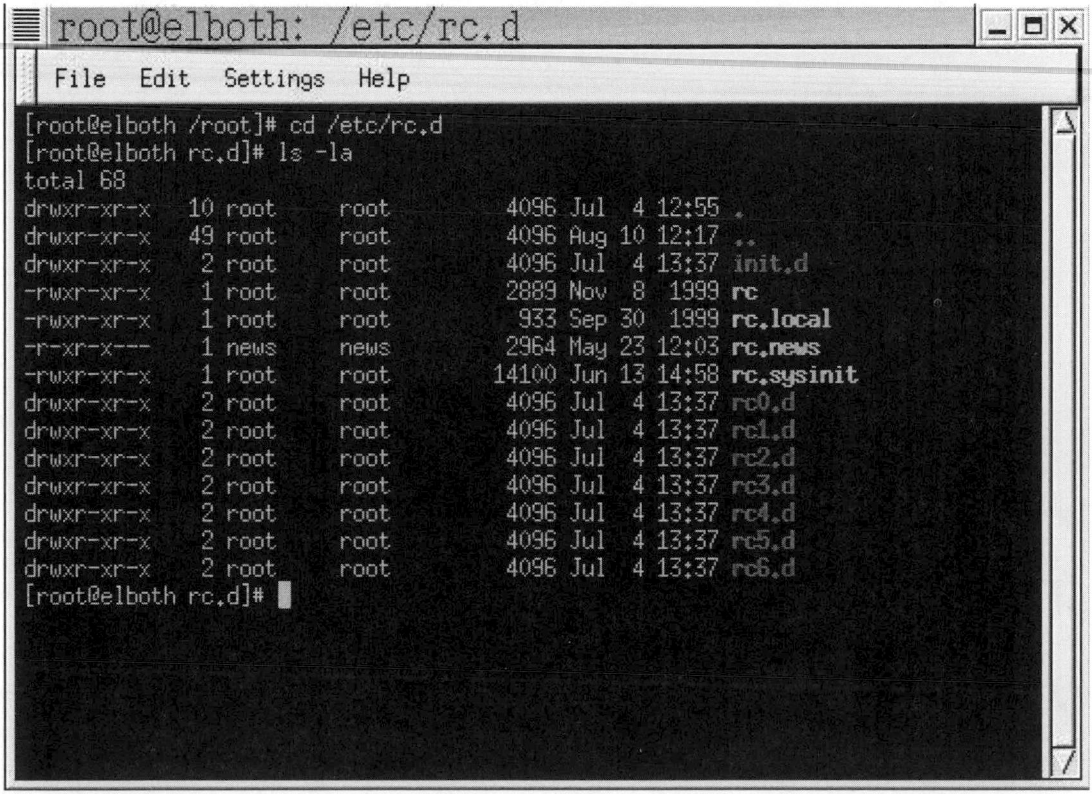

```
root@elboth: /etc/rc.d
File  Edit  Settings  Help
[root@elboth /root]# cd /etc/rc.d
[root@elboth rc.d]# ls -la
total 68
drwxr-xr-x  10 root   root        4096 Jul  4 12:55 .
drwxr-xr-x  49 root   root        4096 Aug 10 12:17 ..
drwxr-xr-x   2 root   root        4096 Jul  4 13:37 init.d
-rwxr-xr-x   1 root   root        2889 Nov  8  1999 rc
-rwxr-xr-x   1 root   root         933 Sep 30  1999 rc.local
-r-xr-x---   1 news   news        2964 May 23 12:03 rc.news
-rwxr-xr-x   1 root   root       14100 Jun 13 14:58 rc.sysinit
drwxr-xr-x   2 root   root        4096 Jul  4 13:37 rc0.d
drwxr-xr-x   2 root   root        4096 Jul  4 13:37 rc1.d
drwxr-xr-x   2 root   root        4096 Jul  4 13:37 rc2.d
drwxr-xr-x   2 root   root        4096 Jul  4 13:37 rc3.d
drwxr-xr-x   2 root   root        4096 Jul  4 13:37 rc4.d
drwxr-xr-x   2 root   root        4096 Jul  4 13:37 rc5.d
drwxr-xr-x   2 root   root        4096 Jul  4 13:37 rc6.d
[root@elboth rc.d]#
```

**Figure 17-1**
*The directory structure under /etc/rc.d.*

The default run level is set in `/etc/inittab`. Under most Linux distributions, you will find that the default run level is 3. If you are running Red Hat Linux and you have chosen a graphical environment, your default run level will be 5 (`id:5:initdefault`). Red Hat Linux starts your graphical environment (GUI with Gnome or KDE) in run level 5.

All scripts you find under `/etc/rc.d/rc.local` will run only once, no matter which run level is your default run level.

Only root may change the system init files. In all Linux systems, the system information is displayed at the main console or `syslog`. A simple shell is run at the main console. This shell belongs to the system administrator (root) and is used to control the filesystem. If the filesystem works properly after init level 1, you can choose to run the system at higher run levels. If the filesystem does not work properly, the `fsck` program starts automatically. This program fixes filesystem problems (see Chapter 19). When the filesystem has been fixed, you are ready to boot your system at the selected run level.

When the system is at run level 1, the system will read the `/etc/rc` system file and all files in `/etc/rc.d/rc/.d`. At run level 2, the system will read the files in the `/etc/rc.d/rc2.d` directory.

When moving from a lower run level, e.g., level 1 to level 2, all files in `/etc/rc.d/rc2.d` (see Figure 17-2) starting with `S*` are read (Unix also reads the `rc2.d` directory). When moving from a higher run level, e.g., level 3 to level 2, all command files in the `/etc/rc.d/rc3.d` directory that start with `K*` are read with the `stop` option. All other files that don't start with `S` or `K` are completely ignored in the `/etc/rc.d/rc3.d` directory. The `S*` and `K*` files are always read in ASCII-sorted order.

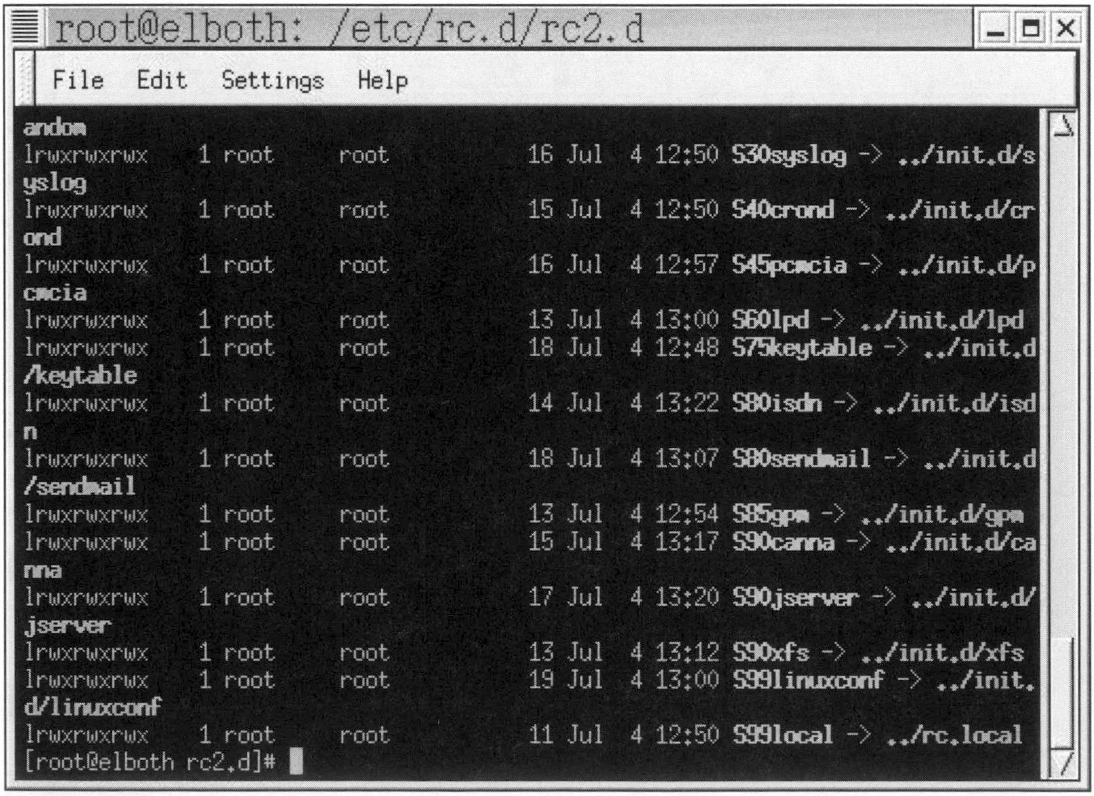

```
root@elboth: /etc/rc.d/rc2.d
File  Edit  Settings  Help
andom
lrwxrwxrwx    1 root     root           16 Jul  4 12:50 S30syslog -> ../init.d/s
yslog
lrwxrwxrwx    1 root     root           15 Jul  4 12:50 S40crond -> ../init.d/cr
ond
lrwxrwxrwx    1 root     root           16 Jul  4 12:57 S45pcmcia -> ../init.d/p
cmcia
lrwxrwxrwx    1 root     root           13 Jul  4 13:00 S60lpd -> ../init.d/lpd
lrwxrwxrwx    1 root     root           18 Jul  4 12:48 S75keytable -> ../init.d
/keytable
lrwxrwxrwx    1 root     root           14 Jul  4 13:22 S80isdn -> ../init.d/isd
n
lrwxrwxrwx    1 root     root           18 Jul  4 13:07 S80sendmail -> ../init.d
/sendmail
lrwxrwxrwx    1 root     root           13 Jul  4 12:54 S85gpm -> ../init.d/gpm
lrwxrwxrwx    1 root     root           15 Jul  4 13:17 S90canna -> ../init.d/ca
nna
lrwxrwxrwx    1 root     root           17 Jul  4 13:20 S90jserver -> ../init.d/
jserver
lrwxrwxrwx    1 root     root           13 Jul  4 13:12 S90xfs -> ../init.d/xfs
lrwxrwxrwx    1 root     root           19 Jul  4 13:00 S99linuxconf -> ../init.
d/linuxconf
lrwxrwxrwx    1 root     root           11 Jul  4 12:50 S99local -> ../rc.local
[root@elboth rc2.d]#
```

**Figure 17-2**
*The directory structure under /etc/rc.d/rc2.d.*

Most of the scripts in the directories under /etc/rc.d/ have start and stop options that permit services to be started and stopped manually. For example:

```
[root@nittedal /root]# /etc/rc.d/init.d/lpd stop
[root@nittedal /root]# /etc/rc.d/init.d/lpd start
```

Stops/starts the lpd process. Init reads the name and argument. If the process is to be terminated, the "K" script (for example, K12lpd) runs. If the process is to be started, the "S" script (for example, S60lpd) runs.

## 17.4 System file /etc/inittab

Booting Linux is dependent on a special init program (see also Chapters 11 and 21). This init program starts as the last part of loading the Linux kernel.

The init process is the first process (although swap has PID number 0) that starts on the system and gets PID number 1. The init process starts all other processes that are described in the /etc/inittab file. This file contains the instructions for /etc/init. The Linux init process reads the /etc/inittab in these situations:

- **When booting up Linux (boot).**
- **When a process uses init.**
- **When the system administrator starts init (or the related program, /bin/telinit).**

Whenever the system changes run level, /etc/inittab is analyzed for instructions. The /etc/inittab file contains four fields:

```
Identification:init mode:action:process
```

The Identification is a text string with up to four characters. init mode specifies at which run level the process starts. The levels are from 1 to 6. Levels may be combined. When init runs at level 1 or S, the system is in single-user mode. The action field describes what to do. The process field points to the physical process. The most usual actions (Column #3) are:

| Column # 3 | Description |
|---|---|
| off | Switched off. |
| respawn | Starts specified process if it isn't already running. If the process dies, it is restarted. |
| wait | Waits to start specified process. |
| once | Starts the specified process once only. If the process dies, it is not restarted. |
| initdefault | Default init level for the Linux system. |

An example of `/etc/inittab-fil` for Linux:

```
#
# inittab       This file describes how the INIT process
should set up
#               the system in a certain run-level.
#
# Author:       Miquel van Smoorenburg,
<miquels@drinkel.nl.mugnet.org>
#               Modified for RHS Linux by Marc Ewing
and Donnie Barnes
#

# Default runlevel. The runlevels used by RHS are:
#   0 - halt (Do NOT set initdefault to this)
#   1 - Single user mode
#   2 - Multiuser, without NFS (The same as 3, if you do
not have networking)
#   3 - Full multiuser mode
#   4 - unused
#   5 - X11
#   6 - reboot (Do NOT set initdefault to this)
#
id:5:initdefault:

# System initialization.
si::sysinit:/etc/rc.d/rc.sysinit

l0:0:wait:/etc/rc.d/rc 0
l1:1:wait:/etc/rc.d/rc 1
l2:2:wait:/etc/rc.d/rc 2
l3:3:wait:/etc/rc.d/rc 3
```

```
l4:4:wait:/etc/rc.d/rc 4
l5:5:wait:/etc/rc.d/rc 5
l6:6:wait:/etc/rc.d/rc 6

# Things to run in every runlevel.
ud::once:/sbin/update

# Trap CTRL-ALT-DELETE
ca::ctrlaltdel:/sbin/shutdown -t3 -r now

# When our UPS tells us power has failed, assume we have
a few minutes
# of power left.  Schedule a shutdown for 2 minutes from
now.
# This does, of course, assume you have powerd installed
and your
# UPS connected and working correctly.
pf::powerfail:/sbin/shutdown -f -h +2  "Power Failure;
System Shutting Down "

# If power was restored before the shutdown kicked in,
cancel it.
pr:12345:powerokwait:/sbin/shutdown -c  "Power Restored;
Shutdown Cancelled "

# Run gettys in standard runlevels
1:2345:respawn:/sbin/mingetty tty1
2:2345:respawn:/sbin/mingetty tty2
3:2345:respawn:/sbin/mingetty tty3
4:2345:respawn:/sbin/mingetty tty4
5:2345:respawn:/sbin/mingetty tty5
6:2345:respawn:/sbin/mingetty tty6
# Run xdm in runlevel 5
# xdm is now a separate service
x:5:respawn:/etc/X11/prefdm -nodaemon
```

The first `active` line (`id:5:initdefault`) sets the default run level at `5`. Virtual terminal sessions are defined at six different consoles (`tty1-tty6`). At the end of the file, you'll see that at `run level 5`, the graphical logon program xdm will start.

## 17.5 Terminal file /etc/termcap

In Linux, you'll find two databases for defining terminals. You can choose to use either `/etc/termcap` or `/usr/lib/terminfo`. The latter is a compiled database which is faster to use than `/etc/termcap`.

Below is an example that shows a terminal definition in an `/etc/termcap` file. The terminal definitions are for a Linux terminal. The terminal definition "`linux`" is normally run when logging on to a Linux box at the main console before starting X Window. The example describes control codes for moving the cursor, blanking the screen, and defining function keys. See the Linux man pages for a more detailed description. F1 to F9 are the function key definitions.

```
#
# From: Eric S. Raymond <esr@snark.thyrsus.com> 9 Nov
1995
#
# added linux-lat as an alias — theline drawing
#  characters aren't right, but
# I think everything which uses line-drawing chars uses
terminfo anyway — ewt
linux|linux-lat|linux console:\
        :am:eo:mi:ms:ut:xn:xo:\
        :co#80:it#8:li#25:\
...
```

Under `/usr/lib/terminfo`, you'll find one category for each letter of the alphabet. Under the letter "`a`," all terminal definitions beginning with an "`a`" are listed. Examples of terminal types beginning with an "`a`" are `ansi` and `adds`. The commands and codes in the compiled terminal database are different from `/etc/termcap`.

If you want to make a terminal definition in `/usr/lib/terminfo`, you start by making a terminal definition file in text file format. Compile this text file with the `tic` Linux command. Finally, move the file to the appropriate directory, for example, to `/usr/lib/terminfo/a` if the terminal and file are called `ansi`. You'll find out more about terminal definitions in the Linux man pages.

## 17.6 Communication file /etc/gettydefs

In connection with terminals, modems, printers, etc., the last column in the `/etc/inittab` file is used to specify the communication speed and tty settings used by `getty` on the various devices. These parameters are defined in the system file `/etc/gettydefs`.

Example:

```
[root@nittedal /etc]# more gettydefs
# [ put this file in /etc/gettydefs ]
#
# This file contains the startup and final flags for the
# tty lines.  Each line starts with a SPEED value; this
is
# the same SPEED that you pass to [uu]getty.  Note that
the
# SPEED identifier is just a string; use whatever names
# you want.
#
# The blank lines in this file are important (so I
hear).
#
# The flags are the same flags you would pass to the
stty
# program.
#
# Format: <speed># <init flags> # <final flags> #<login
string>#<next-speed>
#
#
# Virtual Console entry
VC# B9600 SANE CLOCAL # B9600 SANE -ISTRIP CLOCAL #@S
login: #VC

# 38400 fixed baud Dumb Terminal entry
DT38400# B38400 CS8 CLOCAL CRTSCTS # B38400 SANE -ISTRIP
CLOCAL CRTSCTS #@S logi
n: #DT38400
...
```

In the first and last column of the file `/etc/gettydefs`, the name of the communication definition is given; for example, `DT38400`, `DT9600`, `F57600`,

F19200, etc. The terminal speed (baud) may be from 9600 to 115200. Different flags may be set for each speed definition. The `HUPLC` flag means that the line is terminated when there is no longer contact between a terminal and the Linux machine. `SANE` is a compound flag that sets several parameters. `TAB3` converts all tabs to spaces. The `ECHOE` and `IXANY` flags are connected to handling characters. The last column to the right defines which logon program to use.

## Exercises for Chapter 17

1. Why is the first part of the boot procedure identical under Windows 98, Unix, and Linux?
2. Name the two binary files that are needed to boot Linux.
3. Is it possible to boot Windows from Linux LILO?
4. What happens when a Linux system is booted?
5. Which process is the mother of all other processes?

CHAPTER
18

# Logging in to the Linux System

## 18.1 Logging procedures

Unless you use a graphical logging procedure, getty (/sbin/mingetty) is the first program that communicates with you as a user. The first message from the Linux system always comes from getty.

If you run a graphical login, gdm (see Figure 18-1) will be the first program that communicates with you as a user.

When the user has entered their username, the name is read by the login program, which in turn checks and verifies whether the user is defined in the system. This check runs through the files /etc/passwd (/etc/shadow) and /etc/group. If the user has a password, this must be entered. All users should have a password, including root (which is the system administrator's username).

**Figure 18-1**
*The GDM graphical login screen.*

`getty` waits for your reply and starts the real login program with your answer as an argument. For example, `getty` will check if your terminal can handle upper-case as well as lower-case characters. If your terminal can't handle lower-case characters, the login prompt will be displayed in upper-case characters. `getty` can also automatically control speed.

Figure 18-2 confirms that init is the parent process of all `gettys` and `gdms`.

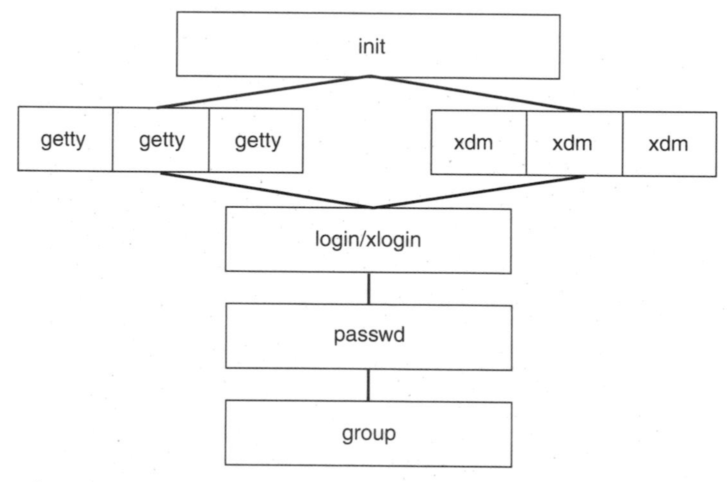


**Figure 18-2**
*Processes and files involved in your login.*

When entering your username and password at the terminal, the login program checks that both are valid.

The screen that is displayed after a character-based login is defined in the system file `/etc/motd`.

## 18.2 The /etc/passwd file

The choice of command interpreter (shell) is made in the `/etc/passwd` file. The columns in the password file have the following fields:

- **User name (`user-id` used at login).**
- **Password (your password).**
- **User number (`user-id` is mapped to a user number).**
- **Group number (your group ID number is mapped to a group name).**
- **Text field (text field that describes user).**
- **User area (your user area).**
- **Shell (default shell for user).**

Username is the name that the system administrator (see Figure 18-3) has defined for the user. The username normally consists of lower-case characters only.

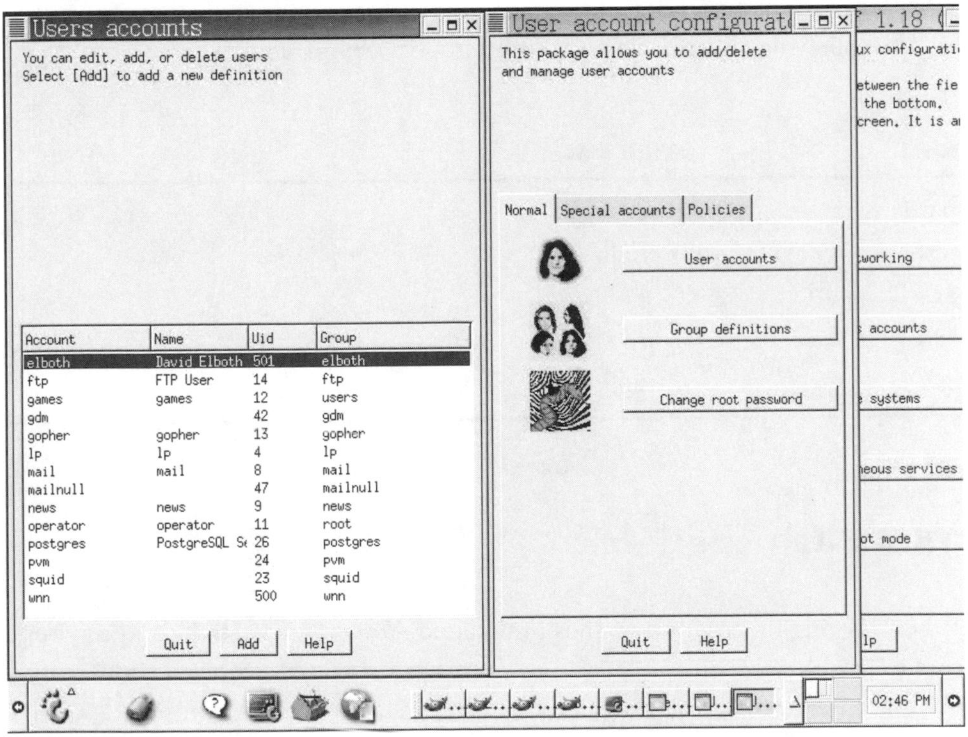

**Figure 18-3**
*From* `linuxconf` *system administrator defines users and groups.*

The next field is the password. In most systems, this field is set to handle multiple functions. If the user has to change their password at the next login or the password has passed a certain date, this may be specified in this field with a certain code. In Linux systems, you will see that the password has been encrypted in this field. If your Linux system uses the `/etc/shadow` file, the encrypted password will be moved to `/etc/shadow`. There will only be a `*` in the password field in your `/etc/passwd` file.

The user number is a unique number that points to the username. The group number indicates which groups the user is a member of. The names of the groups are found in `/etc/group`.

In most systems, the text field can be a maximum of 38 characters. This field may contain a text description of the user.

The user area shows the location of the user's working area. Some examples of working areas are `/home/ole`, `/usr/anne`, `/u/john`, `/usr2/peter`, `/home1/smith`, etc.

The shell is an interactive program that works as a command interpreter (see Chapters 7, 8, and 16.)

The following abbreviations are used in `/etc/passwd`:

| Shell | Shell Name |
|---|---|
| bash | Bash shell. |
| tcsh | T shell. |
| csh | C shell. |
| ksh | Korn shell. |
| zsh | Z shell. |

## 18.3 Bash shell

When logging in, certain key files are loaded. You may use shells and environment variables. Environment variables in bash shell are set with the `export` command and are displayed in upper-case characters. The commands in the system files `.bash_profile` and `.profile` are executed when you log in as bash shell user.

### 18.3.1 Environment Variables

The table below shows the most important bash shell environment variables:

| Bash Shell Environment Variables | Description |
|---|---|
| DISPLAY | Displays the screen session (X Window). |
| HOME | Search path to your home directory. |
| HOSTNAME | Name of host. |
| HOSTTYPE | Uniquely describes type of machine. |
| IPS | Defines field separator. |
| LOGNAME | Your login name. |
| MAIL | Search path to your e-mail file. |
| LANG | Your language. |
| MAILCHECK | Checks mail. |
| PATH | Command search path. |
| PS1 | Defines prompt. |
| PS2 | Defines secondary prompt. |
| SHELL | Search path to your shell. |
| TERM | Your terminal type. |

Environment variables are, for example, terminal type, mailbox, whether there is new mail, etc. If you enter `printenv`, the currently active variables are displayed.

Example:

```
[david@nittedal david]$ printenv | more
USERNAME=
HISTSIZE=1000
HOSTNAME=nittedal.c2i.net
LOGNAME=david
HISTFILESIZE=1000
MAIL=/var/spool/mail/david
TERM=vt100
HOSTTYPE=i386
PATH=/usr/local/bin:/bin:/usr/bin:/usr/X11R6/bin:
/home/david/bin
```

```
HOME=/home/david
SHELL=/bin/bash
PS1=[\u@\h \W]\$
USER=david
BASH_ENV=/home/david/.bashrc
OSTYPE=Linux
SHLVL=1
_=/usr/bin/printenv
[david@nittedal david]$
```

The bash shell specifies standard values for the environment variables PATH, PS1, PS2 and IFS if they have not been defined. On the other hand, HOME is set by login. MAIL must be set, as it has no value.

To activate environment variables, you must execute the export command after defining them. The general syntax is:

*export variable=value*

Example:

```
[david@nittedal /etc]$ export HOME=/home/david
```

Environment variables are always typed in upper-case characters. They always define the user's environment. Defining them like normal variables sets environment variables. Future shells inherit environment variables.

- **DISPLAY**—When running X Window, setting the DISPLAY variable is important. For example:

```
[david@nittedal /etc]$ export DISPLAY=elboth:0.0
```

The syntax of the DISPLAY variable is: *hosts:screen:screen session*

- **HOME**—The name of the user's home directory is defined as an environment variable called HOME. You may, for example, use HOME in the environment variable PATH.

- **HOSTNAME**—Gives you the name of your computer. On many Unix machines, this name is often found in /etc/hostname.
  Example:

```
[david@nittedal /etc]$ echo $HOSTNAME
nittedal.c2i.net
```

- **HOSTTYPE**—Gives you the name of your computer architecture.
  Example:

```
[david@nittedal /etc]$ echo $HOSTTYPE
i386
```

- **IPS**—Specifies the field separator variable. Normal internal field separators are space, tab, and newline.
  Example:

```
[david@nittedal /etc]$ export IPS=,
```

  Here the , (comma) is defined as field separator.

- **LOGNAME**—Defines your login name.
  Example:

```
[david@nittedal david]$ echo $LOGNAME
david
```

- **LANG**—Defines your language. You will find out more about language and keyboard layout in Chapters 3 and 19.
  Example:

```
[david@nittedal david]$ echo $LANG
en_US
```

- **MAIL**—The name of the user's electronic mailbox is normally placed in `/usr/spool/mail`. The `MAIL` variable is, in most cases, used to change the search path and filename of the mailbox.
  Example:

```
[elboth@nittedal elboth]$ export MAIL=/var/spool/-mail/
`logname`
```

- **MAILCHECK**—This parameter specifies how frequently (in seconds) your mailbox is checked.
  Example:

```
[david@nittedal david]$ export MAILCHECK=360
```

This checks the mailbox every 6 minutes (1 minute = 60 seconds). The default value of `MAILCHECK` is 10 minutes (600 seconds), unless a different value is specified. If you set `MAILCHECK=0`, the mail system will check every time you receive a new prompt (i.e., every time you press ENTER).

- **`PATH`**—The special shell variable `PATH` controls the programs that can be executed. `PATH` holds information about the search path for the shell interpreter. Without the `PATH` command, you can only execute the programs and commands that are located in your local directory. If you get the error message `Command not found`, this may mean that the bash shell cannot find the program in any directory specified in the search path (`PATH`). The search path in `PATH` is normally set up in the file `.bash_profile` or `.profile`.
  Example:

```
[david@nittedal /etc]$ export PATH=/bin:/usr/bin:
$HOME/bin:.
```

- **`PS1`**—In bash and tcsh, the variable `PS1` defines your prompt. The standard prompt value for a bash user is the `$` symbol, and for a tcsh user, the `%` symbol.
  Example:

```
[david@nittedal david]$ export PS1='Give command:'
```

Here, I define the text `Give command` as the prompt.

```
[david@nittedal david]$ export PS1='Date: \d Time: \t-> '
Date: Sat Feb 27 Time: 21:34:53->
```

Here, I define today's date and time as the prompt. You may change the system variable `PS1` to define C as the prompt. Then the user will get a feeling of using a PC with the Windows and DOS operating systems.

- **`PS2`**—`PS2` is a secondary prompt that displays when your shell expects additional input. This environment variable is by default set to >.
  Example:

```
[david@nittedal david]$ export PS2=+
```

The secondary prompt is defined as + (plus).

- **`SHELL`**—The environment variable `SHELL` gives information about which shell you are using. You may redefine the shell.
  Example:

```
[david@nittedal david]$ echo $SHELL
/bin/bash
```

- **`TERM`**—When the message terminal type is displayed on your screen, Linux has used the `TERM` variable to define the terminal type. If you wish to set a fixed terminal type in the `.bash_profile` or `.profile` file, you may, for example, enter:

```
[david@nittedal david]$ export TERM=vt100
```

This sets the terminal type to `vt100`.

```
[david@nittedal david]$ export TERM=linux
```

This sets the terminal type to `linux`.

### 18.3.2 Aliases and Shell Commands

In this section, you will learn about alias definitions and other useful commands.

| Bash Shell Variables | Description |
|---|---|
| `alias` | Creates aliases, i.e., defines new names for commands. |
| `unalias` | Removes aliases. |
| `history` | Remembers commands. |
| `source` | Updates bash environment. |

- **`alias`**—When you want to define an alias you write the command `alias`, new alias name, equal, and Linux command.

Example:

```
[david@nittedal david]$ alias l="ls -la"
```

Here are some examples of useful aliases:

```
[david@nittedal david]$ alias rm="rm -i"
[david@nittedal david]$ alias cp="cp -i"
[david@nittedal david]$ alias mv="mv -i"
[david@nittedal david]$ alias lsf="ls -color"
```

The last of these examples adds colors to filenames.

- **unalias**—When you want to remove an alias, you may use the `unalias` command. Here are some examples:

```
[david@nittedal david]$ unalias lsf
[david@nittedal david]$ unalias print
```

If you run the tcsh shell and want to include arguments with an alias, you may use the character combination `\!*`. When using `\!*` or other special characters, you must use single quotation marks (') .

Example (tcsh shell):

```
[anne@delboth ~]% alias print= 'pr -n \!:* | lpr '
```

If you don't specify any arguments with the `alias` command, all aliases connected with the shell are displayed.

- **history**—When setting up the `history` command, the tcsh and bash shells will remember the number of commands that you specify. In most cases, between 10 and 25 commands are defined. Commands are set by typing `set history=n`, where `n` is the number of commands to be remembered.

Example (tcsh shell):

```
[david@nittedal david]$ set history=20
```

You can refer to the list created by the history command when you want to rerun a command or a part of a command.

If you type history only, a list of remembered commands is displayed. All references to the history list start with an exclamation mark (!).

- **source**—If you have altered the `.bash_profile`, `.bashrc`, `.profile`, `.tcshrc`, `.login`, or `.cshrc` files, you can update your environment by entering the `source` command and the name of your configuration file. By doing this, you don't have to login again to make the update.

Example (tcsh shell):

```
[david@nittedal david]$ source .tcshrc
```

## 18.4 User system files

All bash shell users have /etc/profile as their global init file. Only the system administrator may change this file. Local $HOME/.profile is run by all bash users at login. A $HOME/.bash_profile can also be created for each user. If there is no .bash_profile, .profile is used instead. This file executes when you log in as a bash user. It is also a good idea to have a $HOME/.bashrc. All non-login copies of bash execute this file.

| Bash Shell | Description |
|---|---|
| .bash_profile | At login. |
| .bashrc | Each time a new shell is started, e.g., when you enter bash. |
| /etc/profile | At login (global profile file). |
| $HOME/.profile | At login. |
| $HOME/.bashrc | When starting a shell, e.g., when entering bash. |
| $HOME/.bash_logout | At logout. |

When you are set up as a tcsh user, the common profile /etc/csh.login is run at login. $HOME/.tcshrc is run at login and by all new copies of tcsh. $HOME/.login is run only at login followed by .tcshrc. If there is no local .tcshrc file, the .cshrc file is used if it exits. You'll find more about tcsh in the Linux man pages.

Example of a system /etc/profile:

```
[david@nittedal /etc]$ more profile
# /etc/profile
```

```
# System wide environment and startup programs
# Functions and aliases go in /etc/bashrc


PATH="$PATH:/usr/X11R6/bin"
PS1="[\u@\h \W]\\$ "


ulimit -c 1000000
if [ `id -gn` = `id -un` -a `id -u` -gt 14 ]; then
        umask 002
else
        umask 022
fi
USER=`id -un`
LOGNAME=$USER
MAIL="/var/spool/mail/$USER"
HOSTNAME=`/bin/hostname`
HISTSIZE=1000
HISTFILESIZE=1000
ulimit -c 1000000
if [ `id -gn` = `id -un` -a `id -u` -gt 14 ]; then
        umask 002
else
        umask 022
fi
USER=`id -un`
LOGNAME=$USER
MAIL="/var/spool/mail/$USER"
HOSTNAME=`/bin/hostname`
HISTSIZE=1000
HISTFILESIZE=1000
export PATH PS1 HOSTNAME HISTSIZE HISTFILESIZE USER LOG-
NAME MAIL
for i in /etc/profile.d/*.sh ; do
        if [ -x $i ]; then
                . $i
        fi
done

unset i
[david@nittedal /etc]$
```

When you want to display the variables that are defined in the bash shell, enter `printenv`, `export`, or `env`. In the bash shell, you can define an environment variable by giving it a value and export the variable with the `export` command. In the tcsh shell, it is enough to give the variable a value.

## 18.5 Ending a terminal session

Under bash, the system looks for a logout file `$HOME/.logout` (under tcsh `$HOME/.tcsh_logout`) when you log out (see Figure 18-4). This gives you the opportunity to make your own security practice. Each time you want to remove a file, you can move it rather than delete it.

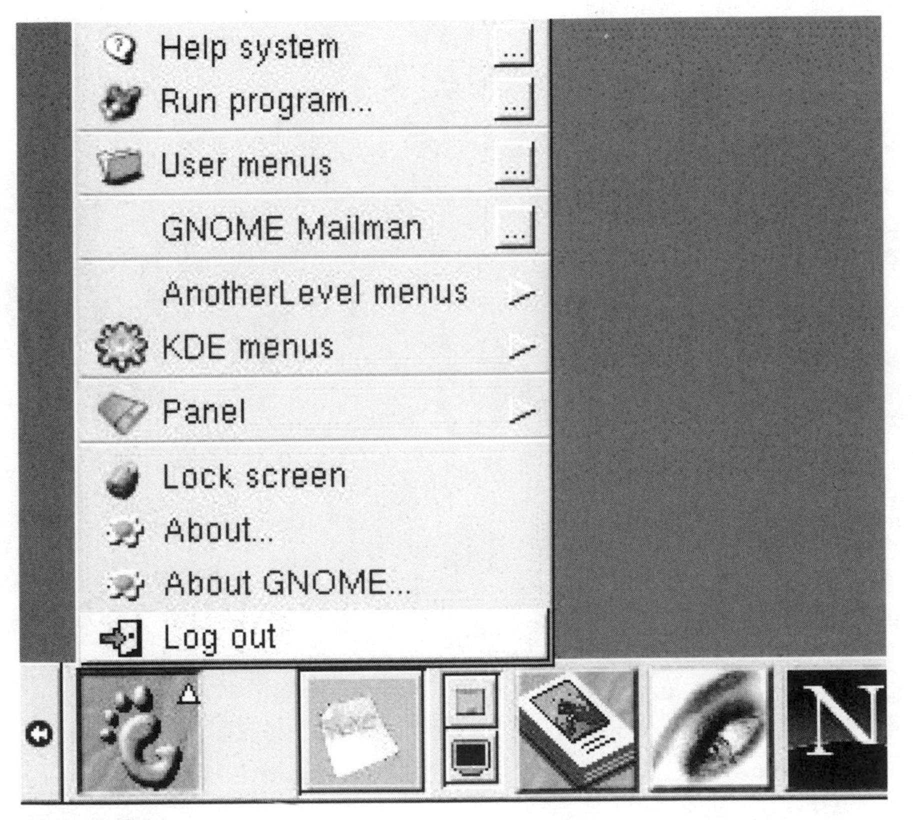


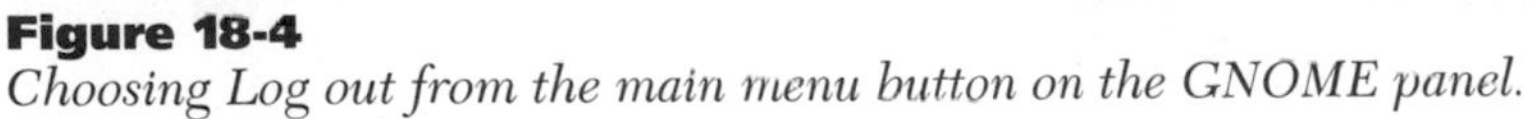

**Figure 18-4**
*Choosing Log out from the main menu button on the GNOME panel.*

In the example below, I have made an alias for the Linux command `re`. Instead of deleting the file, I move it to the `tmp` directory.

An example of `$HOME/.tcsh_logout` in the tcsh shell:

```
#
#   .tcsh_logout file
#
clear
find $TRASH \( -mtime +2 -o -size +15 \) -exec /bin/rm -
f {}
\;
```

The following must be updated in your `$HOME/.tcshrc` file:

```
setenv TRASH $HOME/.Trash
alias rm 'mv \!* $TRASH'
```

## Exercises for Chapter 18

1. What is the function of the `getty` (`/sbin/mingetty`) process and `gdm` process? Which process is the mother process of `getty` and `gdm`?
2. Which shell are you set up in if `/etc/passwd` contains the following: tcsh, sh, bash, ksh?
3. Under which shell is the Linux system administrator always set up?
4. Which logon files are used under the bash shell?
5. What functions do the `PS1` and `IFS` commands have under bash shell?
6. Define some useful aliases.
7. Make your own key files under bash (`.bash_profile`, `$HOME/.bashrc`).

CHAPTER
19

# Linux System Commands

## 19.1 Introduction

In this chapter, we'll take a look at different commands and tools that help you with system administration. Administering a Linux system doesn't differ much from administering a Unix system. If you are running X Window, most functions described in this chapter can also be executed from the control panel (*[root@nittedal /root]#* **control-panel &** ).

## 19.2 Linux key files

| Key File | Description |
|---|---|
| /etc/at.deny | Lists users that are not allowed to use the at command (background jobs). |
| /etc/bashrc | Global startup environment for bash shell users. |
| /etc/crontab | A crontab file for (fixed background jobs) all systems; valid for Red Hat Linux only. |
| /etc/exports | This file is set up when you want to share your filesystems with other Linux/Unix machines. |
| /etc/gettydefs | This is a system file that controls terminal polling. |
| /etc/group | Group definitions for users and system. |
| /etc/inittab | Describes the different init levels (system levels) with different system processes. |
| /etc/issue | Text file that controls the text to be shown prior to the login prompt. |
| /etc/issue.net | Text file that controls the text to be shown prior to the login prompt when connecting via the network. |
| /etc/ld.so.conf | Specifies where the dynamic loader looks for Linux libraries. |
| /etc/motd | Text message that is always displayed when you log in (not in X Window) via a character-based terminal. |

There are many files in Linux that need administration and supervision. They may be manually supervised, or you may use dedicated tools.

| Key File | Description |
|---|---|
| /etc/mtab | mtab is created as the filesystems are mounted. mtab is used to read the information, while /etc/fstab is the key file when configuring and defining filesystems. |
| /etc/passwd | User and system password file. |
| /etc/shadow | When you want increased security, the encrypted password is placed here. This is a condition if you want security-level shadow password or C2 (Orange Book). |

| Key File | Description (*Continued*) |
| --- | --- |
| /etc/syslog.conf | This file specifies the location of the log files. |
| /var/lock | Directory of locked files. |
| /var/log | Directory where all log files are placed. |
| /var/spool/cron/crontabs/ | Here you may keep a crontab file for each individual user. My recommendation is that you use /etc/crontab. |
| /var/spool/lpd | Directory that contains printer spooling area, control files, and printer queues. |
| /var/spool/mail | Directory for incoming mail. |
| /var/spool/mqueue/ | Directory where sendmail's mail queues are placed. |

I have already gone through many of these key files. Some of the other key files will be described in this chapter and later in this book.

## 19.3 Setup devices and system definitions

It is not necessary to reinstall the system when you want to reconfigure a Red Hat Linux system. The simplest method is to run the setup program. With the setup program, you may change:

- **Authorization configuration.**
- **Keyboard configuration.**
- **Mouse configuration.**
- **System services.**
- **Sound card configuration.**
- **Time zone configuration.**
- **X configuration.**

It is up to you whether you prefer to run setup from an X Window terminal window or directly from a character-based terminal session.

```
[root@nittedal /root]# setup
```

The setup program (see Figure 19-1) is menu based and simple to use.

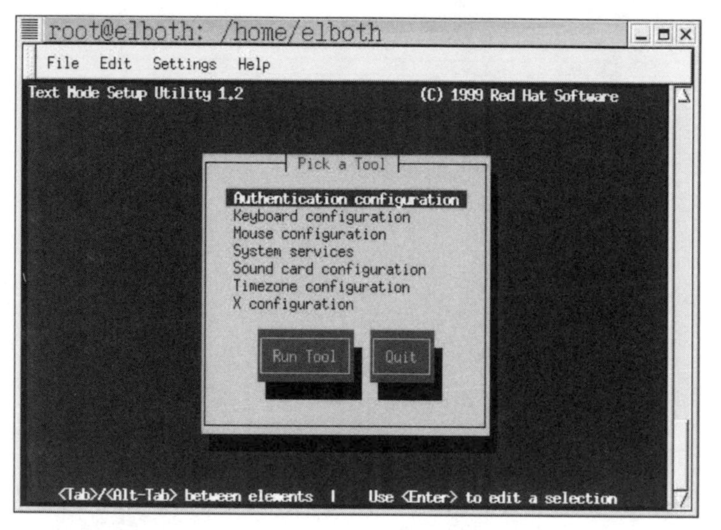


**Figure 19-1**
*The main menu in the Red Hat setup program.*

| Command | Description |
|---|---|
| `authconfig` | Defines the authorization level used by Linux for passwords. The options are NIS password, LDAP, and Kerberos. |
| `kbdconfig` | Sets up the desired keyboard. |
| `mouseconfig` | Use this command to alter mouse emulation. This command tries to analyze what kind of mouse you are using. |
| `ntsysv` | Sets the services to be run on your machine. |
| `sndconfig` | This command has simplified setting up a sound card. Now you load the required modules only. It is not necessary to generate a new Linux kernel. Loadable modules are found in the `/lib/modules/2.X/misc` directory. |
| `timeconfig` | Configures your time zone. |
| `Xconfigurator` | Sets up your X Window system. |

The table above gives an overview of commands that can be used to change various parts of the system. Be aware that all commands require that you be logged in as system administrator (root). There is a certain risk connected to the commands (menu options).

The first menu option lets you define the authorization level (see Figure 19-2) to be used for passwords. See the description in Chapter 3.

root@elboth: /home/elboth
File Edit Settings Help
authconfig 4.0.6 - (c) 1999, 2000 Red Hat, Inc.
User Information Configuration
[ ] Use NIS
[ ] Use LDAP
[ ] Use Hesiod
Next
Cancel
<Tab>/<Alt-Tab> between elements | <Space> selects | <F12> next screen

**Figure 19-2**
*Defining authorization level from the Red Hat setup program* (`authconfig`).

The second menu option lets you change the keyboard (see Figure 19-3). The normal choice is `US-latin1` or us (see also Chapter 3, "Installation").

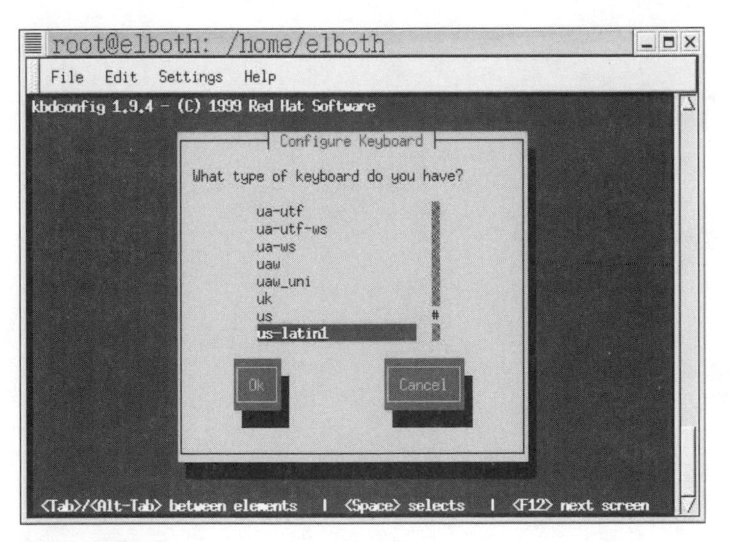


**Figure 19-3**
*Defining keyboard from the Red Hat setup program* (`kbdconfig`).

The next menu option lets you change mouse emulation (see Figure 19-4). This command tries to analyze what kind of mouse you are using.

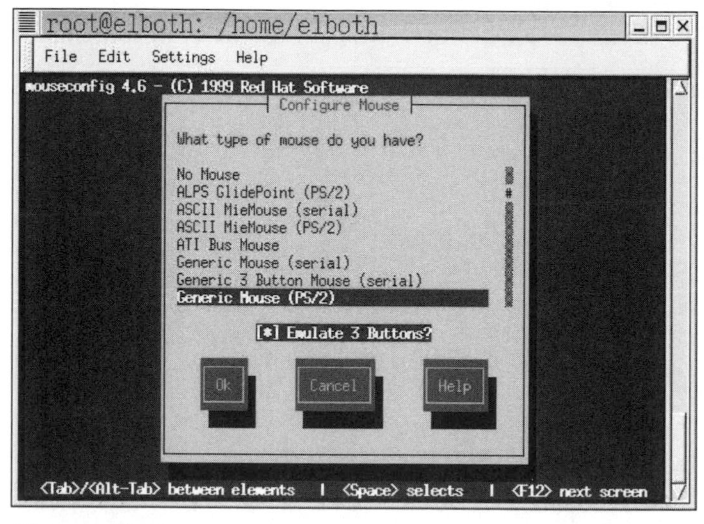


**Figure 19–4**
*Defining mouse emulation from the Red Hat setup program* (`mouseconfig`).

With the next option, you can choose the services (see Figure 19-5) you want to run on your system.

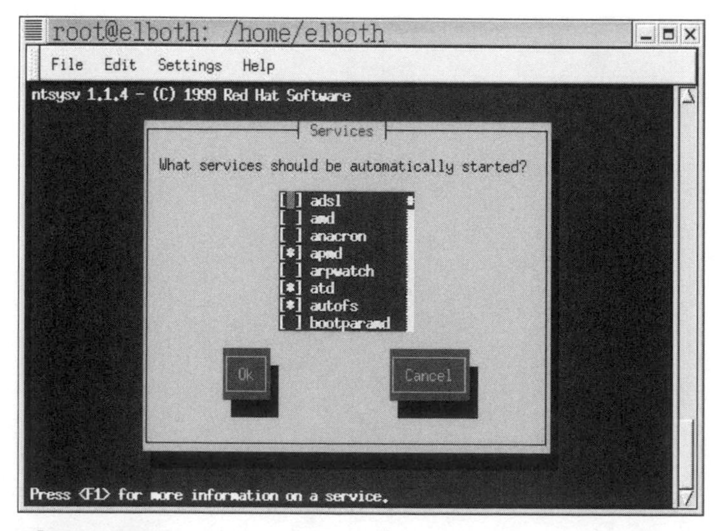


**Figure 19–5**
*Defining services from the Red Hat setup program* (`ntsysv`).

With the next menu option, you can configure the sound card (see Figure 19-6). Only the required modules are loaded. Before running this routine, you should get your sound card setup details like interrupts, DMA channels, and I/O addresses. If you have a plug-and-play sound card, setting up the sound card can be difficult in many cases. Sometimes, you will need to disable plug-and-play on the card (via jumpers or card setup tools). If you still have problems with `snd-config`, there are a couple of other ways to attack the problem. `sndconfig` tries to set up a good set of default values for the plug-and-play settings, and then load the right sound modules. If it can't find a good set of values itself, you can force `sndconfig` not to use default values by writing the command `/usr/sbin/sndconfig - noautoconfig`. Now you can use your own values.

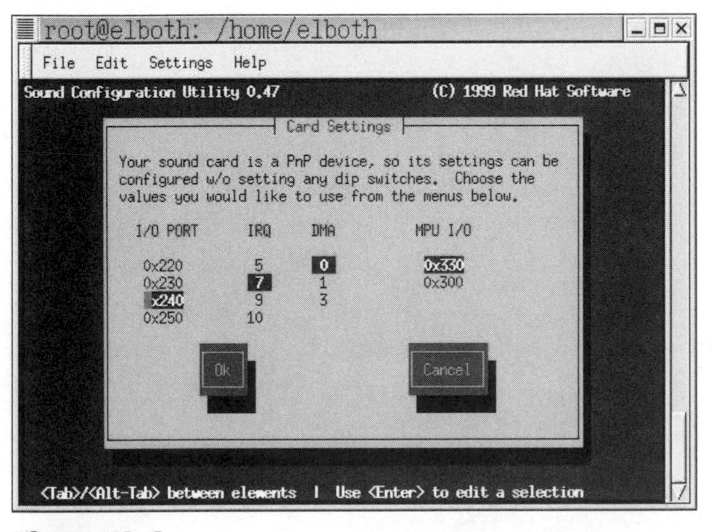


**Figure 19-6**
*Configuring the sound card from the Red Hat setup program* (`sndconfig`).

The next menu option lets you define the geographical location (see Figure 19-7) of your PC (time zone). This is described in more detail in Chapter 3.

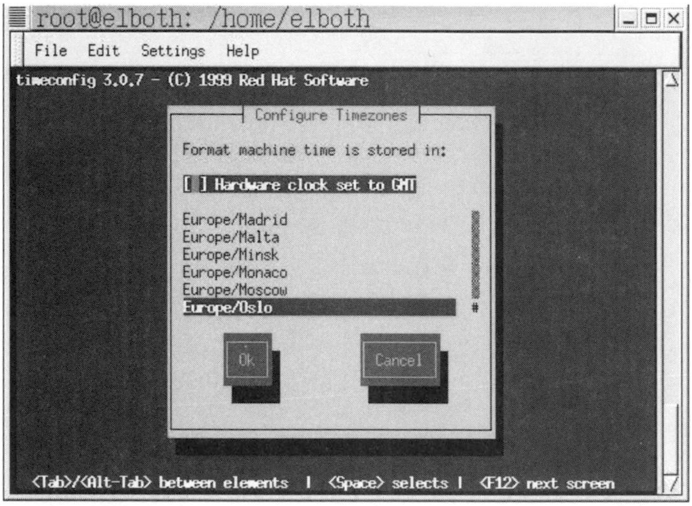

**Figure 19-7**
*Defining your geographical location (time zone) from the Red Hat setup program* (`timeconfig`).

With the last menu option, you can change your graphic display card (X Window system; see Figure 19-8). This is only necessary if you have changed the display card after installation. You'll find more about X Window in Chapter 10.

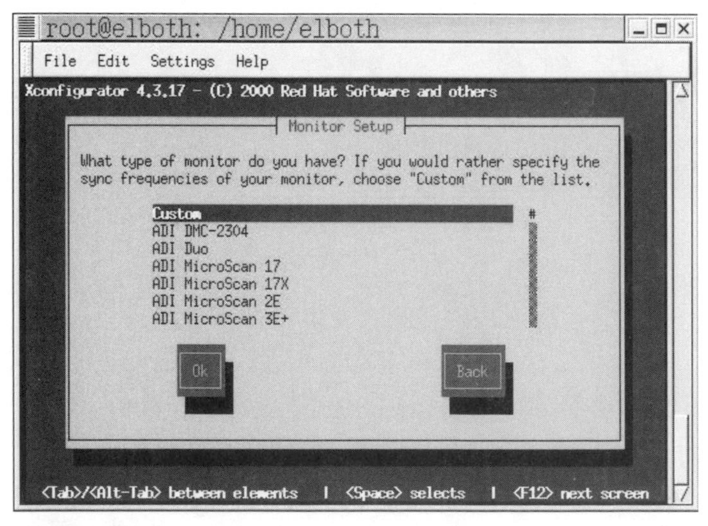


**Figure 19-8**
*Defining your monitor/display (X Window system) from the Red Hat setup program* (`Xconfigurator`).

If Xconfigurator cannot find your card, you'll see a list of potential graphic display cards. You must at least know this:

- **Name of graphic display card.**
- **Chipset used by display card.**
- **Amount of memory on display card.**
- **Type of display (or horizontal/vertical sync frequency).**

After selecting the display card, you must mark off the type of display you are using. You must enter the technical specifications of your display, e.g., horizontal sync, vertical sync, etc., if the system cannot find your display. You'll find this information in the documentation that came with your display. It is essential not to choose a display type with higher technical specifications than the actual display, as this may damage your display. Luckily, most modern displays are smart enough to avoid this.

When you have selected a graphic display card, you will be asked how much memory is on your card. If you have chosen a graphic display card that supports a dedicated clock chip, Xconfigurator will display a list of different clock chips. The simplest solution is to select "No Clockchip Setting". In most cases, Xfree86 will figure out which clock chip to use. Finally, you can select the most suitable display mode (640x480, 800x600, 1024x786, 1200x1024, 1600x1200, etc.). 800x600 or 1024x786 is best suited for a 15" display; 1024x768 is fine for a 17" display; 19" and 21" displays work well with 1200x1024. For some high-quality 19" and 21" displays, you can also use 1600x1200. Now, save your X Window setup. The X Window setup is saved in the `/etc/X11/XF86-Config` file. There is more about installing X Window in Chapter 10.

## 19.4 Defining users

Under Linux, new users can be defined with the `adduser` command, through X Window (`usercfg`), or by manually updating the key files. The files that must be updated are `/etc/passwd`, `/etc/shadow`, and `/etc/group`. In addition, you must make a home directory, e.g., `/home/hansen`. If the users have special requirements, you must also make the right login files. When defining a user, you should know the following:

- **The user's ID (login name) and associated user number.**
- **The user's password.**

- **The group ID and associated group number.**
- **Which user shell (tcsh, bash, sh, ksh) to set for the user.**
- **Description of user.**
- **Where to place user (filesystem, directory).**

Under Linux, user numbers are in the range from 100 to 60,000. In some Unix dialects, the user number range is from 100 to 9,999. Linux group numbers are between 100 and 60,000. In some Unix dialects, the range is from 50 to 100 or 200.

Usernames and group names are unambiguously mapped to user numbers and group numbers, respectively.

Before a user can be removed:

- **All files and subdirectories must be removed from the user area.**
- **The mail file must be removed from `/var/spool/mail/"usr"`.**

In the `/etc/passwd` file, you can see the relationship between username and user number; for example:

```
[root@nittedal /root]# more /etc/passwd
root:BDzbOHOS/sf76:0:0:root:/root:/bin/bash
bin:*:1:1:bin:/bin:
daemon:*:2:2:daemon:/sbin:
...
david:lhs2mCR4tlm/A:500:110::/home/david:/bin/bash
vigdis:nxJQBhoNTYqYA:502:114::/home/vigdis:/bin/bash
simon:hy43qBUeSJ/9s:504:112::/home/simon:/bin/bash
[root@nittedal /root]#
```

In the `/etc/group` file, you can see the relationship between group name and group number; for example:

```
[root@nittedal /root]# more /etc/group
root::0:root
bin::1:root,bin,daemon
...
postgres:x:233:
Support:x:110:
service:x:112:
regnskap:x:114:
[root@nittedal /root]#
```

## 19.5 User administration – useradd

When you want to define new users, edit existing users, or remove users, you can run the `useradd` script, use the X Window `usercfg`, or execute `linuxconf`. It is also possible to update all files manually. From `useradd` and `usercfg`, you can also define the minimum allowed password length and the maximum number of weeks a password may be used.

**useradd Command – User Administration**

| | |
|---|---|
| Command | `useradd [options...] [argument...]` |
| Function | Defines or changes user definitions. |
| Argument | See the Linux man pages. |
| Options | See the Linux man pages. |

Examples:

```
[root@nittedal /root]# useradd -u 502 -g books -d
/home/anne -s /bin/bash anne
[root@nittedal /root]# useradd -u 504 -g service -d
/home/simon -s /bin/bash simon
```

Here, I define two new users (see Figure 19-9), `anne` and `simon`, with the associated user numbers `502` and `504`. They are defined in different groups: `books` and `service`. They are both set up in the bash shell.

```
[root@nittedal /root]# passwd anne
New UNIX password:
Retype new UNIX password:
passwd: all authentication tokens updated successfully
[root@nittedal /root]# passwd simon
New UNIX password:
Retype new UNIX password:
passwd: all authentication tokens updated successfully
[root@nittedal /root]#
```

When you define the users, you set their password (see Figure 19-9). You can also set the password from the `useradd` command by using the `password`

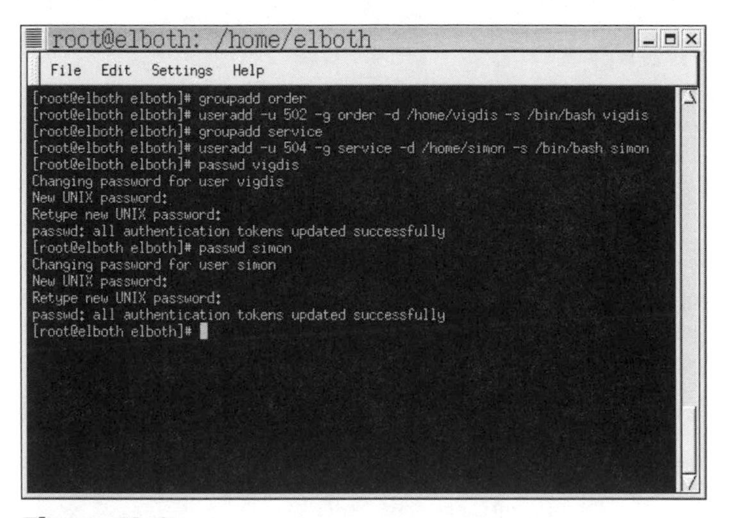


**Figure 19-9**
*User administration from* `linuxconf`.

option. If you want to simplify it, just enter:

```
[root@nittedal /root]# useradd bill
```

You can also define Bill from `linuxconf` (see Figure 19-10). `useradd` will define all new users under `/home`, unless otherwise specified. `bill`'s new home

```
User account creation
You must specify at least the login name
and the full name

Base info | Params | Privileges
The account is enabled
Login name
Full name
group (opt)
Supplementary groups
Home directory(opt)
Command interpreter(opt)    /bin/bash
User ID(opt)

Accept  Cancel  Del  Tasks  Help
```

**Figure 19-10**
*Defining users in* `linuxconf`.

directory is `/home/bill`. His default shell is `/bin/bash`. As a new user just has been defined with user number 504 (`simon`), the next user will get ID number 505. `bill`'s group ID will be the same as his `user-id`. The password for this user is set with `passwd`, but may also be set from `linuxconf` (see Figure 19-11).

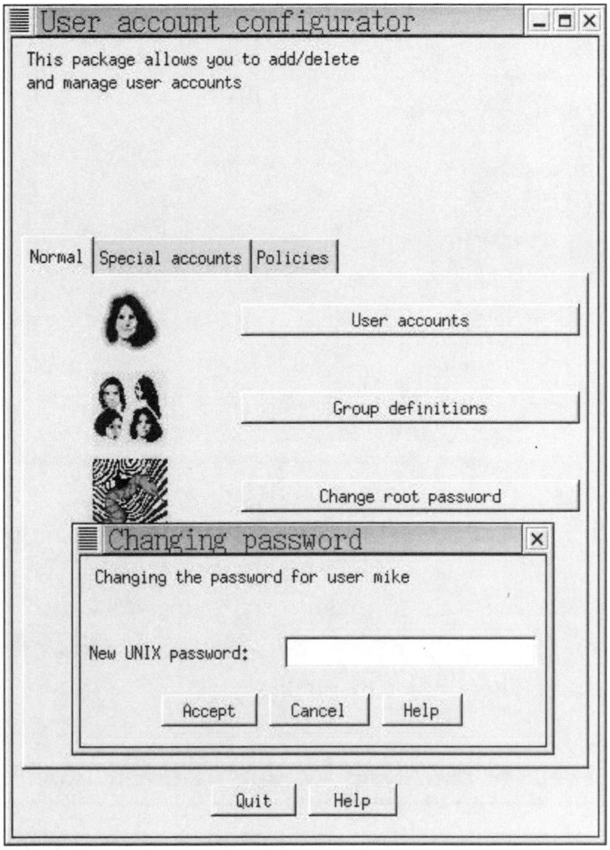

**Figure 19-11**
*Defining new password from* `linuxconf`.

Your security is best controlled from `linuxconf` (see Figure 19-12).

If you as a regular (non-root) user forget your password, you must call the system administrator, or root. Only root may change any password. For example (as root): `passwd david`. This will prompt for a new password for the user `david`. There is no need for knowing the old password. If you forget the root password, you must boot Linux in single mode. (At the `lilo` prompt, you type `linux single`.) You can now log into the system automatically as root without the Linux system asking you for a password. As root, you may change the root password using the Linux `passwd` command.

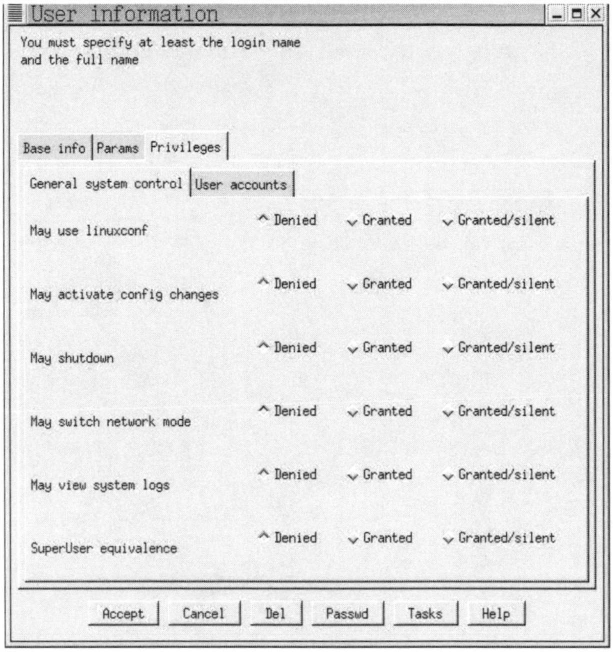

**Figure 19–12**
*Defining security from* `linuxconf`.

## 19.6 Group administration – groupadd

When you want to make new groups, edit existing groups, or remove groups, you can run the `groupadd` script, X Window's `usercfg`, `linuxconf`, or you can update all files manually.

**groupadd Command – Group Administration**

| | |
|---|---|
| Command | `groupadd [-g group id] [group name]` |
| Function | Defines or changes group definitions. |
| `-g group id` | New group number. |
| `group name` | New group name. |

Example:

```
[root@nittedal /root]# groupadd -g 112 service
[root@nittedal /root]# groupadd -g 114 books
```

This defines two new groups, `service` and `books`. The groups have group numbers `112` and `114`.

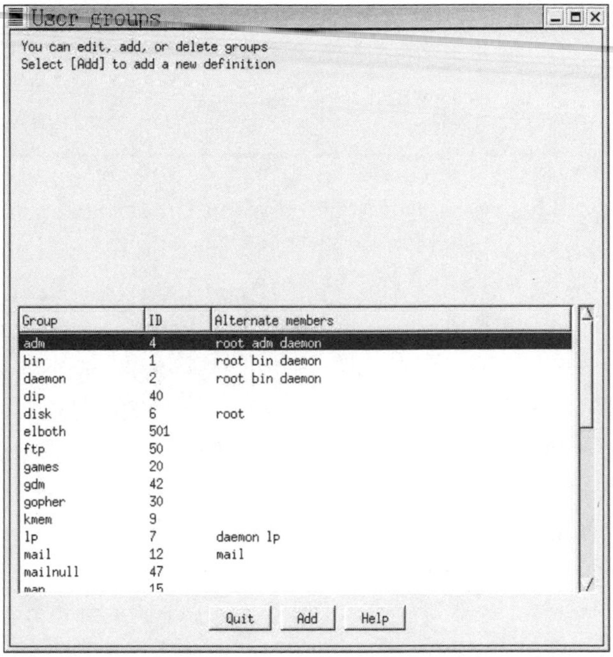

**Figure 19–13**
*Defining groups from* `linuxconf`.

You can also define groups from `linuxconf` (see Figure 19-13).

## 19.7 Check filesystems – fsck

All Linux systems have at least one filesystem called root. It is represented with the symbol /. The root filesystem consists of programs and directories. It is possible to have a total of 16 filesystems on one physical hard disk drive (PC architecture). The most frequently used names of filesystems are: `/usr`, `/usr/src`, `/usr/local`, `/var`, `/var/spool`, `/home`, etc. Linux filesystems normally have a 1KB block size.

| Filesystem | Type |
| --- | --- |
| `e2fsck (fsck.ext2)` | Linux default. |
| `e3fsck (fsck.ext3)` | New Linux filesystem. |
| `fsck.minix` | Minix filesystem. |
| `xfsck (fsck.xiafs)` | Xia file system. |
| `Ext-FS` | Extended FS filesystem |

| Filesystem | Type (*Continued*) |
|---|---|
| `DOS/VFAT` | MS-DOS filesystem. |
| `System V` | Unix System V filesystem. |

The system administrator's maintenance work is simplified with multiple filesystems. When you have a specific filesystem for users, it is simpler to run backups and to clean up. If you have free hard disk capacity (with a defined filesystem), a new filesystem can be mounted with the `mount` command.

In most flavors of Unix, different filesystems can be defined. Today, Linux supports many different file systems. The list above is just a selection.

Whenever you start your Linux system, the status of your Linux filesystems is checked. The Linux filesystem is a structured collection of data that only functions when the structure is well-maintained.

Under normal conditions, the OS maintains the filesystem, but whenever there is a physical failure in the system, i.e., power cut, hard disk drive failure, etc., a cleanup is necessary. Under Linux, `fsck` will start automatically after a power cut.

The `/etc/fsck` command is available to check and fix filesystems. Whenever possible, the `fsck` command will fix references and clean up the filesystem.

Before repairing the filesystem with `fsck`, the system must be taken down and rebooted in single user mode.

**fsck Command - Cleans Up Filesystems**

| | |
|---|---|
| Command | `/etc/fsck [option] [file system type] ...` |
| Function | Analyzes the filesystem, and interactively repairs damaged filesystems. If the filesystem is consistent, the number of files, number of used blocks, and number of free blocks are reported. Be aware that `fsck` is not always capable of saving all data. |
| Argument | See the Linux man pages. |
| Options | See the Linux man pages. |

It is important to remember that you cannot clean up active filesystems.

Examples:

```
[root@nittedal /]# /etc/fsck -A
```

The program checks all filesystems defined in `/etc/fstab`. This command normally starts from `/etc/rc.d/rc.sysinit`.

```
[root@nittedal /]# /etc/fsck -A -R
```

Checks all filesystems except root.

```
[root@nittedal /]# /etc/fsck  -A -R -t e2fsck
```

Checks all filesystems of the `e2fsck` type. The filesystem cannot be root.

When the `fsck` program starts, it normally runs through several phases. Here are the six logical phases.

- **Phase 1**—In the first phase, blocks and sizes are checked. This means that `fsck` reads the inode list and registers file sizes and the locations of data blocks.
- **Phase 2**—In phase 2, pathnames to the various files are checked. Files with a duplicate set of data blocks are removed by `fsck`. In this phase, it is suggested that you take part in the process as root and decide what is to be removed and what is to be kept.
- **Phase 3**—In phase 3, files that have no references are placed in a directory called `lost+found`. Because the directory where the file was kept before has been damaged, the file has no filename. The file is just given a number in the `lost+found` directory.
- **Phase 4**—In phase 4, link references to files that have survived the previous phases are checked. In some cases, you will find files that had no pointer in the directory structure, although they had an inode that could be connected to the filesystem in the `lost+found` directory.
- **Phase 5**—In phase 5, the list of free blocks is updated. The `fsck` command analyzes the list of free blocks and adds up missing and unused blocks. When `fsck` finds an inconsistency, a new list of free blocks will be generated.
- **Phase 6**—In phase 6, the new list of free and used blocks from the changed filesystem is saved. You may have to run the `fsck` command several times before a complete system is error-free.

System files: `/etc/fstab` and filesystems

## 19.8 Make filesystems – mke2fs

With the `mke2fs` command, you can make filesystems by writing to a specified device driver. The name of the device driver depends on where you want to make the filesystem. You can, for example, generate a filesystem on a floppy disk or a hard disk drive. This equals formatting a floppy disk under MS-DOS or Windows.

**mk2fs Command – Makes Filesystems**

| | |
|---|---|
| Command | `/etc/mke2fs [-V] [-T file system type] [fs-options] [file system] [blocks]` |
| Function | Makes filesystems. |
| Argument | See the Linux man pages. |
| Options | See the Linux man pages. |
| `-V` | Verbose execution. |
| `-T filesystem` | What filesystem you want to create. |

Examples:

```
[root@nittedal /root]# mke2fs /dev/fd0 1140
```

Here, I generate a filesystem on a 3.5" 1.44MB floppy disk. I reserve 1400 blocks (each block has 1024 bytes).

See also: `fsck`, `mkfs`, filesystems

## 19.9 Mount filesystems – (u)mount

With the `mount` command, you can mount local or external filesystems. The filesystem can be placed on the hard disk that holds your root filesystem (there must be sufficient free space on the hard disk drive), on a different hard disk drive, on a CD-ROM, or on a floppy disk.

To connect, the `mount` command is used; to disconnect, use the `umount` command. You can also use X Window (user mount tool; *[root@nittedal /root]#* **usermount &**), which is considerably easier to use.

If you want automatic mounting, there are several solutions. Red Hat has its own process called automount (RPM package) which lets you enter, for example, cd /misc/cd (the CD disk) or cd /misc/fd (floppy drive) without mounting the medium first.

**mount/umount Commands – (Un)Mounts Filesystems**

| | |
|---|---|
| Command | `mount [options] device \| dir`<br>`umount [options] device \| dir [...]` |
| Function | Mounts and unmounts file structures (filesystems). The file structure connects to a directory that must be made in advance. This directory becomes the root directory for the new file structure. The directory should be empty before being connected to a filesystem. If there are files in the directory, these will be invisible as long as the directory is mounted. |
| Argument | See the Linux man pages. |
| Options | See the Linux man pages. |

You can from linuxconf edit, add, or delete mounts (see Figure 19-14).

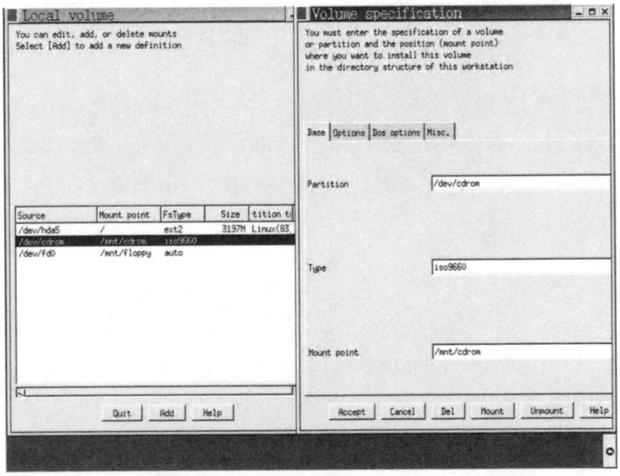

**Figure 19-14**
*Edit, add, or deleting mounts from GNOME.*

The mount and umount commands keep their own tables of connected units. If you enter mount with no arguments, the Linux system displays all mounted filesystems, which directory they belong to, whether the file structure is read- and write-enabled or read-only, and the date when the units were connected.

The umount command removes file structures that are connected to specific directories. Only the system administrator may use the `mount` and `umount` commands.

Examples:

```
[root@nittedal /root]# mount /dev/cdrom /mnt/cdrom
```

This connects `/dev/cdrom` to `/mnt/cdrom`. `/mnt/cdrom` must be a directory (node).

If you want to keep your private files on a floppy disk, you can make a private filesystem on a floppy by means of `mkfs` (see Chapter 15 and the Linux man pages).

```
[root@nittedal /root]# mke2fs /dev/fd0 1440
[root@nittedal /root]# mount -t ext2 /dev/fd0 /mnt
```

This mounts the filesystem. The data is available with the `cd` command.

```
[root@nittedal /root]# cd /mnt
```

To unmount the node, enter:

```
[root@nittedal /root]# umount /mnt
```

The floppy disk cannot be in use when you execute the `umount` command. You cannot be inside the floppy directory structure either.

The following command mounts all filesystems except systems of the `msdos` and `ext` types:

```
[root@nittedal /root]# mount -a -t nomsdos,ext
```

This example shows how to mount remote filesystems via NFS (Network Filesystem):

```
[root@nittedal /root]# mount -t nfs pluto:/data/tmp /mnt
```

The host `pluto` must be defined in your `/etc/hosts` table. The system administrator (root) for the `pluto` machine must make the filesystem `/data/tmp` accessible to you via the `/etc/export` file.

See also: `fsck`, `umount`, `mount` and filesystems
System files: `/etc/mnttab` mount table

## 19.10 Taking the Linux system down

When the system administrator takes the system down, there is more to it than just physically turning the machine off. Before turning the computer off, open files must be closed and processes finished. We'll have a look at the three most usual methods for taking a Linux system down. These commands may be used by root only.

You can also take down the system from the GNOME GUI environment (see Figure 19-15).

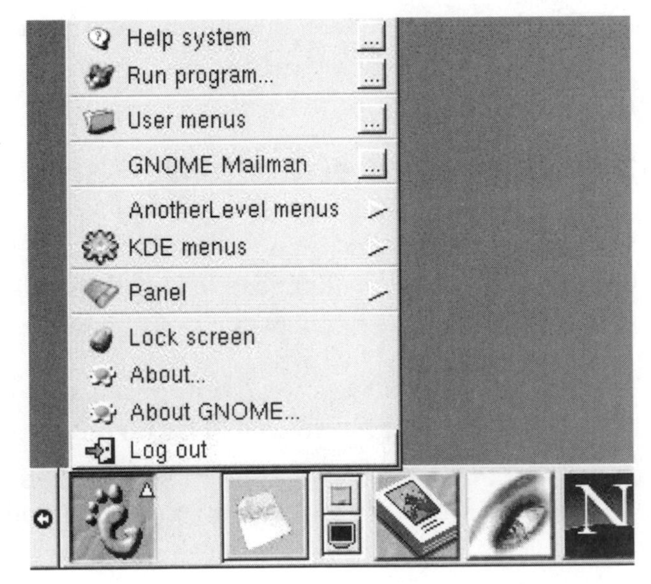


**Figure 19-15**
*From the main menu button on the panel you find the label Log out.*

## 19.11 Fast reboot – reboot

The `reboot` command closes the filesystem, stops the CPU, and locks the hard disk drive's read/write heads before it starts the system again. The `reboot` command acts immediately, so all users should be logged out. This command is recommended on single-user Linux workstations only.

**reboot Command – Takes the Linux System Down and Up Again**

| | |
|---|---|
| Command | `reboot [options]` |
| Function | Updates the super block (see Chapter 7 about the inode system), closes the filesystem, stops the CPU, and locks hard disk drive heads. Then takes the system up. |
| Argument | See the Linux man pages. |
| Options | See the Linux man pages. |

```
[root@nittedal /root]# reboot
```

This command first takes the system down, then boots it again.

See also: `shutdown` and `inittab`

## 19.12 Normal shutdown – shutdown

When other users are active on the system, it is best to take the Linux system down softly with the `shutdown` command. This command terminates all processes. The following happens when you execute the `shutdown` command:

- **All users that are logged in to the system get a message telling them that the system will be taken down.**
- **All processes are terminated.**
- **All filesystems and super blocks are updated.**

**shutdown Command – Shuts the Linux System Down**

| | |
|---|---|
| Command | `shutdown [-h] [-r] time [message]` |
| Function | Softly shuts the Linux system down. |
| Argument | See the Linux man pages. |
| Options | See the Linux man pages. |
| `-h` | Locks the Linux system after shutdown. |
| `-r` | Boots the Linux system after shutdown (default). |
| Time | You decide how long a full shutdown takes. Use hours:minutes, only minutes, or you can use the word **now**, which is an alias for +0. |
| Message | Text message sent to all users. |

Examples:

```
[root@nittedal /root]# shutdown -h 100 System will be in
operation again at 14:00 hours.
```

This shuts the system down after 10 minutes. No automatic reboot is included. A message informs the users that the system is in operation again at 14:00 hours (2 p.m.).

```
[root@nittedal /root]# shutdown -r  10
```

Shuts the system down immediately. Because the `-r` option is included, the system automatically reboots.

See also: `reboot` and `init`

System files: `/fastboot`, `/etc/inittab`, `/etc/init.d/halt`, `/etc/init.d/reboot`, `/etc/shutdown.allow`

## 19.13 Process control initialization – init

The system levels, also called init levels, are defined in `/etc/inittab`. There are eight different system levels in a Linux system. Only a certain group of processes may be run at each level. The different levels are called 0, 1, 2, 3, 4, 5, 6, S, and s, where S, s, and 1 are identical.

**init Command – Set Linux System Level**

| | |
|---|---|
| Command | `init [option]` |
| Function | Runs the OS at different init levels. |
| Argument | See the Linux man pages. |
| Options | See the Linux man pages. |
| `0` | Shuts system down. |
| `1` | Takes system into single-user mode. |
| `2` | Takes system into multi-user mode. |
| `3` | This mode is an extension of multi-user mode. NFS (Network Filesystem) is added; is also called NFS mode or server mode. |
| `4` | Alternative multi-user mode. Normally not in use, but |

**init Command – Set Linux System Level (*Continued*)**

| | |
|---|---|
| | may be configured for special purposes. |
| `5` | Boots the system in X11 (xdm) mode. |
| `6` | Shuts system down and reboots. Not recommended. |
| `s, S` | Shuts system down in single-user mode. The terminal that executes this command becomes the system console. All connected filesystems remain active. Only processes are removed. |
| `7-9` | Exists, but there's no documentation. |

Examples:

```
[root@nittedal /root]# init 0
```

This shuts the system down in the normal manner. It has the same function as `shutdown -h`.

```
[root@nittedal /root]# init s
```

Shuts the system down in single-user mode.

```
[root@nittedal /root]# init 2
```

Takes the system in multi-user mode. If you want server mode, enter `init 3`.

See also: `shutdown`, `reboot`, `inittab`

System files: `/fastboot`, `/etc/inittab`, `/etc/init.d/halt`, `/etc/init.d/reboot`, `/etc/shutdown.allow`, `/etc/initscript`, `/etc/ioctl.save`, `/dev/console`, `/var/run/utmp`, `/var/log/wtmp`, `/dev/initctl`

## 19.14 Configure services – ntsysv

The services that run on your Red Hat Linux machine depend on the installation class you selected when you did your installation.

Under Red Hat Linux you could choose:

- **GNOME Workstation or KDE Workstation**
- **Server**
- **Custom**

After installation, you may change the services you want in operation at any time by running:

```
[root@nittedal /root]# /usr/sbin/ntsysv
```

A more complicated but quicker method is using the `/sbin/chkconfig` program.

## 19.15 Installation packages – rpm

RPM, Red Hat Packet Manager, and the Debian package system, Deslect, are the most frequently used systems for handling program packages under various Linux distributions. You may use RPM only when the program you are installing is supplied in RPM format. Under Red Hat, program packages may be installed or uninstalled either via the GUI (see Figure 19-16) or by using the RPM command from a terminal prompt. If you have X Window, my recommendation is that you use `gnorpm`, which is an elegant GUI for installing, upgrading, uninstalling, and examining program packages.

```
[root@nittedal /root]# gnorpm &
```

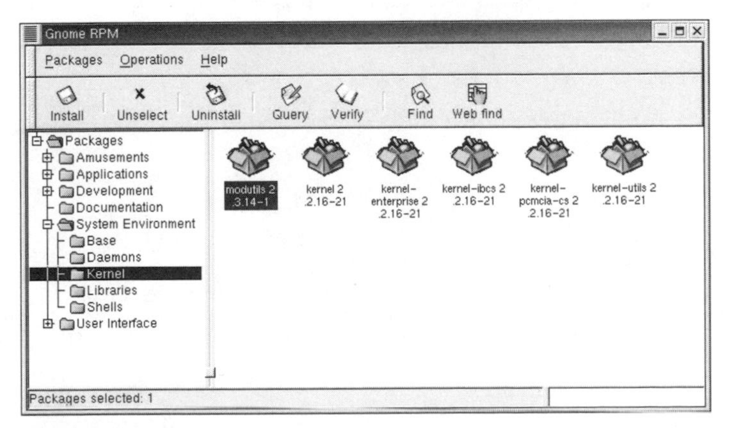


**Figure 19-16**
*The main menu from GNOME RPM (`gnorpm`).*

From the command line, use the RPM command directly as described in this table:

**rpm Command – (Un)Installs Program Packages**

| | |
|---|---|
| Command | `rpm [option]` |
| Function | Advanced Linux package program. |
| Argument | See the Linux man pages. |
| Options | See the Linux man pages. |

| **Mode** | **Description** |
|---|---|
| Installation | `rpm -ivh <program file.rpm>` (`i` means installer, `v` means give clear error messages, `h` means show what you are doing by displaying the # character during the process.)<br>To reinstall a program that has been installed once before:<br>`rpm -ivh -replacepkgs <program file.rpm>`<br>To reinstall a program that has been installed once before by a different method than `rpm` (this option overwrites existing files):<br>`rpm -ivh -replacefiles<program file.rpm>` |
| Uninstall | `rpm -e <program name>` |
| Upgrade | `rpm -Uvh <program file.rpm>` |
| Verification | To verify all programs:<br>`rpm -V <program name>` |
| Queries | To see an overview of all RPM packages installed on your system:<br>`rpm -qa`<br>To query for a single program:<br>`rpm -qdf <file name>`<br>(`q` means query, `d` means show documentation files, `f` means examine the program package that "owns" this file.)<br>For example:<br>*[root@nittedal /root]#* **rpm –qdf /bin/bash**<br>To configure files that are part of a certain program |

| Mode | Description *(Continued)* |
|---|---|
| | package: `rpm -qc <program name>` To check if all files are included: `rpm -qs <program name>` To see the files in an RPM package and where they will be installed: `rpm -qlp <program file.rpm>` |

Examples:
To install Xfree86-Mach8, enter:

```
[root@nittedal /root]# rpm -ivh Xfree86-Mach8
```

You must be in the same directory as the file you are installing; in this example, /root.

When you need more information about a program that you are using, you may enter:

```
[root@nittedal /root]# rpm -qdf /bin/tcsh
```

When missing a file, verify this with the `rpm` command. For example:

```
[root@nittedal /root]# rpm -Vf /bin/bash
```

In the example below, I remove the program package doom:

```
[root@nittedal /root]# rpm -e doom-1.8.9
```

Below is an example of upgrading:

```
[root@nittedal /root]# rpm -Uvh Xfree86-Mach8.rpm
```

When you want to query about one single program package, enter:

```
[root@nittedal /root]# rpm -q Xfree86-Mach8
```

The Red Hat Packet Manager is easiest to use from the GNOME GUI. You can easily choose an `rpm` package and install it (see Figure 19-17).

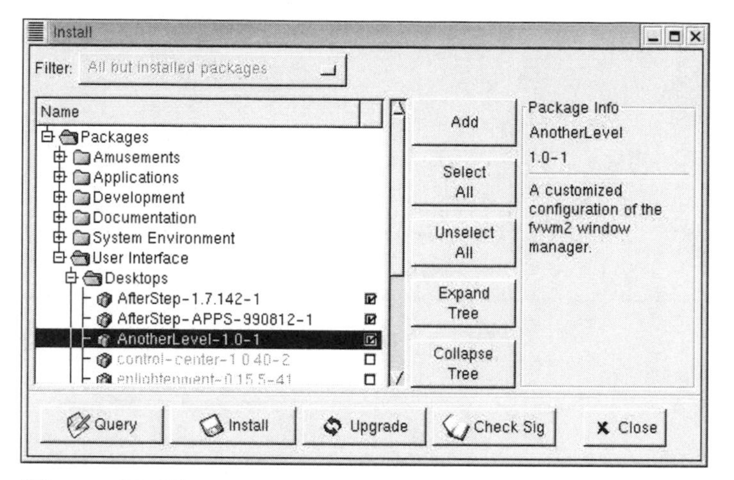


**Figure 19-17**
*Example with GNOME gnorpm choosing three* `rpm` *packages.*

To find out which files are included in the package `doom-1.8.9.rpm`, you must enter:

```
[root@nittedal /root]# rpm -qlp doom-1.8.9.rpm
```

You must work from the same directory as the RPM package or enter the full search path to the RPM package.

If you need more information about how to use RPM, refer to this Web site: http://www.rpm.org

## 19.16 Compiling source code

Using RPM has many advantages with respect to keeping track of and maintaining programs. However, some programs are only supplied with source code as `tar.gz` files. It is also quite common that new versions of programs are first published in `tar.gz` format and after some time in RPM format. For that reason, it is useful to be able to install these programs too. You must have the necessary development tools installed on your computer. Different programs may require different tools, but if you included development tools when installing a Linux distribution like Red Hat, you should have the most important ones.

The first step is to copy the `tar.gz` file to a suitable directory, e.g.,

/home/david/prog. You move to this directory and unpack the file with the tar -xvzf <filename> command.

A catalog tree is made for this program packet under /home/david/prog. Move into this directory and look for files called README, etc. These files contain more information about the installation.

The elements that make up an installation may vary. Many program installations start with ./configure. This is a program that surveys your computer environment and sets some parameters that are needed during the compilation process. Sometimes you will find switches that give you some control over the program details. Check if ./configure -help holds some information.

The ./make command starts the compilation process and makes the binary files that the program uses. Many programs also support the ./make install command, which places files in the correct directories.

These compilers and tools are frequently used:

| Compiler/Tool | Description |
|---|---|
| cc | C compiler. |
| CC | C++ compiler (a more object-oriented development tool than C). |
| gcc | GNU C compiler (cc is linked to gcc, which uses egcs). |
| g++ | GNU C++compiler (CC is linked to g++ which uses egcs). |
| ld | System links and loads. |

Use the Linux gcc compiler if you are only compiling one single file. Ninety five percent of all Linux code is written in C. See Figure 19-18 for an example C program.

I used the vi editor to make the program. The compiling tool I used was cc.

```
[david@nittedal david]$ cc -o intro intro.c
```

In the example above, intro is the result file when compiling the source file intro.c. The finished program can be run directly by entering:

```
[david@nittedal david]$ ./intro
```

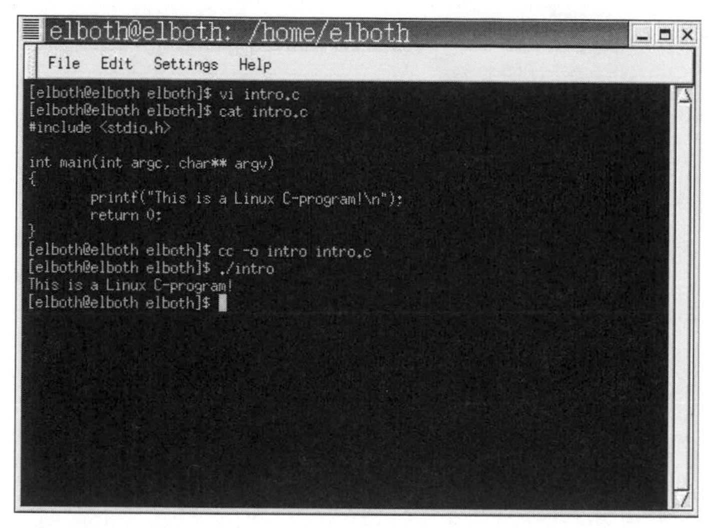


**Figure 19–18**
*Making a C-program.*

## 19.17 Installation example

Below you will find an example describing how to install Netscape Communicator 6.2. The installation files in this example are packed and in `tar` format on a CD-ROM disk (`/netscape/communicator-v62-export.x86-unknown-linux2.2.tar.gz`).

I start by logging in as root. If X Window is not already running, I start X Window from the terminal prompt with `startx` (*[root@nittedal /root]#* **startx**). From X Window, I start a terminal window. Then I make a temporary directory for the installation files.

```
[root@nittedal /root]# mkdir /tmp/netscape
```

I copy the files from the CD to the hard disk drive:

```
[root@nittedal /root]# cp /mnt/cdrom/netscape/communica-
tor-v62-export.x86-unknown-linux2.2.tar.gz /tmp/netscape
```

I move down to the `/tmp/netscape` directory:

```
[root@nittedal /root]# cd /tmp/netscape
```

Then I unpack the installation files:

```
[root@nittedal /tmp/netscape]# gzip -dc communicator-v62-
export.x86-unknown-linux2.2.tar.gz | tar -xvf
```

(You may also enter `tar -xvzf communicator-v62-export.x86-unknown-linux2.2.tar.gz`)

I move down to the Netscape directory:

```
[root@nittedal /tmp/netscape]# cd communicator-v62-
export.x86-unknown-linux2.2
```

Then I run the installation program:

```
[root@nittedal /tmp/netscape/communicator-v62-export.x86-
unknown-linux2.2]# ./ns-install
```

I move back to my home directory:

```
[root@nittedal /tmp/netscape/communicator-v62-export.x86-
unknown-linux2.2]# cd
```

I start the new Netscape Communicator 6.2 by entering the following text in a terminal window under X11:

```
[root@nittedal /root]# /usr/local/netscape/netscape &
```

I respond to the instructions given on-screen.

## 19.18 Terminal parameters – stty

With the `stty` command, you can set various terminal parameters on yours or someone else's terminal. You may use a number of different options to the `stty` command.

**stty Command - Displays/Changes Terminal Parameters**

| | |
|---|---|
| Command | `stty [-options]` |
| Function | Sets various terminal parameters. |

**stty Command - Displays/Changes Terminal Parameters** ***(Continued)***

| | |
|---|---|
| Argument | See the Linux man pages. |
| Options | See the Linux man pages. |
| `50 ... 56000 (115000)` | Speed (terminal baud speed; for example, 1200 baud = 1200 bits per second). |
| `echo` | Prints all entered characters to the screen. |
| `istrip` | Starts stripping all incoming characters to 7 bits. |
| `istrip` | Stops stripping incoming characters. |
| `ixoff` | Starts the START/STOP control of incoming data. |
| `-ixoff` | Stops the START/STOP control of incoming data. |
| `lcase` | Characters entered in lower-case are displayed in upper-case. |
| `-LCASE` | Characters entered in upper case are displayed in lower-case. |
| `sane` | Resets all parameters as default. |
| `tabs` | Replaces tabs with spaces. |

If there is a - (hyphen) preceding an option, the option will be turned off or inverted. The `stty` command without any options prints the terminal setup to the screen.

Examples:

```
[root@nittedal /root]# stty
speed 9600 baud; line = 0;
-brkint -imaxbel
[root@nittedal /root]#
```

```
[root@nittedal /root]# stty intr ^c
```

The interrupt key is set to Control-c.

```
[root@nittedal /root]# stty lcase
```

All text entered in lower-case is printed in upper-case.

```
[root@nittedal /root]# stty sane
```

Sets all parameters to the default.

```
[root@nittedal /root]# stty tabs
```

Tabs are replaced by spaces.

```
[root@nittedal /root]# stty 9600
```

Sets the speed to 9600 bit/s.

## 19.19 Linux and national character sets

Linux is based on the ISO 8859 character set standard, which is the same character set that Microsoft Windows 98 is based on. In most Linux distributions, it is important to define which special characters you want activated via your keyboard. A brief example:

Under Red Hat Linux, you'll get the English (U.S.) character set when selecting **us** at installation. Be aware that if you choose a different character set than **us** and you want national support also in your terminal prompt (in your bash shell), you must also set a few lines in your `.profile`:

```
set meta-flag on
set convert-meta off
set output-meta on
export LC_CTYPE=ISO-8859-1
export LC_ALL=C
export LESSCHARSET=latin1
```

In GNOME or KDE, add the following in the init file `/etc/profile` to get your character set:

```
GDM_LANG= secondary_locale_code
LC_ALL= secondary_locale_code
LANG= primary_locale_code
LINGUAS= primary_locale_code
export GDM_LANG LC_ALL LANG LINGUAS
```

You will find the correct system locale default language code from the program:

```
[root@nittedal /root]# locale_config
```

| Country | Locale Code |
|---|---|
| Spanish (Spain) | es_ES |
| French (France) | fr_FR |
| India (ID) | in_ID |
| Norway (Norway) | no_NO |
| Russian (Russia) | ru_RU |

In GNOME or KDE, add the following in the init file /etc/profile to get a French character set:

```
GDM_LANG=fr_FR
LC_ALL=fr_FR
LANG=fr
LINGUAS=fr
export GDM_LANG LC_ALL LANG LINGUAS
```

In GNOME or KDE, add the following in the init file /etc/profile to get a Norwegian character set:

```
GDM_LANG=no_NO
LC_ALL=no_NO
LANG=no
LINGUAS=no
export GDM_LANG LC_ALL LANG LINGUAS
```

If you also want menus and help text under GNOME in a foreign language, add the following in the global /etc/profile file:

```
LANGUAGE=primary_locale_code
export LANGUAGE
```

If you use an Italian keyboard, your locale code is it. You then need to add the following in the global /etc/profile file:

```
LANGUAGE=it
export LANGUAGE
```

If you wish to use emacs and gnus with full ISO 8859 support, including different European character sets, the following must be present in .emacs:

```
(standard-display-european t)
(require 'iso-syntax)
(set-input-mode nil nil 1)
```

In emacs 20, add the following to i .emacs:

```
(standard-display-european t)
(require 'latin-1)
(set-input-mode nil nil 1)
```

In irc, you must make this ~/.ircrc file:

```
set translation latin_1
set eight_bit_characters on
```

## Exercises for Chapter 19

1. Which command must be run to set up a sound card?
2. What function does the system file /etc/shadow perform?
3. Is it possible for two users to have the same user and group number? Which parameters must be known before you can define a new user? What is important to remember when removing a user?
4. Log in as system administrator and define two users, user1 and user2. Set user1 in bash shell and user2 in tcsh shell. Analyze the various login files generated by the system for these users.
5. Which command is used to repair a Linux filesystem?
6. Why must special commands be executed before you can turn a Linux computer off? Shut the Linux system down with the shutdown command. Give the users a chance to log out; 10 minutes is ample waiting time. Send a message to all users warning them that the system will be shut down.
7. Change the system from multi-user mode (2) to single-user mode (1) and back to 2 again with the init command.
8. What is the difference between the init 1 and init s commands?
9. From which init mode will NFS normally start?

10. Make a filesystem on a floppy disk and copy all your data files to the floppy with the Linux command `cp`.
11. What do you enter to install the program package `ergosoft-2002-01.rpm`?
12. Which character set (code) should be selected when installing Red Hat Linux if you want a German character set?

CHAPTER
20

# Backup/Restore and Media under Linux

## 20.1 Introduction

Backing up your data is important. If your hardware breaks down, you might face huge expenses if your data hasn't been backed up.

Under Linux, there are several ways of making backups. The simplest method is backing up from the menu-controlled program `taper` or from the Linux X Window program BRU 2000.

In this chapter, we'll take a look at commands like `tar`, `cpio`, and `dd`, which are behind these simple interfaces. `tar` as well as `cpio` packs all files together in one large file. The programs offer various options that allow a selective back-up procedure based on, for example, date and filename. The `cpio` program works together with the `find` program, which makes it more flexible than `tar`. Both `tar` and `cpio` have simple restore procedures for single files.

The `dd` program is a general conversion tool and backup program. With the help of `dd`, you can quickly copy a complete filesystem from one hard disk drive to another. If you want to convert data from one system to another, for example, from EBCDIC to ASCII, `dd` is the right tool for the job. When you have read this chapter, you will be able to make backup copies to different media with various Linux commands.

## 20.2 Format and device drivers

Device driver programs are used to communicate with different devices like hard disk drives, floppy disk drives, keyboards, displays and your mouse. All device drivers are placed in the `/dev` directory. Under `/dev`, there may be separate directories for network drivers (`/dev/inet`), floppy drive drivers (`/dev/fd`), etc.

It is important to understand the meaning of the names of device drivers to use them properly. The name structure of device drivers for floppy drives (`/dev` directory) is defined in the table below:

| **Description** | **(fd)(e)( h/H/d/D/E/C)(bbbb)** |
|---|---|
| `fd` | Floppy drive. |
| `e` | Device number; 0, 1, 2, or 3; 0=A, 1=B, etc. |
| `h/H/d/D/E/C` | Indicates size and density of media:<br>`h,d` = 5.25" floppy.<br>`H,D` = 3.5" floppy.<br>`E,C` = 3.5" high-density floppy. |
| `bbbb` | Number of kilobytes. |

If you want the device driver to have a shorter name, you may link it to a new file name. If you, for example, want to link `/dev/fd0H1440` to `/dev/A`, enter:

```
[root@nittedal /root]# ln /dev/fd0H1440 /dev/A
```

The device driver `/dev/fd0` corresponds with the first floppy drive (A under MS-DOS), and `/dev/fd1` corresponds with the second floppy drive (B:).

Below is a list of device drivers for floppy drives that are automatically recognized. The list below also shows the format and capacity of various types of floppy disks.

**5.25" Device Drivers with Double Density**

| Name | Cap. | Cyl. | Sect. | Heads | Base |
|---|---|---|---|---|---|
| `fdnd360` | 360K | 40 | 9 | 2 | 4 |

**5.25" Device Drivers with High Density**

| Name | Cap. | Cyl. | Sect. | Heads | Base |
|---|---|---|---|---|---|
| `fdnh360` | 360K | 40 | 9 | 2 | 20 |
| `fdnh410` | 410K | 41 | 10 | 2 | 48 |
| `fdnh720` | 720K | 80 | 9 | 2 | 24 |
| `fdnh880` | 880K | 80 | 11 | 2 | 80 |
| `fdnh1200` | 1200K | 80 | 15 | 2 | 8 |
| `fdnh1440` | 1440K | 80 | 18 | 2 | 40 |
| `fdnh1476` | 1476K | 82 | 18 | 2 | 56 |
| `fdnh1494` | 1494K | 83 | 18 | 2 | 72 |
| `fdnh1600` | 1600K | 80 | 20 | 2 | 92 |

**3.5" Device Drivers with Double Density**

| Name | Cap. | Cyl. | Sect. | Heads | Base |
|---|---|---|---|---|---|
| `fdnD360` | 360K | 80 | 9 | 1 | 12 |
| `fdnD720` | 720K | 80 | 9 | 2 | 16 |
| `fdnD800` | 800K | 80 | 10 | 2 | 120 |
| `fdnD1040` | 1040K | 80 | 13 | 2 | 84 |
| `fdnD1120` | 1120K | 80 | 14 | 2 | 88 |

**3.5" Device Drivers with High Density (HD)**

| Name | Cap. | Cyl. | Sect. | Heads | Base |
|---|---|---|---|---|---|
| fdnH720 | 720K | 80 | 9 | 2 | 16 |
| fdnH820 | 820K | 82 | 10 | 2 | 52 |
| fdnH830 | 830K | 83 | 10 | 2 | 68 |
| fdnH1440 | 1440K | 80 | 18 | 2 | 28 |
| fdnH1600 | 1600K | 80 | 20 | 2 | 124 |
| fdnH1680 | 1680K | 80 | 21 | 2 | 44 |
| fdnH1722 | 1722K | 82 | 21 | 2 | 60 |
| fdnH1743 | 1743K | 83 | 21 | 2 | 76 |
| fdnH1760 | 1760K | 80 | 22 | 2 | 96 |
| fdnH1840 | 1840K | 80 | 23 | 2 | 116 |
| fdnH1920 | 1920K | 80 | 24 | 2 | 100 |

**3.5" Device Drivers with Extra High Density (HD)**

| Name | Cap. | Cyl. | Sect. | Heads | Base |
|---|---|---|---|---|---|
| fdnE2880 | 2880K | 80 | 36 | 2 | 32 |
| fdnCompaQ | 2880K | 80 | 36 | 2 | 36 |
| fdnE3200 | 3200K | 80 | 40 | 2 | 104 |
| fdnE3520 | 3520K | 80 | 44 | 2 | 108 |
| fdnE3840 | 3840K | 80 | 48 | 2 | 112 |

Below you'll find a list of hard disk drivers that are automatically recognized. The list also includes the format and capacity. Standard device drivers, for example, for IDE, MFM, and RLL, are given names like /dev/hda, /dev/hdb, etc. The disk partitions get device drivers called /dev/hda, /dev/hda1, /dev/hda2, etc.

| Description | Device Driver |
|---|---|
| First hard disk drive (the complete drive) | /dev/hda |
| First hard disk drive, primary partition 1 | /dev/hda1 |
| First hard disk drive, primary partition 2 | /dev/hda2 |

| Description | Device Driver (Continued) |
|---|---|
| First hard disk drive, primary partition 3 | /dev/hda3 |
| First hard disk drive, primary partition 4 | /dev/hda4 |
| First hard disk drive, primary partition 1 | /dev/hda5 |
| First hard disk drive, logical partition 2 | /dev/hda6 |
| Second hard disk drive (the complete drive) | /dev/hdb |
| Second hard disk drive, primary partition 1 | /dev/hdb1 |

SCSI hard disk drives normally use other device drivers; for example:

| Description | Device Driver |
|---|---|
| First SCSI hard disk drive (the complete drive) | /dev/sda |
| First SCSI hard disk drive, primary partition 1 | /dev/sda1 |
| Second SCSI hard disk drive (the complete drive) | /dev/sdb |
| Second SCSI hard disk drive, primary partition 1 | /dev/sdb1 |

The SCSI drives are called `/dev/sda`, `/dev/sdb`, etc., and get partition names like `/dev/sda1`, `/dev/sda2`, etc. SCSI tape units are normally called rmt0, nrmt0 etc. You may create a symbolic link from `rmt0` to `tape`:

```
[root@nittedal /root]# ln /dev/rmt0 /dev/tape
```

## 20.3 Formatting floppies – fdformat

With the `fdformat` command, you can format (prepare for use) floppies for your Linux system. If you want to format multiple floppies, this may be done from the command prompt or from X Window. The default floppy drive normally uses the device driver `/dev/fd0H1440`.

**fdformat Command – Formats Floppies**

| | |
|---|---|
| Command | `fdformat [options] device driver` |
| Function | Low-level floppy formatting. |
| Options | See the Linux man pages. |
| `-n` | The floppy will not be verified. |
| Device driver | Name of device driver to be used. If you don't specify the device driver, the format program selects the default driver, for example, `/dev/fd0H1440`. In the `/etc/fdprm` file, you'll find an overview of the various floppy disk parameters. |

If you want the `fdformat` program to point to the same device driver every time you format a floppy disk, you can set the format once and for all with the `setfdprm` command.

Examples:

```
[root@nittedal /root]# setfdprm -p /dev/fd0 1440/1440
```

Now, whenever you use the `/dev/fd0` device name, it will point to the `/dev/fd0H1440` device driver. This device driver represents the same floppy disk drive, drive A with 3.5" floppies and 1.44MB storage capacity.

```
[root@nittedal /root]# fdformat /dev/fd0
```

This formats the floppy in floppy disk drive A. The device driver points to the `/dev/fd0` device name, which is linked to the `/dev/fd0H1440` device driver (1.44MB).

```
[root@nittedal /root]# fdformat /dev/fd1h1200
```

This formats a 5 1/4" floppy in the second floppy disk drive (B). The floppy is formatted to a capacity of 1.2MB.

```
[root@nittedal /root]# fdformat -n /dev/fd0H720
```

This formats a 3.5" floppy in the first floppy disk drive. The floppy is formatted to a capacity of 720KB. Because I used the `-n` option, the floppy will not be verified.

Tape media normally don't require formatting.

See also: `mformat` (MS-DOS filesystem)

## 20.4 Archive and restore files – tar

The `tar` (tape archiver) command allows copying data from one medium to another. `tar` is not a zip program in itself, but it sequentially groups files specified on the command line. The storage medium normally is a hard disk drive, a floppy, or a tape. `tar` is frequently used to group many files into one on the hard disk drive. Key parameters decide how to copy, which format and device drivers to use, etc. The selected file argument decides which files to back up or restore.

**tar Command – Archives and Restores Files**

| | |
|---|---|
| Command | `tar [-][option] device [argument]` |
| Function | Backs up data to file, floppy, or tape. |
| Device | Device driver or device name. |
| Argument | May be a file(s) or directory(ies). |
| Options | See the Linux man pages. |
| `A` | Prevents the files/directories from getting the same position in the hierarchy as before (original position). `A` is used together with `x` only, i.e., when restoring data. |
| `b` | Makes `tar` use the next argument as a block factor (`b`= block). The default block factor is normally 20 (each block is 512 bytes). The block factor is how much data is read and stored to media simultaneously. This option is normally used in connection with magnetic tape media. When using `x` and `t`, the blocks size is read automatically. |
| `x` | The specified files are extracted (`x` =extract), i.e., restored. If a filename equals a directory, the file is read and placed recursively on the disk, i.e., in the original hierarchical structure. If the filename is not given, the complete tape will be restored. |
| `u` | The specified files are added, unless they are already there, or unless the files have been modified since last archiving. |

**tar Command – Archives and Restores Files (*Continued*)**

| | |
|---|---|
| `C directory` | Moves to the specified directory; for example, `C /home/david`. |
| `c` | (`c` = create) Makes a new archive from the beginning of the medium. Use `c` the first time you copy to a file, floppy, or a tape. All data on the medium will be erased. |
| `v` | (`v` = verbose) Copy process displayed on-screen. Normally, `tar` does not inform the user about its progress. Use `v` when you need to supervise the copying process. |
| `o` | The one who runs the `tar` program owns the files, rather than the registered owner of files and directories on the tape. |
| `p` | Files are extracted with original owner attributes. |
| `t` | (`t`=table) The directory and other information about all files on file, floppy, or tape is displayed on screen. The format of the directory is the same as the `ls -l` command. |
| `z` | (z=zip) Filters the archive through gzip. |

```
[david@nittedal david]$ tar cvf /dev/fd0 textfile
```

Copies the file `textfile1` to floppy (floppy drive A). If the text file is a directory, the entire directory is copied to floppy. The `c` option means that I make a new file on the floppy, and `f` followed by a device driver points to the destination for the `textfile1` (file or directory), which is the floppy disk (`fd0`).

```
[david@nittedal david]$ tar xvf /dev/fd0
```

Restores all the data from the floppy to the hard disk drive. Directories and files are put in their original locations. The `x` option means that data is to be restored from floppy.

```
[david@nittedal david]$ tar tvf /dev/fd0
```

Displays the contents of a 1.44MB floppy.

```
[elboth@nittedal elboth]$ tar -cvf Linuxdoc.tar
/home/elboth/Linuxbok/*
```

What happens here is that the contents, including all directory references to /home/elboth/Linuxbook/, are grouped in one file, Linuxdoc.tar.

tar files are frequently compressed with other programs like gzip or compress. For the tar command, you may also use the z and Z options. When using z, the archive filter is gzip. When using Z, the archive filter is compress. Here are some examples:

```
[elboth@nittedal elboth]$ tar -cvzf Linuxdoc.tar.gz
/home/elboth/Linuxbook/*
```

Zips files.

```
[elboth@nittedal elboth]$ tar -xvzf Linuxdoc.tar.gz
```

Unzips files. You'll often find that file suffixes like .tgz are used for files that are both packed and compressed (gz=gzip files).

```
[david@nittedal david]$ tar -cvf /dev/fd0 -C /tmp test-
file
```

This is an example with multiple option groups. The -C option enables copying from the /tmp directory. The copied file is called testfile.

```
[david@nittedal david]$ tar cvf /dev/fd0D360 *
```

All files and directories are copied to floppy. I use a Linux device driver. This program refers to a floppy (floppy drive A), which is formatted to 360KB.

```
[david@nittedal david]$ tar cvf /dev/fd1H1440 corel
```

The corel text file or directory is copied to floppy (floppy drive B), which is formatted to 1.44MB.

```
[david@nittedal david]$ tar cvf /dev/fd1
```

All files and directories are copied to floppy. The device driver refers to a floppy that is formatted to 1.44 MB.

```
[david@nittedal david]$ tar cvbf 20 /dev/fd0 *
```

All files and directories are copied to floppy. Only `20` blocks are allocated to the floppy. One block is normally 512 bytes. The b key makes the `tar` command use the next argument as the block factor, i.e., allocates 20 blocks (10KB).

```
[david@nittedal david]$ tar cvbf 140 /dev/fd0 /home/arne
/home/david
```

The `/home/arne` and `/home/david` files or directories are copied to floppy. `140` blocks, 512 bytes each, are allocated (i.e., 70KB) to a storage area on the floppy.

```
[david@nittedal david]$ tar xvf /dev/fd0H720
```

Specifies a different device driver (`720`KB).

```
[david@nittedal david]$ tar xvAf /dev/fd1
```

The files that are copied from floppy (floppy drive B, 1.44 MB) are placed in the directory from which you ran the `tar` program.. Unless the A key is used, the data that is copied from floppy or tape will be located in the Linux hierarchy as specified when copying. If the search path was `/etc/termcap` when backing up to floppy or tape, the file (`termcap`) will be restored to the same location (`/etc/termcap`) when restoring without the A option.

If you enter `tarcvf/dev/fd0 /usr/ole/letter` and restore the file with `tarxvf/dev/fd0`, the file, of course, is stored in the same location in the hierarchy as the original file, i.e., `/usr/ole/letter`. If you work from the `/usr/nils` directory and enter `tar xvAf /dev/fd0`, the file `letter` will be placed under `/usr/nils/usr/ole`.

```
[david@nittedal david]$ tar cvf /dev/tape /home/david
/bin/prog
```

Backs up to tape with the `tar` command. The files or directories `/home/david` and `/bin/prog` are backed up to tape. You must know that `/dev/tape` is the tape streamer on this system. A tape streamer normally has the name `/dev/rmt0`.

```
[david@nittedal david]$ tar cvf /dev/rmt0 ./corel
```

The `corel` directory is copied to tape.

```
[david@nittedal david]$ tar cvf /dev/rmt0
```

The working directory is copied to `/dev/rmt0`.

```
[david@nittedal david]$ tar xvf /dev/rmt0
```

Restores from tape to the hard disk drive.
See also: `cpio`, `cp`, `dd`

## 20.5 Backing up data with cpio – cpio

The `cpio` program is as old as the `tar` program, but due to a somewhat complicated syntax, it is not frequently used nowadays. But when transferring data from one Linux system to another or from one Unix system to another, it is an excellent tool. With the `cpio` and `find` commands, you can back up any data from any Linux or Unix system.

**cpio Command – Backs Up and Restores Data**

| | |
|---|---|
| Command | `cpio -o [Bvc]`<br>`cpio -i [Bcdmvtu] [file ...]`<br>`cpio -p [dmvu] directory` |
| Function | With `cpio -o`, you can copy directories and files from one device driver to another; for example, from a root filesystem to tape. The `cpio -i` (copy in) command copies files that have been archived with `cpio -o`. When you need to copy complete directories, use `cpio -p`. The `cpio` command is frequently used for tape backups. |
| Device | Device name. |
| Argument | May be files or directories. |
| Options | See the Linux man pages. |
| `-B` | Sets the block size for in and out data (default block size in Linux is 512 bytes). |

**cpio Command – Backs Up and Restores Data** ***(Continued)***

| | |
|---|---|
| -c | Writes header information in ASCII format for increased portability. Use this option when source and destination machines are different (Linux – Unix). |
| -d | The `cpio` command automatically makes directories when required. |
| -m | When this option is not used, the `cpio` program automatically changes "last modified" to today's date. |
| -t | Prints an index of the files that are read as standard in data. When using the `-t` option, no files are copied. This option is only used when you want to look at what has been backed up to tape. |
| -v | When using this option, you can see what the `cpio` command does. If you use the `t` option at the same time, the contents will be formatted in the same way as with the `ls -l` command. |

Examples:

```
[david@nittedal david]$ ls | cpio -o >>/dev/fd0
```

Copies all files in the current directory (subdirectories included) to floppy.

```
[david@nittedal david]$ ls | cpio -o >>/dev/rmt0
```

When working from the `/home/david` directory, this command will copy all files in the `/home/david` directory (subdirectories included) to tape.

```
[david@nittedal david]$ ls | cpio -oc > class
```

Copies all files in the current directory (subdirectories included) to the file `class`. The `c` option makes the file portable to other machine platforms. Instead of the `ls` command, you can, for example, use Linux commands like `find`, `echo`, and `cat`.

```
[david@nittedal david]$ cpio -i < class
```

Restores all files that are saved in the file `class`.

```
[root@nittedal /root]# cpio -iBdm /etc/termcap <
/dev/tape
```

Reads the file `/etc/termcap` from tape.

```
[david@nittedal david]$ cpio -itvc </dev/fd1
```

Gives you the index of the floppy (B).

```
[root@nittedal /root]# cpio -i </dev/fd0 wpterm
```

Copies the `wpterm` file from floppy to the hard disk drive.

```
[root@nittedal /root]# cpio -i < /dev/rmt0 *
```

Copies all files from tape to the directory in which you are working.

```
[root@nittedal /root]# cpio -itv </dev/rmt0
```

Prints the contents of the tape (`dev/rmt0`) on the terminal screen.

```
[root@nittedal /root]# find . -print | cpio -o >
/dev/fd0
```

Copies the contents of the directory to an archive in the floppy disk drive.

```
[root@nittedal /root]# find / -depth -print | cpio -odv
> /dev/rmt0
```

Backs up all files to tape. When you want to restore everything, just enter:

```
[root@nittedal /root]# cpio -idmv /* < /dev/rmt0
```

See also: cp, filesystem, `find`, dd, `tar`

## 20.6 Converting and copying data – dd

The `dd` program copies data from a specified in file (device driver) to specified out file (device drivers). Data can be converted during the copy. You may specify the size of the in and out blocks to benefit from the different physical units, for example, tape drives. You can choose freely among device drivers when copying data.

The `dd` program is frequently used for copying files between different filesystems and between different tape/floppy formats.

**dd Command – Converts and Copies**

| | |
|---|---|
| Command | `dd [option=value]` |
| Function | Copies data from a specified in file to a specified out file with the option of simultaneous data conversion. |
| Argument | May be files or directories. |
| Options | See the Linux man pages. |
| `if=file` | Enter name of input file (device driver). |
| `of=file` | Enter name of output file (device driver). |
| `ibs=n` | Input block size. |
| `obs=n` | Output block size. |
| `bs=n` | Sets the size of in and out blocks. This parameter overrules the `ibs` and `obs` options. |
| `seek=n` | Reads through `n` blocks before copying starts. |
| `count=n` | Copies `n` blocks only. |
| `conv=ascii` | Converts from EBCDIC to ASCII. |
| `conv=ebcdic` | Converts from ASCII to EBCDIC. |
| `conv=lcase` | Converts from upper-case to lower-case. |
| conv=ucase | Converts from lower-case to upper-case. |

Examples:

```
[root@nittedal /root]# dd if=/dev/fd1h1200
of=/dev/fd0H1440
```

Copies everything from a 1.2MB source floppy to a 1.44MB destination floppy. This is the simplest way of converting programs/data to a different floppy format.

```
[root@nittedal /root]# dd if=/dev/fd0 of=/dev/rmt0
```

Copies from the source floppy A (1.44MB) directly to tape.

```
[root@nittedal /root]# dd if=/dev/rmt0 of=/dev/rmt1
ibs=20k
```

Copies content from the tape drive `/dev/rmt0` to the tape drive `/dev/rmt1`. The in data block size is set at 20K.

```
[root@nittedal /root]# dd if=/dev/rmt0 of=datafile
ibs=800 cbs=80 conv=ascii,lcase
```

This command reads from a tape where the data is stored in EBCDIC format. The in block size is `800` bytes, and the buffer size is set at `80` bytes. The data from tape is converted to ASCII, and all upper-case characters are converted to lower-case. Everything is stored to disk as one file (`datafile`).

You may specify the block size as a multiple of 1KB. For a block size of 20KB, you can enter:

```
[root@nittedal /root]# dd if=file of=/dev/fd1h1200 bs=20K
```

In the example above, I read from one file and placed the data on a 1.2 MB floppy. The size of the in and out blocks was set at 20K.

```
[root@nittedal /root]# dd if=/dev/hda1 of=/dev/rmt0 bs=1K
count=400
```

Copies `400` blocks from a filesystem in `/dev/hda1` to tape `/dev/rmt0`. The block size is set at 1K (1024 bytes) both ways. To create a Linux boot disk, I use the `dd` command:

```
[root@nittedal /imagefd]# dd if=boot.img of=/dev/fd0
bs=1440k
```

You can also use the `rawrite` command in the `/dosutils` directory on the

Red Hat CD-ROM. There is documentation on using `rawrite` in `/dosutils/rawrite3.doc`.

See also: `cpio`, `cp`, filesystem, `tar`

## 20.7 Menu program for backup – taper

A backup program called Taper (see Figure 20-1) is included in many Linux distributions. This program, which was developed by Yusaf Nagree, makes backing up to tape simple.

**taper Command – Simple Tape Backup**

| | |
|---|---|
| Command | `taper -T [media] [options]` |
| Function | Makes it simple to back up directories and files to tape media. |
| Options | See the Linux man pages. |
| Media | Type of backup media (driver) to be used. |

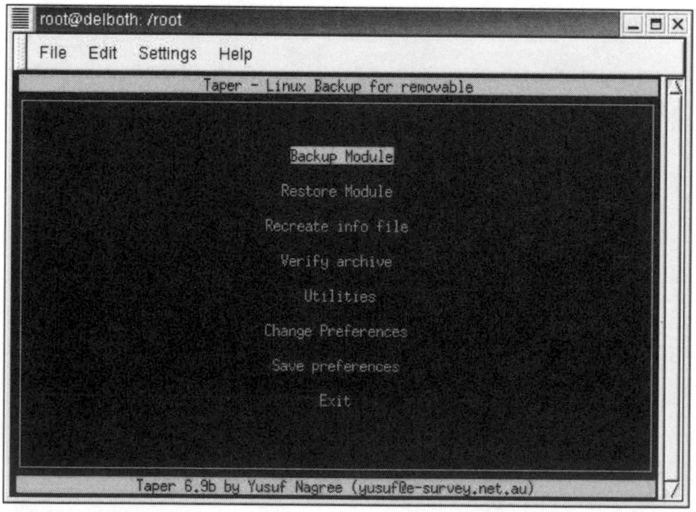

**Figure 20-1**
*The Linux menu-based backup program* `taper`.

Below you'll find a list of tape drive types supported by Taper:

| Description | Media Support |
|---|---|
| Default floppy controller I | tape |
| Default floppy controller II | ftape |
| Newer floppy controller | ztape |
| Tape streamer using SCSI | SCSI |
| Tape streamer using IDE controllers | IDE |
| Tape streamers based on disk controllers that support removable/interchangeable disks | Removable |

Example:

```
[root@nittedal /root]# taper -T ftape
```

Before the actual backup procedure starts, you are asked about which files to back up. If you don't have a tape streamer, you can try and use the media type `removable`.

```
[root@nittedal /root]# taper -T removable
```

The Taper program will use the default floppy drive `/dev/fd0` (A). There are many options in the Taper program. Check the Linux documentation `/usr/doc` (`TAPER.txt`).

## 20.8 Other backup programs

There are many different ways of backing up your data. If you have a primary NFS server (network file server=Linux file server for Linux/Unix as well as DOS/Windows) in your LAN, you may copy your data directly to the NFS server. If you have a tape streamer that only works under DOS, you may copy Linux files to a DOS partition. The next time you boot MS-DOS or Windows, you can back up these files.

You can also make dedicated Linux filesystems on a standard floppy disk. The procedure is the same as on a hard disk drive.

Examples:

```
[root@nittedal /root]# mke2fs /dev/fd0 1440
```

Here, I have made a filesystem of 1400KB (1.44 MB) on the floppy /dev/fd0 (A). You can make other types of filesystems on the floppy. When doing this, specify the type in the mount command. When you want to access the floppy, just mount the filesystem as usual.

```
[root@nittedal /root]# mkdir /floppy_a
[root@nittedal /root]# mount -t ext2 /dev/fd0 /floppy_a
```

Here, I first make the empty directory /floppy_a, then I mount the floppy /dev/fd0 (A) under the /floppy_a directory. Now I can copy my Linux files to the floppy.

```
[root@nittedal /root]# cp /home/david/*  /diskett_a
```

Copies all files from /home/david to the floppy.

```
[root@nittedal /root]# umount  /floppy_a
```

or

```
[root@nittedal /root]# umount /dev/fd0
```

The two last commands unmount the floppy (A). It is also possible to use the automount under Red Hat Linux. The auto-mount will mount or unmount both the floppy disk and CD-ROM automatically.

## 20.9 X Window and backup – BRU

If you have installed Red Hat Linux and you run X Window, BRU 2000 is the simplest backup program to use. This program is a mini version of the original package from the U.S. company Enhanced Software Technologies. If your backup requirements are modest, you will not need to buy the full package.

Before you can use BRU 2000, you must enter the BRU Configuration Utility and define the device driver that you want the tape streamer to use. There are more than 40 device drivers to choose from. If you cannot find the tape streamer that you have installed, select OTHER. Then specify, for example, /dev/rft0 as device driver (with automatic rewind). After selecting the device driver, save your setup by entering `SAVE` in the BRU Configuration window.

To start a backup, insert a tape in the tape streamer and go into the BRU File Selection window. From this window, you can select filesystems, directories, and/or single files. You will see that the BRU program has many different functions like data compression, the ability to run selective jobs, and verification of archives.

## Exercises for Chapter 20

1. What are the device drivers for your floppy disk drives and your hard disk partitions?
2. Back up your user area to floppy or tape. Use the `tar` command. Log on as a different user and restore some of the data to the other user. Are there any special details to remember? (Hint: Use the `o` and `A` options.)
3. Make a full backup of your system with `cpio`. Use the same command to make a complete restore.
4. Define the right device driver for your backup program `taper`, and take a complete backup of your home directory.

CHAPTER
21

# Linux – Logs and Kernel

## 21.1 Introduction

In this chapter, you'll learn about commands that enable surveillance of users, their processes, and the condition of your Linux OS. There are several different commands for this purpose, but we'll concentrate on a few only. We'll also take a look at how simple it is to create your own Linux kernel.

## 21.2 System messages

Boot messages and system error messages that are sent to the system console are also placed in the `/var/log/messages` file.

```
[root@nittedal /root]# less /var/log/messages
Nov 14 22:13:57 nittedal kernel: Swansea University
Computer Society TCP/IP for
Nov 14 22:13:54 nittedal syslogd 1.3-3: restart.
Nov 14 22:13:56 nittedal kernel: klogd 1.3-3, log source
= /proc/kmsg started.
Nov 14 22:13:56 nittedal kernel: Cannot find map file.
Nov 14 22:13:56 nittedal kernel: No module symbols
loaded.
Nov 14 22:13:56 nittedal kernel: Console: 16 point font,
400 scans
```

The system administrator can look at this file by using commands like `more`, `less`, and `cat`, or they can use the `vi` editor for the same purpose. When the host has been running Linux for a long time, this file tends to grow large. It is a good idea to delete the contents of this file regularly. If you installed the Linux package `logrotate`, the size of the log file will be automatically reduced.

## 21.3 Active system parameters

Active system parameters that are set in your Linux system are placed in the `/proc` directory. Here, you'll find all kinds of information about your system; for example, how much memory and swap there is in your system. The directories under `/proc` hold more specific information, e.g., about your LAN and your SCSI devices.

```
[root@nittedal /root]# cd /proc
[root@nittedal /proc]#
```

The `devices` file gives an overview of hardware devices.

```
[root@nittedal /proc]# less devices
```

The `interrupts` file gives an overview of interrupt devices.

```
[root@nittedal /proc]# less interrupts
```

The `dma` file gives an overview of DMA (Direct Memory Access) devices.

```
[root@nittedal /proc]# less dma
```

Look in the `pci` file to see a list of PCI devices.

```
[root@nittedal /proc]# less pci
```

The `partition` file gives an overview of partitions.

```
[root@nittedal /proc]# less partitions
```

You'll find an overview of system memory in the `meminfo` file.

```
[root@nittedal /proc]# less meminfo
```

You should now be able to use the Linux commands `more` and `less` to look at any file in the `/proc` directory.

## 21.4 Process accounting - accton

With the `accton` command, you start process accounting. The program will start automatically if you set up `accton` in an init file (in the `/etc/init.d` directory). The next time you boot the system, the `accton` program will run automatically.

If you enter accton without file arguments, the process accounting program is turned off.

**accton Command – Turns Process Accounting On or Off**

| | |
|---|---|
| Command | `accton [argument]` |
| Function | Starts/stops the supervision and process accounting program (`accton`). |
| Arguments | Filename (log supervision file). `/var/log/pacct` file (under Unix V.4, the `/usr/adm/pacct` file is used). |

`accton` will, for example, tell you which commands the specified user has run and how much CPU and memory resources have been used. You can also analyze the load the user has put on terminal and parallel ports.

Examples:

```
[root@nittedal /root]# accton /var/report/fil01
```

Initiates the `accton` process accounting program. A log supervision file is stored in /var/report/fil01. If you type less /var/report/fil01, you will see that the file grows as the user logs in and starts various programs or executes Linux commands.

```
[root@nittedal /root]# accton
```

This last example switches the process accounting program off.

The sa command (explained next) shows which parameters you can list. Alternatively, you may look at the data in the supervision file /var/log/pacct.

## 21.5 Summarize accounting information – sa

After running the accton program for a while, you can get various statistical data. For example, you can figure out what kinds of commands a user has used, the CPU load, and memory usage. You can also have a look at I/O devices and find out who has used a specific terminal and which programs have been run on the terminal, its memory, and CPU load.

The sa command reads from a specified file or from /var/log/pacct when nothing is specified. A printout from the sa program consists of, among other information: COMMAND, NAME, USER, TTYNAME, START TIME, END TIME, REAL (SEC), CPU (SEC), and MEAN SIZE (K).

**sa Command – Summarizes Accounting Information**

| | |
|---|---|
| Command | sa [option] [user-id] |
| Function | Displays a statistical overview of data gathered by the accton program. |
| Argument | user-id (user name). |
| Options | See the Linux man pages. |
| -a | Lists all names. |
| -b | Sorts the output by the sum of user and system time divided by the number of calls. |

Examples:

```
[root@nittedal /root]# sa -a
```

Lists all usernames.

## 21.6 User terminal data – ac

As system administrator, you may supervise a Linux system, register when users log on, and calculate how long any user was logged in today, this year, or you can summarize their total login time. The `ac` command does not require a background program because it reads the `/var/log/wtmp` file only.

**ac Command – Prints Statistics about Users' Connect Time**

| | |
|---|---|
| Command | `ac [option] [user-id]` |
| Function | Displays an overview of login time for each user. The result is given in hours, based on the `/var/log/wtmp` file. |
| Argument | `user-id`. |
| Options | See the Linux man pages. |
| `-d` | Prints totals for each day. |
| `-y` | Prints total login this year. |
| `-p` | Prints total login per user. |

Examples:

```
[root@nittedal /root]#  ac -d root
Nov 15  total        20.45
Nov 21  total         7.24
Nov 22  total         6.49
Nov 24  total         0.21
Nov 26  total        13.69
...
```

Shows the total login time in hours per day for `root`.

```
[root@nittedal /root]# ac -y david
                       total       225.67
[root@nittedal /root]#
```

Shows `david`'s total login time in hours this year.

## 21.7 Display Status of CPU processes – top

As system administrator, you can easily get an overview of the processes that are currently active by using the Linux command `top`. With the `top` command, you can easily sort the processes with regard to CPU and memory usage and current status. You can also get an overview of the most CPU-intensive processes running on your system.

**top Command – Displays Status of CPU Processes**

| | |
|---|---|
| Command | `top [-d`**`delay`**`] [-q] [-c] [-s] [-S] [-i]` |
| Function | Gives information about working processes in your Linux system. |
| Argument | None. |
| Options | See the Linux man pages. |
| `-d`**`delay`** | Specifies the delay between screen updates. |
| `-q` | Real-time update of `top`. If the user has administrator access (root), `top` has maximum priority. |
| `-c` | Displays full search path to programs, not only filename. |
| `-s` | Makes `top` run in safe mode, which disables potentially dangerous interactive commands. |
| `-S` | Displays total CPU time spent by the program, subprocesses included – rather than CPU usage now. |
| `-i` | Top ignores any idle, inactive, or dead programs. |

The `top` command can, for example, give the following result:

```
55 processes, 53 sleeping, 2 running, 0 zombie, 0
stopped
CPU states: 10.2% user, 4.2% system, 0.0% nice, 85.7%
idle
Mem: 30684K av, 29996K used, 688K free, 12172K shrd,
308K buff
Swap: 130748K av, 29348K, 101400K free
```

```
Pid   User    Pri  Ni  Size   Rss   Share Stat Lib  %cpu %mem Time   Command
141   root    19   0   10936  8236  696   R    0    9.6  26.8 82.24  X
7635  cschal  5    0   1416   1108  800   S    0    2.3  3.6  10.23  Wterm
126   squid   0    0   60     0     0     SW   0    0.0  0.1  0:00   Dnsserver
```

This is a small extract from the process list. The PID is the system ID of a process. It may be useful to know this ID if a program has hung and is occupying system resources. With the `kill` command and PID number, you can make Linux force the program to stop.

Example:

```
[root@nittedal /root]# top
12:12pm  up  3:47,  5 users,  load average: 0.06, 0.02, 0.00
63 processes: 62 sleeping, 1 running, 0 zombie, 0 stopped
CPU states: 12.0% user, 11.8% system,  0.0% nice, 76.2% idle
Mem:  47004K av,  29628K used,  17376K free,  46792K shrd,  5636K buff
Swap:  66492K av,      0K used,  66492K free               12240K cached
PID USER    PRI  NI  SIZE  RSS SHARE STAT  LIB %CPU %MEM   TIME COMMAND
```

If you enter `h` after starting `top`, you will get a help list. Below you'll find a table of commands:

| Command | Description |
|---|---|
| `uptime` | Describes how long the system has been up. |
| `processes` | The total number of current processes. |
| `CPU states` | CPU load in user and system mode. Tells you the share of CPU power that the program occupies. |
| `PID` | Process ID for each process. |
| `PPID` | Parent process ID. |
| `UID` | Program owner's ID number. |
| `USER` | Username of the owner of program/process; it is important to remember that you are not necessarily listed as a user even if you started the program. |
| `PRI` | Priority of program. |
| `NI` | NICE value (priority) of program (–20 is top priority and 19 lowest priority). |
| `TSIZE` | Size of program code. |
| `DSIZE` | Size of program's data and stack. |

| Command | Description (*Continued*) |
|---|---|
| | Resident size of text code. |
| `SWAP` | Size of swapped program code. |
| `D` | Marked packets (memory packets). |
| `LIB Size` | Size of library pages in use. |
| `RSS` | Total amount of physical memory utilized by program. |
| `SHARE` | Shared code. |
| `STAT` | Program status (`S`=sleeping, `R`=running, `Z`=zombies, `T`=stopped, `N`=NICE>0, `W`=swapped program). |
| `WCHAN` | Kernel function accessed by program. |
| `TIME` | Total CPU time used by program since start. |
| `%CPU` | CPU share currently used by program. |
| `%MEM` | Program's share of physical memory. |
| `COMMAND` | Name of program/process. |

See also: `kill`

## 21.8 Make your own Linux kernel

Programs that are installed on a Linux computer can be split into two categories: those that make changes to the Linux kernel and those that don't. Standard applications like WordPerfect, StarOffice, ApplixWare, DBMaker, and LinuxMail do not require regeneration of the Linux kernel.

Applications that require the installation of new hardware devices, e.g., hard disk drive, intelligent I/O, etc., may require regeneration of the Linux kernel. Additionally, it may be necessary to make a new Linux kernel when changing or tuning the OS.

To make a new Linux kernel, the following must be installed:

- **Linux kernel headers.**
- **Linux source code.**

You will find useful information about the Linux kernel on the Web site http://www.kernel.org/.

Before you start changing your kernel, you must determine the version of your current kernel. Try the following command:

```
[root@nittedal /root]# rpm -q kernel kernel-headers
kernel-ibcs \
kernel-pcmcia-cs kernel-source > /kernel.txt
```

Your kernel version is now in the text file `kernel.txt`. The Linux kernel version numbers will tell you if the kernel in question is a development kernel or a stable release kernel. If the second number is even, the kernel is stable; if odd, it is development. So 2.4.x is stable, and 2.5.x is development.

If you downloaded a new Linux kernel from the Internet and you want to install it in your existing environment, do the following:

```
[root@nittedal /root]# cd /usr/src
```

Here, you move to the Linux kernel source directory.

```
[root@nittedal /usr/src]# tar xvzf linux-2.4.5.tar.gz
```

Extract out your new kernel. In this case, we have downloaded the `linux-2.4.5` kernel.

```
[root@nittedal /usr/src]# rm -f /usr/src/linux
```

Remove the old kernel source. You can also rename the old kernel if you want to be on the secure side. Here is the command:

```
[root@nittedal /usr/src]# mv  /usr/src/linux
/usr/src/linux.old
[root@nittedal /usr/src]# ln -s linux-2.4.5 linux
```

In the last command, I made a symbolic link from `linux-2.4.5` to `linux`.

When changing the Linux kernel, it is a good idea to have a known starting point. This can be established by entering:

```
[root@nittedal /usr/src/linux]# make mrproper
```

This command checks the configuration files and references. It removes any configuration files or references that have no function in the kernel.

Now you are ready to make your own configuration file, in which you will include the desired functions of the new kernel. The contents of the configuration file will depend on your own preferences and the hardware you are using. There are three different methods for configuring a new kernel in Linux:

- *[root@nittedal /usr/src/linux]#* **make config**
- *[root@nittedal /usr/src/linux]#* **make menuconfig**
- *[root@nittedal /usr/src/linux]#* **make xconfig**

Linux Kernel Configuration

| | | |
|---|---|---|
| Code maturity level options | I2O device support | Console drivers |
| Processor type and features | Network device support | Sound |
| Loadable module support | Amateur Radio support | Kernel hacking |
| General setup | IrDA (infrared) support | |
| Plug and Play support | ISDN subsystem | |
| Block devices | Old CD-ROM drivers (not SCSI, not IDE) | Save and Exit |
| Networking options | Character devices | Quit Without Saving |
| Telephony Support | USB support | Load Configuration from File |
| SCSI support | Filesystems | Store Configuration to File |

**Figure 21-1**
*Linux Kernel configuration from* `linuxconf`.

The first method, `make config`, has been around as a solution in the Linux environment for a long time. As a user, you enter an interactive, character-based program where you may pick various components by entering `Y` (yes), `N` (no), or `M` (module). The second alternative, `make menuconfig`, is a character-based program that resembles Red Hat Linux's old installation program. You pick the menu options that you want to be included with `Y` (yes), `N` (no), or `M` (module). The last alternative, `make xconfig` (see Figure 21-1), is an X Window program. In `make xconfig`, you can pick the various menu levels with the mouse. The options are the same: `Y` (yes), `N` (no), `M` (module). I personally prefer `menuconfig` because `config` is very cumbersome and `xconfig` is excluded because X Window is not always accessible.

If you have already made a configuration file, e.g., `/usr/src/linux/.config` (normally you call the file `.config`), by one of the methods above, you can run:

*[root@nittedal /usr/src/linux]#* **make dep**

This makes sure that all the dependencies within the source are correct. If you get any errors here, you have problems with the kernel source itself.

If you want support for kerneld and other kernel modules, it is important that you enter `Y` (yes) at the question about kerneld support and supply the module version.

```
[root@nittedal /usr/src/linux]# make clean
```

The `make clean` command deletes old, unneeded files (like old copies of the kernel).

```
[root@nittedal /usr/src/linux]# make bzImage
```

Here, I compile and create a compressed Linux kernel. If you have configured any part of the kernel as a module, you must run the following commands to compile the modules:

```
[root@nittedal /usr/src/linux]# make modules

[root@nittedal /usr/src/linux]# make modules_install
```

The last command installs the modules in the `/lib/modules/2.4.5` directory. One way to simplify compiling your kernel is to execute all the `make` commands in one line by typing `make dep clean bzImage modules modules_install`. If you've just patched your kernel, then type `make oldconfig dep clean bzImage modules modules_install`.

To make sure that the system will boot following whatever happens with the new kernel, you must save the old kernel. It is simple to add the new Linux kernel to the LILO menu. Normally, the name of `/boot/vmlinux` is changed first:

```
[root@nittedal /usr/src/linux]# cp /boot/vmlinux-2.2.16-
21 /boot/vmlinux.old
[root@nittedal /usr/src/linux]# cp /usr/src/linux-
2.4.5/arch/i386/boot/bzImage
/boot/vmlinux-2.4.5
```

Here, I copy the new kernel to the `/boot` directory. The new kernel has the name `vmlinux-2.4.5`.

```
[root@nittedal /usr/src/linux]# cp /usr/src/linux-
2.4.5/System.map
/boot/System.map-2.4.5
```

I copy and rename the new system.map file to the /boot directory.

```
[root@nittedal /usr/src/linux]# rm -f /boot/System.map-
2.2.16-21
```

We don't need the old system.map, so I remove it.

```
[root@nittedal /usr/src/linux]# ln -s /boot/System.map-
2.4.5 /boot/System.map
```

Here, I create a new symbolic link to the default system.map.

```
[root@nittedal /usr/src/linux]# mkinitrd /boot/initrd-
2.4.5.img 2.4.5
```

Here, I create a new ramdisk for the new kernel.

The last step is to prepare LILO for the new kernel. I have added some lines to /etc/lilo.conf. This example is from one of my PCs:

```
[root@nittedal /root]# more /etc/lilo.conf
boot=/dev/hda
map=/boot/map
install=/boot/boot.b
prompt
timeout=50
image=/boot/vmlinuz-2.2.16-21
         label=linux
         root=/dev/hda5
         read-only
other=/dev/hda1
         label=dos
         table=/dev/hda
[root@nittedal /root]#
```

/etc/lilo.conf is updated with four new lines. The new lines are printed in bold.

```
[root@nittedal /root]# more /etc/lilo.conf
boot=/dev/hda
map=/boot/map
install=/boot/boot.b
prompt
timeout=50
image=/boot/vmlinuz-2.4.5
```

```
        label=linux
        root=/dev/hda5
        read-only
image=/boot/vmlinuz.old
        label=old
        root=/dev/hda5
        read-only
other=/dev/hda1
        label=dos
        table=/dev/hda
[root@nittedal /root]#
```

After updating `/etc/lilo.conf` (see Figure 21-2), you must run the `/sbin/lilo` routine. If you forget this, your machine probably won't boot without a floppy disk.

```
[root@nittedal /root]# /sbin/lilo
```

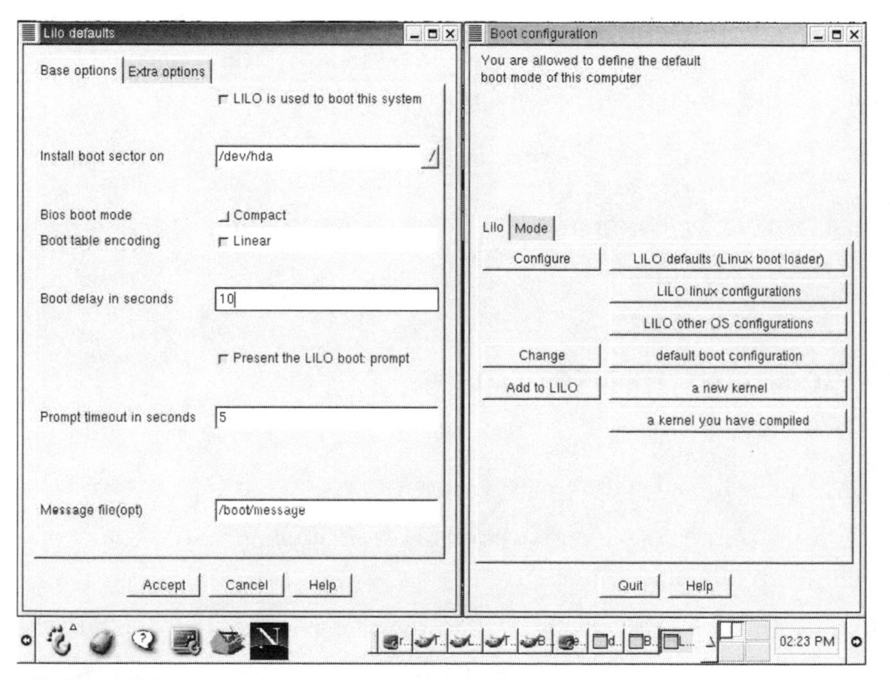


**Figure 21-2**
*Updating LILO defaults from* `linuxconf`.

When the system is loading, the `LILO boot` prompt displays. By pressing Tab, you can choose from the various kernels.

```
LILO boot:
linux     old   dos
```

When choosing the new kernel it is a good idea to look out for error messages. If the machine doesn't boot, you must load the old kernel.

If you want more information about generating new kernels, have a look at the kernel HOWTO pages.

## 21.9 Tuning the hard disk drive

By using `hdparm`, you may tune your hard disk drives. The drawback is that `hdparm` is a command application only. This command has many options. Use option help to get a description of the most frequently used options.

```
[root@nittedal /root]# hdparm -h
```

The `hdparm` command can give you an extraordinary performance increase, but if you pick the wrong options, the consequences are severe.

```
[root@nittedal /root]# hdparm  /dev/hda5 -i
```

This is a request for `hdparm` to identify the hard disk unit (the partition) `/dev/hda5`.

## Exercises for Chapter 21

1. To which file are all system messages sent?
2. Which program do you start when you need to supervise the usage of applications and performance?
3. How do you read data from the `accton` database? What does the `ac` command do?
4. What simple method displays the status of system processes?
5. What are the steps you must go through to generate a new Linux kernel?
6. Which command do you use if you want to tune your hard disk without tuning the Linux kernel?

CHAPTER
22

# Network Communication

## 22.1 Introduction

Linux supports the networking protocols TCP/IP, IPX/SPX, and Apple Talk. In this chapter, we'll focus on the TCP/IP (Transmission Control Protocol/Internet Protocol) networking protocol (see Figure 22-1). The Internet is based on the TCP/IP networking protocol. TCP/IP enables communication with users and machines on the Internet via electronic mail, USENET, news, and telnet (terminal emulation). With TCP/IP, you can also transfer data between two machines; for example, with FTP, NFS (Network Filesystem), electronic mail, World Wide Web, and USENET news.

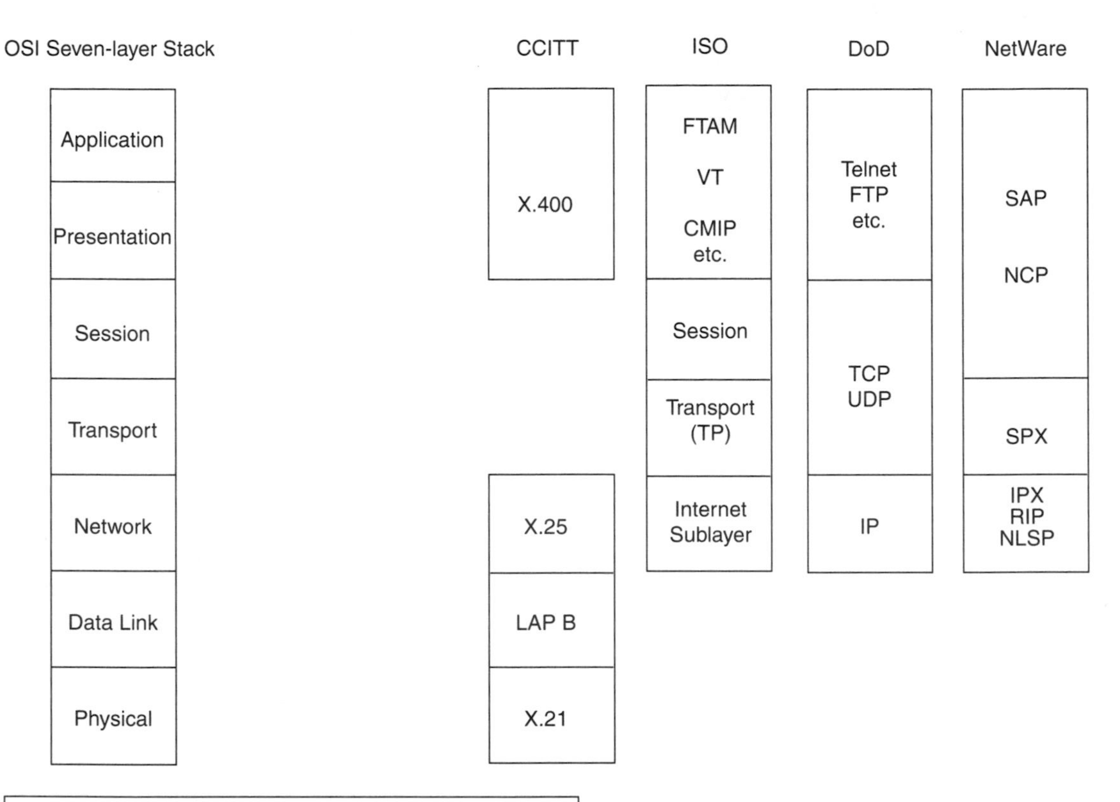


| IEEE 802.2 (Logical Link) | | | |
|---|---|---|---|
| 802.3 | 802.4 | 802.5 | FDDI |
| CSMA/CD | Token Bus | Token Ring | Token Ring |
| 802.3 | 802.4 | 802.5 | FDDI |
| Base/Broad-band Coax UTP | Broadband Optical Analog signal | Shielded Twisted Pair (STP) | Optical |

**Figure 22–1**
*The DoD model for TCP/IP compared with other communication protocols like ISO and Novell Netware IPX/SPX.*

## 22.2 TCP/IP – the networking glue

TCP/IP is a networking product that was developed around 1970 by the DoD (Department of Defense). TCP/IP has given users the possibility of exchanging information independently of their location and the type of equipment they use. Several important organizations have contributed to the development of the TCP/IP standard. Some of them are:

- **NASA (National Aeronautics and Space Administration).**
- **NSF (National Science Foundation).**
- **DoE (Department of Energy).**

In cooperation with the DoD, these organizations today are working with a WAN (Wide Area Network), called the DARPA Internet, which is composed of ARPANET, MILNET, and NFSNET.

## 22.3 The phrase "Internet"

The ARPANET was the network that, more than 20 years ago, connected most universities and research centers in the U.S. and the rest of the world. The DARPA Internet is composed of several different networks. The Internet today is a development of ARPANET, with TCP/IP as the cornerstone of the network. The phrase "Internet" describes the result of all the networks connected. Machines in the Internet are usually referred to as hosts or nodes.

TCP/IP was designed for use via telecommunication lines (X.25) in the ARPANET. TCP/IP was regarded as too bulky and slow for use in LANs like Ethernet and Token Ring networks. Today, TCP/IP may be run in most networks: Ethernet, Token Ring, ARCnet, StarLAN, etc. In addition, you may use dial-up lines (SLIP and PPP), X.25, and satellite connections.

Linux today supports TCP/IP in network interface cards (NICs), as well as asynchronous connections (RS-232=serial port). Linux supports a large number of popular Ethernet cards and interfaces with PCs, including all known NICs from suppliers like 3COM and SMC, D-Link pocket Ethernet adapters for portable computers, etc. Linux also supports asynchronous PPP and SLIP. With PPP or SLIP, you may connect to the Internet via modem or ISDN. If you prefer to communicate via the serial port, Linux supports the low-level protocols

PPP, SLIP and UUCP. UUCP (Unix-to-Unix copy) is used for file transfer, electronic mail, and electronic news between Unix machines. UUCP was originally designed to enable communication between Unix machines via modems connected to telephone lines. Today it is also possible to run UUCP over a TCP/IP-based network.

## 22.4 Protocols

TCP/IP is more than the TCP (Transmission Control Protocol) and IP (Internet Protocol) protocols. It is a whole family of service protocols and commands. Here is a description of the most frequently used protocols:

- **TCP (Transmission Control Protocol)**—Is responsible for chopping messages into network messages and joining them together at the other end, and also resending lost packages. TCP also checks that everything arrives in the right order.
- **IP (Internet Protocol)**—Is responsible for finding a path for network messages. IP only knows the IP address of the destination machine. IP does not have any knowledge of how one network message relates to other network messages. IP is simply a package routine, while TCP ensures stable data transfer.
- **UDP (User Datagram Protocol)**—Is a compact and simple transport protocol without handshaking. This protocol is used by, for example, nftp and NFS.
- **ARP (Address Resolution Protocol)**—Converts an IP address into a physical Ethernet address.
- **ICMP (Internet Control Message Protocol)**—Cooperates with IP and controls error information. This protocol cannot be accessed by the host system.
- **SMTP (Simple Mail Transfer Protocol)**—Sends messages to a list of destinations (mailboxes) on the Internet. SMTP is known as electronic mail.
- **RIP (Routing Information Protocol)**—Is responsible for routing TCP/IP packages from one network to another.
- **SLIP (Serial Line Internet Protocol)**—Is used for sending TCP/IP packages via serial lines (asynchronous).

- **PPP (Point-to-Point Protocol)**—Is used for sending TCP/IP packages via serial lines (asynchronous). Today, PPP is normally used rather than SLIP. Whereas SLIP must be preconfigured at both ends of the connection, PPP is able to negotiate the communication parameters while connecting. PPP also enables authentication and dynamically assigns IP addresses when connecting. PPP also makes it possible to connect to the Internet from different locations. If you are using a modem or ISDN with Linux, I recommend that you use PPP.

### 22.4.1 Addressing

Every node on the Internet has a 32-bit network address that includes a network number and a machine number. There are three network address classes: small, medium, and large. These are called A, B, and C. The larger the network is, the more nodes it has. Network addresses are set up in the hosts file (in most systems, `/etc/hosts`) or via DNS (server). A network address may be 89.0.0.2. Each decimal figure equals an octal number in a 32-bit address.

### 22.4.2 Routing

The different networks that form the Internet are connected via so-called routers; these are machines that are connected to one or more networks. Routers are able to forward TCP/IP packages from one network to another. If the destination network is known, the package will be sent directly to the correct node (host). If the destination network is unknown, the package is sent from router to router until the correct network segment is found.

### 22.4.3 Applications

There is always a bunch of standard user applications like `ftp`, `Telnet`, and a set of commands called R (remote) commands, included in TCP/IP. The R commands come from Berkeley Unix. Linux is also supplied with a standard sockets programming interface. This permits, for example, a C program using TCP/IP to read/write network data. Linux X-server uses TCP/IP, which lets you display applications that are running on a different system on your Linux screen. You'll find out more about X Window in Chapter 10.

## 22.5 TCP/IP configuration files

Before you can update all the configuration files, you need to have some key data like the IP address, netmask, default gateway, and DNS server (name server). You will also be asked about these key data when installing Linux (see Chapter 3). You can update this data using Linux `linuxconf` (see Figure 22-2).

Example:

```
[root@nittedal /root]# linuxconf &
```

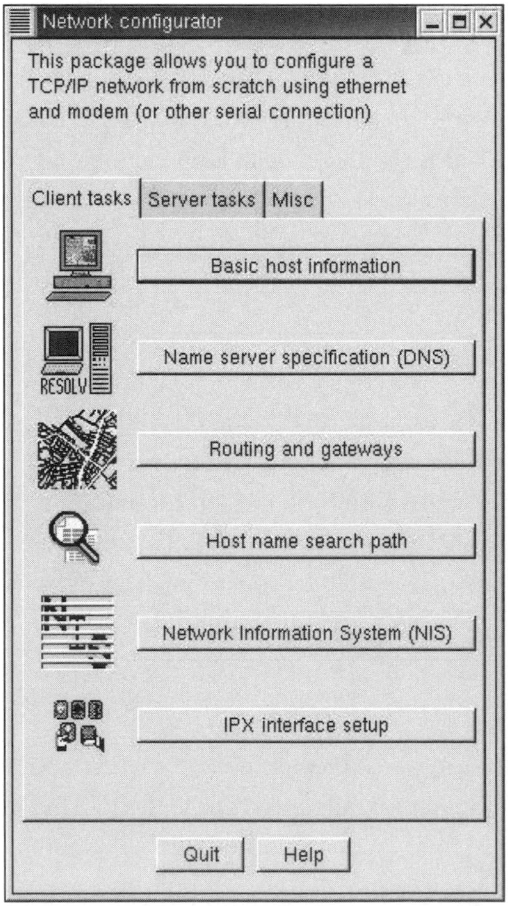

**Figure 22-2**
*Using network configurator from* `linuxconf`.

Every machine on the Internet has a unique IP address. When you want to test the TCP/IP software, you may use the loopback address, 127.0.0.1. The loopback address is a test address that you'll find on every TCP/IP node. The address is placed in the `/etc/hosts` file and is always the same (127.0.0.1). My current Linux workstation has the IP address 207.117.119.15.

If you connect your machine to the Internet via PPP (the most frequently used protocol for connecting to the Internet via dial-up connections), your IP address may be assigned statically or dynamically. If you have a static assignment, you get the same IP address every time you connect to the Internet. If you have a dynamic assignment, you may get a different IP address (although from an interval of IP addresses) every time you connect to the Internet.

The network mask (netmask) decides which part of the IP addresses is reserved for the network number and which part is reserved for the machine address. This is, most of all, the following type of message to the routers in the network: "This part of the IP address is a network address. Check if this package is already in the correct network or if it must be sent to another network." If the network mask is not set up correctly, TCP/IP routing will not function. Network addresses are divided into three main classes. Class A uses network mask 255.0.0.0. This means that there is a maximum of 255 different Class A network numbers, and in each network there can be 255*255*255 (=16581375) different nodes/host addresses. Class B uses network mask 255.255.0.0. This means that there is a maximum of 255*255 (= 65025) different network numbers and the same number of different nodes/host addresses. Class C uses network mask 255.255.255.0. This means that there is a maximum of 255*255*255 (=16581375) different network numbers with up to 255 different nodes/host addresses in each subnet.

The `ifconfig` command starts the NIC and sets the network addresses. This command is normally executed as part of the computer's booting procedure. Afterwards, it is mostly used when searching for errors and when fine-tuning the system. From the command line, without parameters, the `ifconfig` command gives information about the different network interfaces. When setting up an Ethernet card in a Unix-based system, you will find different names for network interfaces.

| Supplier | Operating System | Interface |
|---|---|---|
| Open Source | Linux | eth0/eth1/tr0/tr1 |
| Sun | Solaris | le0 |
| Compaq | Ultrix/OSF/Unix 64 | ln0 |

| Supplier | Operating System | Interface (*Continued*) |
|---|---|---|
| HP | HP-UX | lan0 |
| IBM | AIX | en0 |
| SGI | IRIX | ec0 |

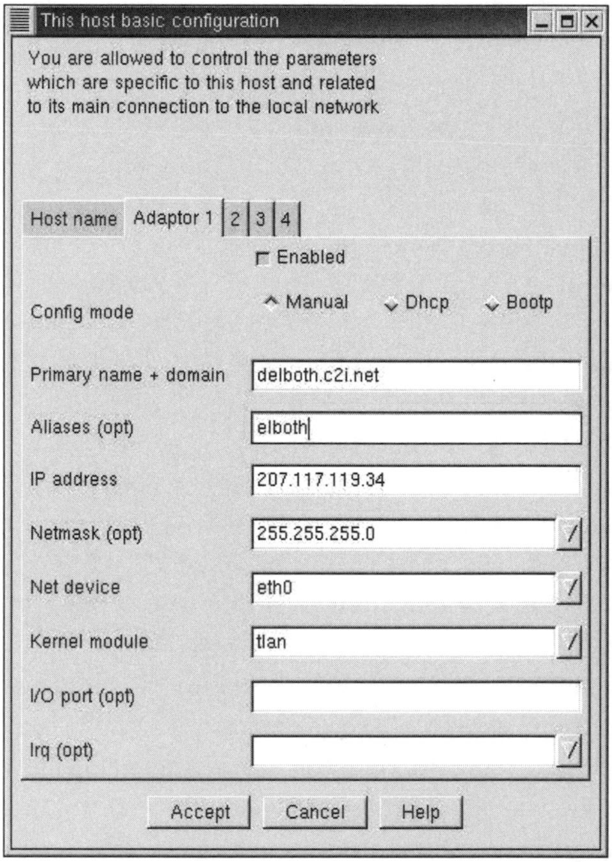

**Figure 22-3**
*Host configuration from Network configurator* (`linuxconf`).

You will find that eth0 (see Figure 22-3) is the first Ethernet interface and eth1 the second Ethernet interface under Linux. If you are using Token Ring, the names are tr0 and tr1. The following is an example from my Linux machine.

```
[root@nittedal /etc]# ifconfig eth0 207.117.119.15 net-
mask 255.255.255.0 broadcast 207.117.119.255
```

In this example, I set the IP address, the netmask, and the broadcast address for the eth0 Ethernet interface.

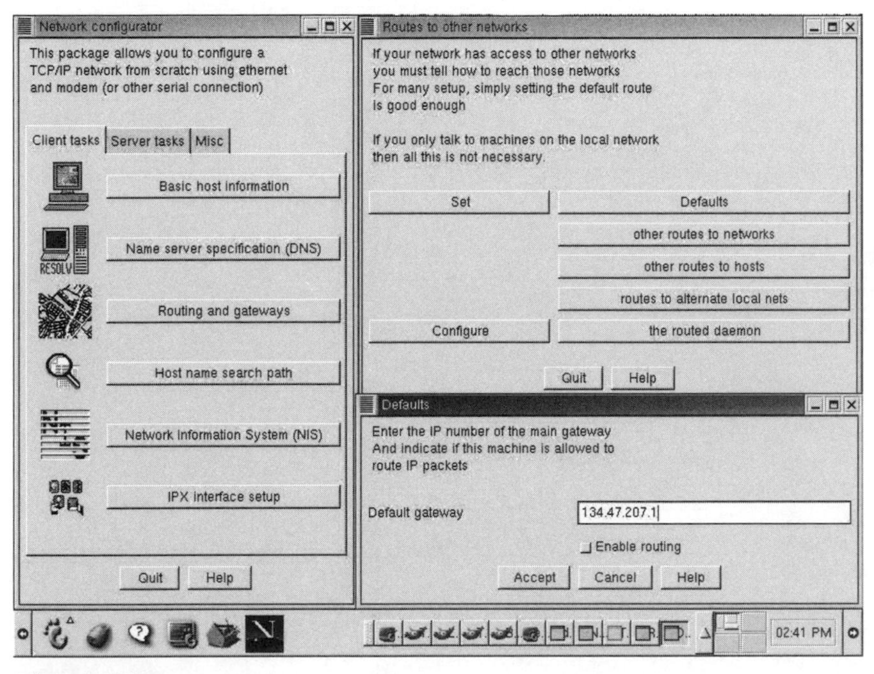


**Figure 22-4**
*Defining the default routes to other networks from Network configurator* (`linuxconf`).

The default gateway (see Figure 22-4) is the address you need to access the outside world. If you access the Internet via a router, the default gateway address normally has a 1 (one) in its last decimal place. In my case, it is 207.117.119.1. When using an asynchronous connection via a modem or ISDN, your ISP will give you default gateway address. You can set all network parameters from X Window's `linuxconf` (`#` **`linuxconf &`**) from the GNOME or KDE interface. If you only need to check the network interfaces, try `usernet` (`#` **`/usr/bin/usernet &`**).

When you want to surf the Internet, your machine must have a way of translating machine names into machine addresses. People find it easier to remember names rather than a bunch of figures. To register your own domain, you send a request to the Internic at this address: rs.internic.net. Every machine on the Internet communicates with a name server (DNS; see Figure 22-5) that translates domain names (hostnames) into IP addresses. Your ISP will give you the name of one or more name servers.

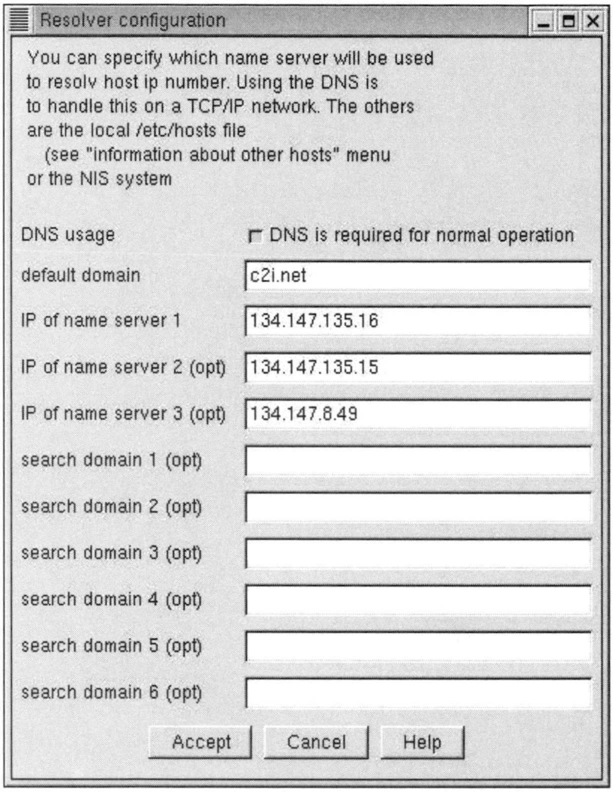

Resolver configuration

You can specify which name server will be used
to resolv host ip number. Using the DNS is
to handle this on a TCP/IP network. The others
are the local /etc/hosts file
(see "information about other hosts" menu
or the NIS system

DNS usage — DNS is required for normal operation
default domain — c2i.net
IP of name server 1 — 134.147.135.16
IP of name server 2 (opt) — 134.147.135.15
IP of name server 3 (opt) — 134.147.8.49
search domain 1 (opt)
search domain 2 (opt)
search domain 3 (opt)
search domain 4 (opt)
search domain 5 (opt)
search domain 6 (opt)

Accept Cancel Help

**Figure 22-5**
*Defining DNS servers from Network configurator* (`linuxconf`).

The DNS servers that you want to use are set up in `/etc/resolv.conf`. Here is an example:

```
[root@nittedal /etc]# more resolv.conf
search c2i.net
nameserver 193.216.1.10
nameserver 193.216.69.10
```

The important system files in a TCP/IP network are `/etc/hosts`, `/etc/hosts.equiv`, and `$home/.rhosts`. In the `/etc/hosts` file (see Figure 22-6), all other TCP/IP machines are defined with a unique address, name, and alias. When you want to communicate with other hosts, you may use their address, name, alias, or complete domain name.

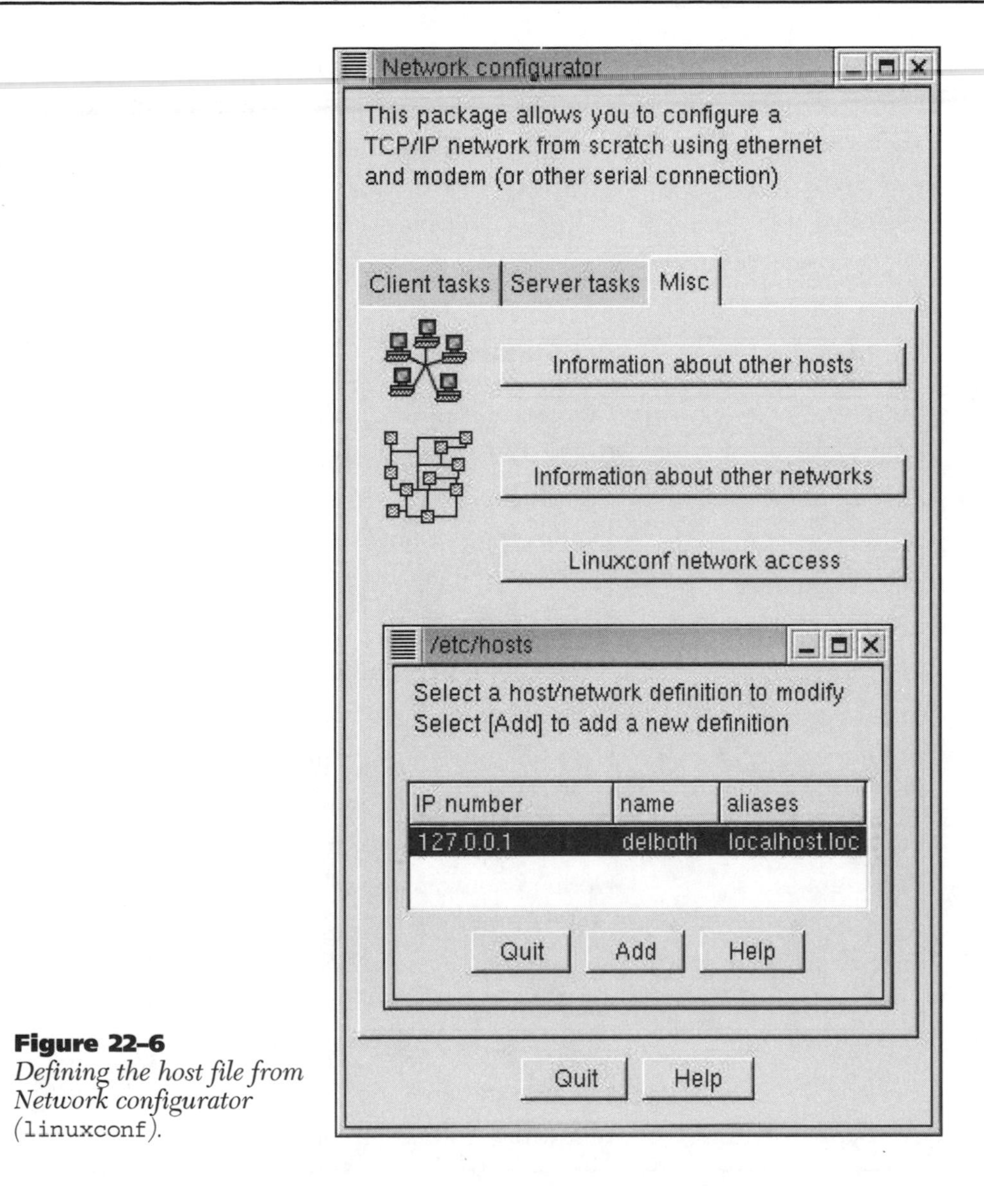


**Figure 22-6**
*Defining the host file from Network configurator* (`linuxconf`).

The `/etc/hosts.equiv` file contains a list of so-called entrusted machines. This file works only when you use remote commands like `rlogin`, `rcp`, and `rsh`. These commands can normally be used between machines running the Linux, Unix, VMS, Mac, and Windows operating systems only. In the `.rhosts` file, which is located in your home directory, you decide which users you entrust on your account. This file has two columns: the first column contains the machine name (host); the second column contains the username of the user who is allowed to log in without a password.

The difference between /etc/hosts.equiv and $HOME/.rhosts is that $HOME/.rhosts is a local file that allows the user to connect their different user-ids (one single user defined at multiple Linux machines), whereas /etc/hosts.equiv works globally for everyone on each single machine. Be aware that the /etc/hosts.equiv and $HOME/.rhosts files make it easier to enter your Linux system.

| Key Files | Description |
|---|---|
| /etc/exports | Filesystem export (sharing) via NFS. |
| /etc/fstab | Controls filesystem mounting. |
| /etc/ftpaccess | Controls FTP access to your FTP server. |
| /etc/ftpgroups | Defined FTP groups. |
| /etc/ftpusers | Defined FTP users. |
| /etc/ftphosts | Defined FTP hosts. |
| /etc/HOSTNAME | Name of your Linux PC. |
| /etc/hosts | Local mapping between hostname and IP address. |
| /etc/hosts.lpd | Host file for remote printer access. |
| /etc/hosts.equiv | Host file for remote commands. |
| /etc/nsswitch.conf | Defines TCP/IP services and location of key files. |
| /etc/networks | Defined networks (used in connection with static TCP/IP routing). |
| /etc/resolv.conf | Domain name and DNS server setup. |
| /etc/smb.conf | Samba setup (file server software). |
| /etc/services | TCP/IP services connected to port numbers. |
| /etc/yp | Yellow pages configuration file. |
| /etc/ypserv.conf | Yellow pages configuration file. |

In the examples with rsh, rcp, and rlogin below (Sections 22.14-22.16), it is a requirement that /etc/hosts.equiv and/or $HOME/.rhosts be set up correctly.

## 22.6 Connecting via modem

It is simple to connect to the Internet via an analog modem with Red Hat Linux as long as you use X Window. Under GNOME, you'll find configuration tools

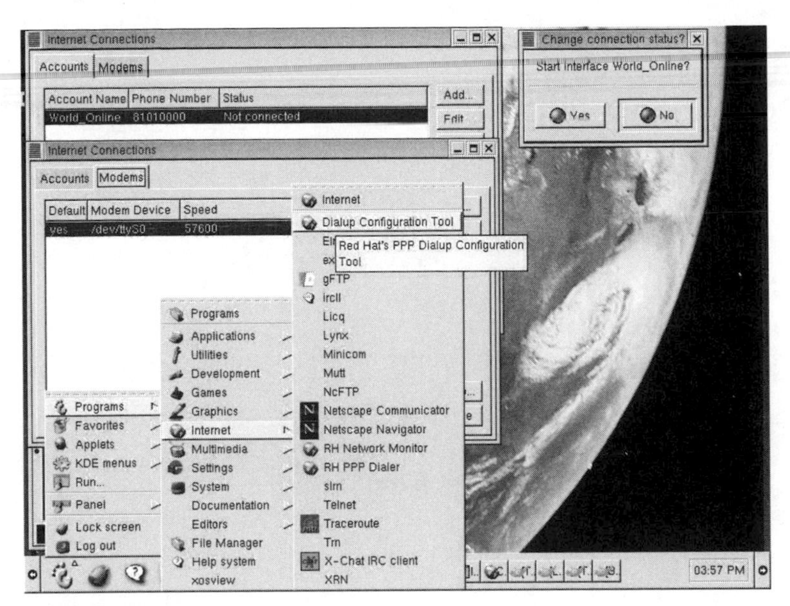


**Figure 22-7**
*Red Hat's PPP Dialup Configuration Tool.*

for Dialup (Internet) and RH PPP Dialer (see Figure 22-7).

Under KDE, you'll find the Kppp program. It is a matter of taste as to what to use, but my recommendation is the Kppp program. The program should be run from the KDE interface.

The modem is normally connected to a serial port; for example, COM1 or COM2. The names of serial ports in Linux are defined below:

| MS-DOS Name | Linux Name | Device Driver |
|---|---|---|
| COM1 | cua0 | ttyS0 |
| COM2 | cua1 | ttyS1 |
| COM3 | cua2 | ttyS2 |
| COM4 | cua3 | ttyS3 |

As the Linux names cua0, cua1, cua2, and cua3 are being phased out (as of kernel 2.2), you should use the ttySx names.

For a 2.0.X kernel, you should use:

```
[root@digital /root]# ln -s /dev/cuaX /dev/modem
```

For a 2.2.X kernel, you should use:

```
[root@digital /root]# ln -s /dev/ttySX /dev/modem
```

The simplest way of connecting to the Internet via modem is by using the Kppp program. Before using this program, run a backup of the PPP configuration file and make the pppd program accessible to all users. Select the terminal icon and execute the following commands:

```
[elboth@digital elboth]$ su -
Password:
[root@digital /root]# chmod +s /usr/sbin/pppd
[root@digital /root]# chmod a+x /usr/sbin/pppd
[root@digital /root]# mv /etc/ppp/options
/etc/ppp/options.000
[root@digital /root]# exit
[elboth@digital elboth]$ exit
```

It is simple to start Kppp (see Figure 22-8) from a GNOME or KDE interface. My recommendation is that you use KDE.

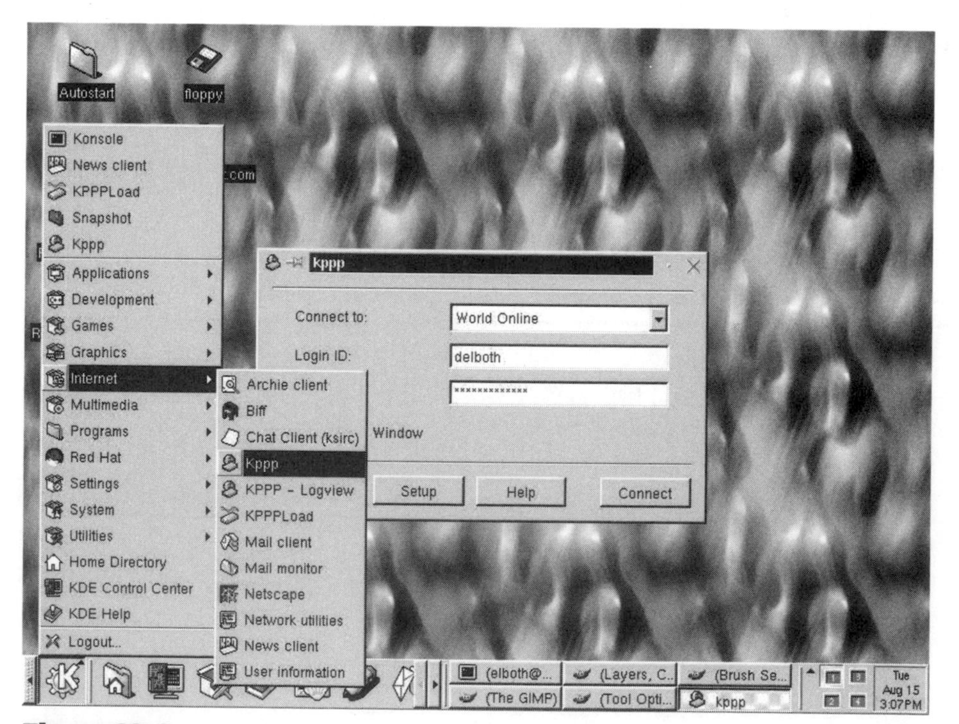

**Figure 22-8**
*The Kppp program under the KDE GUI environment.*

When in the KDE interface, this is the method to use:

1. Click on the KDE foot on the taskbar at the bottom of your screen.
2. Select Internet, and then Internet connection.
3. From Kppp, select the Setup tab. This takes you to the Kppp Configuration window (see Figure 22-9).

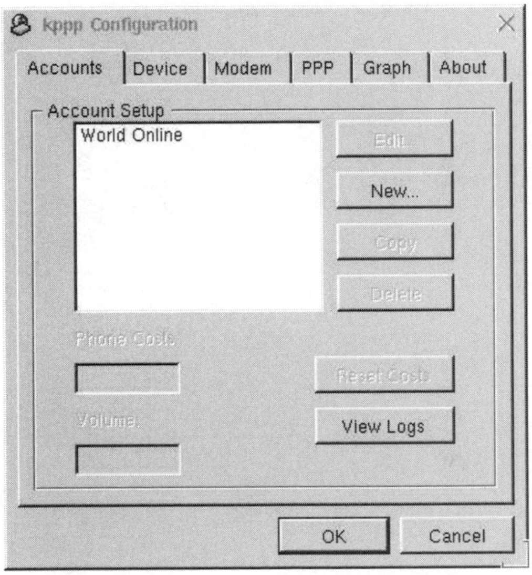

**Figure 22-9**
*The Kppp configuration program.*

4. Select the Accounts tab, and then click New. You enter a new window that allows you to configure your ISP connection. Fill in your name and telephone number.
5. Click the IP tab. Here you can choose between a dynamic and static IP address. The most usual option is dynamic address. This means that your ISP assigns a new IP address every time you connect.
6. Click the DNS tab and define the domain name and DNS servers to your ISP.
7. If you need to define a gateway (see Figure 22-10), logon script, or accounts, go to each tab. Finish by clicking OK.
8. Now, from Kppp, select the Device tab. Choose Modem Device. In most cases, the standard setup, `/dev/modem` or `/dev/ttyS0`, should work fine. If this is wrong, you will get an error message when trying to connect

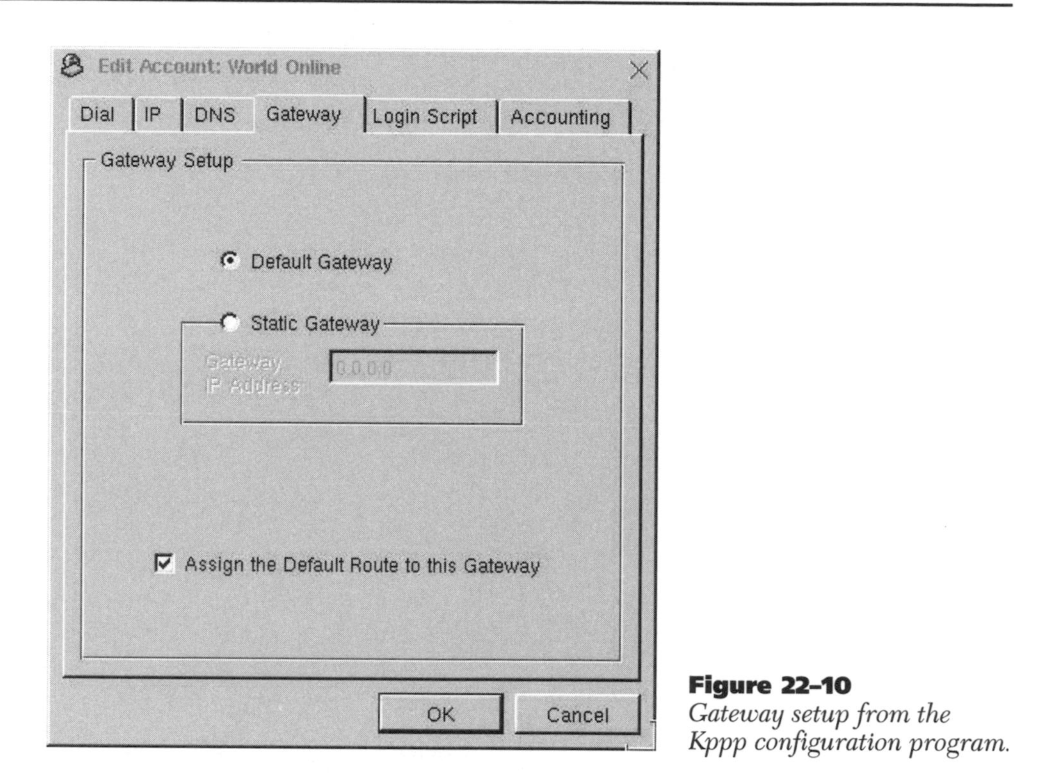


**Figure 22-10**
*Gateway setup from the Kppp configuration program.*

to your ISP. The selection of device drivers is listed in the table above. Finish with OK.

9. In the Kppp connection form (see Figure 22-11), enter your username and password, click Connect, and you are connected to your ISP.
10. Start Netscape from the taskbar. You are now ready to surf the Internet.

**Figure 22-11**
*Connecting to local ISP with the Kppp program.*

## 22.7 Connecting via ISDN

A good way of connecting to the Internet is using an external ISDN terminal adapter (I use an ISDN router at home). You will find that setting up ISDN is similar to setting up a modem connection. The only difference is the chatscript. ISDN is only supported if you have a Linux kernel that supports ISDN (Linux kernel 2.2 or later). Using the ISDN program isdn-config is the easiest way of connecting to the Internet via ISDN. This program can be started from the GNOME foot in the taskbar at the bottom of your screen. Here, you choose System, and the isdn-config.

With Red Hat Linux 7.0, you will find that it is as simple to set up an ISDN terminal adapter as it is to set up a modem. More information about ISDN under Linux can be found under the different Linux HOWTOs (Kernel HOWTO, ISDN HOWTO) and Web sites like www.redhat.com, www.suse.com, www.corel.com, www.millenniumx.de. Also check the different Linux newsgroups.

## 22.8 Start/stop scripts

In the table below, you'll find the most important start/stop scripts for TCP/IP communications services on a machine running Red Hat Linux.

| **Important Network Processes** | **Description/Configuration** |
|---|---|
| `/etc/rc.d/rc2.d/S10network [start] [stop]` | Starts and stops Linux NICs. Configuration files: `/etc/sysconfig/files=network..pcmica` `/proc/sys/net/ip4/files`, `/etc/hosts`, `/etc/networks`, etc. |
| `/etc/rc.d/rc2.d/K50inet [start] [stop]` | Starts and stops TCP/IP. Configuration files: `/etc/sysconfig/network`, `/etc/inetd.conf`, `/etc/hosts`, `/etc/networks`, etc. |
| `/etc/rc.d/rc2.d/K50snmp [start] [stop]` | Starts and stops TCP/IP SNMP. Configuration files: `/etc/snmp/snmpd.local.conf` `/etc/snmp/snmpd.conf`, |

| Important Network Processes | Description/Configuration (*Continued*) |
|---|---|
| | /usr/share/snmp/snmp.local.conf, /usr/share/snmp/snmp.conf, /etc/sysconfig/network, /etc/inetd.conf, /etc/hosts, /etc/networks, etc. |
| /etc/rc.d/rc2.d/K55routed [start] [stop] | Starts and stops TCP/IP RIP Configuration files: /etc/sysconfig/routed, /etc/gateway, /etc/sysconfig/network, /etc/inetd.conf, /etc/hosts, /etc/networks, etc. |
| /etc/rc.d/rc2.d/K85nfsfs [start] [stop] | Starts and stops NFS mounting Configuration files: /etc/fstab, /etc/exports (remote hosts), /etc/sysconfig/network, /etc/inetd.conf, /etc/hosts/, /etc/networks, etc. |
| /etc/rc.d/rc2.d/S65dhcp [start] [stop] | Starts and stops dhcp. Configuration files: /etc/sysconfig/network, /etc/dhcpd.conf |
| /etc/rc.d/rc2.d/K15http [start] [stop] | Starts and stops Apache WWW server. Configuration files: /etc/httpd/conf/access.conf, /etc/httpd/conf/httpd.conf, /etc/httpd/conf/srm.conf |
| /etc/rc.d/rc2.d/K20nfs [start] [stop] | Starts and stops nfs. Configuration files: /etc/sysconfig/network, /etc/exports |
| /etc/rc.d/rc2.d/K20rusersd [start] [stop] | Starts and stops remote users. Configuration files: /etc/sysconfig/network, /etc/hosts* |

| Important Network Processes | Description/Configuration (*Continued*) |
|---|---|
| /etc/rc.d/rc2.d/K20rwall [start] [stop] | Starts and stops rwall. Configuration files: /etc/sysconfig/network, /etc/hosts* |
| /etc/rc.d/rc2.d/K35smb [start] [stop] | Starts and stops smb SAMBA. Configuration files: /etc/sysconfig/network, /etc/hosts*, /etc/smb.conf |
| /etc/rc.d/rc2.d/K45named [start] [stop] | Starts and stops DNS server Configuration files: /etc/sysconfig/network, /etc/hosts*, /etc/named.conf |

All scripts are links to /etc/rc.d/init.d. Many of the same scripts are also linked to system level 3, i.e., /etc/rc.d/rc3.d. The R* daemons are often considered a security problem and are rarely run. Routed should normally not be run.

## 22.9 Security

When you are surfing the Internet, you should limit the access to your machine. Update /etc/hosts.deny with ALL: ALL. This stops all access, including your own. Opening your own access is done by updating /etc/hosts.allow with the loopback address ALL: 127.0.0.1. You should also define the loopback address and your network in the /etc/network file; for example:

```
[root@nittedal /root]# more /etc/networks
loopback          127.0.0.0
localnet          207.117.119.0
```

You will find more about Linux security on the Web sites http://www.rootshell.com and http://insecure.org.

## 22.10 Using a browser

If you have a low-bandwidth connection, Lynx may be a good browser alternative. Lynx is included in Red Hat. Most users prefer running X Window, and need a browser with a GUI. The most frequently used GUI browsers are Netscape (included in Red Hat Linux 7.x (see Figure 22-12)) Mosaic, Opera, and Chimera.

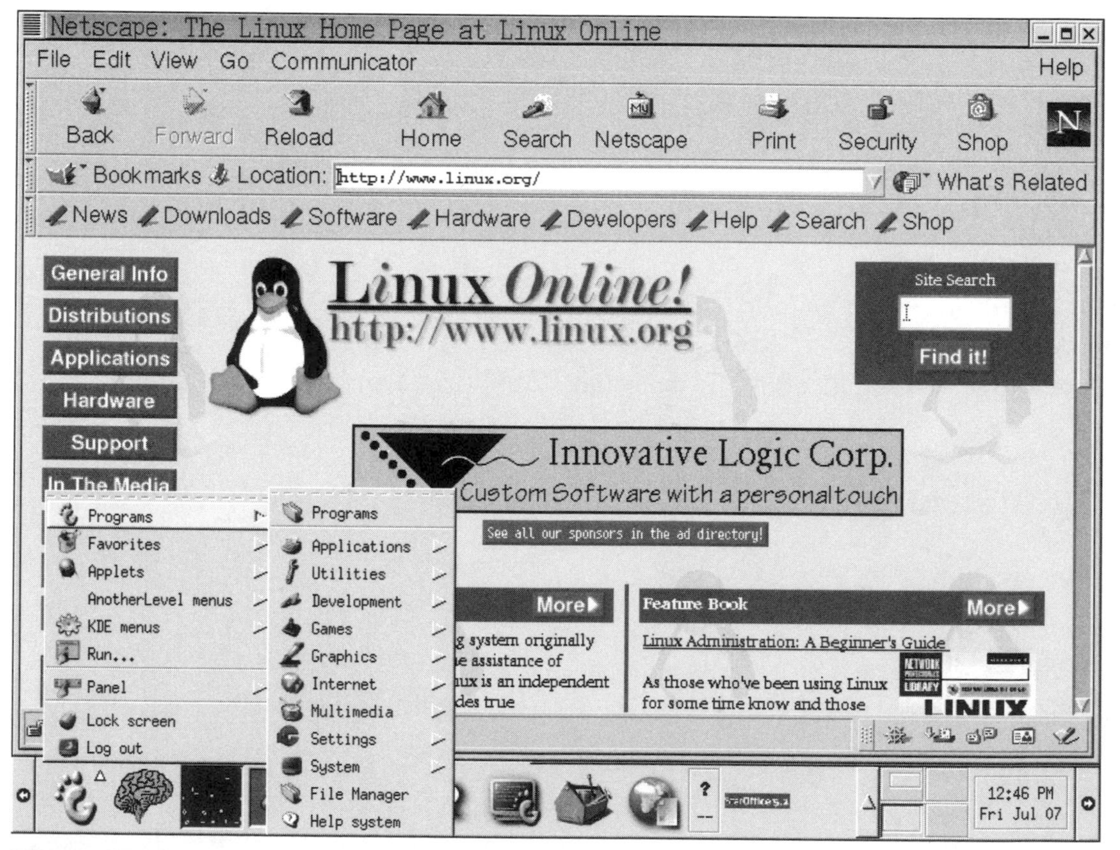


**Figure 22-12**
*Using the Netscape GUI browser under Linux.*

For more information on Chimera, go to:

ftp://ftp.nvg.unit.no/pub/linux/sunsite/system/Network/info-systems/www/chimera-1.65.bin.ELF.tar.gz

or

http://www.unlv.edu/chimera/

For more information on Mosaic, see the following FTP sites:

- ftp://ftp.nvg.ntnu.no/pub/linux/sunsite/system/Network/info-systems/Mosaic-2.7b1-aout.tgz
- ftp://ftp.NCSA.uiuc.edu/Web/Mosaic/Unix/binaries/2.6

## 22.11 Contact – ping

When you are connected to a TCP/IP network, you can check whether you have contact with other active machines by using the `ping` command. The `ping` program forwards a data package to a specified host (machine). If there is contact with the machine, the data package is returned. `ping` sends ICMP (Internet Control Message Protocol) packages.

**ping Command – Contact/Interface Check**

| | |
|---|---|
| Command | `ping [-c count] [-i interval] [-s packetsize] host` |
| Options | See the Linux man pages. |
| Function | Checks whether you have contact with your own interface (NIC, serial port) or a specified host in the network. |
| `-c count` | Stops after specified count of packages. (If you don't specify a count of packages, `ping` will go on forwarding packages.) |
| `-i interval` | Waits the specified number of seconds before forwarding a new package. |
| `-s packetsize` | Specifies the number of data bytes to be sent. The default is 56, which translates into 64 ICMP data bytes when combined with the 8 bytes of ICMP header data. |
| `host` | Name of the machine that you want to communicate with. You may use the hostname, complete domain name, or IP address. |

Examples:

```
[david@nittedal david]$ ping ftp.powertech.com
```

Here, I try to get in touch with the machine ftp.powertech.com.

```
[david@nittedal david]$ ping -s 64 207.117.119.9
PING 207.117.119.9 (207.117.119.9): 56 data bytes
64 bytes from 207.117.119.9: icmp_seq=0 ttl=64 time=2.7
ms
64 bytes from 207.117.119.9: icmp_seq=1 ttl=64 time=2.6
ms
64 bytes from 207.117.119.9: icmp_seq=2 ttl=64 time=2.6
ms
64 bytes from 207.117.119.9: icmp_seq=3 ttl=64 time=2.6
ms
-- 207.117.119.9 ping statistics --
4 packets transmitted, 4 packets received, 0% packet
loss
round-trip min/avg/max = 2.6/2.6/2.7 ms
[david@nittedal david]$
```

Here, I try and make contact with the machine that has the IP address 207.117.119.9. I use the -s option, which specifies the number of data bytes to be sent.

System files: /etc/hosts, /etc/hosts.equiv, $home/.rhosts

## 22.12 Terminal emulation – telnet

Telnet is a user application that makes it possible to connect to another machine on the network. This means that any terminal, vt52, vt100, vt220, wyse60, 3270, etc., can be connected to a network host. Use Telnet when you need to work on another machine via terminal emulation. Just enter telnet and the name of the machine you want to connect to. When the connection has been established, your screen acts like a terminal to the other machine. You can also run Telnet to machines that run operating systems other than Linux.

**telnet Command – Terminal Emulation**

| | |
|---|---|
| Command | telnet [options] [host] [port] |
| Function | Sets up a terminal connection to a specified machine. |
| Options | See the Linux man pages. |

**telnet Command – Terminal Emulation (*Continued*)**

| | |
|---|---|
| `host` | The name of the machine you want to communicate with. You may use the hostname, complete domain name, or IP address. |
| `port` | Select which port number to use for your Telnet connection. The default port is 23. An overview of ports is found in the `/etc/services` file. |

It is also possible to just enter `telnet`. You'll get a new prompt (`telnet>`). From this prompt, you can give various commands; for example:

```
telnet>help
```

Here, you get a complete overview of available commands.

```
telnet>open host
```

Connects you to the host specified by the machine name.

```
telnet>close
```

Closes a Telnet session.

```
telnet>quit
```

Quits the Telnet program.

Examples:

```
[david@nittedal david]$ telnet davelin
Trying 207.117.119.9...
Connected to davelin.c2i.net.
Escape character is '^]'.


Red Hat Linux release 7.0 (Guinness)
Kernel 2.2.16-22  on an i686
login:
```

Starts Telnet emulation to the host `davelin`. You log in to the new machine with your username and, if applicable, your password.

```
[david@nittedal david]$ telnet ftp.c2i.net 25
```

The Telnet program is also useful when you want to check other TCP/IP services, e.g., SMTP, which is port number 25.

See also: `rlogin`

System files:

`/etc/hosts`, `/etc/hosts.equiv`, `$home/.rhosts`

## 22.13 Transfer files - ftp

The most frequently used method for transferring data in a TCP/IP network is via FTP (File Transfer Protocol). The FTP program is used to transfer files between different machines (although ncftp is more fun and easier to use). The FTP program uses the FTP protocol. The FTP program is found on most computers, no matter which OS they use. FTP supports a range of transfer formats, including ASCII, EBCDIC, and binary files.

**ftp Command - Transfers Files between Two Machines**

| | |
|---|---|
| Command | `ftp [-d] [-i] [-n] [-v][host]` |
| Function | Transfers files between two machines connected via TCP/IP. |
| Options | See the Linux man pages. |
| `-d` | Turns FTP analysis mode (debugging) on. |
| `-i` | Turns off interactive queries during file transfer. |
| `-n` | Prevents auto logging from your login name. |
| `-v` | Displays all messages. |
| `host` | The name of the machine you want to communicate with. You may use the hostname, complete domain name, or IP address. |

FTP is an interactive program. When giving the FTP command, you get a new prompt (`ftp>`) (see Figure 22-13).

From this prompt, you can give a number of commands; for example:

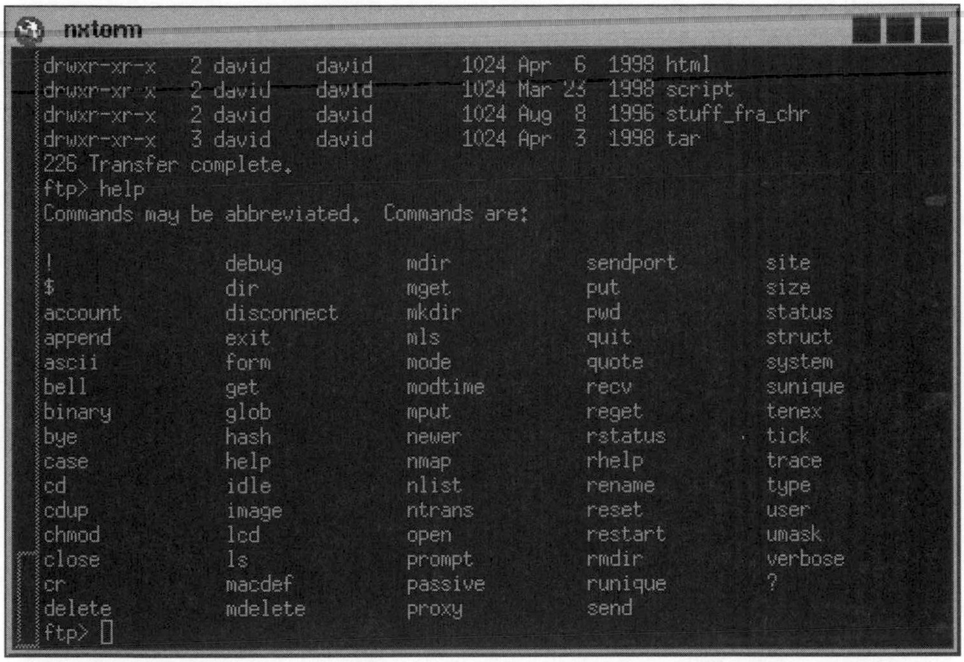

```
nxterm
drwxr-xr-x   2 david    david        1024 Apr  6  1998 html
drwxr-xr-x   2 david    david        1024 Mar 23  1998 script
drwxr-xr-x   2 david    david        1024 Aug  8  1996 stuff_fra_chr
drwxr-xr-x   3 david    david        1024 Apr  3  1998 tar
226 Transfer complete.
ftp> help
Commands may be abbreviated.  Commands are:

!               debug           mdir            sendport        site
$               dir             mget            put             size
account         disconnect      mkdir           pwd             status
append          exit            mls             quit            struct
ascii           form            mode            quote           system
bell            get             modtime         recv            sunique
binary          glob            mput            reget           tenex
bye             hash            newer           rstatus         tick
case            help            nmap            rhelp           trace
cd              idle            nlist           rename          type
cdup            image           ntrans          reset           user
chmod           lcd             open            restart         umask
close           ls              prompt          rmdir           verbose
cr              macdef          passive         runique         ?
delete          mdelete         proxy           send
ftp> []
```

**Figure 22-13**
*Using ftp from a terminal session.*

*ftp>***help**

This gives a complete overview of available commands.

*ftp>***open ftp.powertech.com**

Connects you to the host specified by the machine name.

*ftp>***close**

Closes an FTP session.

When you need to move to the directory on the local machine that you want to transfer files to or from, use commands like `cd`, `pwd`, and `dir`. When you are transferring files from a remote host, you must use `get` and the filename.

For example:

*ftp>***get datafile**

When transferring a file to a remote host, use `put` and the filename.

For example:

```
ftp>put datafil
```

When copying multiple files simultaneously, you can use `mget` and `mput`. The usual wildcard characters can be used.

More and more users prefer ncftp. This program makes it easier to use FTP, and it supports all the necessary older features. You'll find more information about ncftp on the Linux man and help pages.

See also: `nftp` and `rcp`

System files: `/etc/hosts`, `/etc/hosts.equiv`, `$home/.rhosts`, `/etc/ftpgroups`, `/etc/ftpusers`, `/etc/ftphosts`

## 22.14 Run remote programs – rsh

With `rsh` (remote shell), you can execute commands on other Linux machines. This is the simplest way of executing (running) programs between two Linux machines that are connected via TCP/IP. To execute an `rsh` command, the `/etc/hosts.equiv` and/or `$home/.rhosts` files must be updated.

**rsh Command – Execute Remote Commands**

| | |
|---|---|
| Command | `rsh [-l username] [host] [command]` |
| Function | Executes remote commands between two machines connected via TCP/IP. |
| Options | See the Linux man pages. |
| `-l username` | Login name of the remote user. When this option is not used, `rsh` presumes that you are using your login name. |
| `host` | The name of the machine that you want to communicate with. You may use the hostname, complete domain name, or IP address. |
| command | Here you enter the command you want to execute on the remote host. |

Examples:

```
[david@nittedal david]$ rsh linuxadm ps axl
```

Registers process status on the Linux machine `linuxadm`.

```
[david@nittedal david]$ rsh linuxadm uname -a >
local.file
```

Sends the result of the remote command `uname -a` to the local file `local.file`.

```
[david@nittedal david]$ rsh linuxadm 'uname -a >
remote.file'
```

Sends the result of the remote command `uname -a` to `remote.file` at a remote host.

```
[david@nittedal david]$ rsh linuxadm lpr -P hpprinter2 <
/etc/hosts
```

Sends a print of the `/etc/hosts` file to a printer controlled by the spooling system in the Linux machine `linuxadm`.

See also: `rlogin` and `rcp`

System files: `/etc/hosts`, `/etc/hosts.equiv`, `$home/.rhosts`

## 22.15 Remote copy – rcp

`rcp` is the simplest method of copying files between two Linux machines that are connected via TCP/IP. This command works the same way as the Linux command `cp`, but in addition, you specify the names of the Linux machines. To execute an `rcp` command, the `/etc/hosts.equiv` and/or `$home/.rhosts` files must be updated.

**rcp Command – Remote Copies**

| | |
|---|---|
| Command | `rcp [-p] [from_file] [to_file]`<br>`rcp [-p] -r [from_files] [to_directory]` |
| Function | Transfers files between two Linux machines that are |

**rcp Command – Remote copies (*Continued*)**

| | |
|---|---|
| | connected via TCP/IP. |
| Options | See the Linux man pages. |
| `-p` | Preserves the original bits at the time of file changes (time, date). |
| `r` | Copies subdirectories, too. |
| `from_file` | File you are copying from. |
| `to_file` | File you are copying to. |
| `from_files` | Files you are copying from. |
| `to_directory` | Directory you are copying to. |

Where required, you must include the hostname before the filename. For example, `host:to_file`, `remote_user@host:path` (file located relative to the home directory of `remote_user` at host), `host:/home/david`, `host:~search path` (located relative to your home directory). You'll find the hostname in your local `/etc/hosts` file.

Examples:

```
[david@nittedal david]$ rcp linuxadm:/home/david/letter
```

Copies the file `letter` from the `linuxadm` machine to the machine and directory from which you executed the command.

```
[david@nittedal david]$ rcp offer
linuxadm:/home/david/offer
```

Copies the file `offer` from the local machine to the `linuxadm` machine.

```
[david@nittedal david]$ rcp applix.ag
linserv.linux.com:~lecture/linux.ag
```

Copies the Applix file `applix.ag` from my active directory (local host) to the `lecture` directory (which is a subdirectory of my home directory) on the remote host `linuxserv.linux.com`. The file gets the name `linux.ag` on the remote host.

See also: `rlogin` and `rsh`

System files: `/etc/hosts`, `/etc/hosts.equiv`, `$home/.rhosts`

## 22.16 Remote login – rlogin

There are some advantages of using rlogin over Telnet. It is a requirement that the following is defined:

- You are defined as a user on the remote host.
- The /etc/hosts.equiv and/or $home/.rhosts system files on the remote host are updated.

Now you can log in to the remote host without specifying your username and password. If you are not defined in the /etc/hosts.equiv and $home/.rhosts files, your password will be requested.

**rlogin Command – Remote Terminal Emulation**

| | |
|---|---|
| Command | `rlogin [-8] [echar] [-l login name] host` |
| Function | Sets up a remote terminal connection to a specified host. The machine name is the name of the host you want to communicate with. |
| Options | See the Linux man pages. |
| `-8` | Allows 8-bit characters (default), except escape characters. |
| `-echar` | Sets the escape character to char. |
| `-l login name` | Sets the login name of the remote system. |
| `host` | The name of the machine you want to communicate with. You may use the hostname, complete domain name, or IP address. |

Examples:

```
[david@nittedal david]$ rlogin -8 -eg linuxadm
```

Starts a terminal connection with the linuxadm machine. I have support for 8-bit characters. The escape character is g.

See also: telnet, rsh, rcp

Other system files: /etc/hosts, /etc/hosts.equiv, $home/.rhosts

## 22.17 Trace package – traceroute

With the `traceroute` command, it is possible to trace the route that your TCP/IP packages are using. The packages are slightly delayed each time they pass through a router. `traceroute` gives an overview of the routers that are passed. With the UDP and ICMP (Internet Control Message Protocol) protocols, the `traceroute` program traces the route of the TCP/IP packages.

**traceroute Command – Traces Packages**

| | |
|---|---|
| Command | `traceroute [-m max] [-q packages][-w wait_time] host` |
| Function | Traces the route of your TCP/IP traffic. |
| Options | See the Linux man pages. |
| `-m max` | Sets the maximum number of hops (1 hop is 1 router passage) allowed getting to the remote host. Default value is 30. |
| `-q packages` | Sets the number of packages to be sent in each hop. |
| `-w wait_time` | Sets the time to wait for an analysis. |
| `host` | The name of the machine that you want to communicate with. You may use the hostname, complete domain name, or IP address. |

Example:

```
[root@nittedal /root]# traceroute -m 20 ftp.c2i.net
```

Here, you see the number of hops required to get from where the `traceroute` command is executed to `ftp.c2i.net`. Each line represents one hop. The time in milliseconds is the time required to get from your current location to the displayed hop.

See also: `rlogin`, `rcp`

System files: `/etc/hosts`, DNS

## 22.18 TCP/IP traffic – tcpdump

The tcpdump command gives information about the traffic on the network. It is a useful command when analyzing traffic patterns or looking for errors.

**tcpdump Command – TCP/IP Traffic**

| | |
|---|---|
| Command | `tcpdump [-a] [-c count] [-i interface] [-r file] [-w file] [expression]` |
| Function | Gives information about the TCP/IP traffic on the network. |
| Expression | String. |
| Options | See the Linux man pages. |
| `-a` | Tries to convert network and broadcast addresses to names. |
| `-c count` | Quits after receiving the count number of TCP/IP packages. |
| `-i interface` | Listens to the NIC. The first Ethernet card in a machine is, for example, eth0. |
| `-r file` | Reads packets from file (which was created with the -w option). |
| `-w file` | Prints information to file, not to screen. |

The table above gives some of the most important options only; there are many more. Use the man tcpdump command for more information.

```
[root@nittedal /root]# tcpdump -i tr0
```

Gives information about network traffic on the first Token Ring card.

```
[root@nittedal /root]# tcpdump -a -i eth0
```

Gives information about the network traffic on the first Ethernet card (see Figure 22-14). All network and broadcast addresses are converted to names. tcpdump has several uses for different categories of Linux users. If you are a new Linux user, tcpdump is a useful tool for connecting a couple of machines in a network.

```
nxterm
                        0000 00
21:13:43.645860 0:10:4b:7e:e4:5c > Broadcast sap e0 ui/C len=81
                        ffff 0050 0014 0000 0000 ffff ffff ffff
                        0455 0000 0000 0010 4b7e e45c 0455 0001
                        0000 0000 0000 0000 0000 0000 0000 0000
                        0000 00
21:13:44.185860 0:10:4b:7e:e4:5c > Broadcast sap e0 ui/C len=81
                        ffff 0050 0014 0000 0000 ffff ffff ffff
                        0455 0000 0000 0010 4b7e e45c 0455 0001
                        0000 0000 0000 0000 0000 0000 0000 0000
                        0000 00
21:13:44.725860 0:10:4b:7e:e4:5c > Broadcast sap e0 ui/C len=183
                        ffff 00b7 0004 0000 0000 ffff ffff ffff
                        0455 0000 0000 0010 4b7e e45c 0455 000b
                        4441 5649 4445 2020 2020 2020 2020 2020
                        4543 53
21:13:44.725860 0:10:4b:7e:e4:5c > Broadcast sap e0 ui/C len=217
                        ffff 00d9 0014 0000 0000 ffff ffff ffff
                        0553 0000 0000 0010 4b7e e45c 0553 0000
                        0000 0000 0000 0000 0000 0000 0000 0000
                        0000 00
21:13:44.725860 207.117.119.10.netbios-dgm > 207.117.119.255.netbios-dgm: udp 20
1
```

**Figure 22-14**
*Example with the* `tcpdump` *command.*

The system administrator can use `tcpdump` as a tool to find out why the network's performance has been declining. `tcpdump` can, for example, find out when a machine is sending a lot of calls into the network due to an error.

## 22.19 Anonymous FTP server

When you want to use your Linux machine as an anonymous FTP server on the Internet, you must set up the following:

- Domain name.
- The FTP daemon.
- Password and group files.
- FTP directory structure.
- Security.

The machine should have a domain name. It gets too complicated if users must specify IP addresses. A domain name can, for example, be `ftp.osi.org`.

The FTP daemon (the process) must be defined in /etc/inetd.conf. Check if it starts from /etc/inetd.conf. The following should be defined in /etc/inetd.conf:

```
ftp stream tcp nowait root /usr/sbin/tcpd  in,ftpd -l -a
```

Below is an example of /etc/password:

```
ftp:*:800:45:Anonymous FTP access:/source/ftp:/bin/false
```

In this case, I defined a group, 45 (the group is defined in /etc/group). The FTP area was put into a dedicated filesystem. I used the shell /bin/false, which gives the user limited options. I made these directories:

```
/source/ftp/bin
/source/ftp/etc
/source/ftp/in
/source/ftp/out
```

In the /source/ftp/bin directory, I placed the Linux ls command, which allows user execution of the ls command. /etc/passwd and /etc/group are placed in the /source/ftp/etc directory. These files contain only the user- id and group ID definitions of FTP. Uploadable files must be placed in /source/ftp/in to be loadable to the Linux machine. Downloadable files are placed in /source/ftp/out. Finally, the directories should be protected.

```
[root@nittedal /root]# chown root /source/ftp
[root@nittedal /root]# chmod ugo-w /source/ftp
[root@nittedal /root]# chown root /source/ftp/bin
[root@nittedal /root]# chmod ugo-w /source/ftp/bin
```

Sets the following rights in the etc directory:

```
[root@nittedal /root]# chown root /source/ftp/etc
[root@nittedal /root]# chmod ugo-w /source/ftp/etc
```

Sets the following rights in the out directory:

```
[root@nittedal /root]# chown root /source/ftp/out
[root@nittedal /root]# chmod ugor-w /source/ftp/out
```

Sets the following rights in the `in` directory:

```
[root@nittedal /root]# chown root /source/ftp/in
[root@nittedal /root]# chmod ugo+w /source/ftp/in
```

By following this setup, you can make a secure anonymous FTP server solution.

## 22.20 Other TCP/IP programs

Here is a list of useful character-based and X Window-based TCP/IP programs:

| Command | Function |
|---|---|
| `ncftp` | Available as character-based and X-based FTP client (ncftp is more advanced and offers more possibilities than the traditional FTP client). |
| `whois [-h hostname] name` | Finds DNS information. Try `whois help`. |
| `nslookup [option] [host]` | Gives information about the Internet DNS server (name server). |
| `snmpwalk [arguments] [Object-ID]`<br>`snmpwalk 134.47.141.170 public \| more` | Communicates with the network interfaces via SNMP GET (a good network analysis tool for hackers). |

| Command | Function |
|---|---|
| `rwho [-a]` | Finds out who is logged on to a local machine via the network. |
| Netscape Navigator | A browser. |
| Netscape Communicator | Browser, e-mail and many other functions. |
| `wget` | `wget`, a good copy program for the Web, may also be used instead of `ftp`. `http://ftp.powertech.no/`. |
| `x3270` | X-based 3270-emulator (emulates an |

| Command | Function (*Continued*) |
|---|---|
| | old IBM terminal standard). |
| xgopher | X-based gopher (menu-based search system). |

## Exercises for Chapter 22

1. What does TCP/IP mean?
2. What is defined in the /etc/hosts file?
3. In which file do you define your DNS servers?
4. Which simple command can be used to check that TCP/IP works on your machine and that you can access the Web?
5. Which command requires that the /etc/hosts.equiv and/or $home/.rhosts files be updated to function properly?
6. Mention two ways of copying a file from one Linux machine to another.

CHAPTER
23

# Messages

## 23.1 Introduction

In this chapter, we'll take a look at the commands that make it possible for us to communicate with other users on the same machine, via the LAN or the Internet by means of services like `write`, `talk`, `mail`, and `news`. Many of the services mentioned in this chapter require that you have set up your network connection (TCP/IP) to the Internet.

## 23.2 Internal communication – write

With the `write` command, you can write a message directly to another user on the same machine. What you type on your screen is sent to the other user's terminal.

To receive the message, the user must be logged in and allow other users to send messages. The `mesg` command is used to permit other users to send messages to your terminal.

**write Command – Writes to Other Users**

| | |
|---|---|
| Command | `write [user-id] [ttyport]` |
| Function | Writes directly to another user's terminal; works only if the recipient is logged in. |
| Options | See the Linux man pages. |
| `user-id` | The user's `user-id`. |
| `ttyport` | Specifies which display port the message is sent to (`ps ax`). |

If the user you are writing to is logged in to several terminals, you may use the username as well as the terminal name.

The username is the name used by the recipient to log in to the system and the terminal name is the name of the device driver that controls the recipient's terminal session.

Example:

```
[david@nittedal david]$ write john
The system will be down in 20 minutes.
<Ctrl-d>
```

A communication session is always initiated with a message on the recipient's screen; for example: `Message from david ttyp`.

When two users are in communication with one another, for example, David and Anne, everything entered at David's terminal will also be displayed on Anne's terminal, and vice versa. The text line is sent after pressing the ENTER key.

Each user rounds off writing text by entering `o` (over). A conversation is rounded off with `oo` (over and out). If you want to exit `write`, press <Ctrl-d>.

See also: `mail`, `mesg`, `who`, `talk`

## 23.3 Message to all – wall

If you are the system administrator (root), you can write to all users with the `wall` command.

**wall Command – Sends Messages to All**

| | |
|---|---|
| Command | `wall [message]` |
| Function | Writes to all logged in users. |
| Options | See the Linux man pages. |
| Message | Text message to be sent to all. |

Example:

```
[root@nittedal /root]# wall
System is going down, log out!!
oo
<Ctrl-d>
[root@nittedal /root]#
```

Here, the system administrator sends a message to all. It is impossible not to receive messages (in the terminal window) sent from the `wall` command.

## 23.4 Permission to receive message – mesg

When you want to permit or deny users to send messages to your terminal, you can use the `mesg` command.

**mesg Command – Permission to Receive Messages**

| | |
|---|---|
| Command | `mesg [argument]` |
| Function | Permits or denies messages to the user's terminal. |
| Options | See the Linux man pages. |
| Argument | `y` or `n` (permits or does not permit receiving messages to your console). |

If you enter the mesg command without options, you will see whether others have permission to write to you.

Examples:

```
[david@nittedal david]$ mesg y
```

The mesg y command permits all messages to your terminal session.

```
[david@nittedal david]$ mesg n
```

mesg n stops all messages, except messages from system administrator (root). The who -T command gives an overview of the users that you can send messages to. You'll find more about the who command in Chapter 5.

See also: mail, who, write, talk

## 23.5 External communication – talk

The talk command is a more powerful variation of write. With talk, you can communicate with other machines on the Internet, not only users on the machine that you are logged in to.

The simplest talk client program (see Figure 23-1) is kvt (*[david@nittedal david]$* **kvt -e talk &**), which comes with Red Hat Linux under KDE. The announcement program is called ktalkdlg (*[david@nittedal david]$* **ktalkdlg &**) under KDE.

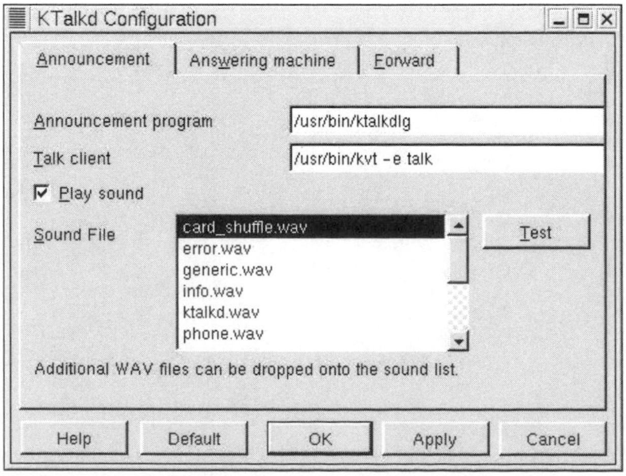

**Figure 23-1**
Talk *configuration program.*

Here is a description of a character-based `talk` command that comes with all Linux distributions.

**talk Command – Writes to Other Users**

| | |
|---|---|
| Command | `talk user-id [ttyport]` |
| Function | Writes directly to another user's terminal. Works only if the user you want to communicate with is logged in. |
| Options | See the Linux man pages. |
| `user-id` | Here you enter the user's `user-id` if you want to contact a local user. If you want to talk with someone else in the network, use the syntax `user@machine`. The machine name can be defined in your `/etc/hosts` file. |
| `ttyport` | Specifies which display port the message will be sent to (`ps ax`). |

`talk` is a development of the `write` command. When using the `talk` command, the screen is split in two. The text that you enter shows up in the upper part, and the reply is displayed in the lower part.

Examples:

```
[david@nittedal david]$ talk john
```

John is a username. To get a two-way communication, John must also start the `talk` program.

```
[david@nittedal david]$ talk david@server
```

Here, I want to talk with the user `david` who is logged in to the machine `server`.

```
[david@nittedal david]$ talk david@server ttyp5
```

Here, I use the terminal name `ttyp5` in addition to the user's username. This may be useful when the user you want to talk to is logged in to several machines. Using terminal names follows the same syntax as the `write` command.

See also: `mail`, `mesg`, `who`, `write`

## 23.6 Electronic mail

Sendmail must be set up when you want your own mail services on your Linux machine. This system uses the TCP/IP protocol SMTP to send and receive electronic mail. If you only need to read and send e-mail from your ISP, you can use the POP protocol. A simple and user-friendly solution is using Netscape Communicator.

Linux offers many different software solutions for e-mail. All e-mail solutions under Linux offer the possibility to:

- **Make mail.**
- **Send mail.**
- **Receive mail.**
- **Forward mail.**
- **Reply to mail.**

You can send e-mail to one or more recipients at the same time. You can send mail even if the recipient is not logged in. This means that you can send messages that the recipient will get after logging in. When logging in, they will get a message telling them that there is new mail. All users on a Linux system have their own electronic mailbox that holds mail from other users.

The simplest mail solution on a Linux machine is local e-mail. When using this, you are limited to sending e-mails to users on your system only. If you want to send mail to users outside of your local machine, TCP/IP or UUCP must be set up. How you send e-mail to users on the Internet will depend on which software you use.

The simplest alternative for e-mail is using your ISP as an e-mail server. You won't need to set up sendmail. All you will need to do is set up a POP client; for example, Netscape Communicator. If you choose to use an e-mail reader (that uses the POP protocol), this is considerably simpler than using an e-mail sender (that uses the SMTP protocol).

Setting up sendmail, for example, can be quite complicated. Sendmail takes care of both local and remote e-mail. If you want your own e-mail service, Smail is a simpler solution than sendmail.

## 23.7 E-mail – mail

The simplest mail client software (see Figure 23-2) is kmail (*[david@nit-tedal david]$* **`kmail &`**), which comes with Red Hat Linux under KDE.

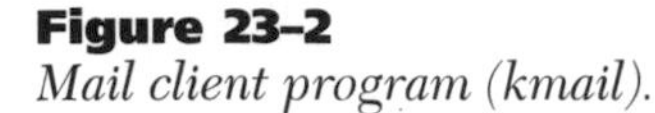

**Figure 23-2**
*Mail client program (kmail).*

When you start kmail for the first time, you'll be asked about the most important configuration parameters. If you want a command-based solution, the `mail` command is the right choice.

**mail Command – e-mail**

| | |
|---|---|
| Command | `mail [options] [argument]` |
| Function | Sends electronic mail to local users or Internet users. |
| Options | See the Linux man pages. |
| `-u user` | Reads the user's mailbox. |
| `-f mailbox` | Reads from a file (local mailbox) instead of from your mailbox. |
| `-s subject` | Specifies a text headline. |
| Argument | May be a username or an alias. |

For the `-u` option, you must have a username as an argument; for the `-f` option, you must have the name of a mailbox (a file) as an argument; and for the

-s option, you must have a text string as the subject.

Examples:

```
[david@nittedal david]$ mail jim
```

After entering mail and a username, the mail system asks for a subject. Here, you may give a short description of the message, e.g., "lunch meeting," "project," "seminar," etc. After specifying the subject, just press RETURN and type the message. Finally, press <Ctrl-d>, which finishes the file (the message).

```
[david@nittedal david]$ mail jim mary anne
```

Here, I send mail to three users at the same time. You can also send documents written with other word processing software than the simple system in mail. Here, I send a letter to mary:

```
[david@nittedal david]$ mail mary < letter.offer
```

The mail command has a very useful option: -s "subject", which is used to specify a mail headline in command mode.

Example:

```
[david@nittedal david]$ mail -s "Linux replaces  Windows" john
jim anne < report.ag
```

In this last example, electronic mail is sent to john, jim, and anne. The subject is defined by using the -s option and the letter has the name report.ag (Applix file).

The first time you log in to a new system, you get mail from the OS. You get the following message:

```
You have mail! (at login)
You have new mail (while being logged in)
```

Try the mail command:

```
[david@nittedal david]$ mail
```

After starting mail, all mail that you have received will be listed. For example:

```
Red Hat Linux release 7.0  (Guinness)
Kernel 2.2.16-22 on an i686
```

```
delboth login: david
Password:
Last login: Thu Mar  4 21:18:46 from 207.117.119.10
You have new mail.
 [david@nittedal david]$ mail
Mail version 8.1 6/6/93.  Type ? for help.
"/var/spool/mail/david": 3 messages 3 new
>N  1 root@nittedal.c2i.ne  Wed Mar 10 19:25  16/380
"Linux news"
 N  2 root@nittedal.c2i.ne  Wed Mar 10 19:26  18/384
"Server changes"
 N  3 root@nittedal.c2i.ne  Wed Mar 10 19:26  16/392
"Server problems"
&
```

To get an overview of available commands, you can enter `?` (question mark). The most frequently used commands in the mail system are:

| | |
|---|---|
| n | Displays next message. |
| d [list] | Removes the next message or specified list of messages. |
| p | Displays the same message again. |
| - (hyphen) | Shows the previous message. |
| q | Quits and saves unread mail. |
| x | Quits without changing the contents of the mailbox, i.e., all mail is saved. |
| ? | Help. |
| s [list] | Saves one or more letters. |
| w [list] | Saves one or more message text headlines. |

You can now enter `n` to look at the first message. If you enter `n` once more, you'll see the next mail. You can go on like this until you have read all your mail. If you want to read the previous message, enter `p`. If you want to read one specific mail, enter `t` and the number of the wanted mail. If you are sending mail to users on the Internet, the username is not a sufficient address; You must have a complete Internet address; for example, john.smith@aol.com.

## 23.8 Sendmail and references

Sendmail is a script that is based on SMTP. SMTP takes a pre-defined port number (see your `/etc/service` file). If there are firewalls or routers between your machine and the Internet, you must make sure that the port number of SMTP gets through. As sendmail is a daemon, it is most interesting to users that have a fixed connection. Sendmail spools mail that cannot be delivered and waits until it can be delivered. The alternative is to start sendmail when you have connected to your ISP.

You can start sendmail manually by running the script:

```
[root@nittedal /root]# /etc/rc.d/rc2.d/S80sendmail start
```

You can stop sendmail manually by running the script:

```
[root@nittedal /root]# /etc/rc.d/rc2.d/S80sendmail stop
```

The setup parameters in sendmail are controlled by the configuration file `/etc/sendmail.cf`. The default configuration file may work very well if you have a fixed connection to the Internet and an official domain address. If you don't have an official address, you should correct the following line in `/etc/sendmail.cf`:

```
# who I masquerade as (null for no masquerading)
DMacme.net
```

It is assumed that the local username is the same as your ISP username. Sendmail is now set up to send directly to the recipient. Normally, using the ISP as a hub is preferable, as you avoid long telephone connections when the connection to the recipient's machine is poor. This is done by setting the DS field:

```
# "Smart" relay host (may be null)
DSmail.acme.net
```

Receiving mail may be a problem if you do not have a public address. The best and simplest solution is to use, for example, Netscape Communicator as your e-mail client (POP as transport mechanism) instead of sendmail and SMTP.

The Linux Mail HOWTO gives you more information about different e-mail programs for Linux and how to set them up. If you want to send remote e-mail, you must understand how TCP/IP or UUCP functions and what to use. You will see that many e-mail programs can be downloaded by anonymous FTP from metalab.unc.edu in the `/pub/Linux/system/Mail` directory. You'll find a solution based on fetchmail instead of the POP client from the site ftp://ftp.ccil.org/pub/esr/fetchmail/.

## 23.9 News from the news server – tin

The Linux news software consists of two parts: the server and the client. If you work in a large company, it probably makes sense to have a dedicated news server. The newsreader is the program that connects to the server and lets the users read and post news. In this section, I'll only explain how to connect a newsreader to a news server.

You'll find most of the Linux newsgroups under comp:

- **comp.os.linux.announce.**
- **comp.os.linux.hardware.**
- **comp.os.linux.misc.**
- **comp.os.linux.networking.**
- **comp.os.linux.x.**

On the Internet, there are more than 50,000 different newsgroups. The list above only contains a few of the Linux-related newsgroups.

If TCP/IP is set up correctly on your machine, you can read news from different news servers.

The simplest news client software (see Figure 23-3) is krn (*[david@nittedal david]$* **krn &**), which comes with Red Hat Linux under KDE. When you start krn for the first time, you'll be asked about the most important configuration parameters. I have also included a description of the newsreader `tin`, which comes with all Linux distributions as well.

**tin Command – News Reader (Internet)**

| | |
|---|---|
| Command | `tin [-n] [-q] [-r]` |
| Function | Displays news from various newgroups. `tin` is a character-based news program that simplifies reading newsgroups. Use the cursor to select and activate newsgroups. |

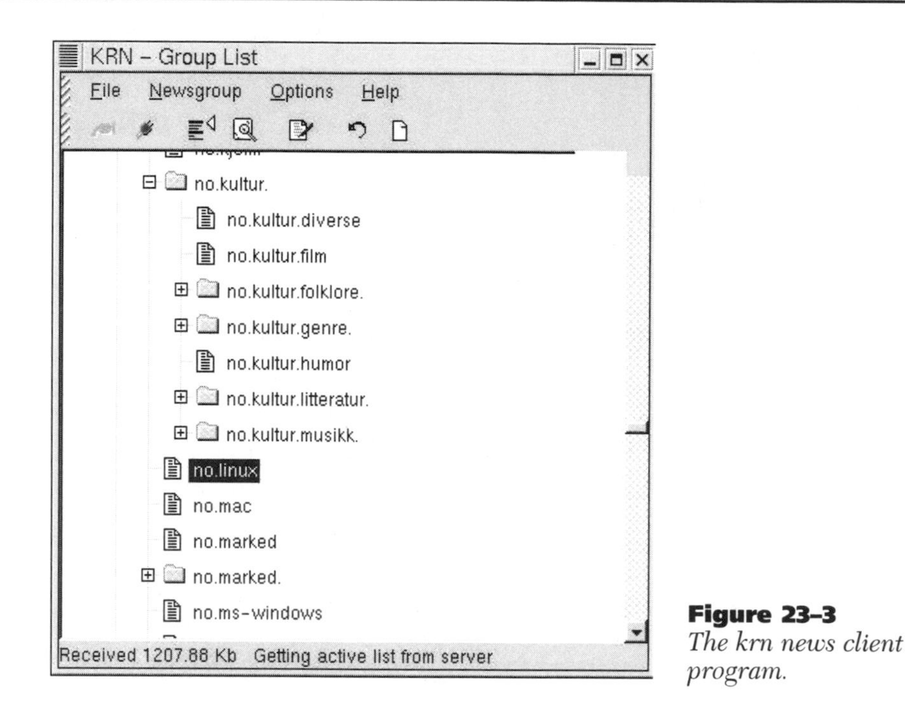


**Figure 23–3**
*The krn news client program.*

**tin Command – News Reader (Internet)** ***(Continued)***

| | |
|---|---|
| Argument | File, directory, and/or wildcards. |
| Options | See the Linux man pages. |
| `-n` | Loads only active newsgroups (`.newsrc`). |
| `-q` | Reads news fast, without checking for newsgroups. |
| `-s` | Reads news remotely from a specified news server as defined in the `/etc/nntpserver` file or in the variable `NNTPSERVER`. |

The `tin` program reads the newsgroups that are defined in the `.newsrc` file in your home area. Your ISP, for example, AOL, must support the newsgroups that you want to access. You must list the newsgroups that you want to use in your local `/home/"user-id"/.newsrc`. In addition, the name of your ISP's news server must be updated in the `/etc/nntpserver` file.

Example:

```
[root@nittedal /root]# cat /etc/nntpserver
news.powertech.no
```

Example:

```
[root@nittedal /root]# cat /etc/nntpserver
news.c2i.net
```

Instead of using the `/etc/nntpserver` file, you can use the global variable `NNTPSERVER`. Then you don't need to log in as system administrator (root).

Example:

```
[david@nittedal david]$ NNTPSERVER='news.c2i.net'
[david@nittedal david]$ export NNTPSERVER
[david@nittedal david]$ source /etc/profile
```

When this is done, you can use the `tin` newsreader:

```
[david@nittedal david]$ tin -nqr
```

This downloads the newsgroups that I have defined in my `.newsrc` file. If you haven't set up your box for Internet use and you haven't yet read Chapters 3 and 22 in this book, the `tin` command may be difficult to understand. You can check the Linux News HOWTO from metalab.unc.edu in the directory `/pub/Linux/docs/HOWTO` to get more information.

System files: `/usr/lib/news/*`, `$HOME/.newsrc`

See also: login files, `env`, `slrn`

## 23.10 Using a fax

Today there are several different fax solutions for Linux. Fax software is included in the Red Hat Linux KDE user interface. (KDE button – Graphics - Faxviewer).

If you haven't got the KDE interface, you may download one of the most popular fax solutions for Linux, HylaFAX. You can download it from:

ftp://ftp.sgi.com/sgi/fax/binary/

or

http://www.vix.com/hylafax/

The HylaFAX software may be set up to receive and send faxes.

## Exercises for Chapter 23

1. What are the `write` and `talk` commands used for?
2. What is the difference between the `write` and `talk` commands? When can you use `talk` only?
3. Write to other users with `write` and `talk`.
4. Try to stop messages with the `mesg` command. What status do you get with the `who -T` command for users that have set `mesg n`?
5. If you are system administrator: Try and write to all using the `wall` command. Does it help the user to write `mesg n`?
6. Send mail to some users and read your own mail. If you are connected, you may try the POP mechanism with the Netscape Communicator program.

CHAPTER
24

# File Services with NFS and Samba

## 24.1 Introduction

In this chapter, I'll go through how to share files, directories, and printer resources in heterogeneous networks.[1] The most frequently used solutions under Linux today are Samba and NFS (Network Filesystem). Both file services enable both Linux and Windows to work as file servers as well as file clients in a LAN or over the Internet.

[1]A heterogeneous network consists of clients and servers with different operating systems like Windows, Mac, Linux, and Unix.

## 24.2 What is Samba?

Samba is based on the SMB (Server Message Block) protocol, which means that we can communicate with all PC networks using SMB, e.g., Windows 95, Windows 98, Windows NT 4.0, Windows 2000 Professional, and Windows 2000 Advanced Server. Other network operating systems that talk SMB are, among others, SCO XENIX-net (SCO UnixWare), IBM LAN Server, and 3COM's 3 +OPEN.

The Samba tools, which were made by Andrew Tridgell, permit Linux machines to share disks and printers with Windows workstations or servers. With Samba, all Linux machines in the network appear as one or more logical folders to DOS and Windows users. A DOS or Windows user with TCP/IP and NetBEUI will see the Samba resources in the same way as an external DOS or Windows disk drive or a printer in a Windows network.

With the smbfs tools made by Paal-Kr. Engstad and Volker Lendecke, Linux machines can connect to shared (shared under Windows) SMB directories from a Windows or Samba host (Linux or Unix). A Linux client sees SMB file servers as Linux filesystems. The Linux client can also share printers in the Windows environment.

## 24.3 Installing Samba

Before you start configuring Samba, your machines, i.e., both Linux and Windows workstations, must be set up with TCP/IP. I described how to set up TCP/IP under Linux in Chapter 22. Refer to your Windows user manual for information on how to set up TCP/IP under Windows. Note that SMB protocols cannot be routed. This means that you may not use this service via traditional routers without applying special techniques. Today, traditional routers and, for example, Novell servers like NetWare 5.x, support IP tunneling.

If you have a complete installation of Red Hat Linux on your PC, the Samba distribution is included. The alternative is to run the `rpm` command and install both the server and client packages. Here is an example:

```
[root@nittedal /root]# rmp -ivh samba-common-2.0.7-
20.i386.rpm
[root@nittedal /root]# rmp -ivh samba-client-2.0.7-
20.i386.rpm
```

The client package smbfs makes it possible for Linux clients to access other SMB servers like Windows 98, Windows NT 4.0, Windows 2000 Professional, and Windows 2000 Advanced Server.

The most recent source code version of Samba is available from ftp://ftp.samba.org/. After retrieving the source code, you should read the README file that comes with the installation. The file `docs/INSTALL.txt` describes how to do the installation. You compile by running `make`. Be aware that in the Samba package, you must specify the location of the `smb.conf` file (Samba configuration file) in the file `Makefile`. The most frequently used location is the `/etc` directory. In the remaining parts of this chapter, I assume that `smb.conf` file is located in the `/etc` directory.

After the installation, you should check that the SMB and nmbd (assigns NetBIOS name server support to clients) daemons are running. You can easily check this with the `ps` command:

```
[root@nittedal /root]# ps ax | grep smbd
972 ?       S      0:00 smbd -D
997 pts/0   S      0:00 grep smbd
[root@nittedal /root]# ps ax | grep nmbd
981 ?       S      0:00 nmbd -D
995 pts/0   S      0:00 grep nmbd
```

The daemons are located in the `/usr/sbin` directory. The SMB daemons `/usr/sbin/smbd` and `/usr/sbin/nmbd` start from the `/etc/rc.d/init.d` (see Figure 24-1) directory under Red Hat Linux.

In the table below, you'll find an overview of the most important files in a Samba installation. The binary files are found under `/usr/bin`.

| Command | Description |
|---|---|
| `smbclient` | SMB client for Linux machines. Gives an FTP-like interface. |
| `smbprint` | SMB client for Linux machines. |
| `smbstatus` | Gives active Windows (SMB) connections to your local machine. |
| `smbrun` | Ready shell script that runs applications on Windows machines (SMB). |
| `/etc/smb.conf` | SMB configuration file. |

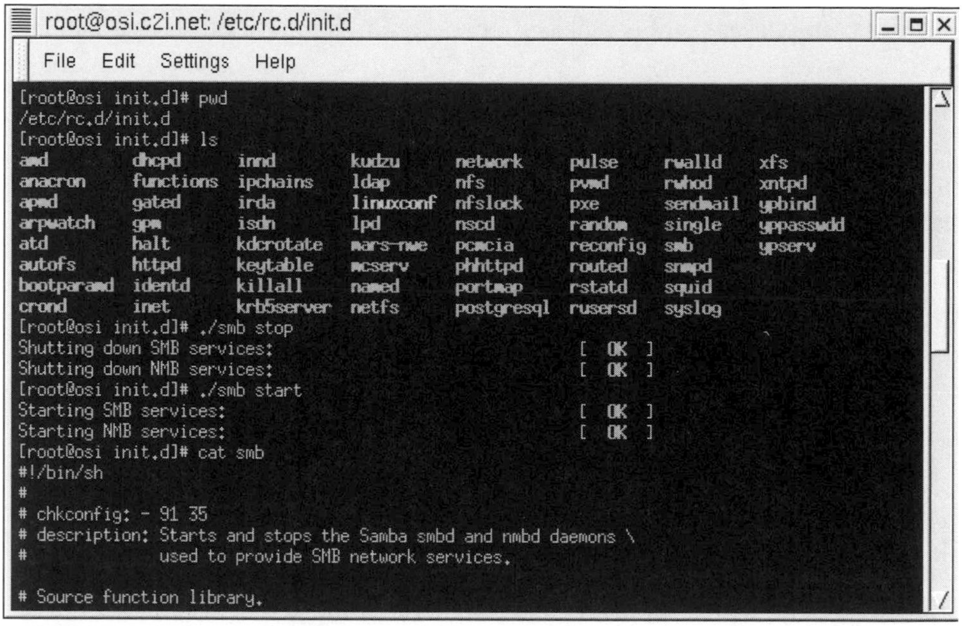

```
root@osi.c2i.net: /etc/rc.d/init.d
File  Edit  Settings  Help
[root@osi init.d]# pwd
/etc/rc.d/init.d
[root@osi init.d]# ls
amd         dhcpd      innd        kudzu      network     pulse     rwalld    xfs
anacron     functions  ipchains    ldap       nfs         pvmd      rwhod     xntpd
apmd        gated      irda        linuxconf  nfslock     pxe       sendmail  ypbind
arpwatch    gpm        isdn        lpd        nscd        random    single    yppasswdd
atd         halt       kdcrotate   mars-nwe   pcmcia      reconfig  smb       ypserv
autofs      httpd      keytable    mcserv     phhttpd     routed    snmpd
bootparamd  identd     killall     named      portmap     rstatd    squid
crond       inet       krb5server  netfs      postgresql  rusersd   syslog
[root@osi init.d]# ./smb stop
Shutting down SMB services:                                   [  OK  ]
Shutting down NMB services:                                   [  OK  ]
[root@osi init.d]# ./smb start
Starting SMB services:                                        [  OK  ]
Starting NMB services:                                        [  OK  ]
[root@osi init.d]# cat smb
#!/bin/sh
#
# chkconfig: - 91 35
# description: Starts and stops the Samba smbd and nmbd daemons \
#              used to provide SMB network services.

# Source function library.
```

**Figure 24-1**
*Stopping and starting the smb services.*

| Command | Description (*Continued*) |
|---|---|
| `/usr/local/man` | SMB man pages. |
| `smbmount` | Mounts Windows folders under Linux. |
| `smbumount` | Unmounts Windows folders under Linux. |

It is important that the following ports are set in `/etc/service`:

*[root@nittedal /root]#* **cat /etc/service**

```
netbios-ns        137/tcp      nbns
netbios-ns        137/udp      nbns
netbios-dgm       138/tcp      nbdgm
netbios-dgm       138/udp      nbdgm
netbios-ssn       139/tcp      nbssn
```

If you have a Linux distribution that runs the daemons from `inetd`, you should read the documentation in the README file or read the SMB-HOWTO to learn about the configuration file `/etc/inetd.conf`.

## 24.4 Configuring Samba

When you have installed all Samba files, you are left with the `smb.conf` file. Before you start configuring Samba, I recommend that you first make a copy of the original configuration file, `smb.conf`. It's a good idea to make a hard copy of the file, too.

```
[root@nittedal /root]#  cp /etc/smb.conf
/etc/smb.conf.000
[root@nittedal /root]#  lpr /etc/smb.conf
```

You can also configure the file directly from the GUI configuration tool for Samba, GnoSamba (see Figure 24-2; www.open-systems.com/gtksamba.html). You can also configure the file manually with the vi editor. (The vi editor is described in Chapter 12.) With GnoSamba, you can read and edit `/etc/smb.conf` or an alternative Samba configuration file. GnoSamba requires installation of the GNOME libraries. If you have installed Red Hat Linux 7.0 with the GNOME interface, the GNOME libraries are included.

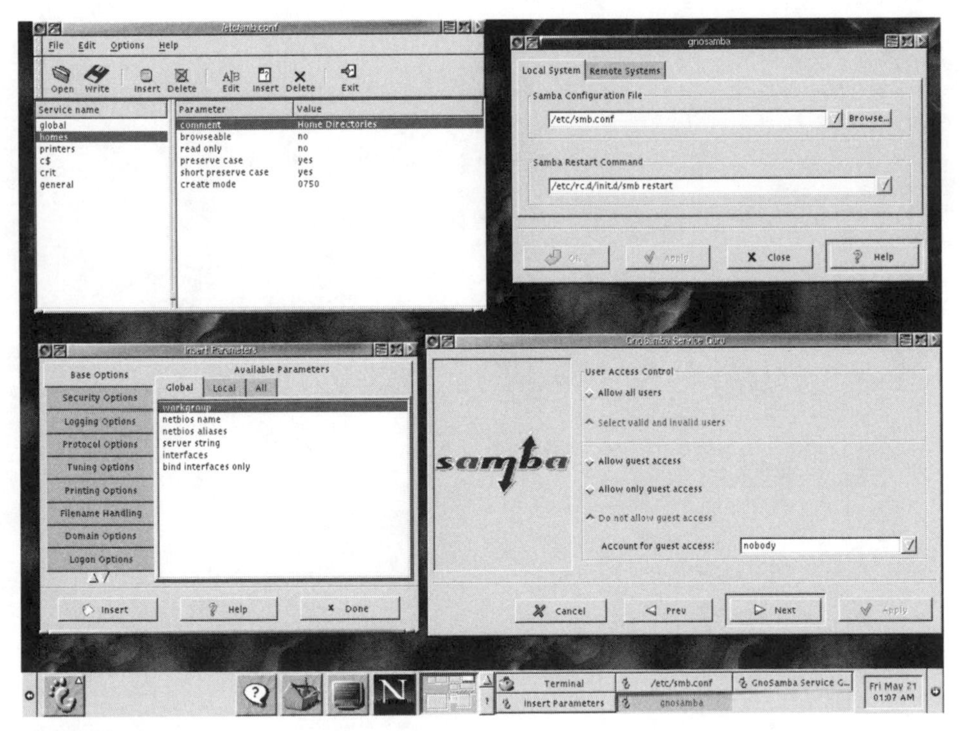


**Figure 24-2**
*The GUI configuration tool for Samba.*

## 24.5 Setting global parameters

Note that all sections in the `smb.conf file` start with a section header, e.g., `[global]`, `[homes]`, `[printers]`, etc. In the `[global]` section, you will find variables that Samba uses to define how to share all resources. Below is a list of the default contents of the `[global]` section:

```
[root@nittedal /root]#  cat /etc/smb.conf
...
[global]

# workgroup = NT-Domain-Name or Workgroup-Name
   workgroup = MYGROUP

# server string is the equivalent of the NT Description
field
   server string = Samba Server

# This option is important for security. It allows you
to restrict
# connections to machines which are on your local net-
work. The
# following example restricts access to two C class net-
works and
# the "loopback" interface. For more examples of the
syntax see
# the smb.conf man page
;   hosts allow = 192.168.1. 192.168.2. 127.

# if you want to automatically load your printer list
rather
# than setting them up individually then you'll need
this
   printcap name = /etc/printcap
   load printers = yes

# It should not be necessary to spell out the print sys-
tem type unless
# yours is non-standard. Currently supported print sys-
tems include:
# bsd, sysv, plp, lprng, aix, hpux, qnx
;   printing = bsd
```

```
# Uncomment this if you want a guest account, you must
add this to /etc/passwd
# otherwise the user "nobody" is used
;  guest account = pcguest

# this tells Samba to use a separate log file for each
machine
# that connects
   log file = /var/log/samba/log.%m

# Put a capping on the size of the log files (in Kb).
   max log size = 50

# Security mode. Most people will want user level secu-
rity. See
# security_level.txt for details.
   security = user
# Use password server option only with security = server
;   password server = <NT-Server-Name>

# Password Level allows matching of _n_ characters of
the password for
# all combinations of upper and lower case.
;  password level = 8
;  username level = 8

# You may wish to use password encryption. Please read
# ENCRYPTION.txt, Win95.txt and WinNT.txt in the Samba
documentation.
# Do not enable this option unless you have read those
documents
;  encrypt passwords = yes
;  smb passwd file = /etc/smbpasswd

# The following are needed to allow password changing
from Windows to
# update the Linux system password also.
# NOTE: Use these with 'encrypt passwords' and 'smb
passwd file' above.
# NOTE2: You do NOT need these to allow workstations to
change only
#        the encrypted SMB passwords. They allow the
Unix password
#        to be kept in sync with the SMB password.
;  unix password sync = Yes
```

```
;  passwd program = /usr/bin/passwd %u
;  passwd chat = *New*UNIX*password* %n\n *ReType*new*UNIX*pass-
word* %n\n *passwd:*all*authentication*tokens*updated*successful-
ly*

# Unix users can map to different SMB User names
;  username map = /etc/smbusers

# Using the following line enables you to customize your config-
uration
# on a per machine basis. The %m gets replaced with the netbios
name
# of the machine that is connecting
;   include = /etc/smb.conf.%m

# Most people will find that this option gives better perfor-
mance.
# See speed.txt and the manual pages for details
socket options = TCP_NODELAY SO_RCVBUF=8192 SO_SNDBUF=8192

# Configure Samba to use multiple interfaces
# If you have multiple network interfaces then you must list
them
# here. See the man page for details.
;   interfaces = 192.168.12.2/24 192.168.13.2/24

# Configure remote browse list synchronization here
#  request announcement to, or browse list sync from:
#   a specific host or from / to a whole subnet (see below)
;   remote browse sync = 192.168.3.25 192.168.5.255
# Cause this host to announce itself to local subnets here
;   remote announce = 192.168.1.255 192.168.2.44

# Browser Control Options:
# set local master to no if you don't want Samba to become a
master
# browser on your network. Otherwise the normal election rules
apply
;   local master = no

# OS Level determines the precedence of this server in master
browser
# elections. The default value should be reasonable
;   os level = 33
```

```
# Domain Master specifies Samba to be the Domain Master
Browser. This
# allows Samba to collate browse lists between subnets.
Don't use this
# if you already have a Windows NT domain controller
doing this job
;   domain master = yes

# Preferred Master causes Samba to force a local browser
election on startup
# and gives it a slightly higher chance of winning the
election
;   preferred master = yes

# Use only if you have an NT server on your network that
has been
# configured at install time to be a primary domain con-
troller.
;   domain controller = <NT-Domain-Controller-SMBName>

# Enable this if you want Samba to be a domain logon
server for
# Windows95 workstations.
;   domain logons = yes

# if you enable domain logons then you may want a per-
machine or
# per user logon script
# run a specific logon batch file per workstation
(machine)
;   logon script = %m.bat
# run a specific logon batch file per username
;   logon script = %U.bat

# Where to store roving profiles (only for Win95 and
WinNT)
#         %L substitutes for this servers netbios name,
%U is username
#         You must uncomment the [Profiles] share below
;   logon path = \\%L\Profiles\%U

# All NetBIOS names must be resolved to IP Addresses
# 'Name Resolve Order' allows the named resolution mech-
anism to be specified
# the default order is "host lmhosts wins bcast". "host"
```

```
means use the unix
# system gethostbyname() function call that will use
either /etc/hosts OR
# DNS or NIS depending on the settings of /etc/host.con-
fig, /etc/nsswitch.conf
# and the /etc/resolv.conf file. "host" therefore is
system configuration
# dependant. This parameter is most often of use to pre-
vent DNS lookups
# in order to resolve NetBIOS names to IP Addresses. Use
with care!
# The example below excludes use of name resolution for
machines that are NOT
# on the local network segment
# - OR - are not deliberately to be known via lmhosts or
via WINS.
; name resolve order = wins lmhosts bcast

# Windows Internet Name Serving Support Section:
# WINS Support - Tells the NMBD component of Samba to
enable it's WINS Server
;   wins support = yes

# WINS Server - Tells the NMBD components of Samba to be
a WINS Client
#   Note: Samba can be either a WINS Server, or a WINS
Client, but NOT both
;   wins server = w.x.y.z

# WINS Proxy - Tells Samba to answer name resolution
queries on
# behalf of a non WINS capable client, for this to work
there must be
# at least one  WINS Server on the network. The default
is NO.
;   wins proxy = yes

# DNS Proxy - tells Samba whether or not to try to
resolve NetBIOS names
# via DNS nslookups. The built-in default for versions
1.9.17 is yes,
# this has been changed in version 1.9.18 to no.
   dns proxy = no

# Case Preservation can be handy - system default is
```

```
_no_
# NOTE: These can be set on a per share basis
;   preserve case = no
;   short preserve case = no
# Default case is normally upper case for all DOS files
;   default case = lower
# Be very careful with case sensitivity - it can break
things!
;   case sensitive = no
```

- **workgroup**—This parameter sets the Windows workgroup name or the Windows NT domain name. If the name is MYGROUP, a Windows or Windows NT system on your network will see the name MYGROUP when clicking Network Neighborhood.
- **server string**—This parameter gives a description of your Samba server that will be visible to Windows clients. Write a text that describes the kind of server that you have.
- **printcap name**—This parameter specifies where the printer definition file is located. All printer definitions under Linux are found in this file. You'll find more about the `printcap` file in Chapter 14.
- **load printers**—This parameter tells Samba to automatically make local printers accessible to any SMB client. You only need to set this parameter if you want to make Linux printers accessible to SMB clients. It checks whether the printers in `/etc/printcap` are to be loaded by default. If you do this, there is no reason to set the printers up individually. In the [`printers`] section, you specify the features of the printers that you want to define. These definitions are not required if you have loaded all by "load printers". If your printing system doesn't work this way (BSD), you must set up a dummy `printcap` file (or use the print command technique as described below). For more information on the `printcap` system, see the Printing HOWTO.
- **printing**—Here, you can select the desired spooling system. It should not be necessary to change the default setting, which is `printing=bsd`. You'll find more about this in Chapter 14.
- **log file**—This parameter gives the filename of the Samba log, `filen`. By default, there is one log file made per client.
- **max log size**—This parameter controls the maximum log file size

in kilobytes. In most cases, 50KB is more than sufficient.

- `security`—This is the most important of all the global parameters. It indicates how SMB handles client authentication. There are three variants:

  - user.
  - share.
  - server.

  If you have selected `user`, the Samba server will tell the client to pro-duce a username and a password for authentication. This solution is preferred if you have the same `user-id` and password under Windows and Linux. If you select `share`, the Samba server will ask for a password for each service. Choose this alternative if you don't use the same `user-id` and password for your Linux and Windows systems.
  For the last option, the Samba server requires that the client produce a `user-id`/password that another Windows (SMB) server (Windows NT) authenticates. A requirement for this is that you set the password server parameter, which gives the name of the SMB authentication server (`password server = <NT-Server-Name>`).
- `encrypt passwords`—Currently, Windows 98 (with Service Pack 3 or higher), Windows NT 4.0 (with Service Pack 3 or higher), Windows 2000 Professional, and Windows 2000 Advanced Server use encrypted passwords by default. Samba uses unencrypted passwords, and this removes the possibility of mounting anonymously. You are left with two options: configuring Samba for encrypted passwords or configuring the Windows machines to use unencrypted passwords.

This is how you can make Windows work with unencrypted SMB passwords:

*Windows 95/98*

1. From Windows 95/98 with Service Pack 3 or higher, start the Registry editing tool (`regedit`). This program can also be started from the DOS prompt in Windows by entering `regedit`.
2. Make the following registry entry:
   `HKEY_LOCAL_MACHINE\System\CurrentControlSet\Services\`
   `VxD\VNETSUP`
3. Add a new DWORD value: Value name: **EnablePlainTextPassword**

4. Place the following data in the new variable: **0x01**
5. Save and reboot your PC.

*Windows NT 4.0*

1. From Windows NT 4.0 with Service Pack 3 or higher, start the Registry editing tool (`regedit`).
2. Make the following registry entry: `HKEY_LOCAL_MACHINE\System\CurrentControlSet\Services\Rdr\Parameters`
3. Add a new DWORD value: Value name: **EnablePlainTextPassword**
4. Place the following data in the new variable: **0x01**
5. Save and reboot your PC.

Remark: When you have found VNETSUP (Windows 9x) or Parameters (Windows NT) in the Registry tree, select Edit and New, then select a new DWORD value. `regedit` gives you the possibility to select a new value in the Registry. The new value is: **EnablePlainTextPassword**. When you double-click this new variable, you get a new dialog box where you can add a value to the new variable. Set the new variable to **0x01**.

The last alternative is configuring Samba to using encrypted passwords. Just add the following in the `[global]` section of `/etc/smb.conf`.

```
encrypt passwords = yes
smb passwd file = /etc/smbpasswd
```

There is more information about this in the Samba documentation files, `ENCRYPTION.txt`, `Win95.txt`, and `WinNT.txt`. Be aware that clients and servers that use encrypted passwords will not be allowed to browse through accessible, shared directories on the server before you have made the first connection with correct authentication. You make the first connection by manually entering the name of the shared directory. Do this by going into Explorer like this: '`\\<host name>\ <directory name>`'. Log into the server with a valid username and password.

- **`socket options`**—Here, TCP_NODELAY is normally set. This increases Samba's file access service. You'll find more about this parameter in the README files.

- **interfaces**—If you have multiple network interfaces (NICs) on your Samba server you can configure Samba to utilize all of them. The setup is described in the man pages.
- **dns proxy**—If this parameter is set at yes, nmbd server will handle NetBIOS names as Internet domain names and try and resolve the names with the DNS protocol. Leave this parameter at no.

## 24.6 The [homes] section

The [homes] section gives a connected user access to their own (and only their own) home directory on the local Linux machine. This means that if a Windows user tries to connect to a shared resource from their Windows machine, they will be connected to their personal home area. Note that you must have an account on the Linux box to do this. The smb.conf file below will allow other users from other machines to put their home directories on the local machine and write to a temporary directory:

```
[homes]
   comment = Home Directories
   browseable = no
   writable = yes
```

The Linux box (PC) must be part of the LAN so that a Windows user can see these shared directories. Then, the local user can just connect to a network hard disk from Windows File Manager or Windows Explorer.

## 24.7 Sharing a Linux disk

It is simple to set up smb.conf to share your Linux disk drives with others. Below is an example of the settings in the [public] section:

```
# A publicly accessible directory, with read and write.
[public]
comment = Public Stuff
path = /home/data
```

```
public = yes
writable = yes
printable = yes
```

If you want the directory to be readable to all and writable to those in the `staff` group only, the [`public`] section should look like this:

```
  # A publicly accessible directory, but read only,
except for people
# in the "staff" group
[public]
comment = Public Stuff
path = /home/data
public = yes
writable = yes
printable = no
write list = @staff
```

## 24.8 Printing Windows - Linux

Before sharing a printer with a Windows environment, you must check that the printer works from Linux. Under Linux, you set up the printer from `printtool` under X Window or by updating the `/etc/printcap` file. This is described in Chapter 14. When you want to share a Linux printer under Windows, you update the following in `/etc/smb.conf`:

```
[global]
        printing = bsd
        printcap name = /etc/printcap
        load printers = yes
        log file = /var/log/samba-log.%m
        lock directory = /var/lock/samba
```

In the [`printers`] section, you may, for example, have the following:

```
     [printers]
        comment = All Printers
        security = server
        path = /var/spool/lpd/lp
        browseable = no
        printable = yes
        public = yes
```

```
    writable = no
    create mode = 0700
[hpjet]
    security = server
    path = /var/spool/lpd/lp
    printer name = lp
    writable = yes
    public = yes
    printable = yes
    print command = lpr -r -h -P %p %s
```

It is important that the `hpjet` driver's name and search path are set correctly in `/etc/printcap`. Note that the Windows machine's account name (the machine attempting to use the Linux printer via Samba) should be the same as the Linux username of the Linux box. If you have a user `john` on your Windows workstation (`windowspc`) who wants to print to the `printq1` printer on the Linux machine `webserv` (`\\webserv\printq1`), there should be a user `john` on the Linux machine. The simplest solution is using the same `user-id` and password on both the Linux and Windows machines. A password is requested when setting up the printer from Windows (Printer – Add printer). Even if you define the printer as public in the `smb.conf` file, you will be asked for a password in Windows.

## 24.9 Linux clients – SMB servers

There are two ways of accessing data with Linux from a Windows server. You can run the `smbclient` program that gives you an FTP-like interface on the command line, or you can mount the logical Windows folders and see them as local filesystems.

Before using `smbclient`, all or part of, for example, the C folder on your Windows machine must be shared. You'll find a description of how to do this in your Windows user manual. Remember to update the Linux clients with `/etc/hosts` files containing the names and IP addresses of each Windows PC. This is not required if your machine is running DNS.

With `smbclient`, you can view the directories that are accessible on a certain server.

```
/usr/sbin/smbclient -L machine name
```

After entering this, you will get a list of server services names, i.e., names for disk mapping or printers that the machine can share with you. If you haven't configured any kind of security, you will not be asked for a password. The password may be the guest account that you have defined on the Linux machine.

Here are some examples:

```
[root@nittedal /root]# smbclient -L osi
added interface ip=207.117.119.50 bcast=207.117.119.255
nmask=255.255.255.0
Password:

   Sharename     Type      Comment
   -------       ----      -----
   C             Disk
   IPC$          IPC       Remote Inter Process Communication

   Server                  Comment
   -----                   -----
   OSI                     Howard's Office

   Workgroup               Master
   -------                 -----
   MARLINK                 SIMON
   WORKGROUP               OSI

[root@nittedal /root]# smbclient -L simon
added interface ip=207.117.119.50 bcast=207.117.119.255
nmask=255.255.255.0
Password:

   Sharename     Type      Comment
   -------       ----      -----

   F             Disk
   E             Disk
   D             Disk
   C             Disk
   IPC$          IPC       Remote Inter Process Communication

   Server                  Comment
   -----                   -----
   SIMON                   166 MHz CPU, 82 MB RAM, 5.1 GB

   Workgroup               Master
```

```
--------                    -----
MARLINK                     SIMON
WORKGROUP                   OSI
```

Now you can get a list that shows other SMB servers that have resources available on the network. When you want to access a service, you must enter:

```
/usr/bin/smbclient service <password>
```

If you, for example, want to access a directory that has been shared on a machine called `osi`, the syntax is:

```
[root@nittedal /root]# /usr/bin/smbclient //osi/c
```

Every backslash must be included as special characters because the Linux shell cannot handle backslashes directly. If everything is entered correctly, you will see the `smbclient` prompt:

```
added interface ip=207.117.119.50 bcast=207.117.119.255
nmask=255.255.255.0
smb: \>
smb: \> dir
WINDOWS           D          0    Mon Jul  3 21:09:08 2000
BOOTLOG.PRV      AH      31538    Mon Jul  3 21:53:56 2000
SUHDLOG.DAT     AHR       7738    Tue Jan 26 13:36:06 1999
FRUNLOG.TXT       A       4648    Mon Jul  3 21:47:18 2000
COMMAND.COM       R      94600    Sat May 16 04:01:00 1998
...
fundak            D          0    Mon Sep 18 18:36:20 2000
Tmpdata           D          0    Mon Sep 11 10:29:00 2000

61777 blocks of size 131072. 41617 blocks available
smb: \> quit
```

I recommend that you enter `h` to get the required help. If you are used to FTP, you will soon get the hang of it.

```
smb: \>
smb: \> h
  ls          dir         lcd     cd         pwd
  get         mget        put     mput       rename
  more        mask        del     rm         mkdir
```

```
md          rmdir       rd      prompt      recurse
translate   lowercase   print   printmode   queue
cancel      stat        quit    q           exit
newer       archive     tar     blocksize   tarmode
setmode     help        ? !
smb: \>
```

Below you'll find an example where I restore a backup copy of linux_book.tar to the share myshare on the osi machine. No password is set for the share.

```
[root@nittedal /root]# smbclient //osi/myshare "" -N
-Tx linux_book.tar
```

Because we are using the N option, the password prompt is not required. Here, -Tx is a tar option for extracting data from a local tar file to a share.

```
[elboth@acer elboth]$ cat message | smbclient -M osi
added interface ip=207.117.119.50 bcast=207.117.119.255
nmask=255.255.255.0
Connected. Type your message, ending it with a Control-D
sent 45 bytes
[elboth@acer elboth]$
```

In this last example, I send the text in the message file to the osi machine. The -M option makes it possible to send messages to other clients or servers. If you want two-way communication, you must enter the messages after entering smbclient -M netbios_name. At the end of every sentence, you must enter <Ctrl-d>. To receive messages, the Windows PCs must run the WinPopup program.

## 24.10 Mounting Windows folders

If you are familiar with the mount/unmount commands under NFS, you will quickly see how the smbmount and smbumount commands work. As with smbclient, you only need to share all or parts of, for example, the C folder on your Windows machine.

To access Windows servers from Linux clients by mounting, it is required that you have Samba client tools installed (as described before under "Installing

Samba"). smbfs support must be compiled in the kernel to use these tools.

The default syntax for the `smbmount` command is:

```
smbmount //windows-server/path /mount point options
```

Below is an example:

```
[root@acer elboth]# smbmount //osi/c /mnt/data
```

Here, the name of the Windows server (SMB) is `osi`. The folder that I want to access is `c`. I want to mount to the local directory, `/mnt/data`. I have already made the empty directory `/mnt/data`. The `smbmount` command uses, in principle, the `mount` command with the `-t smbfs` options. Alternatively, you can enter:

```
[root@acer /root]# mount -t smbfs -o username=simon,
password=simon //osi/c /mnt/data
```

Here, I specify username and password. With the `mount` command you can see that the filesystem has been mounted:

```
[root@acer elboth]# mount
```

When you want to unmount, simply enter:

```
[root@acer elboth]# smbumount /mnt/data
```

Alternatively you can unmount with the `umount` command:

```
[root@acer elboth]# umount /mnt/data
```

More information about `smbmount` and `smbumount` is available from the man pages.

## 24.11 Printing Linux - Windows

It is also possible to connect to a printer that is controlled by a Windows server. The solution is using the `smbclient` command. The general syntax is:

```
smbclient //windows-server/sharedprinter options
```

Before using the `smbclient` command, you must define a Windows user that can access the printer. Do not define a password for the Windows user. Check that you get print output in Windows from the new Windows user. In the example below, we connect to the Windows machine `osi`. The name of the printer that is set up as a shared unit is `epson`. In Windows, you can decide which names to give to the shared units.

```
[root@acer elboth]# smbclient //osi/epson -U simon -N
added interface ip=207.117.119.50 bcast=207.117.119.255
nmask=255.255.255.0
smb: \>
```

In our example, the username is `simon`. The `-U` option is used to specify the username `simon` as we make the connection. When using the `-N` option, the password prompt is not required if the unit itself doesn't require a password.

```
[root@acer elboth]# lpr -P windows_printer letter.ps
```

When you are connected to the Windows printer from Linux, you can print directly with the Linux command `lpr`.

## 24.12 Testing a configuration

After making your changes, you can test your new `smb.conf` file with the `testparm` tool. This tool is included in the Samba distribution. This command checks the syntax of all lines in your `smb.conf` file. You don't necessarily get a straight error message, but possibly a warning. The warnings will tell you whether you have safety defects in your configuration.

```
[root@acer /root]# testparm /etc/smb.conf
```

Whatever is wrong with your `smb.conf` file will be reported by the `testparm` command.

## 24.13 Samba references

In your Linux distribution, you will find the Samba documentation as a part of the Samba distribution. Check if the distribution is available at: ftp://ftp.samba.org/. Here you will find:

- **HOWTO SMB**
- **The Linux Printing HOWTO.**
- **The Print2Win Mini-HOWTO.**
- **Protocol Standard For A NetBIOS Service On A TCP/UDP Transport. RFC 1001**
- **Concepts and Methods. RFC 1002 Detailed Specifications.**

If you need more information about Samba, look at Samba's Web site: http://www.samba.org/. You can also have a look at the com.protocols.smb newsgroup. Among many good books about Samba, I recommend John D. Blair's *SAMBA: Integrating UNIX and Windows*, Specialized Systems Consultants, Inc., ISBN: 1-57831-006-7. Another alternative is Gerald Carter and Richard Sharpe, *Sam's Teach Yourself Samba in 24 hrs*, Sam's Publishing, 1999. ISBN 0-672-31609-9.

## 24.14 What is NFS?

NFS (Network Filesystem) defines the connections in a multi-supplier network. NFS is based on the TCP/IP network protocol. It is a requirement in NFS that the TCP/IP protocol runs on all NFS servers and clients. Today NFS is a de facto standard for integrating Unix/Linux machines. When you want to integrate Windows or Mac workstations, PC-NFS or Mac-NFS must be installed on clients.

NFS supports a variety of access methods; for example, Ethernet, Token Ring, RS-232 port, and parallel port. NFS facilitates file sharing between the Linux, Unix, VAX, DOS, Windows, and Macintosh operating systems.

## 24.15 Installing NFS

NFS used to have performance problems. Now, with NFS version 3, you can connect to other Unix machines and get high performance and considerably better record lock functionality than under NFS 2. If you have made a complete Red Hat Linux installation on your PC, NFS is included. The alternative is to run the rpm command and install the server and client packages. Here is an example:

```
[root@elboth /root]#  rpm -ivh nfs-client-version.386.rpm
[root@elboth /root]#  rpm -ivh nfs-server-version.386.rpm
```

Note that the NFS server package is based on RPC (Remote Procedure Call). If you get an error message about missing files, you are missing the RPC libraries. These libraries are included in the RPM package portmap. If you want the newest version of NFS, look at:

ftp://nfs.sourceforge.net/pub/nfs/nfs-version.tar.gz.

When downloading a newer NFS implementation, the nfs-utils package must be installed. Before you download the nfs-utils package, the Linux kernel parameters CONFIG_NFS_FS, CONFIG_NFSD, and CONFIG_NFSD_SUN must be set to m. The last kernel parameter is only required if the Linux machine will be an NFS server for Sun Solaris. Updated versions of NFS (rpc.rquotad, rpc.mountd, and rpc.nfsd) and nfslock (rpc.lockd and rpc.statd) are included in the nfs-utils rpm package. You may (not necessary with Red Hat Linux 7.0) have to update the init level information as follows:

```
[root@elboth /root]# /sbin/chkconfig nfs on
[root@elboth /root]# /sbin/chkconfig nfslock on
[root@elboth /root]# /sbin/chkconfig --list | grep nfs
```

After installation, you should check that the NFS daemons are running. This can easily be done with the ps and rpc info commands. Now the NFS server/client machine should be all set!

## 24.16 Defining an NFS server

When setting up an NFS server, you must export one or more filesystems. For a Linux or Unix NFS server, the /etc/exports file controls the filesystems to share with (export to) other machines. If you need to modify the `/etc/exports` file, you must log in as root. Select an editor that you are familiar with. It is easiest to use the vi editor. An alternative is to use the NFS export option from `linuxconf` under the GNOME or KDE GUI environment (see Figure 24-3 and 24-4).

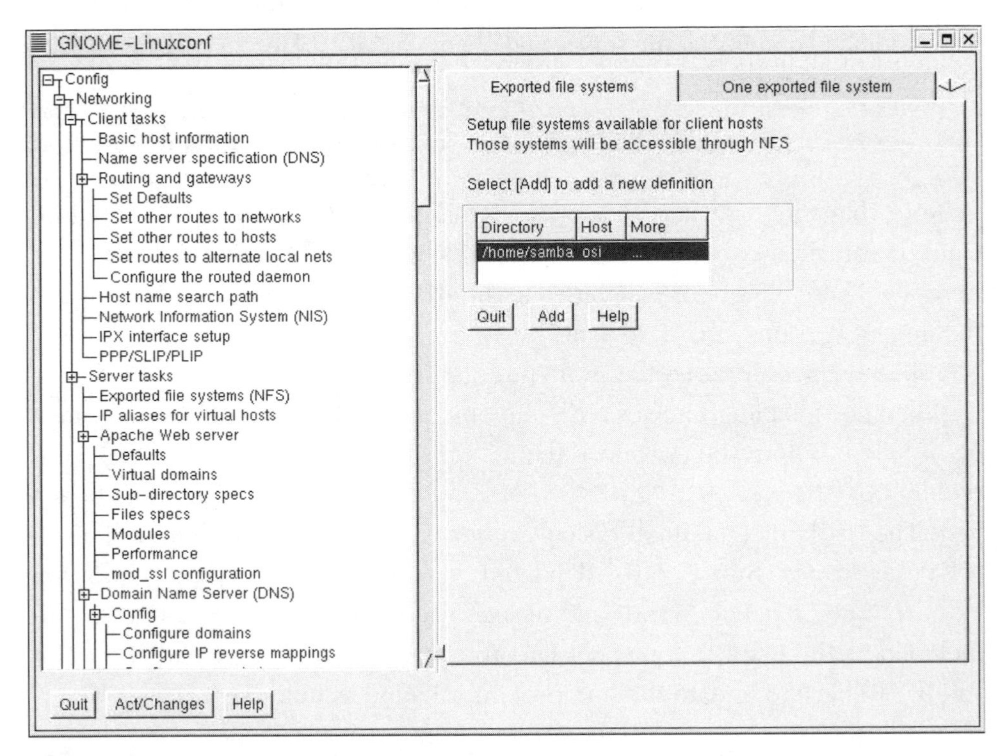


**Figure 24-3**
*Exporting file systems from* `linuxconf`.

Example:

We want the `/home/elboth/local` directory and CD-ROM on the `nittedal` machine to be accessible to the `hakadal` machine. I have therefore defined the following in the `/etc/exports` file of the `nittedal` machine:

```
[root@nittedal /root]# cat /etc/exports
/home/elboth/local   hakadal(rw)
/mnt/cdrom           hakadal(ro)
```

This gives `hakadal` read/write access to `/home/elboth/local`. Instead of `rw`, I can enter `ro` (read-only). If nothing is specified, the result is read-only. In the next line, I have set readonly for the CD-ROM. There are other options you can find by using the Linux `man` command:

```
[root@nittedal /root]# man exports
```

If you are running NIS (NIS was earlier known as YP), you can alternatively get a list of all hosts by using net groups, entering the domain "wildcard," and defining IP subnets as hosts with permission to mount. When using this kind of authorization, you should carefully consider who might get unauthorized access to the server.

Note that the `exports` file under Linux uses a syntax that differs from other Unix implementations.

Now you are ready to start `mountd` (it may be called `rpc.mountd`), and then `nfsd` (which may be called `rpc.nfsd`). Both will read the `/etc/exports` file.

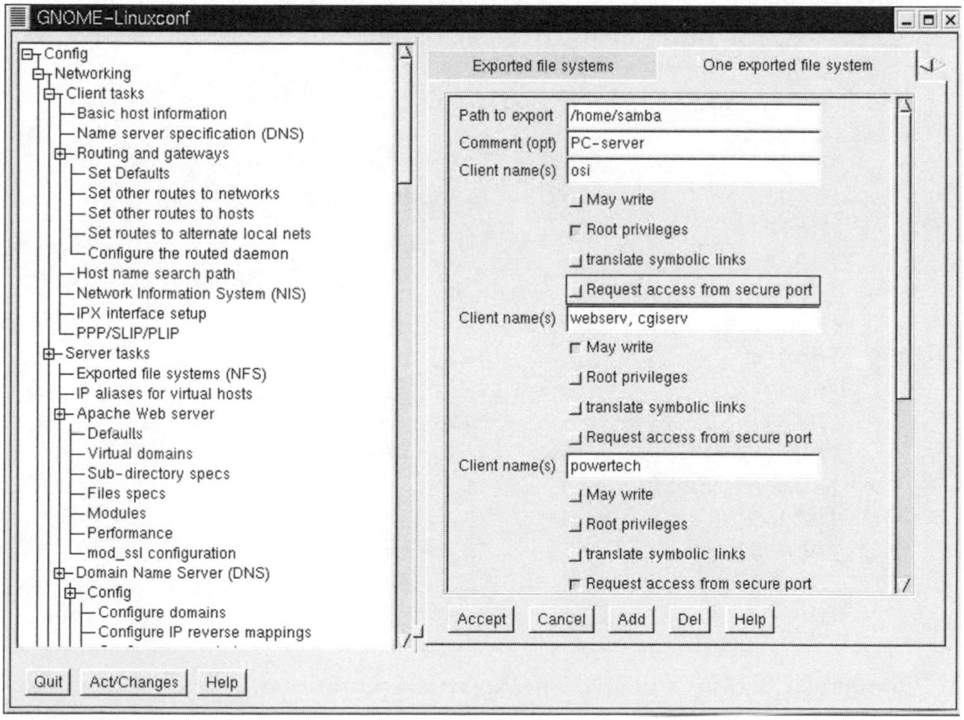

**Figure 24-4**
*Defining NFS exporting file systems parameters from* `linuxconf`.

When editing /etc/exports, you must make sure that nfsd and mountd know that the files have been altered. The most frequently used method is running exportfs. Many Linux distributions don't have an exportfs program. If you don't have exportfs, you can enter the following script:

```
[root@nittedal /usr/sbin]# cat exportfs
#!/bin/bash
killall -HUP /usr/sbin/rpc.mountd
killall -HUP /usr/sbin/rpc.nfsd
echo "File systems are exported"
```

You can, for example, save the file as /usr/sbin/exportfs. Remember to run the chmod command:

```
[root@nittedal /usr/sbin]# chmod u+rx exportfs
```

After you have changed the exports file, run exportfs as root. If you are running Red Hat Linux, you will find that exportfs is included.

Now you should check that mountd and nfsd are running properly. First use rpcinfo -p. The result should be similar to this:

```
[root@nittedal /root]# rpcinfo -p
program vers proto   port
     100000    2    tcp     111  portmapper
     100000    2    udp     111  portmapper
     100021    1    udp    1024  nlockmgr
     100021    3    udp    1024  nlockmgr
     100021    1    tcp    1024  nlockmgr
     100021    3    tcp    1024  nlockmgr
     100024    1    udp     967  status
     100024    1    tcp     969  status
     100011    1    udp     742  rquotad
     100011    2    udp     742  rquotad
     100005    1    udp     750  mountd
     100005    1    tcp     752  mountd
     100005    2    udp     755  mountd
     100005    2    tcp     757  mountd
     100003    2    udp    2049  nfs
```

Some distributions will give you the rpcbind process instead of portmapper. In this example, we see portmapper, mountd, and nfs.

If you get the error message "rpcinfo: can't contact portmapper:

RPC: Remote system error - Connection refused" or similar, portmapper is not running.

After checking that portmapper reports the correct services, you can also check with the ps command. Note that portmapper will continue to report services even if the programs that use them have crashed. So, a check with ps ax is a good idea if something seems to be wrong.

Of course you must modify the rc files on the system to start mountd, nfsd, and portmapper when booting. The scripts probably already exist on your machine. All you have to do is remove the comments or activate them for the correct init level. If you are running Red Hat Linux, you will find the NFS init in /etc/rc.d/init.d/nfs. Starting NFS on different init levels is found in the /etc/rc.d/rc2.d and /etc/rc.d/rc3.d directories. Below you'll find an example describing manual start and termination of NFS under Red Hat Linux.

```
[root@nittedal /etc/rc.d/init.d]# ./nfs start
[root@nittedal /etc/rc.d/init.d]# ./nfs stop
```

## 24.17 Defining NFS clients

You can mount external filesystems (NFS server) with the mount command.

**mount/unmount Command – Mounts or Unmounts External Filesystems**

| | |
|---|---|
| Command | mount [options] [-t options] unit directory<br>umount directory |
| Function | Makes it possible to connect a directory to an external machine. Directories are viewed as local directories. |
| Options | See the Linux man pages. |
| Unit | Normally a server name (hostname) and external directory. |
| Directory | Directory (internal directory) to which the external file system is connected. |

When you want to mount external filesystems, you must log in as root. From the prompt, you enter the mount command, including the correct options. Here is an example:

I wish to mount the /home/elboth/local filesystem from nittedal on the hakadal NFS client:

```
[root@hakadal /root]# mount -o rsize=1024,wsize=1024 nittedal:/home/elboth/local /mnt/data
```

The filesystem is now accessible under /mnt/data. Use the Linux commands cd and ls. Everything works as if it were a local filesystem, except the speed, which will be slightly lower than a local system. If you get the error message "nittedal:/home/elboth/local /mnt/data failed, reason given by server: Permission denied", you must check your exports file. If you get the error message "mount clntudp_create: RPC: Program not registered", either nfsd or mountd is not running on the NFS server.

To umount the filesystem, enter:

```
[root@hakadal /root]# umount /mnt/data
```

You can also unmount or mount from the GNOME or KDE GUI environment (see Figure 24-5).

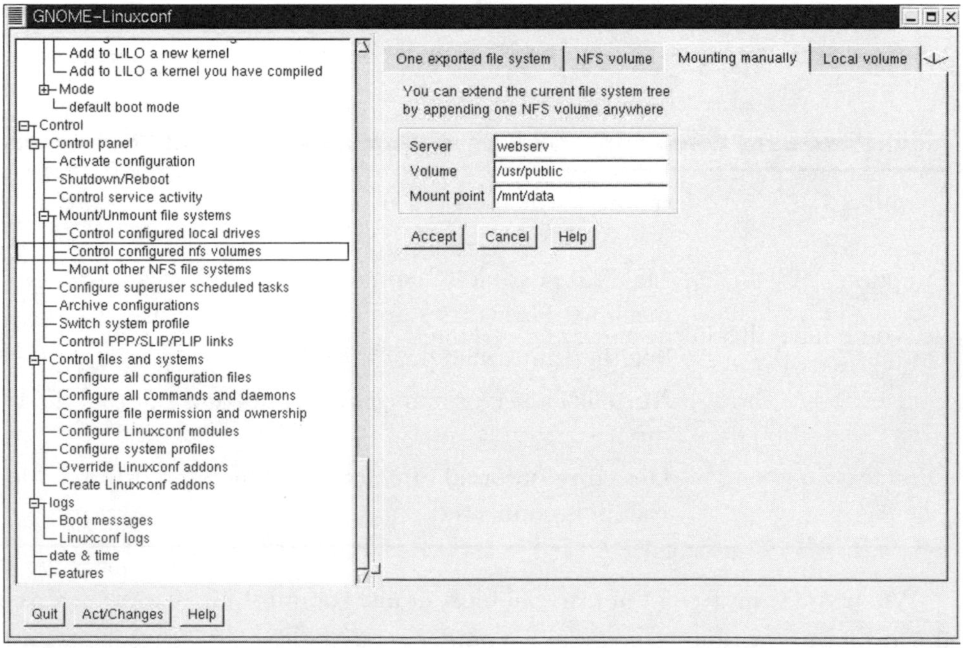

**Figure 24-5**
*Mount/unmount file systems from* linuxconf.

To make the system mount an NFS filesystem when booting, edit /etc/fstab. In this example, you'll need a line like this:

```
[root@hakadal /root]#  cat /etc/fstab
/dev/hda5    /           ext2    defaults            1 1
/dev/cdrom  /mnt/cdrom iso9660 noauto,owner,ro     0 0
/dev/hdb1    /usr        ext2    defaults            1 2
/dev/fd0     /mnt/floppy auto    noauto,owner        0 0
none         /proc       proc    defaults            0 0
none         /dev/pts    devpts gid=5,mode=620      0 0
/dev/hda6 swap           swap    defaults            0 0
nittedal:/home/elboth/local   /mnt/data nfs
rsize=1024,wsize=1024   0 0
```

## 24.18 NFS mounting options

To avoid server hangs, there are some important options and selections that you can use when mounting external filesystems. The two most important ones are soft and hard.

When you select soft mode, the NFS client will report processes that are trying to get to a file on an NFS-mounted filesystem. Only a few programs handle this in a secure way, so I do not recommend this option. When you select hard mode, the program that tries to access a file in an NFS-mounted filesystem will hang when the server crashes. The process will not be disturbed or killed unless you terminate the process. When the NFS server is back on the network, the program will continue undisturbed. This is probably how you want things to be. Use `hard,intr` on all NFS-mounted filesystems. Based on our previous example, you'll have this in the /etc/fstab file:

```
nittedal:/home/elboth/local /mnt/data nfs
rsize=1024,wsize=1024, hard,intr 0 0
```

## 24.19 NFS and asynchronous connections

If there is no NIC in your Linux machine and you need to transfer data between machines, there are several ways of doing this. You can use the serial port or the parallel port of your machine. If you want to use the serial port, you will need to make a null modem cable. If you have 9-pin serial ports, this means connecting pin # 2 to pin # 3, pin # 3 to pin # 2, and pin # 5 to pin # 5. The command for connecting is `pppd` and the maximum transfer speed is 115 Kb/s. Any TCP/IP service can be run between the machines, e.g., Telnet and FTP. On top of TCP/IP, you can run NFS via the serial port or the parallel port. The fastest solution is using the parallel port and the `plip` program.

I set up the `nittedal` machine as follows:

```
[root@nittedal /root]#  pppd passive lock local
/dev/ttyS0 115200 10.0.0.1:10.0.0.2
```

Then I set up the `hakadal` machine:

```
[root@hakadal /root]# pppd lock local /dev/ttyS0 115200
defaultroute
```

In this example of describing an asynchronous connection, the `nittedal` machine got the address `10.0.0.1` and the `hakadal` machine got the address `10.0.0.2`. From the `nittedal` machine, I exported the desired filesystems to the `hakadal` machine. Here's an example of the `/etc/exports` file:

```
[root@nittedal /root]# more /etc/exports
/cgi                     10.0.0.2 (insecure,rw)
/home                    10.0.0.2
```

On the `hakadal` machine, I can now mount these filesystems:

```
[root@hakadal /root]# mount -t nfs 10.0.0.1:/cgi /mnt1
[root@hakadal /root]# mount -t nfs 10.0.0.1:/home /mnt2
```

After a bit of fine-tuning (see optimalizing NFS), you can select the correct rsize and wsize plus the hard option if required. Note that the NFS server machine must have an updated `/etc/exports` file. If you boot the machine with an empty `/etc/exports` file, `mountd` and `nfsd` will die.

## 24.20 Optimizing NFS

Normally, if no rsize or wsize options have been set, NFS will read and write blocks of 4096 or 8192 bytes. Blocks of this size are probably not optimal, and some combinations of Linux kernels and NICs cannot handle them. It is probably a good idea to experiment. Try various combinations and use an rsize and wsize that work and work fast.

I start by mounting the filesystem:

```
[root@hakadal /root]# mount -o rsize=1024,wsize=1024 nit-
tedal:/home/elboth/local /mnt
```

The sequential print performance is tested with this command:

```
[root@hakadal /root]# time dd if=/dev/zero of=/mnt/test-
file bs=16k count=4096
```

I make a 64K file with null bytes. (This should be large enough to avoid caching being a significant part of the performance. Use a larger file if you have plenty of memory.) Do this a few times and record the average time. Use elapsed or wall clock time. The read performance can be read in this file:

```
[root@hakadal /root]# time dd if=/mnt/testfile
of=/dev/null bs=16k
```

Do this a few times and find the average. Then unmount and mount again with a larger rsize and wsize. Use multiples of 1024 bytes and no value higher than 16384 bytes as this is the maximum size in NFS version 2. Immediately after mounting, test the mounted filesystem. This is simple with the Linux commands `cd` and `ls`. When you explore the filesystem with the `ls` command, you are actually checking whether the filesystem is consistent. If rsize or wsize is too large, you may experience strange symptoms that are not necessarily absolutely obvious. One typical symptom is an incomplete file list. After making sure that the given rsize/wsize work, you can run the performance test again. Different server platforms generally have different optimal sizes. Sun Solaris is normally much faster with 4096 blocks than with any other size.

Newer Linux kernels utilize pre-reading of any rsize larger than or equal to the machine's page size. For Intel CPUs, the page size is 4096 bytes. Pre-reading significantly increases the reading speed of NFS, so use 4096-byte rsize on Intel machines whenever possible. Finally, you must edit `/etc/fstab` with the new rsize and wsize.

It is also possible to increase the write performance of the NFS server on a

Unix machine by switching synchronous writing off on the server. The NFS specifications indicate that NFS writing is not considered finished until the data that has been written is saved to a non-volatile medium (normally the hard disk drive). This limits the write performance a bit, while asynchronous writing will increase NFS performance.

Linux nfsd cannot perform synchronous write operations, as they are not permitted by the Linux filesystem. But everywhere, except on Linux servers, the performance can be increased this way by adding the following to the `/etc/export` file:

```
/dir      -async,access=linux_machine
```

## 24.21 NFS and poor bandwidth

Modem and ISDN connections are frequently used, even though they offer quite slow connections. NFS is basically a slow protocol; nearly "everything" is faster than NFS. The following services are faster than NFS: FTP, HTTP, rcp, and ssh. NFS's standard options are made for fast connections. If you use these options on lines with heavy traffic, the consequences may be errors, halted operations, files that pretend they are shorter than they really are, and generally strange operation.

Avoid using the soft mount option. This will cause timeout errors that the software probably won't be able to handle. Use the hard mount option instead. When hard mode is active, it will go on polling "forever," i.e., a timeout won't stop the NSF client. The next thing you must do is control the "timeo" and "retrans mount" options. These are explained on the NFS man page.

## 24.22 Exporting NFS (Unix)

If you want to export filesystems across various Unix platforms, you will see that NFS is not consistent. The two OS platforms that differ most are Linux and Sunsoft Solaris 2. To make sure that the syntax is right, you must check the user manuals or user man commands `nfs`, `/etc/exports`, and `exportfs`. Here are some examples:

We want to export /home/data (hakadal) to the webgo machine with read/write access. Our NFS server runs IRIX, HP-UX, Digital-Unix, Ultrix, SunOS 4 (Solaris 1), and AIX. All these operating systems use the Sun export format. Enter the following in /etc/export:

```
/home/data -rw=webgo
```

Then run exportfs to export the filesystem:

```
[root@hakadal /root]# exportfs -av
```

We want to export /home/data to the webgo machine with read/write access. The NFS server is a Solaris 2.8. Enter the following in /etc/dfs/dfstab:

```
share -o rw=webgo -d "Home local" /home/data
```

Then run shareall to export the filesystem:

```
[root@hakadal /root]# shareall
```

You will find more information about how to set up NFS under Solaris 2.8 by using the Solaris command share.

## 24.23 Security and NFS

As long as you can trust your colleagues, there is no reason to worry if you are part of a closed network. Check that there is no way of calling into the network, and that there is no connection to other networks where you cannot trust all.

There is a basic security problem in NFS. The client will trust in the NFS server and vice versa unless they are told otherwise. This may be hazardous. It means that if someone breaks into the root account of the server, it is simple to access the client's root account, too, and vice versa.

## 24.24 NFS references

In your Linux distribution, you will find the NFS documentation as a part of the NFS distribution. Also read Nicolay Langfeldt's NFS HOWTO. Other HOWTOs that I recommend are NIS HOWTO and NFS Root HOWTO. In addition, you can read the CERT advices on NFS. See ftp.cert.org/01-README for an updated list of CERT advices.

## Exercises for Chapter 24

1. What is Samba?
2. Which services are available in Samba?
3. Which transport protocol/media are supported by Samba?
4. Can the SMB protocol be routed?
5. How can you test a Samba configuration?
6. How can Samba be a security hazard?
7. What is NFS?
8. Which transport protocol/media are supported by NFS?
9. How can NFS be set up when you want to run it via a serial interface?
10. How can NFS be a security hazard?

CHAPTER 25

# Cost/Benefit Analysis

## 25.1 Introduction

In this chapter, you'll find some points to consider about the technological and financial factors connected to choosing Linux as your OS platform. It's a fact that these factors are boosting the growth of Linux. An increasing number of companies are looking for reduced IT costs and finding that Linux gives a good cost/benefit ratio.

I have to add that the total cost of an IT solution is strongly influenced by costs other than the initial investment. The costs of support and training offered by the supplier are significant considerations for many companies. Another important cost element that many companies will emphasize is how well the different suppliers cooperate.

Your company's current status and strategy will of course influence the factors that are given the highest priority.

The considerations below will be most relevant for companies that put strong emphasis on IT and also have substantial IT resources.

## 25.2 Protect your investments

Today, Linux is the OS that gives the best protection of your former hardware investments. Linux runs effectively on platforms from Intel 80386 to Pentium III. Linux also supports other CPU architectures like, for example, SPARC, Alpha, PowerPC, MCXXX, and StrongARM. Linux uses standard components much more efficiently than, for example, Microsoft Windows 95 and Windows 2000 Professional.

The best illustration of this is my own LAN. I run, among other machines, an old Acer PC with a 16MHz Intel 80386 CPU (16-bit data bus) with 8MB RAM and a 2.5GB hard disk drive. Nowadays, I use this machine as an NFS server for my two workstations (one HP workstation Apollo Series 700 and one Dell OptiPlex). The Acer PC is also used as a Samba server for a Windows 98 machine. In addition, the Linux machine is the Apache Web server for my intranet.

My primary workstation is a Dell OptiPlex PII 350MHz. Today, Dell can offer computers with Windows or Red Hat Linux preinstalled. Hence, PC device drivers are normally no problem on Dell PCs.

## 25.3 Differences between Open Source Linux and Windows

Following, you'll find a comparison of Microsoft Windows 95, Windows 2000 Professional, and Linux.

| Service/Option | Windows 95[1] | Windows 2K[2] | Linux 2.4 |
|---|---|---|---|
| **Cost of operating system** | $109 | $319 | Free |
| **Application cost** | 100% | 100% | Around 1/3 of the Windows prices. |
| **Administration cost** | 100% | Slightly lower. | 20% lower administration cost. |
| **Hardware requirements** | 486DX/100MZ, 16MB RAM, 150MB HD, CD-ROM | 486DX/100MZ, 32MB RAM, 150MB HD, CD-ROM | 386SX/16MZ, 4MB RAM, 150MB HD, CD-ROM |
| **Standard** | Proprietary (has become a "de facto" standard).[3] | Proprietary (has become a "de facto" standard). | Open (partly "de jure"[4] standard). |
| **Development platform** | Can be bought from Microsoft. | Can be bought from Microsoft. | Free (C, C++, FORTRAN, Perl). |
| **Stability** | Unstable in complex DLL[5] environments. | Slightly more stable. Still with blue screens. | Thoroughly tested and more stable than Windows. |
| **Development model** | Normally closed. | Normally closed. | Open Source. |
| **Protocol support** | TCP/IP, NetBEUI | TCP/IP, NetBEUI, IPX/SPX, AppleTalk | TCP/IP, NetBEUI, IPX/SPX, AppleTalk, DECnet |
| **Future** | Windows 2K | Next version. | Continuous upgrades. |

[1]Microsoft Windows 95 with Internet Explorer Version Upgrade CD-ROM.

[2]Microsoft Windows 2000 Professional English North America CD Encryption Coded Software CD-ROM.

[3]A well-known proprietary (owned by one company) standard.

[4]Bylaw – made by government or standard committees.

[5]Dynamic Link Libraries (DLLs) under the Windows platform.

Linux has low running and administration costs. This is where the real savings can be realized; not in the initial buying cost. GartnerGroup claims that upgrading to Windows 2000 Professional will cost at least $1500 per seat. But what is the running cost for a Windows solution?

## 25.4 Microsoft's license policy

Today most companies use Microsoft products and licenses. The cost of licenses depends on the total number of seats. Recently, Microsoft has launched more liberal licensing alternatives called Open Business and Open Volume License. Even with discounts up to 28 percent off normal retail prices, the total cost is considerable. A typical company will spend large amounts of money buying client products (Microsoft Windows 95 or Microsoft Windows 2000 Professional) and server products (Microsoft Windows 2000 Advanced Server).

What does an average company spend per annum to automatically upgrade their Windows operating systems and Office products? Depending on the licensing program, a company with 10,000 seats based on Microsoft Office and Windows 95 will probably spend some $300 per seat, totaling $3 million per year. Adding server licenses (Microsoft Windows 2000 Advanced Server) and mail systems (Exchange Server Enterprise Edition), the grand total easily amounts to $5 million per year. Smaller companies have even larger costs per seat. If the company also replaces their PCs every three years, about $109 OS cost must be added per PC. This cost is normally hidden in the hardware cost.

## 25.5 Cost differences

To illustrate the cost differences between Microsoft and Linux solutions, we'll take a look at a company with 100 employees. This company needs a Web hotel solution internally and externally. The Web hotel will serve employees as well as customers. Additionally, the company needs a file and mail server solution for their employees.

Microsoft's Web site suggests these solutions:

| Service | Microsoft Product | Cost in Dollars |
|---|---|---|
| Server OS | Windows 2000 Advanced Server | $3,596 |
| Client OS | Microsoft Windows 95 with Internet Explorer Version Upgrade CD-ROM ($109 per workstation) | $10,900 |
| Web server | Internet Information Server | Included |
| E-mail | Exchange Server Enterprise Edition | $7,895 |
| Database | SQL Server Enterprise Edition | $17,215 |
| Proxy server | Microsoft Proxy Server | $995 |
| Total cost | | $40,601 |
| Cost per seat | | $406 |

Red Hat and other Linux suppliers offer these solutions:

| Service | Linux Solution | Cost in Dollars |
|---|---|---|
| Server OS | Linux Red Hat Professional version 7.2 | $179.95 |
| Client OS | Linux Red Hat Professional version 7.2 (Copy) | 0 |
| Web server | Apache Web server | Included |
| E-mail | Sendmail, IMAP, POP3 | Included |
| Database | Just Logic SQL | $219 |
| Proxy server | Squid Object Cache | 0 |
| Total cost | | $398.95 |
| Cost per seat | | $3.99 |

If you think that the Red Hat solution is inadequate, you are wrong! Did you know that sendmail today is the most frequently used e-mail solution for the Internet? Sendmail allows aliases, supports multiple protocols, and also supports a large number of filter mechanisms. Perhaps you have a suspicion that sendmail doesn't scale as well as Exchange? The largest mail installations in the world today are based on sendmail. All the largest players use sendmail; for example, AOL and CompuServe. A number of large Microsoft Exchange installations have stability problems.

When suggesting that you use sendmail as a mail engine, I presume that you are using an e-mail front-end like, for example, Netscape Communicator (included in Red Hat Linux). If you need advanced calendar functions like those supported by, for example, Exchange, you must choose alternative products.

The JustLogic SQL database that I suggest is not a minimal solution; it is, for example, used by USAF, NEC, and CompuServe. The Apache Web server is the current market leader according to Netcraft. More than 55% of all companies use Apache today.

If the company also buys a complete Office package per user, the gap between a Microsoft-based solution and a Linux-based solution grows even larger. A Microsoft Office solution costs $499[6] per seat. If you choose Linux instead, most Office packages are about one-third the cost. StarOffice (www.sun.com) comes for free with SuSE Linux, and is generally available for both personal and business use at no cost. A complete ApplixWare (www.vistasource.com) 5.0 Standard Office Suite for Linux Intel package costs $99. If you want ApplixWare or Microsoft Office for 100 users with automatic updates, you must discuss the price with your distributor.

Here are some more sources of information:

- http://www.microsoft.com/office/
- http://www.vistasource.com/
- http://www.sun.com/products/staroffice/

Generally, you will find that software solutions under Linux are considerably cheaper than comparable solutions for Windows or Unix. But you don't save money only when buying software. A Linux environment is more stable and simpler to keep running than a traditional, Microsoft Windows-based system. This is very noticeable in large networks. Your company will save money by being able to reduce the number of IT staff.

The next time you want to reduce your company's running cost, avoid Microsoft and go for Linux. For help, contact http://home.c2i.net/delboth.

[6]Microsoft Office 2000 Win32 English North America CD-ROM.

CHAPTER
26

# Open Source/Linux Information

## 26.1 Information through the Internet

Do you want to learn more? You will find masses of information about the Linux OS on the Internet. With Internet access, you can download various Linux versions and distributions. You can also read Linux magazines, participate in different Linux newsgroups, etc.

## 26.2 Web (http) resources

Following, you'll find URLs that can give you useful information about Linux kernel development, user groups, and other links.

| WWW Address | Type of Resource |
|---|---|
| http://www.slashdot.org | News for nerds and stuff that matters. |
| http://www.kernelnotes.org | Linux's former headquarters. Lots of information about Linux kernels. |
| http://www.kernel.org | This is where Linus Torvald publishes the newest Linux kernels. |
| http://www.li.org | Here's the top-level administration of Linux development. |
| http://www.linux.org.uk/diary | Alan Cox's diary (kernel updates). |
| http://kt.linuxcare.com | Updated kernel news and patches/updates of Wine and Samba. |
| http://www.linux.org | Lists Linux user groups and links. |
| http://www.linux.com | Lists Linux user groups and links. |
| http://www.linuxresources.com | General information about how to use Linux at work and at home. Many links. |

## 26.3 Distributors' web resources

All Linux distributors have their own Web servers. Many of these have other Web servers that mirror (copy) the original server. Red Hat, Debian, and Slackware Web sites offer complete downloadable versions of their own Linux distributions. Try these different URLs to get more information:

| WWW Address | Type of Resource |
|---|---|
| http://www.caldera.com | Caldera distribution. |
| http://www.cdrom.com | Official Slackware distribution. |
| http://www.debian.org | Debian Linux distribution. |
| http://www.infomagic.com | Linux mirror server. Also sells Linux CDs. |
| http://www.redhat.com | Red Hat distribution. |
| http://www.stampede.org | Optimalized (fast) Linux distribution. |
| http://www.suse.com | SuSE Linux distribution (SuSE has the market's best ISDN support). |

| WWW Address | Type of Resource (*Continued*) |
|---|---|
| http://www.slackware.org | One of the original Linux distributions. |
| http://www.stormlinux.com | Increasingly well-known Linux distribution. |
| http://www.turbolinux.com | TURBO is a compact Linux distribution. |

## 26.4 Linux on a laptop

If you have problems installing Linux on your laptop, the following URLs contain useful information:

| WWW Address | Type of Resource |
|---|---|
| http://www.snafu.de/~wehe/index_li.html | Lots of HOWTOs. |
| http://www.linuxdoc.org/HOWTO/PCMCIA-HOWTO.html | PCMCIA HOWTOs. |
| http://www.cs.utexas.edu/users/kharker/linux-laptop/volunteer.html | A voluntary support database. |
| http://www.linuxce.org | Description of small, physical units (PDAs) that can run Linux. |
| http://www.uclinux.com | Porting Linux to small physical units (PDAs) like a 3Com PalmPilot. |
| http://www.cs.utexas.edu/users/kharker/linux-laptop/ | This site is a good resource when you have general laptop installation problems. |

## 26.5 FTP resources

Here is a list of the most popular FTP servers that offer free downloads of Linux operating systems.

| FTP Address | Type of Resource |
|---|---|
| tsx-11.mit.edu/pub/linux | General Linux archive. |
| ftp.cdrom.com/pub/linux | Home archive for Slackware. |
| ftp.debian.org | Home archive for Debian. |
| ftp.caldera.com/pub/OpenLinux | Linux archive with patches. |
| ftp://metalab.unc.edu/pub/Linux | General Linux archive. |
| ftp://ftp.kernel.org | Source code of various Linux kernels. |

You'll also find many Linux programs at metalab:
ftp://metalab.unc.edu/pub/Linux/

## 26.6 Linux tools and applications

All Linux distributors supply lots of software with their OS packages. Anything from games to word processing is included. For general office use, the popular StarOffice (www.sun.com/staroffice/) is a clone of Microsoft Office. The package is free for private and public use. Abiword (www.abisource.com) is an Open Source word processing program that reads Microsoft Word 97 format. GNU Image Manipulation Program, GIMP (www.gimp.org), is a very good Photoshop clone that comes with most Linux distributions. When you need other themes, fonts, and icons for your GNOME or KDE environment, Themes (www.themes.org) is the place for you. The newest version of GNOME and KDE can be downloaded from http://www.gnome.org and http://www.kde.org. If you are interested in GNOME programs, you should check http://helixcode.com, which is the home page of the company Helixcode. They are specialists on GNOME programs. The home page of the world-renowned web browser Mozilla is www.mozilla.org. News, information, and gossip about Mozilla can be found on the Web site www.mozillazine.org. If you are looking for games, 3-D drivers, etc., have a look at http://linuxgames.com and http://happypenguin.org . A complete database that contains all RPM packages can be found at http://rpmfind.net/linux/RPM/. If you don't depend on the RPM format, you will find masses of Linux software at http://freshmeat.net, http://linuxapps.com, http://www.xnet.com, and http://nextel.linux.tucows.com.

## 26.7 Linux Internet publications

New Linux publications are published on the Internet all the time. Here are the most popular ones right now:

| Linux Publication | Type of Publication |
|---|---|
| http://www.linuxmagazine.com | Monthly magazine (printed) published in the U.S. |
| http://www.linuxjournal.com | Monthly magazine (printed) published in the U.S. |
| http://linuxtoday.com | Daily Linux news. |
| http://lwn.net | Weekly Linux news. |
| http://www.linuxworld.com | Updated Linux news. |
| http://www.linuxgazette.com | Monthly online Linux publication. |

## 26.8 Linux newsgroups

Following, you'll find a list of the most popular Linux newsgroups. By checking your local ISP's news server, you can find additional groups. When looking for information without knowing which newsgroup to visit, http://searchlinux.com, run by C|net, could be of help.

| Newsgroup Name | Type of Newsgroup |
|---|---|
| alt.os.linux.caldera | Caldera-specific. |
| alt.os.linux.slackware | Slackware-specific. |
| comp.os.linux.advocacy | Linux contra other OS. |
| comp.os.linux.alpha | Linux on Digital Alpha. |
| comp.os.linux.announce | Linux announcement. |
| comp.os.linux.answers | Linux Q and A. |
| comp.os.linux.development.apps | Linux porting/development. |
| comp.os.linux.development.system | Linux kernel/device drivers. |

| Newsgroup Name | Type of Newsgroup (*Continued*) |
|---|---|
| comp.os.linux.hardware | Compatible hardware. |
| comp.os.linux.m68k | Linux on MC680X0 CPU. |
| comp.os.linux.misc | Various Linux issues. |
| comp.os.linux.networking | Networking and communication. |
| comp.os.linux.powerpc | Linux on PowerPC. |
| comp.os.linux.setup | Linux installation and system administration. |
| comp.os.linux.x | Linux X Window. |
| linux.debian.announce | Debian Linux announcements. |
| linux.redhat.install | Red Hat Linux installation. |

## 26.9 Electronic documentation

Below is a list of the most popular sites that offer Linux documentation. You'll even find complete books and manuals here. The only thing you'll need is a printer.

| Web Address | Description |
|---|---|
| http://linuxdoc.org | Linux documentation project. |
| http://www.linuxdoc.org/-docs.html#translated | *Linux System Administrator's Guide*, translated into many languages. |
| http://metalab.unc.edu/pub/Linux/-docs/linux-doc-project/users-guide/-!INDEX.html | *Linux Users Guide.* |
| http://metalab.unc.edu/LPD | Linux documentation and information about various Linux projects. |
| http://metalab.unc.edu/mdw/linux.html | This page contains lots of HOWTOs and other HTML documents, plus links to other interesting Linux sites. |

# Index

## Symbols



## A

## B

## C

## D

## G



## H

## I



## J



## K

## L



## M

## N

## O



## P

## Q



## R



## S

## T



## U

## V



## W



## X

## Z